Sebastian Lohsse | Reiner Schulze | Dirk Staudenmayer [eds.]

AI-Contracting

Münster Colloquia on EU Law
and the Digital Economy IX

HART

Nomos

Onlineversion
Nomos eLibrary

The Deutsche Nationalbibliothek lists this publication in the Deutsche Nationalbibliografie; detailed bibliographic data are available on the Internet at http://dnb.d-nb.de

ISBN (Print) 978-3-7560-3345-4 (Nomos Verlagsgesellschaft mbH & Co. KG, Baden-Baden)
ISBN (ePDF) 978-3-7489-6309-7 (Nomos Verlagsgesellschaft mbH & Co. KG, Baden-Baden)

ISBN (Print) 978-1-5099-9778-7 (Hart Publishing)

1st Edition 2026

Table of Contents

Attribution of Knowledge and Pre-Contractual Information Duties

Defects of Consent and Unexpected Outcomes

Introduction

AI Contracting – Challenges, approaches, and the UN Model Law on Automated Contracting as a starting point for adapting contract law

Sebastian Lohsse, Reiner Schulze & Dirk Staudenmayer[*]

I. Autonomous contracting as a possible challenge for contract law

Our economy and society are facing the fundamental challenge of digitalisation, which is bringing about a new digital economy. In this context, the law must adapt, not only because it is part of our economic and societal system. Rather, adaptation of the law can also be employed as a steering instrument in order to ensure from the outset that the digitalisation of our economy and society becomes a success and in order to enable us to reap its benefits, in particular its growth potential. At European level, over the past years, such a steering approach has already resulted in a whole series of new rules and proposals, including those relating to digital content, digital services, smart products, and the emerging data economy. For a while now, however, a further, third wave[1] of potential adaptation has appeared on the horizon: Artificial intelligence (AI), in its more developed forms, is set to become a key player in private law. Its specificities of autonomy and opacity[2] once again present private law with challenges to which the law might have to respond. With respect to tort law many of these challenges have already been addressed in this series of the Münster Colloquia on EU

* Sebastian Lohsse and Reiner Schulze are Professors of Law, Centre for European Private Law, University of Münster. Dirk Staudenmayer represented as Head of Unit in the Directorate General Justice and Consumers of the European Commission the EU in the decisive UNCITRAL negotiations in July 2024; he is also Honorary Professor at the University of Münster. This contribution only reflects the personal opinions of the authors and does not bind in any way the European Commission.

1 As to the waves of adaptation of EU private law to the needs of the digital economy, see Staudenmayer, Der Data Act im Gefüge des europäischen digitalen Privatrechts, Neue Juristische Wochenschrift, 2024, 1377.

2 See for an explanation of these features Lohsse/Schulze/Staudenmayer, in: Lohsse/Schulze/Staudenmayer (eds.), Liability for AI, 2023, pp. 8 et seq.

Law and the Digital Economy.[3] Yet, major challenges are also brought about with a view to contract law.

The legal novelty of contracting with or between AI lies in the cases of "autonomous contracting"[4] which are specific to AI. They are characterised by the fact that AI is no longer subject to the "if – then" scenario of traditional automated contracting.[5] While traditional automated contracting involves (even complex) software being programmed to make decisions when certain pre-determined conditions are met,[6] more advanced forms of AI, especially systems based on advanced machine learning, behave differently. Such autonomous AI systems, while still subject to certain settings, can make decisions with legal consequences which cannot be foreseen or pre-determined. The challenges arising from such AI systems entering into contracts are manifold. Firstly, since several parties may be involved when AI is used, it may seem questionable to whom the behaviour of the AI should be attributed.[7] Furthermore, one may question whether such behaviour can result in a valid contract at all. In particular, it may be doubtful whether there is sufficient intention to be bound and thus sufficient agreement between the parties.[8] If such an agreement is found in the first place, questions specific to AI may then arise with respect to the circumstances in which it is possible to correct *a posteriori* an outcome which does not correspond to the will of a contractual party. This situation may arise not only because the AI made a mistake; rather, it may even have done exactly what it was supposed to do, yet the outcome still does not correspond to what the parties could have expected.[9]

---

3 Lohsse/Schulze/Staudenmayer (eds.), Liability for AI, 2023.

4 For an explanation why the term "autonomous contracting" is more suitable for contracts concluded with or between AI than "automated contracting", see Lohsse/Schulze/Staudenmayer, in: Lohsse/Schulze/Staudenmayer (eds.), Smart Products, 2022, p. 31.

5 Cf. Lohsse/Schulze/Staudenmayer, in: Lohsse/Schulze/Staudenmayer (eds.), Smart Products, 2022, pp. 31, 34 et seq.

6 By and large existing contract laws can handle these cases since quite some time. See for instance for German law Cornelius, Vertragsabschluss durch autonome elektronische Agenten, MultiMedia und Recht, 2002, 353, 354 et seq.; Spindler, in: Spindler/Schuster (eds.), Recht der elektronischen Medien, 4th ed. 2019, Vorbemerkung zu §§ 116 ff. BGB, para 6.

7 See below, ch. IV.2.a)-b).

8 See below, ch. IV.2.c) and Lohsse/Schulze/Staudenmayer, in: Lohsse/Schulze/Staudenmayer (eds.), Smart Products, 2022, pp. 33 et seq.

9 See below, ch. IV.3.

II. Responses at an international level

The aforementioned challenges could be dealt with by each legal system individually. In fact, existing private law rules might be flexible enough to address such challenges through interpretation alone, without requiring adaptation.[10] However, it may well seem questionable whether such interpretation or purely national adaptation would fully allow us to reap the benefits of digitalisation.[11] This is precisely why EU private law has been in the vanguard of the transformation process of digitalisation so far. EU private law has not been at the forefront because it is as such of better quality than national law, because EU institutions find the best solutions, or because the EU legislative process is more efficient than the national one. Rather, so far, acting at the EU level has been a more efficient action level than the national or global level, albeit relevant only for the limited target group of EU Member States.

Apparently, as the process of digitalisation is of a global nature, it might be even better to tackle its challenges globally. However, there would be major questions regarding the adaptation of private law to digitalisation at a global level: For example, how long would it take to reach an agreement and what could be agreed upon? According to a well-known saying among UN practitioners: "There is the time of God, there is the time of man – and somewhere in between is the time of the UN". Specifically, this refers to the adoption by consensus, which has two key weaknesses: it takes a long time and one can only agree on a minimum of basic points. Under normal circumstances, this means that acting at the UN level is not an efficient way to make decisions. Consequently, at least for the first two waves of adapting private law to the challenges of the digital economy, EU law has demonstrated its ability to achieve significant results.[12]

However, with regard to AI contracting, a first step has been made at UN level rather than at EU level. Remarkably, the decision-making process on the UN Model Law on Automated Contracting has bucked the trend. From the mandate to start work in 2021[13] until the UNCITRAL adoption

10 See below, ch. IV.1.

11 For use-cases and possible benefits see also Staikova-van Bommel, The UNCITRAL Model Law on Automated Contracting, ch. I.2.-3., in this volume.

12 Cf. above, fn. 1.

13 UNCITRAL placed the topic of automated contracting on its work programme at its fifty-fourth session, Official Records of the General Assembly, Seventy-sixth Session, Supplement No. 17 (A/76/17), paras. 25 (e) and 236.

in July 2024, the relevant work took only three years. This comparatively fast adoption process, which focused on a few key consensual points, was possible because there was a general consensus on the need for such a UN Model Law; the creation of legal certainty was considered important.[14] This is all the more impressive given that the general political climate at EU level has changed over the last couple of years in response to the large number of legislative acts adopted during the last mandate of the von-der-Leyen I Commission. Further legislation is the envisaged solution only in very exceptional cases.[15] Due to this political trend, it would currently be very difficult to adopt an EU legislative act with the same content as the UN Model Law. Even so, the UN Model Law is important for the process of adaptation of EU private law to the needs of the digital economy. It can be seen as laying the groundwork for the third wave of this adaptation by paving the – international – way for adapting contract law to autonomous contracting. It demonstrates an 'enabling' approach which fits well with the current legal policy discussion on developing digital law altogether. In any case, the UN Model Law provides a basis for a closer examination of the challenges of AI contracting and how to respond to them.

III. The UN Model Law on Automated Contracting: a groundbreaking step towards adapting contract law to AI

The General Assembly of the United Nations (UN) endorsed on 4 December 2024 the Model Law on Automated Contracting,[16] which had been adopted on 11 July 2024 by the UN Commission on International Trade Law (UNCITRAL).[17]

---

14 Resolution 79/119 of the General Assembly, 5th Recital and UNCITRAL decision, 4th Recital.

15 See for instance the withdrawal of the proposal for a Directive on AI Liability, OJ. of 6.10.2025, C/2025/5423.

16 47th plenary meeting, Resolution 79/119.

17 Official Records of the General Assembly, Seventy-ninth Session, Supplement No. 17 (A/79/17), chap. VII and annex IV.

1. Scope of the UN Model Law

It is no coincidence that the UN Model Law addresses precisely the aforementioned questions; there was a consensus that they are key to establishing legal certainty and that they should therefore be regulated. The UN Model Law thus confirms that a contract concluded with or between AI is valid and attributes the contract to a specific person. It also contains a rule on unexpected outcomes.[18] In doing so, the UN Model Law avoids[19] the term of "autonomous contracting" in favour of "automated contracting"[20], as the latter has a broader scope. It covers both "deterministic" and "non-deterministic" systems.[21]

"Deterministic" systems still apply the "if – then" scenario. As they can be handled by existing legislation, including them in the UN Model Law was not strictly indispensable. However, the fact that the UN Model Law includes smart contracts[22] is useful. While the Data Act harmonises certain technical standards for smart contracts,[23] it deliberately refrains from regulating their legal aspects. If one wants to deploy smart contracts more in commercial transactions,[24] the UN Model Law deals with relevant topics for an adaptation of private law in its Arts. 5 and 6 with the validity of smart contracts and their self-executing actions.[25]

---

18 For the details, see below, ch. IV., and Staikova-van Bommel, The UNCITRAL Model Law on Automated Contracting, in this volume.

19 Guide to Enactment and Use, para. 30.

20 Guide to Enactment and Use, para. 4.

21 Art. 1 (2) UN Model Law, Guide to Enactment and Use, para. 29. For details as to the Model Law's scope see also Staikova-van Bommel, The UNCITRAL Model Law on Automated Contracting, ch. II.2., in this volume.

22 Guide to Enactment and Use, para. 10, 12.

23 Article 36 (EU) 2023/2854 of 13.12.2023 on harmonised rules on fair access to and use of data (Data Act).

24 As to the possibility to use smart contracts as a tool for personal information management systems see Staudenmayer, Die Anpassung des Privatrechts an die digitale Wirtschaft, Zeitschrift für Internationales Wirtschaftsrecht, 2020, 151 et seq. For an overview on legal questions of blockchain technology cf. De Filippi/Wright, Blockchain and the Law: The Rule of Code, Harvard University Press, 2018, pp. 72 et seq.; Guggenberger, The Potential of Blockchain Technology for the Conclusion of Contracts, in: Schulze/Staudenmayer/Lohsse (eds.), Contracts for the Supply of Digital Content: Regulatory Gaps and Challenges, 2017, pp. 85 et seq., 94 et seq.

25 For more details, see below, ch. IV.2.c).

"Non-deterministic" systems[26] are used for autonomous contracting and are thus those for whom it is highly valuable to create legal certainty.

Despite this broad scope and the traditional principle of "technology neutrality" of UNCITRAL work, the UN Model Law recognises the specificities of AI and proposes changes to private law. While the principle of technology neutrality is widely used in UNCITRAL work, the way it is explained has shifted slightly. Traditionally, it was meant to clarify that the relevant rules applied to all factual situations covered by the scope of a UNCITRAL instrument, regardless of the technology used.[27] This description of the principle has recently been changed, first implicitly[28] and then explicitly in Art. 4 UN Model Law. Now, the principle of technology neutrality is explained as to not require a specific technology.[29] However, the UN Model Law acknowledges, albeit in careful terms, that the specifics of AI also require technology-specific rules.[30]

The scope of the UN Model Law is broad, covering the entire contract life cycle[31], including the pre-contractual stage, conclusion of the contract, its performance, its termination, and the exercise of possible contractual remedies.[32] It covers both contracts concluded with and between AI[33], i.e. where one or both contractual parties use AI systems. Despite this broad scope, the UN Model Law does not overlap with rules like the AI Act,[34] which covers the design and use of AI systems.[35]

---

26 The Guide to Enactment and Use, para. 29, states explicitly that this notion includes AI.

27 See the United Nations Convention on the Use of Electronic Communications in International Contracts of 2005, 5th Recital and Explanatory note para. 47 et seq. and the UNCITRAL Model Law on Electronic Transferable Records of 2017, Resolution 72/114 of the General Assembly, 5th Recital and UNCITRAL decision, 4th Recital and Explanatory note, para. 18, 44, 143, 154, 197.

28 See UNCITRAL Model Law on the Use and Cross-border Recognition of Identity Management and Trust Services of 2022, Resolution 77/101 of the General Assembly, 4th Recital and UNCITRAL decision, 4th Recital and Guide to Enactment, para. 45, 48, 55, 112, 117.

29 Resolution 79/119 of the General Assembly, 6th Recital and UNCITRAL decision, 6th Recital and Guide to Enactment and Use, para. 12, 43.

30 Guide to Enactment and Use, para. 30, 76.

31 Guide to Enactment and Use, para. 8.

32 Art. 2 (1) UN Model Law, Guide to Enactment and Use, para. 33.

33 Guide to Enactment and Use, para. 32, 46.

34 Regulation (EU) 2024/1689 of the European Parliament and of the Council of 13 June 2024 laying down harmonised rules on artificial intelligence.

35 Art. 2 (2) UN Model Law, Guide to Enactment and Use, para. 7, 13, 36.

While the UN Model Law was conceived to cover B2B contracts, it may also apply to B2C contracts.[36] As UNCITRAL, as displayed by its name, is an organisation concerned with "international trade law" topics, the fact that this Model Law applies also to B2C transactions is a major breakthrough recognising that autonomous contracting can play a significant role also in these transactions.[37] While the use of AI contracting in B2C contracts may raise a number of other issues,[38] the UN Model Law restricts itself to its 'enabling' approach,[39] i.e. it allows that such contracts can be concluded both in B2B and in B2C contexts. The Model Law therefore avoids regulating B2C-specific aspects, concluding that relevant consumer contract law would still apply.[40]

As with other UN legal frameworks,[41] the role of observing good faith in the interpretation of the UN Model Law is explicitly recognised. This is noteworthy because it shows that, despite AI being able to act autonomously, existing key principles applicable to human transactions, like the principle of good faith, are still considered applicable when adapting contract law to AI. As with other examples in EU law,[42] this demonstrates the usefulness of such fundamental principles when regulating new features of the digital economy, such as autonomous decisions that are neither predetermined nor controlled by humans, or emerging dependencies.

2. The 'enabling' approach of the UN Model Law

A particularly noteworthy feature of the UN Model Law is its 'enabling' approach which manifests itself in several dimensions.

---

36 Guide to Enactment and Use, para. 35. See also Staikova-van Bommel, The UNCITRAL Model Law on Automated Contracting, ch. II.2., in this volume.

37 Ibid.

38 See for instance below, ch. IV.2.d.

39 See below, 2.

40 Art. 2 (2), 9 UN Model Law, Guide to Enactment and Use, para. 35 et seq., 84.

41 Beyond the examples of Art. 7 (1) CISG and Art. 3 Model Law on Electronic Commerce, mentioned by the Guide to Enactment and Use, para. 38, see also Art. 5(1) UN Convention on the Use of Electronic Communications in International Contracts.

42 See as to the use of good faith in the Data Act regulating the emerging dependency between "data-haves" and "data-have-nots" in the data economy Lohsse/Schulze/Staudenmayer, in: Lohsse/Schulze/Staudenmayer (eds.), Private Law and the Data Act, 2024, pp. 27 et seq.

Firstly, the UN Model Law was not agreed as a binding convention, but as a model law. While the UN General Assembly recommends that all states "give favourable consideration to the Model Law when revising or adopting legislation on electronic commerce",[43] this is only a recommendation. Not only in this nature, but also in its substantive drafting and narrative, the UN Model Law sends in many instances soothing messages to the states that guard their national contract law jealously. This is evident, for example,[44] in the wording of Art. 5 UN Model Law. Rather than simply conveying the message that contracts concluded with or between AI are valid, it uses an awkward wording with a double negation to express that a contract conclusion or performance is not invalid just because no human was involved. While this wording is indeed used in other UNCITRAL texts – which in itself shows the importance of this narrative for achieving consensus –, this drafting sends the "important signal" (sic!) that national general contract law rules can still apply to the formation and performance of the contract.[45] UNCITRAL is not alone in facing this dilemma; EU law sometimes encounters the same issue.[46]

The second dimension of the UN Model Law's 'enabling' approach is its strong emphasis on party autonomy.[47] While the UN Model Law does not propose the creation of mandatory law between the parties, it recognises that a framework contract, concluded to regulate all more specific contracts covered by it, could be the first source of rules creating legal certainty between the parties about their rights and obligations; likewise there is room for conditions imposed by a third party operating a platform which uses AI and makes autonomous contracting possible.[48]

Beyond this general emphasis on the principle of contractual freedom, the same message is expressed more specifically in two provisions. While the contract is attributed as a matter of principle to the person using AI, a different agreement between the parties takes precedence.[49] Similarly, the UN Model Law explicitly states that the rule on unexpected outcomes only applies if the parties have not agreed on an alternative solution. These

---

43 Resolution 79/119, point 3.

44 See for other examples Art. 2 (2), (4), 7 (4), 8 (2), 9 UN Model Law, Guide to Enactment and Use, para. 7, 35 et seq., 58, 84.

45 Guide to Enactment and Use, para. 4.

46 See the example of the drafting of Art. 9 (1) 2 ECD.

47 Guide to Enactment and Use, para. 15, 37, 40, 42 et seq.

48 Guide to Enactment and Use, para. 15, 43.

49 Art. 7 (1) UN Model Law, Guide to Enactment and Use, para. 64.

clauses, which give precedence to the agreement of the parties, are not actually indispensable, because their effect follows from the aforementioned approach of the UN Model Law. However, they are included because they formed part of compromises reached during the drafting process for provisions where consensus was difficult to achieve and because they reinforce the emphasis on party autonomy.

The third dimension of the 'enabling' approach is its intended commercial and, indirectly, macroeconomic impact. With its willingness to address legal uncertainty,[50] it aims to facilitate and promote the development and implementation of innovative business models, using autonomous contracting and smart contracts. Although the number of such business models is growing,[51] one reason they are not yet widespread is legal uncertainty.[52] By addressing this issue by clarifying key legal uncertainties, the UN Model Law has the potential to contribute to the positive growth effect of such innovative business models.

IV. Challenges for contract law in detail

1. Fundamental questions and overarching perspectives

As previously mentioned, the focal points in the provisions of the UN Model Law may serve as a basis for a more detailed examination of the question in how far contract law is confronted with the challenges of AI contracting and how it might react to these challenges. This question was reflected in the colloquium that gave rise to this volume: It took into account both the UN Model Law and other recently presented drafts (such as the ELI Guiding Principles and Model Rules on Digital Assistants for Consumer Contracts[53] and the Principles for AI in Contracting[54]). Accordingly, it also

---

50 Cf. Resolution 79/119 of the General Assembly, 4th and 5th Recital and UNCITRAL decision, 3rd and 4th Recital; Guide to Enactment and Use, para. 4.

51 Cf. Staikova-van Bommel, The UNCITRAL Model Law on Automated Contracting, ch. I.2., in this volume.

52 Ibid., ch. I.3.

53 ELI Guiding Principles and Model Rules on Digital Assistants for Consumer Law (2025), https://www.europeanlawinstitute.eu/projects-instruments/instruments/eli-guiding-principles-and-model-rules-on-digital-assistants-for-consumer-contracts/.

54 Wendehorst, Discussion Draft: Principles for AI in Contracting (Version 3.0), Annex, in this volume. The previous Version (Wendehorst, Discussion Draft: Principles for AI in Contracting (Version 2.1), https://papers.ssrn.com/sol3/papers.cfm?abstract_id

addressed issues of consumer protection and pre-contractual information duties when contracting with AI.

The individual aspects considered were embedded in a series of cross-cutting issues and themes that were discussed throughout the colloquium. It is sufficient here to highlight the most important of these overarching perspectives. Firstly, the colloquium addressed the fundamental question of whether the increasing automation of the contracting process can adequately be dealt with even in absence of any adaptation of contract law,[55] as it "does not raise any legal concerns",[56] or whether the introduction of technology-specific (and particularly AI-specific) rules in the field of contract law is appropriate.[57] Assuming, in principle, that it is appropriate to establish specific rules regarding AI contracting, the colloquium also addressed the extent to which such rules should recognise this type of contracting[58] and how they should shape its legal framework.

One of the key questions in shaping the content of this legal framework will likely be how to deal with the tension between two fundamentally different types of autonomy: human autonomy, including its legal manifestation as private autonomy, on the one hand, and the autonomy of AI systems, whose actions can be unpredictable even for their creators and operators, on the other hand.[59] In addition to such overarching issues concerning the content of the legal framework for AI contracting, there are also overarching matters regarding which regulatory instruments may be appropriate. For example, this concerns the extent to which provisions should be mandatory or merely take the form of default rules.

=4704081#:~:text=Christiane%20Wendehorst,-University%20of%20Vienna&text=The%20'Principles%20for%20AI%20in,in%20relation%20to%20automated%20contracting.

55 See this conclusion in Mik, Contract Law in the middle on an AI Summer, ch. VI, in this volume.

56 Mik, Contract Law in the middle on an AI Summer, ch. VI., in this volume.

57 Rejecting, in particular with regard to common law, see therefore Mik, Contract Law in the middle on an AI Summer, in this volume.

58 See for example, Rodríguez de las Heras Ballell, Legal Framework for AI-Contracting: Key Rules on Validity, Attribution and Risk Allocation, ch. II., in this volume.

59 See for example, Rodríguez de las Heras Ballell, Legal Framework for AI-Contracting: Key Rules on Validity, Attribution and Risk Allocation, ch. II., in this volume. For overarching issues in this context, including with regard to the principles of UN model law and the ELI Guiding Principles; see also Amodio/Diurni (eds.), Human Vulnerability in Interaction with AI in European Private Law (forthcoming 2025) for a recent discussion of this topic from the perspective of the interaction between AI and human vulnerability in private law.

In this regard, it should be noted that, at least in asymmetrical relationships, the protection needs of one party may argue in favour of introducing mandatory rules. This is likely to be particularly relevant, if consumer law were to be updated in light of the new challenges posed by AI contracting. However, this could also be problematic if new protection needs, such as those of internet users or users of internet-connected devices, are to be assessed beyond the traditional scope of consumer law.[60] Conversely, the normative role of default rules must be considered, particularly in a contractual environment characterised by high automation and low transaction costs, as discussed in more detail in a separate contribution on AI contracting and default rules.[61] In such an environment, AI systems can facilitate the direct transfer of default rules into contract texts and may also compensate for information asymmetries in this context.[62] These considerations imply that default rules as "the legal infrastructure of private autonomy"[63] will be highly significant with regard to future regulations governing AI contracting. Ultimately, in this area – as in other areas of modern private law – the challenge will be to combine these two instruments in a way that reconciles the fundamental principle of private autonomy with a growing number of protection needs.

Taking into account these overarching aspects, the colloquium – and, consequently, this volume – considered the aforementioned recently submitted drafts[64] in order to gain insight from their comparison and critical evaluation with regard to suitable approaches for designing a legal framework for AI contracting. Based on this, the volume addresses the numerous individual aspects of AI contracting within three key areas: Firstly, it deals with the conclusion of contracts and the contracting parties. Secondly, it addresses questions of attribution of knowledge and pre-contractual information obligations. Thirdly, it examines questions of defects of consent and unexpected outcomes.

---

60 See below ch. 2.d.

61 Möslein, AI Contracting and Contract Law (Default) Rules, in this volume.

62 Möslein, AI Contracting and Contract Law (Default) Rules, ch. III.1. and IV., in this volume.

63 Möslein, AI Contracting and Contract Law (Default) Rules, ch. III.1., in this volume.

64 See above fn. 53, 54.

2. Conclusion of contracts and the contracting parties

a) AI as a contracting party?

When it comes to concluding contracts, the most fundamental question is who should be considered the contracting parties. In theory, in addition to or even instead of the natural or legal persons using AI to conclude contracts in their interest, the AI itself could be regarded as a legal entity and thus qualify as a contracting party. However, concerns regarding such legal personhood of AI have been raised on several occasions, with good reason, in the context of a controversial legal-ethical and legal-political discussion (for example, in relation to a resolution of the European Parliament[65] in several statements).[66]

Thus, both the UN Model Law and the aforementioned drafts are based on the principle – also reflected in EU law[67] – that AI does not have legal personality but that it is necessary to attribute its legal actions to the person behind it.[68] While a different agreement between the parties takes precedence (Art. 7 (1) UN Model Law), the contract is attributed by default to the person using AI (Art. 7 (2) UN Model Law).

Such an agreement could be included in the relevant contract itself, in a framework contract covering more specific contracts between the parties, or in the conditions imposed by a third party operating a platform which uses AI and enables autonomous contracting. As the term "action" shows, the scope of the provision is wide, covering the entire life-cycle of the contract.[69] This is important because, while a contract agreed by the parties is necessary, the provision also covers actions prior to the conclusion of the relevant contract.[70]

---

65 The resolution of the European Parliament, of 20 October 2020 (2020/2014(INL)).

66 Liability for Artificial Intelligence and other emerging digital technologies, Expert Group on Liability and New Technologies, New Technologies Formation, 2019, pp. 37 et seq; Policy and Investment Recommendations for trustworthy AI, High-Level Expert Group on Artificial Intelligence, 2019, point 29.7; see also Rodríguez de las Heras Ballell, Legal Framework for AI-Contracting: Key Rules on Validity, Attribution and Risk Allocation, ch. III.1., in this volume.

67 As to the adequateness of this principle and its reflection in EU law, see Lohsse/Schulze/Staudenmayer, in: Lohsse/Schulze/Staudenmayer (eds.), Liability for AI, 2023, pp. 9 et seq.

68 Ibid., para. 60 et seq.

69 See above under 1. and Guide to Enactment and Use, para. 63 and 50.

70 Guide to Enactment and Use, para. 64.

In line with this, the section's opening contribution on the conclusion of contracts and contracting parties summarised that the "obvious conclusion" must be drawn, "that the law, to the extent that the law has actually confronted this question, must be allowing AI systems to function as part of the world of contracts without the AI system having legal personhood".[71] Based on this assessment, the contribution sets out the reasons why AI systems should also not be given the role of "agent" of the user, but rather be regarded simply as a 'tool' that facilitates the conclusion of contracts for its user.[72]

b) Attribution to the user or to the operator

The rejection of legal personality for AI, and the focus on the natural or legal person using the autonomous system in question, implies the need to more precisely define this attribution to a person in order to ascertain the identity of the contracting parties. This raises the crucial and much-discussed issue of which person exactly should be attributed responsibility for AI activities in contract formation, and how this should be done.

Based on overviews of the current legal and academic discourse on attribution in automated contracting, several contributions in this volume address the concept of 'attribution' in relation to AI contracting as well as the determination of the entity to which this attribution refers. With regard to the former, the main focus is on the meaning, relevance and scope of this concept when used in this context. This includes, not least, the question of the extent to which the different levels of autonomy of AI systems must be considered when designing the system of attribution rules and factors.[73] Regarding the latter, the task is to describe and conceptually define the relevant group of persons for attribution. There are good reasons

---

71 Gabriel, What does it mean to have "the intention to contract" in an AI Contract?, ch. II.3.a); as well Twigg-Flesner, Attribution of pre-contractual information and knowledge: the ELI Model Rules on Digital Assistants for Consumer Contracts and beyond, ch. I., both in this volume.

72 Gabriel, What does it mean to have "the intention to contract" in an AI Contract?, ch. II.3.b) and c), in this volume; for more on the issue of agency, see Lohsse/Schulze/Staudenmayer, Contracts for the Supply of Digital Content: Regulatory Challenges and Gaps – An Introduction, in: Lohsse/Schulze/Staudenmayer (eds.), Contracts for the Supply of Digital Content: Regulatory Challenges and Gaps, 2017, pp. 19 et seq.

73 Rodríguez de las Heras Ballell, Legal Framework for AI-Contracting: Key Rules on Validity, Attribution and Risk Allocation, ch. III.1., in this volume.

for considering the (human) user or operator of the automated system in question as the pivotal legal subject for establishing contractual responsibility.[74] By contrast, as is explained in more detail,[75] the developer of the core AI software or the platform provider are not suitable as subjects of such attribution in AI contracting.

The UN Model Law has therefore quite rightly refrained from attributing the contract to any of these individuals. As previously mentioned, its fallback rule in Art. 7 (2) UN Model Law attributes the contract to the person who uses the AI system. From this perspective, the key issue is obviously to determine who "uses" the AI system for the contractual purpose. The Guide to Enactment and Use[76] mentions the "strongest link" to that action as the relevant criterion. This link should be determined objectively in light of all the circumstances. The Guide to Enactment and Use also provides a list of examples of circumstances that can be considered, such as the person deploying the automated system, the control exercised over the operational parameters of the system and the action, the benefit or value derived from the action, the nature and purpose of the contract, and trade usages and the practices established between the parties. These examples do not apply in all cases, but only where relevant.

In principle, Art. 22 of the ELI Guiding Principles and Model Rules on Digital Assistants in Consumer Contracts, and Principle 5 of the Principles for AI in Contracting have a similar focus. However, the latter principles are likely to be considered advantageous in that they offer a somewhat more succinct designation of the attributable subject with the term "operator"[77] than the term "user", which is also used in many other meanings and legal contexts.[78]

74 Schwamberger, The Party to an AI Contract: Navigating Attribution in Autonomous Transactions, ch. III., in this volume.

75 Schwamberger, The Party to an AI Contract: Navigating Attribution in Autonomous Transactions, ch. II.2. and 3., in this volume.

76 Para. 66.

77 For the differences between this term and "deployer" as defined in Article 3(4) of the AI Act, see Schwamberger, The Party to an AI Contract: Navigating Attribution in Autonomous Transactions, ch. IV., in this volume.

78 See for example, the use of this term in different contexts in Art. 3 lit. b DSA; Art. 2 No. 20 and 21 DMA; Art. 2 No. 12 DA.

c) Validity of the Contract

Even with the attribution of the contract to the operator or user of the AI, the question remains as to how its validity can be justified in light of general contract law concepts. This is because the operator or user of the AI may not be able to predict which parties and what content the contracts will involve, even if the other party does not use AI. This lack of predictability could give rise to doubts as to whether the party using AI actually has the "intention to contract",[79] i.e. the intention to be legally bound which is regularly required for the conclusion of a contract. Despite differences in contract law across jurisdictions, such an intention is likely to be a generally recognised prerequisite. It can also be found, for example, in Art. 14 (1) of the UN Convention on Contracts for the International Sale of Goods (CISG) and similarly in Art. 2.2 of the UNIDROIT Principles of International Commercial Contracts.

However, the conclusion that a contract could not be concluded with the aid of AI, given the lack of predictability, seems highly doubtful. Strong arguments against this view have already been put forward. In particular, it has been pointed out that even in absence of AI, contracts are regularly concluded, even though their content is only determined by future events (e.g. contracts relating to future market prices) and that the binding effect and enforceability of such contracts is generally recognised in contract law.[80] Similarly, the fact that the contractual partner may not be fully recognisable is not only relevant to the conclusion of contracts with the assistance of AI, but also to the conclusion of "conventional" contracts with the aid of vending machines, for which the individualisation of a contractual partner recognisable to the operator is usually considered unnecessary.

Correspondingly, Art. 5 and 6 UN Model Law also recognise the validity of contracts involving AI.[81] These articles comprehensively deal with a wide range of situations. While Art. 5 (1) UN Model Law establishes the general principle by recognising that a contract concluded with or between AI is valid, Art. 5 (3) UN Model Law extends this to any action taken in connection with the conclusion or performance of the contract. The term "action"

79 Gabriel, What does it mean to have "the intention to contract" in an AI Contract?, in this volume.

80 Gabriel, What does it mean to have "the intention to contract" in an AI Contract?, ch. III.3.c), in this volume.

81 As to these provisions see also Staikova-van Bommel, ch. II.3., in this volume.

is understood broadly and covers any communication under the contract or any exercise of contractual rights or remedies.[82] Art. 5 (2) UN Model Law[83] clarifies that the validity of a contract is not called into question by the self-executing performance of smart contracts or the autonomous performance of an AI contract.[84]

Art. 6 UN Model Law has a similar structure and content, but tackles specific validity questions of smart contracts and dynamic contracting. So-called smart contracts are not necessarily contracts as such; actually, they are mostly software which allows the automatic execution of contracts. However, they can be entire contracts concluded and expressed in computer code[85] and it is thus useful that Art. 6 (1) UN Model Law recognises the validity of contracts expressed in computer code.

Art. 6 UN Model Law also recognises that dynamic contracting is not putting into question the validity of a contract (Art. 6 (2)) or an action linked to the formation of a contract (Art. 6 (3)). In cases of dynamic contracting, the AI that concludes a contract is fed with data which can lead to the conclusion of the contract with a specific party or at specific terms, e.g. auctioning advertising time in real time to the highest bidder.[86] This information may come from a source which may be internal or external to the relevant contractual party and can be fed continuously or periodically.[87] Different from the approach of Art. 5 UN Model Law, Art. 6 however did not include the stage of performance of a contract.[88]

Other approaches to recognising the validity of contracts in such situations can already be found in discussions in national jurisdictions. Within

82 Guide to Enactment and Use, para. 50.

83 The rule is placed in square brackets, see the footnote accompanying Art. 5 UN Model Law and Guide to Enactment and Use, para. 48. As to the assessment of placing a rule in square brackets see under 3.

84 Guide to Enactment and Use, para. 47.

85 Cf. Guide to Enactment and Use, para. 53 and the references in fn. 24; Staikova-van Bommel, The UNCITRAL Model Law on Automated Contracting, ch. II.3.b, in this volume. As to more fundamental questions of "code is law" (cf. Lessig, Code, 2nd edition (2006), p. 5) and "law is code", cf. De Filippi/Hassan, Blockchain technology as a regulatory technology: From code is law to law is code, First Monday, 5 December 2016, https://firstmonday.org/ojs/index.php/fm/article/view/7113, last accessed on 14.9.2025.

86 For more details on contracts incorporating dynamic information see Staikova-van Bommel, The UNCITRAL Model Law on Automated Contracting, ch. II.3.c), in this volume.

87 Guide to Enactment and Use, para. 55.

88 Guide to Enactment and Use, para. 57.

the framework of the German doctrine of legal transactions, for instance, it is conceivable that the concept of "Geschäftsbewusstsein" ("transactional awareness"; awareness of the specific legal transaction in question) could be adapted without amending the underlying provisions of the Civil Code.[89] Although such approaches may differ between jurisdictions, one may assume that the provisions which are included in the UN Model Law and other drafts on the validity of contracts concluded with AI correspond to a legal situation that is already covered by "pre-digital" contract law. Thus, such provisions are useful because they have a clarifying nature. However, in legal systems that are not sufficiently flexible, the introduction of these models would constitute an important change to contract law.

d) Conclusion of consumer contracts with AI

AI is also increasingly being used to conclude consumer contracts. So far, autonomous systems have primarily been used in this sector by businesses, facilitating the combination of "mass contracting" with personalised contract design, for example. However, the use of such systems is not limited to the contracting businesses. They may also become important for consumers. In particular, consumers are increasingly likely to delegate the decision-making and execution of a variety of everyday contracts to AI systems in the future (from ordering everyday goods to restaurant reservations).[90]

Given the increased use of AI in consumer contract formation, the question arises as to whether specific rules are appropriate for this area, and if so, to what extent and in what manner. This issue is part of the broader question of the future role of the concept of the consumer and related legal institutions in the context of "digital matters", particularly with regard to legal issues concerning the protection of internet users (especially those using certain internet services and connected products, including autonomous systems).[91] In short, the relationship between consumer pro-

89 See for this issue Gsell/Steinhausen, Der intelligente Kühlschrank kauft ein – wirksamer Vertragsschluss beim Einsatz autonomer Agenten?, in: Arroyo/Arbst/Kindl (eds.), Schuldrecht und Digitalisierung (forthcoming 2026).

90 Busch, Enabling Innovation and Protecting Consumers in the Agentic Economy: Why the Digital Fairness Act Should Regulate Agentic AI, ch. I., in this volume.

91 See for example Schulze, El Derecho privado ante los retos del cambio digital y de la sostenibilidad, in: Institut de Dret privat europeu i comparat Universitat de Girona

tection and "user protection" is being examined in relation to various types of internet use and the potential "digital vulnerability" issues that may arise in this context. In this regard, it has been emphasised on several occasions that, alongside consumer protection, new approaches to "user protection" could be given increasing importance.[92] However, moving towards broader "user protection", which includes the protection needs of businesses on the internet as well as consumers, does not rule out the possibility of additional provisions being necessary to protect consumers from the risks arising from digitalisation. These concerns relate to protection needs with regard to many different developments resulting from digitalisation.[93] Accordingly, with regard to the use of autonomous systems, the ELI Guiding Principles[94] have specifically addressed "assistants for consumer contracts". In contrast, the UN Model Law does not contain any consumer-specific rules. However, it also recognises the continuing importance of specific consumer law, expressly allowing for its application alongside its general provisions on AI contracting.[95]

With regard to the further development of consumer law in the field of AI contracting, the issue of consumer protection when using agentic AI systems highlights an important yet previously overlooked aspect. The article dealing with this issue[96] considers such AI systems not only as a potential risk to consumers, but also as a "tool for consumer empowerment".[97] In this respect, it considers AI contracting from the perspective of enabling innovations that benefit consumers rather than from that of digital vulnerability.

Based on this approach, legal certainty is to be regarded as a crucial prerequisite for consumers to take advantage of AI contracting; and ensuring

---

(Coord.), El Dret civil català davant la transformació digital i les exigències de la sostenibilitat, 2025, pp. 61 et seq.

92 See for example Grochowski, Digital Vulnerability in a Post-Consumer Society. Subverting Paradigms?, in: Crea/de Franceschi (eds.), The New Shapes of Digital Vulnerability in European Private Law, 2024, p. 201 et seq.; Schulze, ibid., pp. 521, 534.

93 See for example with regard to IoT Data Sharing Specht-Riemenschneider/El-Rifaai/Mehnert/Bodemann, IoT Data Sharing in B2C: How to Better Serve the Consumer, in: Lohsse/Schulze/Staudenmayer (eds.), Private Law and the Data Act, 2024, pp. 59 et seq.

94 See above fn. 53.

95 See above III.1.

96 Busch, Enabling Innovation and Protecting Consumers in the Agentic Economy: Why the Digital Fairness Act Should Regulate Agentic AI, in this volume.

97 Busch, Enabling Innovation and Protecting Consumers in the Agentic Economy: Why the Digital Fairness Act Should Regulate Agentic AI, ch. IV., in this volume.

legal certainty also requires an update of EU consumer law with regard to the legal framework for the use of agentic AI.[98] This includes creating new protection instruments, particularly against manipulation by and of AI agents – from "poisoned gifts" (where such agents are distributed on favourable terms but are preset to favour certain suppliers) and other algorithmic manipulations to the exploitation of access to personal data.[99] Since no "human consumer" is directly involved when a contract is concluded by an AI agent, the focus shifts to achieving consumer protection through design requirements for the AI agent ("consumer protection by design"). From this perspective, the article on consumer AI agents sets out initial steps for further developing consumer protection with regard to AI contracting, with reference to the ELI Guiding Principles and Rules. It also illustrates how ex ante requirements for designing AI agents can be combined with ex post consumer contract law instruments.

2. Attribution of knowledge and pre-contractual information duties

Turning to the pre-contractual stage of AI contracting, the main focus – as with conventional forms of contracting – is on pre-contractual information duties and the attribution of knowledge. In particular, the question arises for EU consumer law as to whether and, if so, how the extensive existing acquis communautaire should be adapted further in this area with regard to the use of AI. The issues arising in this respect must be carefully distinguished from those we have already encountered in relation to the conclusion of contracts. There the focus was on how and to whom the behaviour of an AI system could be attributed. In the field of pre-contractual information, however, one considers the attribution of information and knowledge received by an autonomous system, whether from the other party or from other sources such as its own data storage, internet searches or access to databases.[100]

98 Busch, Enabling Innovation and Protecting Consumers in the Agentic Economy: Why the Digital Fairness Act Should Regulate Agentic AI, ch. III.2., in this volume.

99 See Busch, Enabling Innovation and Protecting Consumers in the Agentic Economy: Why the Digital Fairness Act Should Regulate Agentic AI, ch. III.2.b), in this volume for more details and a series of examples.

100 Twigg-Flesner, Attribution of pre-contractual information and knowledge: the ELI Model Rules on Digital Assistants for Consumer Contracts and beyond, ch. I., in this volume.

With regard to such diverse types of information or knowledge of the autonomous system, it is probably not an easy task to determine whether and to what extent they can be attributed to the person using the system for contracting purposes. Nevertheless, the article in this volume that addresses this question,[101] does not merely describe this complex problem. Instead, it puts forward further proposals based on a critical analysis of the approaches set out in the ELI Guiding Principles and Model Rules with specific reference to consumer contracts as well as on a comparative study of the UN Model Law and the Principles for AI in Contracting.[102] Above all, the article addresses the challenging issue of defining the scope of "knowledge" that may be relevant to attribution (as opposed to categories such as "opinion"), while also considering the purpose of the relevant legal norm and the specific circumstances of the case, such as, in particular, the technical capability of the AI system in question.[103] Thus, it provides input for further discussion on the final version of any legislative proposals based on the current drafts and offers guidance on criteria for the possible future application of such legal texts.

3. Defects of consent and unexpected outcomes

Finally, using AI to conclude contracts may result in unexpected outcomes. This is obviously the case when the AI has been programmed wrongly. However, more importantly, the stochastic way of proceeding of AI guarantees a certain result (only) with a very high degree of probability but not with absolute certainty. Therefore, unexpected outcomes may occur even when the AI has done exactly what it was supposed to do, i.e. when it has made an autonomous decision that comes as a surprise. This raises fundamental questions for the theory of AI contracting, particularly regarding the relationship between traditional doctrines on defects of consent and new forms of contract conclusion. The assessment of which party (and to

101 Twigg-Flesner, Attribution of pre-contractual information and knowledge: the ELI Model Rules on Digital Assistants for Consumer Contracts and beyond, in this volume.

102 Twigg-Flesner, Attribution of pre-contractual information and knowledge: the ELI Model Rules on Digital Assistants for Consumer Contracts and beyond, in this volume.

103 See Twigg-Flesner, Attribution of pre-contractual information and knowledge: the ELI Model Rules on Digital Assistants for Consumer Contracts and beyond, in particular ch. II. and III., in this volume.

what extent) has to bear the risks of such "unexpected outcomes" is also of outstanding relevance with a view to the economic interests of the parties and the drafting of contracts.

a) A broad spectrum of positions

In terms of the normative handling of such unexpected outcomes, two fundamentally different approaches can be identified. According to one view, the traditional civil law doctrines of defects of consent (or vices of consent) and the existing contract law provisions based on them are sufficient to address the issue of unexpected outcomes in AI contracting.[104] This view is explained in more detail in the present volume with reference to German law and the Principles of European Contract Law.[105] From this perspective, the rules relating to the triad of error, fraud and duress constitute a "common core" of continental European legal systems. This makes it unnecessary to create new, specific sets of rules regarding issues of AI contracting in these legal systems.[106]

However, according to the other view, it may well be appropriate to create specific rules for unexpected outcomes when concluding contracts with AI, although opinions differ on the design of these rules. This view is primarily based on analyses of the peculiarities of contracting with autonomous systems.[107] It focuses on the assumption that increased automation has introduced a new dimension even in relation to conventional electronic contracts.[108] Based on this, various rules for dealing with unexpected outcomes have already been proposed, differing not only in detail, but also in scope. While the ELI approach is specifically tailored to consumer contracts (and is therefore not easily transferable to B2B contracts),[109] the

104 Rüfner, Vices of consent and AI Contracting, in this volume.
105 Rüfner, Vices of consent and AI Contracting, ch. IV., in this volume.
106 Rüfner, Vices of consent and AI Contracting, ch. V., in this volume.
107 See for example IV.2. above; Staikova-van Bommel, The UNCITRAL Model Law on Automated Contracting, ch. II.5.; Rodríguez de las Heras Ballell, Legal Framework for AI-Contracting: Key Rules on Validity, Attribution and Risk Allocation, ch. III.; Schwamberger, The Party to an AI Contract: Navigating Attribution in Autonomous Transactions, ch. II., all in this volume.
108 Staikova-van Bommel, The UNCITRAL Model Law on Automated Contracting, ch. I., in this volume.
109 Wendehorst, When things go wrong – dealing with unexpected outcomes in automated contracting, ch. IV., in this volume.

UN Model Law rules are only intended to apply cumulatively to the contract law of the relevant jurisdiction; the Principles for AI in Contracting, in turn, aim to provide an exhaustive regulation of the matter.[110] Despite their differences, the detailed assessments of the various solutions in this volume[111] show that there certainly is a solid basis for legislative policy decisions to be made in the near future, should the political will to do so arise at national or supranational level.

b) The approach of the UN Model Law

Once again, for the purposes of this introduction, the UN Model Law offers a good starting point for a more detailed analysis of the challenges and possible solutions. The UN Model Law recognises that, in some cases, the outcomes of an AI system may be so unexpected that exceptionally it appears justified to allow the party to whom the contract is attributed not to be bound by this outcome. Art. 8 UN Model Law addresses this situation, which stems from the specific autonomy of AI.[112]

Of all the provisions of the UN Model Law, Art. 8 was the most controversial. Consequently, Art. 8 UN Model Law was discussed at length during the preparation process. It was only agreed during the final, decisive UNCITRAL meeting week in July 2024. Even then it required discussions spanning almost an entire day, followed by a late-evening drafting session.

The controversy stems from the fundamentally different approaches to the balancing of interests in cases of unilateral misunderstanding (error/mistake) by one of the parties to a contract.[113] In simple terms, most continental European laws, while also safeguarding the interests of the

---

110 For more on this and other differences see among others, Wendehorst, When things go wrong – dealing with unexpected outcomes in automated contracting, ch. III. and IV.; Schwamberger, The Party to an AI Contract: Navigating Attribution in Autonomous Transactions, in particular ch. IV.; Rodríguez de las Heras Ballell, Legal Framework for AI-Contracting: Key Rules on Validity, Attribution and Risk Allocation, ch. III., all in this volume.

111 See in particular Wendehorst, When things go wrong – dealing with unexpected outcomes in automated contracting; Schwamberger, The Party to an AI Contract: Navigating Attribution in Autonomous Transactions, in particular ch. IV.; Rodríguez de las Heras Ballell, Legal Framework for AI-Contracting: Key Rules on Validity, Attribution and Risk Allocation, ch. III.

112 Cf. Guide to Enactment and Use, para. 76.

113 See Lohsse, in: Jansen/Zimmermann (eds.), Commentaries of European Contract Laws (2018), Introduction before PECL 4:101, para 4 as regards this distinction.

party relying on the contract, are relatively generous in protecting the mistaken party by allowing this party to avoid the contract. By contrast, legal systems belonging to or following the approach of the common law tradition concentrate on protecting the interests of the party relying on the contract, resulting in a more restrictive approach to contract avoidance. Generally speaking, the former approach primarily considers the mistaken party and restricts the type of relevant mistakes in order to safeguard the interests of the other party. The latter approach is more limited from the outset. Avoidance of the contract for reason of mistake is only permitted if the party relying on the contract was responsible for the mistake.[114]

Art. 8 UN Model Law establishes a rule that adapts the concept of avoidance of contracts in case of errors or mistakes to the specifics of autonomous contracting. However, in order to reach a consensus on adopting its Art. 8, the UN Model Law had to avoid saying so explicitly. Therefore, its Art. 8 (2) pretends that Art. 8 does not affect any rules regarding legal consequences, such as avoidance in case of mistake.[115] This provision aims to reassure UN States that they can retain their national rules on avoidance of contracts. In line with this approach, Art. 8 (1) UN Model Law could not determine the legal consequence of avoidance resulting from fulfilment of its substantive conditions. Instead, the UN Model Law borrows some wording from Art. 13 (5) UN Model on Electronic Commerce.[116] Thus, it affirms that "the other party to the contract is not entitled to rely on that action". When explaining this, the Guide to Enactment and Use states that Art. 8 (1) "effectively deprives that party of the right to assert the legal consequences flowing from the action".[117] In effect, this means that the party which would normally rely on the contract concluded autonomously cannot require the performance of the contract, if the conditions of Art. 8 (1) (a) and (b) UN Model Law are fulfilled. Through this construction, the UN Model Law reaches the result that the national laws on avoidance of contract can continue to exist, while creating a specific rule allowing a party facing an unexpected outcome not to be bound by the contract.

---

114 See Lohsse, in: Jansen/Zimmermann (eds.), ibid., 4:103, para 2 et seq. as to the origins in legal history and para 5 et seq. as to present laws and major restatements; for the different national laws see also the notes I. 1. et seq.; DCFR II.-7:203 in von Bar/Clive (eds.), Principles, Definitions and Model Rules of European Private Law – Draft Common Frame of Reference (DCFR) Volume I (2009).

115 Guide to Enactment and Use, para. 83.

116 Guide to Enactment and Use, para. 79.

117 Ibid.

As this covers both categories of unexpected outcomes, i.e. when the AI is wrongly programmed and when the AI did exactly what it was supposed to do, i.e. taking an autonomous decision the outcome of which is however unexpected, the scope of this rule is even broader than a classical error/mistake, but is adapted to the autonomy of AI.

Another element of the overall agreement is that UN Model Law clarifies in its Art. 7 (3) that an outcome which is unexpected does not change the attribution of the contract to the party which uses the AI. This is in line with an emphasis that a party using AI for the purposes of contracting bears the risk of doing so.[118] The Guide to Enactment and Use[119] sees Article 7 (3) as reaffirming the principle that attribution is not concerned with a person's state of mind,[120] but that other rules like Art. 8 UN Model Law solve the problem of unexpected outcomes. This is a reaction to the perplexities of the common law or those legal orders influenced by it when looking at European continental rules of error and mistake. Art. 8 is indeed designed to intervene only in exceptional cases; in most cases of unexpected outcomes, the contract will still have to be performed as foreseen.

Notably, as a result of the July 2024 compromise Art. 8 UN Model Law was put in square brackets, with its meaning explained in the accompanying footnote. This is supposed to clarify that it is meant for those UN States which want to implement a rule on unexpected outcomes.[121] However, the UN Model Law is by its nature in any case only a recommendation to UN States to implement it into their law. Putting Art. 8 UN Model Law in square brackets means thus basically using 'belts and suspenders'; its added value is purely presentational.

Furthermore, a compromise element also was the explicit priority given in Art. 8 (1) UN Model Law to the parties to agree a different risk allocation.[122] While this reflects the general emphasis of the UN Model Law on party autonomy, it does nothing more than that: it repeats a general principle.[123] It does not harm, but it does not add great value either.

While these two features were of a more nominal relevance, the rule itself uses elements from the two above-mentioned approaches. The EU

118 Guide to Enactment and Use, para. 77.
119 Para. 68.
120 The last sentence of para. 66 follows the same purpose.
121 Guide to Enactment and Use, para. 73 et seq.
122 Guide to Enactment and Use, para. 77.
123 See above, ch. III.2.

contribution to the UNCITRAL negotiations has significantly influenced the substance and drafting of the conditions in Art. 8 (1) (a) and (b) UN Model Law as well as the relevant explanations in the Guide to Enactment and Use. In doing so, it drew from the Common European Sales Law[124] (CESL), like several EU key legal acts in EU digital private law,[125] and from existing EU law. This is the first time that CESL fulfilled its functions as a "quarry"[126] not only in EU law, but also in international law.

The first substantive condition in Art. 8 (1) (a) UN Model Law requires that the party invoking this rule "could not reasonably have expected the action", looking at the situation from the point of view of the party for whom the outcome was unexpected and thus more from an angle known from continental European rules. The Guide to Enactment and Use[127] explains that the reasonable expectations are not subjectively, but objectively determined and that this objective determination takes into account all circumstances of the case at hand. It mentions explicitly the nature and purpose of the contract, the type of transaction, for which the action is carried out, and trade usages and practices established between the parties. This is based on the concept of "reasonable expectations" used in Art. 5 (2) and (1) CESL, a concept that has been deployed in the Digital Content Directive[128] (DCD) and the Sale of Goods Directive[129] (SGD).[130] As the concept of "reasonableness" is very widely used in common law, this was

124 Proposal of 11.10.2011 for a Regulation on a Common European Sales Law, COM(2011) 635 final; withdrawn OJ C 321/40 of 29.9.2020. For an introduction cf. Staudenmayer, Proposal for a Regulation on a Common European Sales Law – Textbook, 2011, pp. VII et seq. For details cf. Schulze (ed.), Common European Sales Law, 2012.

125 As to where the Digital Content Directive (2019/770 of 20 May 2019 on certain aspects concerning contracts for the supply of digital content and digital services), the Sale of Goods Directive (2019/771 of 20 May 2019 on certain aspects concerning contracts for the sale of goods) and the Data Act had already taken over CESL wording in their texts, cf. Staudenmayer, The Directives on Digital Contracts: First Steps Towards the Private Law of the Digital Economy, ERPL, 2020, pp. 223 et seq. and Lohsse/Schulze/Staudenmayer, in: Lohsse/Schulze/Staudenmayer (eds.), Private Law and the Data Act, 2024, p. 19.

126 Lohsse/Schulze/Staudenmayer, ibid.

127 Para. 81.

128 Directive 2019/770 of 20 May 2019 on certain aspects concerning contracts for the supply of digital content and digital services.

129 Directive 2019/771 of 20 May 2019 on certain aspects concerning contracts for the sale of goods.

130 For more details see Staudenmayer in Schulze/Staudenmayer (eds.), EU Digital Law, Art. 8 DCD, para. 93 et seq.

a basis for consensus in UNCITRAL. The "objective determination" stems from Recitals 46 DCD and 24 SGD. Again, the factors to be taken into account originate from Art. 5 (1) CESL and have been used in Recitals 46 DCD and 24 SGD. The Guide to Enactment and Use also adds the explanation that unexpected actions refer to outcomes where the party would not have concluded the contract or would have done so only on fundamentally different contract terms should it have been aware of the action from the outset. The resemblance of this explanation with the wording of Art. 48 (1) (a) CESL is also due to the EU input into the UNCITRAL negotiations. Finally, the Guide to Enactment and Use does not consider information on the design, operation and use of the automated system as a decisive factor, because such information might not be readily understood by the party. This is due to a main EU negotiation aim to ensure that the UNCITRAL rules take into account the situation of SMEs which do not have particular technical knowledge of the functioning of AI.

The second condition in Art. 8 (1) (b) UN Model Law requests that the other party "knew or could reasonably be expected to have known" that the party invoking the rule on unexpected outcomes did indeed not expect the action. This condition looks at the balance of interests from the angle of the other contractual party, as in such cases it would not be justified that this party could rely on the contract. While the first element ("knew") refers to positive, subjective knowledge of the other party, the second element ("could reasonably be expected to have known") introduces a reference to what the party ought to have known, which is to be determined objectively.[131] Again this wording and the respective explanations are influenced by CESL and EU law, as explained above.

V. Conclusion – Follow-up to the UN Model Law

For a legal policy discussion at EU level, which started at the High-Level Forum on Justice for Growth,[132] the UN Model Law raises several questions. Should the UN Model Law be implemented at all? If so, should this be done by the Member States or at EU level? If it should be implemented, should it be implemented by law or through other means? Finally, if it is

131 Guide to Enactment and Use, para. 82.

132 On the discussion in the High-Level Forum on Justice for Growth, see High-Level Fora on Justice for Growth and on the Future of EU Criminal Justice - European Commission, last accessed on 1.11.2025.

implemented, should its content remain unchanged or be adapted? While this introduction cannot address these questions in detail, the preceding considerations at least allow us to put forward a few thoughts.

The way in which the UN Model Law is drafted clearly shows that it was thought to be implemented by law. This is not only the explicit recommendation of UNCITRAL[133] and the UN General Assembly,[134] In addition, the already mentioned[135] emphasis on party autonomy and the explicit references to the parties' ability to decide otherwise, only make sense if the UN Model Law is implemented through default rules. In EU law, the most appropriate place to incorporate the UN Model Law into the EU acquis would be an adaptation of Art. 9–11 E-Commerce Directive (ECD) to technological progress in form of autonomous contracting.[136] Both sets of rules take the same approach to recognising contracts concluded using new technologies.[137]

Following the endorsement of the UN Model Law by the UN General Assembly, the AI Continent Plan of the European Commission had already indicated that the forthcoming Apply AI Strategy would address AI contracting.[138] However, the current political climate and main trends at EU level do not favour the proposal and adoption of further EU legislation. In line with this major political trend, the Commission has chosen a non-legislative approach in its Apply AI Strategy.[139] The strategy recognises AI as a production factor to be supported, particularly with regard to SMEs, which includes AI contracting.[140] It announces that, by the end of 2027, in the context of enhancing opportunities for European startups and SMEs, it will establish a discussion forum with interested stakeholders on reducing risks in AI contracting for SMEs (including start-ups) and provide legal guidance, notably in the form of model contract terms for AI contracts and on the choice of AI contracting systems.[141]

---

133 UNCITRAL decision, point 4.
134 Resolution 79/119 of the General Assembly, point 3.
135 See III.2.
136 Directive 2000/31 of 8 June 2000 on certain legal aspects of information society services, in particular electronic commerce, in the Internal Market (Directive on electronic commerce).
137 Art. 9 (1) ECD; Guide to Enactment and Use, para. 13.
138 COM (2025) 165 final, p. 14.
139 COM (2025) 723 final.
140 Ibid, p. 15.
141 Ibid., Annex 3, p. 8.

Indeed, one of the purposes of the UN Model Law is that it can be used by parties in a possible framework agreement for autonomous contracting.[142] Model contract terms for such a framework contract or also specific contracts could therefore be a means of implementing the UN Model Law. However, model contract terms cannot recognise that autonomous contracts are valid in all legal systems. This can only be achieved through legislation. It may therefore be necessary to clarify, through appropriate means, that the recognition of contracts concluded by electronic means in Art. 9 ECD also extends to the conclusion of autonomous contracts. The Guide to Enactment indeed sees automated contracting as electronic contracting with reduced human involvement.[143]

Finally, as regards the question of possible adaptations of the UN Model Law rules, the detailed examinations of these rules and its comparison with other proposals in this volume hopefully provide a solid basis for all further discussion.

142 Guide to Enactment and Use, para. 7.
143 Guide to Enactment and Use, para. 4, 24.

The UNCITRAL Model Law on Automated Contracting

*Simona Staikova-van Bommel**

I. Context of the Model Law on Automated Contracting

The drafting history of the Model Law on Automated Contracting (Model Law) can be traced back to 2018. At its 51st session the United Nations Commission on International Trade Law (UNCITRAL) mandated exploratory work on the legal effects of automated technologies in contracting, following a proposal from the Government of Czechia. While UNCITRAL at that stage had decades long experience in the field of electronic commerce and distance contracts, innovative technological developments in automation raised new issues. Traditional electronic contracts were concluded by parties communicating with each other at a distance, but increased automation added a new dimension, by enabling contracting even without the direct communication and involvement of the parties. The work on automated contracting was meant to tackle new issues arising from such technological innovations. For a better understanding of the Model Law, it is helpful to first consider the broader context of digital trade and technological developments in contracting automation. The drafting history of the Model Law focused on key contemporary technologies used for the purpose of automated contracting, namely smart contracts and artificial intelligence (AI).[1]

1. Automated technologies in contracting

The smart contracts technology relies on software programmes that execute actions when certain conditions are fulfilled, based on the premise

* EU official working for the European Commission who was involved in the negotiations on the Model Law on Automated Contracting at UNCITRAL. The views expressed in this publication are in a personal capacity and the European Commission cannot be held responsible for the information contained therein.

1 Guide to Enactment on the UNCITRAL Model Law on Automated Contracting, Vienna, 2025, para 16.

'if condition A is fulfilled, action B should be executed'. The term was originally coined by computer scientist Nick Szabo in the late 1990s.[2] Building on preceding decades long experience with Electronic Data Interchange (EDI), he envisaged computerised software resembling contract clauses that would bind each party together in a way that would narrow down 'the opportunities to terminate its performance obligations'.[3] More specifically, as contract terms are expressed in code, performance of actions, is triggered automatically when certain conditions are met. The notion of 'smart contracts' is however misleading, because smart contracts as a technology does not necessarily overlap with the legal notion of a contract.[4] The two can overlap when the technology is used to conclude or perform legal contacts or parts thereof.

The smart contracts technology can be seen as rigid, because once activated it may be hard to stop the automated performance of actions or reverse transactions. Moreover, on the blockchain, there is no single person who controls it.[5] On the other hand smart contracts can enable greater flexibility in contracting, when linked to an external data source called 'an oracle'. The oracle feeds the latest external data on a given indicator, for instance as regards financial data, outside temperature or location. On this basis, performance obligations, such as payment flows can also be up-dated almost in real time.[6]

It should be noted that even though smart contracts are often used in conjunction with distributed ledger technology (DLT), this interlinkage is not a must per se. Historically, smart contracts application expanded and became increasingly linked to DLT with the increased use of Bitcoin and other blockchain based systems.[7] Nevertheless, smart contracts were first conceived and used independently of DLT and can per se be relevant for various use-cases beyond cryptocurrencies and blockchains. Recent

2 *De Filippi/Wright,* Blockchain and the Law, the Rule of Code, Cambridge, Masachusetts, 2019, p. 73.

3 *De Filippi/Wright,* Blockchain and the Law, the Rule of Code, Cambridge, Masachusetts, 2019, p. 73.

4 *Borges,* Smart Contracts for Data Transactions and the Data Act, pp. 7-8.

5 *De Filippi/Wright,* Blockchain and the Law, the Rule of Code, Cambridge, Masachusetts, 2019, pp. 74 et seq.

6 *De Filippi/Wright,* Blockchain and the Law, the Rule of Code, Cambridge, Masachusetts, 2019, p. 75.

7 *De Filippi/Wright,* Blockchain and the Law, the Rule of Code, Cambridge, Masachusetts, 2019, p. 74.

legislative developments[8] reaffirmed that the interlinkage of smart contracts with DLT is not a must. For the purpose of automated contracting, what matters is that the smart contracts is a contemporary technology relevant for automated contracting. It can be deployed in various use-cases and sectors also in the future.

The other key technology increasingly drawing expanding in automated contracting is AI. An AI system, as defined in the AI Act[9] is a machine-based system that can produce outputs based on varying degrees of adaptiveness and autonomy, based on the input it receives. Amongst others, it can generate output in the form of predictions, recommendations, content or decisions. While the difference between AI and non-AI based automated systems has been subject to considerable debate, a simple distinction can be drawn on the basis that non-AI systems perform clearly pre-defined instructions.[10] In that sense their can be traced back to the instructions given by a human and their respective will and intention to that effect. On the other hand, the AI-based systems can be envisaged on a spectrum with different degrees of autonomy. On one end would be 'symbolic', 'deterministic' or 'rule-based' AI which is closer to traditional computer programmes and performs via algorithms based on pre-defined logic and encoded expert knowledge.[11] On the other end of the spectrum is 'autonomous' or 'non-deterministic' AI operating based on machine learning techniques. They apply mathematic models drawing on large scale data sets that should be sufficiently representative for the performance of a specific task.[12] Such autonomous systems are more likely to produce outputs that are not neces-

8 Art. 2 (39) of Regulation (EU) 2023/2854 of the European Parliament and of the Council of 13 December 2023 on harmonised rules on fair access to and use of data and amending Regulation (EU) 2017/2394 and Directive (EU) 2020/1828 (Data Act), (Text with EEA relevance), OJ L, 2023/2854, 22.12.2023.

9 Art. 3(1) of Regulation (EU) 2024/1689 of the European Parliament and of the Council of 13 June 2024 laying down harmonised rules on artificial intelligence and amending Regulations (EC) No 300/2008, (EU) No 167/2013, (EU) No 168/2013, (EU) 2018/858, (EU) 2018/1139 and (EU) 2019/2144 and Directives 2014/90/EU, (EU) 2016/797 and (EU) 2020/1828 (Artificial Intelligence Act) (Text with EEA relevance) OJ L, 2024/1689, 12.7.2024AI Act.

10 Joint Research Centre, 'Novel forms of contracting in the digital economy, AI-enabled autonomous contracting', 2024, p. 25.

11 Joint Research Centre, 'Novel forms of contracting in the digital economy, AI-enabled autonomous contracting', 2024, p. 25.

12 Joint Research Centre, 'Novel forms of contracting in the digital economy, AI-enabled autonomous contracting', 2024, p. 25.

sarily known or intended by the humans deploying the system for specific purposes.

As companies are experimenting by applying different technologies to automate contracting activities, use-cases are emerging in different economic sectors. In practice, the existing use-cases of automated contracting involve systems relying either on smart contracts, artificial intelligence or on both. It is not always obvious how to categorise them in practice.

2. Developing use-cases

It should first be acknowledged that one-sided automation has been widely used by traders at the marketing and pre-contractual stage for a long time, starting with physical vending machines.[13] Nowadays, it is widely used in the online environment and e-commerce and is usually deployed by traders. One example is dynamic pricing which depends on real time and supply and demand in ticket sales by airline companies.[14] Another example are digital assistants or chatbots that can make purchase recommendations to consumers based on their past history. Since the decisions and actions concerning the contract conclusion and performance are still taken by humans, the legal issues arising from such use-cases have not been significant enough to hinder the wider uptake of one-sided automation at the marketing and pre-contractual stage.[15] More complex issues arise with the development of automated systems that are capable to take independent actions and interact with others. Emerging use-cases are increasingly going beyond the pre-contractual phase and focus on the next stages of the contract life cycle, namely contract conclusion and performance.

Recently, the smart contracts technology combined with AI has been deployed in renewable energy trading. The Port of Rotterdam micro-grid introduced one of the first high frequence energy trading systems for renewable energy.[16] It deployed energy trading agents, which can enter into transactions based on user preferences, behaviours and available prices,

---

13 *Borges*, Smart Contracts for Data Transactions and the Data Act, p. 5.

14 Joint Research Centre, 'Novel forms of contracting in the digital economy, AI-enabled autonomous contracting', 2024, p. 79.

15 Joint Research Centre, 'Novel forms of contracting in the digital economy, AI-enabled autonomous contracting', 2024, p. 79.

16 Joint Research Centre, 'Novel forms of contracting in the digital economy, AI-enabled autonomous contracting', 2024, pp. 89 et seq.

considering weather conditions[17] In recent years automated contracting use-cases have also been tested in the real estate trading field, for instance automated contract performance following acquisition of apartments in Kyiv, Ukraine.[18] Smart contracts have recently also been used in industrial and transport services, such as production and delivery of goods, as well as financial transactions.[19]

AI can be used in manufacturing and supply chains, in so called smart factories and smart warehouses. The application fields can vary and include various purposes, such as contract negotiations, automated inventory stocking and purchase order filling, including automated demand prediction anticipating future needs.[20] The use-case of automated negotiations with multiple suppliers was successfully tested by Walmart in a pilot project. It deployed a chatbot to negotiate contracts with thousands of its suppliers.[21] This test case by far exceeded expectations (20% success rate) and reached agreement with 64% of the suppliers, while 83% were satisfied with the experience with the chatbot.[22] Other use-cases including high levels of automation include programmatic advertising,[23] high frequency foreign exchange trading on platforms[24] and algorithmic house pricing of real estate in the US.[25]

Another step towards the development of autonomous AI use-cases is the Amazon Nova Act[26], which aims to enable AI agents to take actions on web browsers. The envisaged examples include an AI agent making weekly orders for food delivery, contracting a repair service for an oven or maybe

17 Joint Research Centre, 'Novel forms of contracting in the digital economy, AI-enabled autonomous contracting', 2024, p. 90.

18 *Filatova,* 'Smart contracts from the contract law perspective: outlining new regulative strategies', IJLIT, 2020, 28, pp. 217-242, p. 223.

19 *Borges,* 'Smart Contracts for Data Transactions and the Data', pp. 6-7.

20 Joint Research Centre, 'Novel forms of contracting in the digital economy, AI-enabled autonomous contracting', 2024, pp. 85 et seq.

21 Joint Research Centre, 'Novel forms of contracting in the digital economy, AI-enabled autonomous contracting', 2024, pp. 86 et seq.

22 Joint Research Centre, 'Novel forms of contracting in the digital economy, AI-enabled autonomous contracting', 2024, pp .86 et seq.

23 Joint Research Centre, 'Novel forms of contracting in the digital economy, AI-enabled autonomous contracting', 2024, pp. 73 et seqq.

24 Joint Research Centre, 'Novel forms of contracting in the digital economy, AI-enabled autonomous contracting', 2024, pp. 70 et seqq.

25 ICF Consortium, 'Novel Forms of Contracting in the Digital Economy', 2025, p. 96.

26 Amazon AGI Labs, 'Introducing Amazon Nova Act', 2025, available at Introducing Amazon Nova Act | Amazon AGI Labs (last accessed: 9.6.2025).

even completing a sequence of complex tasks such as planning a wedding. It is also highly relevant in a business context where its proactive actions could bring high efficiency gains. The envisaged possibilities include proactive restocking of warehouses with potential variations in orders depending on anticipated demand, supplies orders for factories and proactive management of logistic operations to optimise supply chains. Increased complexity may further result from two-way automation, namely scenarios where both contractual parties are acting by means of automated systems.

3. Benefits, costs and risks

The development of innovative technologies in the form of automated contracting systems deployed throughout the contract lifecycle brings many economic benefits. They include reduced costs and more efficient contract management. This is particularly relevant for high volume contracting, involving frequent transactions, multiple parties or both aspects. An additional benefit is improved accuracy and lower rates of errors and respectively lower risk of legal challenges.[27] These translate in increased operational efficiency and customer satisfaction.[28] Another advantage is the ability to conclude contracts or adjust contractual terms in real time based on the analysis of large data sets, while effectively responding to dynamic market developments[29] in real time. This improves the capacity of economic operators to identify favourable conditions and suitable offers to their needs, while improving contract outcomes and contributing to competitiveness.

While automated contracting is still a use-case with relatively limited uptake[30], given the significant benefits, it is likely to increase in the future. As the practical use is growing, costs, risks and uncertainties around the use of automated contracting are also revealing themselves. There are a range of costs and risks that may hold back the likely rapid expansion of automation given its benefits. They include both practical and legal barriers, that may deter potentially interested companies from adopting

27 ICF Consortium, 'Novel Forms of Contracting in the Digital Economy', 2025, p. 101.
28 ICF Consortium, 'Novel Forms of Contracting in the Digital Economy', 2025, p. 103.
29 ICF Consortium, 'Novel Forms of Contracting in the Digital Economy', 2025, p. 99.
30 Joint Research Centre, 'Novel forms of contracting in the digital economy, AI-enabled autonomous contracting', 2024, p. 63.

automation. As regards the assumed adopters of AI in contracting[31], the key barriers are lack of skills, adoption and adaptation costs, lack of access to necessary data, liability and reputational risks and complex algorithms. A distinction between 'revealed barriers' and 'deterring barriers' can be made, respectively considering the perceptions of actual users and on the one hand and prospective users, on the other hand. The latter are only considering using a technology, but may be discouraged to test it due to high risks and costs. The evidence suggests that the same issues impact both groups of users, albeit with small percentage variations.[32]

While practical barriers play a major role, legal uncertainty is one of the key obstacles that affects both existing and prospective users of AI. Legal issues seem to gain importance progressively with the degree of automation and in particular the systems' capacity to perform autonomous actions during the contract lifecycle. The extension of automation to the phases of contract conclusion and performance touches upon decisions and actions that have clear legal consequences. Data suggests that nearly 1 in 2 EU companies interested in AI are dissuaded from adopting it because of concerns about liability and the consequences off use.[33] While liability concerns may relate to contractual or non-contractual issues, evidence suggests that a number of contract-law related obstacles could feed this perception. They include in particular concerns about validity of automated contracts,[34] errors and unexpected outcomes,[35] limited human control[36] and uncertainty about the legal framework.[37]

---

31 Currently Eurostat does not include specific indicators on uptake of AI in contracting. The rate of uptake of AI in contracting can be assumed based on existing broader indicators on use of AI technologies and uptake of AI in general.

32 Joint Research Centre, 'Novel forms of contracting in the digital economy, AI-enabled autonomous contracting', 2024, pp. 73-75, pp. 66 et seqq.

33 Eurostat, ICT usage by enterprises, 2023: 45.5% of EU companies which ever considered to use any AI technologies do not use AI technologies due to a lack of clarity about the legal consequences.

34 ICF Consortium, 'Novel Forms of Contracting in the Digital Economy', 2025, pp. 61 et seqq.

35 ICF Consortium, 'Novel Forms of Contracting in the Digital Economy', 2025, pp. 63 et seqq.

36 ICF Consortium, 'Novel Forms of Contracting in the Digital Economy', 2025, pp. 66 et seq.

37 ICF Consortium, 'Novel Forms of Contracting in the Digital Economy', 2025, pp. 67 et seq.

Market developments substantiate these concerns. The cases below are a couple of recent examples that gained publicity and illustrate how such concerns could materialise. The Zillow case exemplifies the high costs and risks that could materialise due to unexpected actions of an automated system. In 2021, Zillow launched an AI-powered platform for home-buying contracts. However, the AI algorithm guiding the purchasing decisions failed to account for shifting market conditions and overestimated property values. This resulted in Zillow buying properties at a higher price it could sell, which led to $ 300 Million losses and significant job cuts and made the news at the time.[38] An earlier notable example is the landmark Quoine case decided by the Singapore Court of Appeal. The case combines questions around contract validity, mistake, unexpected actions and uncertainty about the application of the current legal framework. The dispute arose in relation to the automated Quoine cryptocurrency exchange platform. B2C2 Ltd could complete trades at a highly beneficial price 250 times more than the market rate, due to an operational oversight by the platform operator, which resulted in the platform not accessing external market data.[39] As the platform operator Quoine cancelled and reversed the transactions after discovering the issue, but B2C2 Ltd challenged this and eventually won the case. While the Quoine decision applied the existing legal framework and clarified important questions around automated contracts, at least in common law, it left other questions open, notably whether the same reasoning could apply under different circumstances, notably involving non-deterministic automated systems.[40]

In this context, the Model Law rightly focuses on the core contractual issues that contribute to legal uncertainty and clarifies them for a wide range of scenarios.

---

38 CNN, 'Zillow's home-buying debacle shows how hard it is to use AI to value real estate', 2021, available at: Zillow's home-buying debacle shows how hard it is to use AI to value real estate | CNN Business (last accessed: 9.6.2025).

39 The Singapore Courts, 'Do Algorithms Dream of Mistaken Contracts?', 2020, available at quoine-pte-ltd-v-b2c2-ltd.pdf (last accessed: 9.6.2025).

40 The Singapore Courts, 'Do Algorithms Dream of Mistaken Contracts?', 2020, p. 7, available at quoine-pte-ltd-v-b2c2-ltd.pdf, (last accessed: 9.6.2025).

II. The Model Law on Automated Contracting addressing key areas of legal uncertainty

1. Definitions

The Model Law takes a technology neutral approach, setting out model rules for 'automated systems', rather than focusing on concrete technologies, such as AI. The term 'automated system' is defined (Article 1(1)(a)), by reference to two key characteristics. First, this a computer system and second, it has capability to carry out actions without the necessary review or intervention by a natural person. This does not preclude a possibility of 'human in the loop' solutions which provide for a human involvement, but this should not be necessary for the system to function. Considering that contract law in various legal systems is human-centric and largely reliant on human intent and more broadly, on human cognitive and volitional states, the lack of necessary human intervention is a key characteristic of automated systems deployed for contracting purposes.

The concept of an automated system in the Model Law (Article 1(2)) is further specified by reference to different types of systems, namely those operating in a 'deterministic' or in a 'non-deterministic' manner. The difference between the two types of systems is elaborated in the Guide to Enactment.[41] It specifies that the notion of 'deterministic' manner refers to 'rules-based' systems which generate predictable output given the same input. It also includes non-deterministic systems that can increasingly take autonomous actions and generate output based on pre-defined objectives, but not necessarily predefined results. Their output may not be predicted in advance, as they operate based on a range of probabilities.

The broad definition of an automated system paves the way for the technology neutral and future-oriented approach of the Model Law. This approach aims to capture various types of automated technologies. The most relevant contemporary technologies meeting the characteristics of an 'automated system' in contracting are smart contracts and artificial-intelligence (AI)-based systems. While presently there is great focus on AI and its growing role in digital trade and the wider economy, the definitions do not include this concept. Not spelling out AI, confirms the technology neutral

41 Guide to Enactment of the UNCITRAL Model Law on Automated Contracting, 2025, para 29.

approach. It also ensures that the rules are future proof and will also be fit to capture future technologies with similar characteristics.

The definitions further include the concept of a 'data message'. It is defined as information, which can be generated and processed by various technological means, including electronic, magnetic, optical (Article 1(b)). It is used in the context of actions forming or performing contract the terms and could relate to the terms of the contract or communications in relation to the contract. The concept of a data message is not specific to automated contracting systems and is well-established in UNCITRAL texts on electronic commerce. Its use in the Model Law ensures consistency with other UNCITRAL texts on electronic commerce.

2. Scope

The scope of application of the Model Law includes the complete contract lifecycle (Article 2(1)). The inclusion of actions in connection with the formation of a contract, such as offer and acceptance, means that also actions at the pre-contractual stage are covered. Furthermore, the performance stage is defined broadly, including contract modification, termination as well as non-performance and the exercise of agreed remedies.[42] Importantly, the scope comprises the use of automated systems either at a single contractual stage, in multiple contractual stages or throughout the whole contract lifecycle.

This approach takes into account various use-cases and business models for deployment of automated contracting in practice. It illustrates the intended broad scope of application of the Model Law. More specifically, automated systems that may be deployed exclusively at the contract formation stage are included. They can be relevant in dynamic pricing, automated offer generation, selection and contract conclusion. Automated system that could be deployed by one party only for the contract performance stage are also covered. This can for instance be relevant for smart contracts-based systems that can be programmed to execute multiple repetitive transactions, such as contract renewal notices for insurance. Finally, an automated system could also be deployed at all stages of the contract life cycle. While it remains to be seen what use-cases in contracting will gain more practical

42 Guide to Enactment of the UNCITRAL Model Law on Automated Contracting, 2025, para 33.

relevance, it is important that the legal framework provides certainty for a broad range of scenarios.

Another important consideration in the scope of the Model Law is that it is not limited to business-to-business contracts. During the development of the Model Law, it was acknowledged that automated contracting is prevalent amongst others in consumer transactions.[43] Its rules are therefore also relevant and can apply to consumer contracts. This is however subject to any limitations that may stem from other laws that prevail, notably consumer protection rules (Article 2(2)). The use of automated systems in consumer transactions could respectively be subject to limitations or even potential prohibitions that may stem from consumer rules that would prevail. Similarly, the application of other laws that may govern the design, commissioning, operation or use of automated systems is safeguarded. The choice not to exclude consumer contracts from the scope is important to note. It is also appropriate, as key general contract law issues affecting business-to-business contracts could equally be relevant for consumer contracts. It difficult to estimate what the actual current and future uptake of automated contracting will be in either business or consumer contracts due to lack of specific statistical indicators. Some stakeholders consider that consumer contracts are more suitable and likely to be automated at scale. An argument to that end is that consumer contracts are less complex and more standardised compared to business-to-business contracts.

The Model Law clearly aims to take an ambitious approach ensuring a broad scope covering various types of use-cases. It is still pragmatic and restrained in terms of the range of legal issues covered. The Model Law as a whole intends to supplement the existing legal framework by bringing legal certainty on key questions for automated contracting. The objective of integrating rules on automated contracting into the broader framework on electronic commerce is specifically acknowledged by the UN General Assembly.[44] The Model Law was therefore not intended to regulate exhaustively all relevant issues to automated contracting in an instrument specific to this topic. Respectively, a number of areas remained outside the scope

43 Guide to Enactment of the UNCITRAL Model Law on Automated Contracting, 2025, para 35.

44 Resolution 79/119 on the 'Model Law on Automated Contracting', adopted by the General Assembly on 4 December 2024. The Preamble envisages that the Model Law 'will constitute a useful addition to existing Commission texts in the area of electronic commerce by assisting States in enhancing their legislation governing the use of automation in contracting, or in formulating such legislation where none exists'.

of the Model Law. They include rules governing the design, commissioning and operation of automated systems, rules on permitted and ethical use of AI and AI governance, rules on information disclosure, personal data and consumer law or other rules regulating transactions with weaker parties (Article 2(2)). The specific rules on automated contracting do not affect the application of other rules and mandatory rules prevail.[45]

3. Validity

The Model Law contains a general rule on legal recognition of automated contracting (Article 5) and a specific provision relating to contracts in computer code and including dynamic information (Article 6). These provisions affirm the validity of automated contracts in various contexts and therefore address a core area of legal uncertainty.

a) The general rule

Legal uncertainty is particularly relevant for legal systems where existing rules on meeting of minds and intent may call into question automated contract conclusion. This is particularly relevant where contracts are concluded by automated systems with a high degree of autonomy and a person is not necessarily aware of all the details[46] at the point of contract conclusion, given that a system can act randomly based on a range of probabilities. The issue is that a person concluding a contract may not even be aware of what is exchanged and on what terms, notably: who is the other party, what are the characteristics of the object of the contract and what are the contract conditions including price. Thus, also the party's intent and agreement to conclude a given contract can be called into question.

The general rule of the Model Law states that contracts formed or performed using an automated system should not be denied legal validity or enforceability on the sole ground that no natural person revised or intervened (Article 5(1)). This wording reflects the approach of standard non-discrimination provisions UNCITRAL e-commerce texts, adapted to

45 Guide to Enactment of the Model Law on Automated Contracting, 2025, para 36.

46 *Wendehorst,* 'Principles for AI in Contracting, Old and New Rules for Old and New Problems', V. Sagaert en J. Vanaroye (ed.), Privaatrecht plenis coloribus. Libur Amicorum Matthias Storme, Mechelen, Kluwer, 2024, 1097-1124. p. 46.

automated contracting. This means that the use of an automated system per se should not lead to invalidity of the contract. The same approach applies to 'actions in connection with the formation of performance of contracts' (Article 5(3)). Legal recognition is given to a wide range of automated contractual actions throughout the contract lifecycle. This includes the pre-contractual phase where a contract has not yet come into being, as well as the performance phase and the exercise of rights and remedies agreed under the contract or permitted by law. Such actions can include communications (declaration, notice, request, offer, acceptance) or other outcomes of a decision-making process.[47]

It should be noted that the Model Law does not preclude the application of other rules that may limit or even rule out the validity of automated contracts (or actions in connection with contracts) for various reasons. As mentioned above, such rules could stem from other areas of law referred to in Article 2(2), such as consumer protection or data protection laws that could require human intervention for various considerations. This is reflected in the wording 'sole ground', i.e. that legal recognition should not be denied.

b) Terms in computer code

The specific rule on legal recognition (Article 6) focuses on issues arising out of particular characteristics of automated systems, that may not be relevant in all cases. It provides important clarifications in relation to contracts including terms expressed in computer code or involving dynamic information. First, legal recognition of validity and enforceability for contracts including terms in the form of computer code is confirmed (Article 6(1)). This is particularly relevant for the smart contracts technology. In practice, it is likely that a contract would be drafted in a natural language and then translated into computer code in a smart contracts system. The contract or certain aspects thereof are then performed if certain encoded conditions are met. They are translated into machine readable instructions, so that the automated system can take respective actions.

Different scenarios for the deployment of smart contracts are possible. They include the formulation of an offer or contract in natural language

47 Guide to Enactment of the UNCTRAL Model Law on Automated Contracting, 2025, para 50.

and then expressing the terms in code for the purpose of automating both conclusion and performance. Another scenario is automating performance of certain obligations after the conclusion of a contract in a natural language. A third scenario, which may be less frequent, but not excluded, is a contract that is exclusively formulated in code. It would then not be available in natural language, such as contracts on the blockchain without verbal negotiations. While it is less likely that someone would enter into a contract expressed in programming language alone, it is not impossible, for instance by performing a required action, such as transfer of digital asset.[48] This scenario could become more relevant in the future with the increased use of smart products with the capacity to perform actions in connection with contracts, as such products could operate based on machine-readable computer languages alone.[49] The Model Law captures all the above scenarios ensuring that contract terms expressed in computer code and respectively smart legal contracts, will not be denied validity or enforceability on that ground alone. A related question the Model Law does not answer is what language should prevail if there is a discrepancy between a contract term expressed in natural language and code language.

c) Dynamic information

The Model Law further clarifies that contracts should not be denied validity or enforceability on the sole ground that they incorporate dynamic information from a data source that changes continuously or periodically (Article 6(2)). Respectively, also actions in connection with such contracts should not be denied legal effects, validity or enforceability (Article 6(3)). The rationale behind these rules is to capture automated systems which incorporate dynamic information into the contract terms or perform actions which could depend on dynamic indicators. The sources of dynamic information could be internal or external to the system, but the core implication is the continuous prospect of changes in the contractual terms or future actions in connection with a contract. In practice, this means for instance that parties to a contract could agree to terms they are not aware of, as the terms are dynamic and may materialise only in the future. Similarly, a

48 *Filatova*, 'Smart contracts from the contract law perspective: outlining new regulative strategies', IJLIT, 2020, 217-242, pp. 228 et seq.

49 *Filatova*, 'Smart contracts from the contract law perspective: outlining new regulative strategies', IJLIT, 2020, 217-242, pp. 228 et seq.

person could end up concluding a contract based on a dynamic indicator that may trigger an action for contract formation in the future.

Questions could arise whether such a rule is justified and warranted in view of considerations of legal certainty. It could also be questioned whether a meeting of minds and agreement to conclude a contract including dynamic contract terms can be ascertained if the respective information in the terms only materialises in the future. The issue could however be overcome. First, the incorporation of terms that are per se not spelled out in a contract is not a novelty in e-commerce. For instance, the Model Law on Electronic Commerce already in 1998 included a rule on incorporation by reference, which did not exclude the possibility of later amendment.[50] The issue could further be addressed by way of instructions authorising a range of acceptable actions and terms that could be given in advance. Furthermore, an essential consideration for the inclusion of this provision is the high relevance of dynamic information for the contemporary realities automated systems. In practice, the ability to process vast amounts of information, assess it and take action in real time is one of the key benefits of AI-based systems, with a higher degree of autonomy based on machine learning. Similarly, oracles add flexibility and agility to smart contracts based automated systems.

In digital trade, the ability to identify and respond to price fluctuations, is a competitive advantage in dynamic environments where multiple parameters are changing continuously and depend on supply and demand. This could be the main reason why an automated system is deployed in the first place. An automated system is more effective in such dynamic environments compared to human operators who normally will not have similar capacity to process vast amounts of information in real time. The relevance of dynamic information is far reaching and not only limited to measuring price as an indicator. Another example is the ability to respond in real time to temperature changes, which can trigger the conclusion of contracts for renewable energy. Automated contracting systems with dynamic information capabilities could also be deployed to monitor the performance of logistic contracts in supply chains, for instance monitoring the location of a moving object and performing certain actions such as a payment once a delivery has reached its final destination.

50 Article 5 bis of the Model Law on Electronic Commerce and Guide to Enactment, 1996, para 46-5.

The above examples demonstrate that the chosen solution to provide for legal recognition of dynamic information is necessary and justified. Denying legal recognition to dynamic information in contracts or related actions would practically exclude from the scope a large number of use-cases where automated contracting can be economically beneficial.

4. Attribution

The question of attribution arises in relation to actions of automated systems, which can produce output with legal consequences throughout the contract life cycle. Since the actions are performed by an automated system, it is not obvious who (or what) should be accountable for them. This has clear implications as regards the legal effects as well as the attribution of risk in relation to the action. The respective rule on attribution (Article 7) is of limited scope and focuses on attribution of actions in connection with a contract, while leaving beyond its scope the question of legal consequences of attribution.

a) Clarifying who is behind an automated action

The Model Law makes a choice and provides an important clarification on the question of attribution, namely that the actions of an automated system should be attributed to a person. This approach is in line with the prevailing view and solutions taken in other areas, for instance with respect to establishing intellectual property rights over output generated by AI systems.[51] The inclusion of the rule on attribution practically discards a widely discussed alternative, which is to give legal personality to AI, respectively the automated system. This is an important clarification as the matter has been widely discussed with arguments supporting different solutions.

There are arguments in favour of awarding legal personality to AI, which take into account its growing capacity to take independent actions with legal consequences. While a potential AI personality could not be equated to a natural person's, it could build on the approach of bestowing a legal personality to companies or to governmental and non-governmental entities. Furthermore, there are examples of objects that have been given legal

51 Guide to Enactment of the Model Law on Automated contracting, 2025, para 61.

personality in various jurisdictions. They include a river in New Zealand, temples in India, an ecosystem in Ecuador, a humanoid robot that was given citizenship in Saudi Arabia and an online system granted residency rights in Japan.[52]

Nevertheless, the Model Law opts for a different solution and reaffirms the prevailing view that an automated system should not have legal personality. Considerations underpinning this position include that a legal personality for AI would 'be fundamentally inconsistent with the principle of human agency, accountability and responsibility'.[53] The creation of a potential electronic personality would shift the risks from the otherwise responsible legal and natural persons who could use this route to avoid liability risks for the output.[54] Furthermore, AI does not have a will and decision-making power of its own. Moreover, it does not have property that would enable it to deal with potential claims, notably liability claims for damages caused.[55]

b) How to attribute an automated action

Having made the choice of attributing actions of automated systems to a person, the Model Law further clarifies the next question, namely how to link a given action to a specific person. Two scenarios are envisaged. First, the primary rule provides for a procedure agreed by the parties (Article 7(1)). An agreement can be expressed in a framework contract between the parties. Such framework contracts or framework arrangements[56] can be particularly helpful for parties which engage in multiple transactions with each other and can agree in advance how the output of the automated system will be attributed in advance. Alternatively, the procedure could be set out in the terms and conditions of a platform to which both parties using an automated system may subscribe to.

---

52 *Chesterman*, 'AI and the Limits of Legal Personality', ICLQ, vol. 69, 2020, pp. 819-844, pp. 821 et seq.

53 Independent High Level Expert Group on Artificial Intelligence, 'Policy and Investment Recommendations for Trustworthy AI' 2019, p. 41.

54 *Chesterman,* 'AI and the Limits of Legal Personality', International and Comparative Law Quarterly, p. 826.

55 *Chesterman,* 'AI and the Limits of Legal Personality', ICLQ, vol. 69, 2020, pp. 819-844, p. 824.

56 *Wendehorst*, 'Version 3.0. of the Principles for AI in Contracting, Old and New Rules for Old and New Problems', Privaatrecht plenis coloribus. Liber Amicorum Matthias Storme, Mechelen, Kluwer, 2024, 1097-1124, p. 1117.

The second scenario is a fall-back rule which deals with a situation where the parties have not agreed a procedure for attribution in advance (Article 7(2)). The rule states that an action should be attributed to a person who uses the system for that purpose. It therefore contains two elements: first, affirming that the attribution should be to a person and second, the reference to a purpose of the action, which contains an element of intent. The scope of this provision is even broader than the primary rule where an agreement exists between the parties. The fall-back rule also covers actions at the pre-contractual stage where a contract has not yet been formed. Therefore, the wording refers to a 'person' rather than 'parties'. Questions as to how that person should be identified are further addressed in the Guide to Enactment. It specifies that attribution should be objective and to the person with the strongest link to a specific action.[57] That link can be identified based on various factors, including system deployment, control, benefit or value from an action, nature and purpose of the contract, trade usages or practices.[58] The factors are neither exhaustive, nor should they be used cumulatively, as different considerations may be relevant for different scenarios.

Earlier drafts of the Model Law explored different wording, namely attribution of a data message to a person on whose behalf an automated system is operated.[59] This formulation was ultimately abandoned, considering amongst others that it may not suit all use-cases. More specifically, the system is not always operated on someone's behalf but could be operated by one of the parties. For instance, an airline company could have its own proprietary system for (dynamic) ticket pricing and online purchases and could operate it via its internal staff. Alternatively, both contracting parties could make use of an automated system operated by a third-party platform. The retained rule on attribution is ultimately not concerned with the role of the person with respect to the system. What matters is the link of a person to a specific action of the automated system for a given purpose.

While the key question of attribution is thus resolved, other related matters remain outside the scope. They include the relationship of the of

57 Guide to Enactment of the UNCITRAL Model Law on Automated Contracting, 2025, para 66.

58 Guide to Enactment of the UNCITRAL Model Law on Automated Contracting, 2025, para 66.

59 Draft Provisions on Automated Contracting, of 14 August 2023, A/CN.9/WG.IV/WP.182, Principle 4 Attribution.

the person(s) using the automated system for contracting with the system developer or operator, which may be a third party responsible for the system design or operation. The rule also does not deal with the legal consequences of attributed actions (e.g. liability). It also does not deal with verifying the identity of a specific person, in the sense of authentication.[60] Legal certainty on the fundamental approach to attribution is nevertheless an essential precondition for dealing with related matters.

Finally, the attribution rule also specifically deals with the question of attribution of unexpected actions. It is particularly relevant for automated systems with higher levels of autonomy which could generate output which the user did not necessarily anticipate or intend. In such situations the question arises whether the actual intention and state of mind of the parties should be taken into account for the purpose of attribution. The Model Law provides a straightforward solution. Namely, attribution should not be denied on the sole ground that an action is unexpected by the person to whom it should be attributed. It is therefore not concerned with the actual state of mind and intention of the person behind the action. This solution ensures legal certainty and avoids abusive practices where a person could easily disavow unfavourable outcomes to the detriment of the other party, on the ground that they were not expected. While unexpected actions should be attributed, other rules may still come into play to deal with the implications. They could include rules on mistake, excused non-performance or specific rules on unexpected actions.

5. Unexpected actions

The Model Law puts forward an optional provision on unexpected actions carried out by automated systems (Article 8). First, it should be noted that the provision is not technology neutral, because the rule applies specifically to actions of automated systems. Secondly, the provision is optional. This reflects the complexity and different views concerning this issue. The very nature of automated systems presumes a limitation or even absence of human involvement in the performance of actions during the whole or parts of the contract lifecycle. The limited control, is one of the reasons for a higher risk that the system can produce actions which are unexpected and

60 Guide to Enactment of the UNCITRAL Model Law on Automated Contracting, 2025, para 60.

importantly, unintended by the person to whom they are attributed. This risk is higher for non-deterministic systems, which operate within a range of probabilities based on complex algorithms. As discussed, below there are also other reasons, such as external interference with the system.

a) The concept of an unexpected action

The first important question to resolve in this context is how to define the notion of an unexpected action. The Model Law does not provide a legal definition but puts forward a broad interpretation of this concept in the Guide to Enactment. The concept comprises three categories of unexpected actions: first those that result from the normal operation of the system; second, errors in programming or transmission and finally, those caused by third-party interference. It should be noted that the concept of unexpected actions is not limited to mistakes, because it explicitly includes scenarios where the system operated correctly. Furthermore, it includes errors in transmission which could occur due to internal or external factors to the system. Finally, external factors are clearly covered by the notion of third-party interference. All these factors are relevant and are appropriately included as potential causes of unexpected actions.

The broad approach to the notion of unexpected actions is a recognition of the practical realities in the digital ecosystem. While over 92% of EU companies had put in place security measures in 2024, more than 21 % experienced a security incident, and suffered various consequences.[61] Security incidents could happen due to non-malicious and malicious reasons.[62] The most frequent type of issue by far is unavailability of ICT services due to hardware or software failures (for non-malicious causes). Nevertheless, it is likely to result in errors in transmission. AI systems that are trained on large data sets could be even more vulnerable, because additional security incidents could affect the data set, notably data corruption or destruction

61 Eurostat, ICT security in enterprises, EU, 2024.

62 Eurostat, Enterprises experienced ICT related security incidents leading to consequences, 2024. Non-malicious causes include unavailability of ICT services due to hardware or software failures (about 18%); destruction or corruption data due to hardware or software failures (about 4%); disclosure of confidential information due to unintentional actions of own employees (about 1%). The malicious incidents involve similar outcomes (combined around 7%) but are intentional and for malicious reasons, such as denial of services attacks, malicious software, etc.

due to malicious or non-malicious reasons.[63] The evidence suggests that security incidents potentially beyond the control of the system user are frequent. The identified potential causes for unexpected actions under the Model Law are therefore in line with the evidence on practical issues.

The Model Law takes a pragmatic approach by implicitly acknowledging that the specific cause for an unexpected action may be complex to identify. First, the complexity of algorithms involved is already a major factor. Second, a range of different ICT security incidents could cause unexpected actions. Yet, as illustrated by Eurostat data, the same type of technical issue could again occur for various reasons - either non-malicious mistakes of the system's programmer, user or operator or due to external factors that could include malicious third-party interference. This assessment alone is likely to be complex and costly. It will be particularly burdensome for smaller economic operators who often may lack the skills for such a complex analysis. As the concept comprises the key relevant causes, it may be easier to invoke the rule when an unexpected action occurs without first investigating the cause behind it.

b) A specific approach to unexpected actions

The second important question is how to deal with unexpected actions when they occur. This has been subject to legal debate also during the development of the Model Law. Different views persisted as regards first the need for such a provision and second, the appropriate approach for risk allocation between the parties concerned by an unexpected action.

As regards the need for a specific provision on unexpected actions, it was acknowledged during the preparation of the Model Law that some jurisdictions considered such a rule unnecessary or even undesirable.[64] One reason is that such a specific rule could interfere with existing fundamental principles and would be unnecessary. In any case, the existing rules could be effectively applied in situations involving unexpected outcomes. They include for instance rules on mistake or force majeur.

Other jurisdictions considered a specific rule was warranted for various reasons. The existing legal framework may not be fit to deal with new

63 Eurostat, Enterprises experienced ICT related security incidents leading to consequences, 2024.

64 Guide to Enactment of the UNCITRAL Model Law on Automated Contracting, 2025, para 73.

technological developments involving increasingly autonomous algorithmic decision-making. First, some unexpected actions may be highly detrimental and clearly beyond the range of reasonable expectations of a trader but may not qualify as mistakes. This is particularly the case where the system operated correctly and none of the contractual parties was mistaken. Nevertheless, even if formally no mistake occurred, it could be unconscionable for one party to benefit from an action they realise is unintended and is highly detrimental to the other. There is legal uncertainty as to how such situations can be addressed and whether they could be effectively dealt with under the current legal framework. At the same time, the related risk and potential costs for users may be difficult to estimate. They could be dissuasive, especially for small and medium sized companies. The Model Law acknowledged the different views on the need for a specific provision on unexpected actions and reconciled them by presenting an optional solution (Article 8). It is available for consideration for those jurisdictions that consider specific regulation of unexpected actions necessary.

c) The delicate balance in risk allocation

As regards the solution on substance, the Model Law again strikes a balance between the different views. A key issue on substance is the risk allocation between the parties and again, there are different viewpoints and approaches. One viewpoint focuses on the importance of fair dealing and the protection of the interests of the non-mistaken party, as well as the broader objective of ensuring legal certainty and predictability in commercial transactions. The argument is that a (non-mistaken) party should be able to rely on an action and contract, which it legitimately expects to be valid and where a contract objectively appears to be concluded. The party responsible for a mistake (respectively, an unexpected action) should not be entitled to assert its subjective view to the detriment of the other party. Alternatively, this would create 'intolerable uncertainty in contractual arrangements'.[65] There is also a concern that the person responsible for the unexpected action could abuse possible exemptions to excuse themselves and avoid unfavourable outcomes. Legal certainty and predictability in commercial transactions is therefore prioritised over the potential costs for an individual party that may have committed a mistake. However, there are counterarguments to this view.

65 Quoine Pte Ltd v B2C2 Ltd [2020] SGCA, para 81.

'There are cases where justice outweighs in the balance the interests of legal certainty'.[66] This quote of Lord Justice Mance reflects the other viewpoint and summarises a range of eloquent arguments developed in his dissenting opinion on the landmark Quoine case, summarised below.[67] In situations when it is obvious that a fundamental computer system breakdown occurred, the considerations for reversal of the transaction can outweigh the faults of a party that may have led to it. Moreover, fundamental errors could occur in computerised exchanges also without any fault. An objective test could be whether a reasonable trader should have thought in such circumstances that a situation was the 'consequence of a gross and unintended "major database breakdown" or error with equivalent effect'.[68] In such situations for an honourable trader it would be unconscionable to benefit from the losses to the other party, especially where was no detriment to themselves or any third party. Depending on the circumstances, in such situations a transaction could be voidable.[69]

Furthermore, there are additional arguments for policy considerations, where the policy objective is to facilitate the use of automated systems. In practice, prospective users of automated systems bear higher risks of unexpected actions, especially where the systems are complex non-deterministic ones. There should be some safeguards for honest traders at least in extreme cases, involving highly unusual circumstances. Considering the higher risk of unexpected actions when automated systems are deployed some potential users may refrain from using automated systems altogether to avoid the associated costs. Therefore, certain safeguards and limited exceptions are necessary to enable parties to claim non-reliance and disavow such unexpected actions, while considering the interests of the other party.

The proposed solution of the Model Law ultimately reflects both viewpoints and seeks to balance them. The main rule is that the party using an automated system bears the risk for unexpected actions. However, it could disavow an unexpected action under strict conditions. Importantly, the interests of the other party are also protected and that is why two

66 Quoine Pte Ltd v B2C2 Ltd [2020] SGCA, Dissenting Opinion by Lord Justice Jonathan Mance, para 184.

67 Quoine Pte Ltd v B2C2 Ltd [2020] SGCA, Dissenting Opinion by Lord Justice Jonathan Mance, para 195-197.

68 Quoine Pte Ltd v B2C2 Ltd [2020] SGCA, Dissenting Opinion by Lord Justice Jonathan Mance, para 200.

69 Quoine Pte Ltd v B2C2 Ltd [2020] SGCA, Dissenting Opinion by Lord Justice Jonathan Mance, para 207.

cumulative conditions should be met to benefit from the specific rule on unexpected actions. These conditions are linked to the knowledge and expectations of both parties. First, the party responsible for an unexpected action should not have reasonably expected the action. The determination of the expectations is objective, taking into account the circumstances of the case, rather than the subjective state of mind of the person concerned. Second, the other party knew or reasonably could have been expected to know that. In this case, the assessment is based on subjective and objective elements.[70] Respectively, the provision creates a possibility to disavow unexpected actions, but only in scenarios where both parties should have been aware of an unexpected action.

It remains to be seen how many jurisdictions will implement this provision. Practice will show how easy or hard it will be to disavow unexpected actions before the courts based on this rule. In the emerging digital trade environment contractual parties are increasingly detached from each other. They may not even directly interact with humans, but with their AI agents and it may be difficult to judge what the expectations of a person for a transaction had been when they deployed an AI agent. An added complication may be to assess what a reasonable trader could expect from or ought to know about the operation of a non-deterministic system, such as an AI agent. Even if the assessment is objective, given the complexity of algorithms involved and limited AI skills of most users, it is likely to be difficult. Furthermore, the assessment of circumstances in a given case may be especially complicated in automated cross-border transactions, as market conditions and practices may vary. While the practical impact of Article 8 remains uncertain, it is at least a noteworthy attempt to acknowledge the issue of unexpected actions and the potential need to deal with it.

6. Other issues

The Model Law touches upon other relevant issues without dealing with them on substance. In particular, it refers to information requirements that may be relevant in the context of using automated systems in contracting (Article 9). Such requirements could concern disclosure, for instance on the design, operation or use of the system. In the development of the

70 Quoine Pte Ltd v B2C2 Ltd [2020] SGCA, Dissenting Opinion by Lord Justice Jonathan Mance, para 207.

Model Law a possible inclusion of disclosure requirements was considered, but ultimately abandoned and left in the remit of other laws. While the text acknowledges that such rules could be relevant, it does not deal with them specifically. This solution helps avoid a duality of disclosure regimes depending on whether an automated system is used.[71]

Another rule is the non-avoidance provision (Article 10). It states that the use of an automated system should not excuse non-compliance with other rules of law. This provision was phrased as 'compliance with applicable laws' in an earlier stage of the negotiations. It required the person on whose behalf the system is operated to ensure 'that the design, operation and use of the automated system in contracting complies with all applicable laws'.[72] This formulation however was considered too broad and onerous, especially for use-cases where the user of the system is neither the designer of the system, nor responsible for its operation. While in some cases users indeed develop and operate their own automated system, in the majority of cases users seem to purchase or access AI systems from external providers.[73] Moreover, one of the key obstacles to the uptake of AI are limited skills.[74] Respectively, a user of a system designed and possibly operated by another party, may not have any control or even understanding of the design and operation of the system. Respectively, they should not be held responsible for ensuring compliance with all applicable laws. Such a requirement would go too far for any user, but the burden would be especially onerous on small and medium-sized enterprises. It could further discourage uptake. Ultimately, the final provision formulated as non-avoidance, is a well-balanced rule which reflects the objective of ensuring compliance with the applicable legal framework without imposing extra burdens.

---

71 Guide to Enactment of the UNCITRAL Model Law on Automated Contracting, 2025, para 84.

72 Draft Provisions on Automated Contracting, of 14 August 2023, A/CN.9/WG.IV/WP.182, Principle 7 on Compliance with applicable laws.

73 Joint Research Centre, 'Novel Forms of Contracting in the Digital Economy, AI Enabled autonomous contracting', 2024, p. 69.

74 Communication from the Commission to The European Parliament, the Council, the European Economic and Social Committee and the Committee of the Regions, AI Continent Action Plan, Brussels, 9.4.2025 COM(2025) 165 final, p. 3.

III. Relevant areas outside the scope of the Model Law on Automated Contracting

While the Model Law deals with important questions, it leaves other issues outside its scope. Important areas outside the scope are liability, the contractual relationship between the automated system provider and its user, as well as product design rules.

Taking account of this broader context, the European Law Institute in its Guiding Principles and Model Rules on Digital Assistants for Consumer Contracts (ELI DACC Rules), specifically acknowledges two contractual relationships in automated contracting.[75] The first one is 'a contract for the supply of a digital assistant', meaning the automated contracting system used by consumers.[76] The other relationship is 'the algorithmic contract', concluded by means of the automated system, between a consumer and business. The ELI DACC Rules also focus on the interlinks between product design and automated contracting. Such rules could be formulated either as binding or non-binding provisions. While product design requirements are not a contract law matter per se, they could largely influence the contracting lifecycle between parties. For instance, the degree of control over contractual actions may practically depend on the ability to set and modify parameters of the automated system, as well as to deactivate it altogether. Possible design features could also enable the user to mitigate risks of unexpected actions, for instance by setting more concretely the contracting parameters and/or options to confirm or object to transactions.[77] Importantly, all these features should be available to the user before a contract is even concluded. The Model Law however does not venture into this area, which in any case goes beyond the domain of contract law.

The link between product design in contract law has also been reflected in EU law, albeit in another field. The obligation to repair[78] applies to goods covered by reparability requirements under eco-design rules. The repara-

75 European Law Institute, Guiding Principles and Model Rules on Digital Assistants for Consumer Contracts , 19.3.2025, pp. 2 et seq.

76 European Law Institute, Guiding Principles and Model Rules on Digital Assistants for Consumer Contracts, 19.3.2025, pp. 2 et seq.

77 European Law Institute, Guiding Principles and Model Rules on Digital Assistants for Consumer Contracts, 19.3.2025, Chapter 2.

78 Art. 5 (1) and Annex II of Directive (EU) 2024/1799 of the European Parliament and of the Council of 13 June 2024 on common rules promoting the repair of goods and amending Regulation (EU) 2017/2394 and Directives (EU) 2019/771 and (EU) 2020/1828 (Text with EEA relevance), OJ L, 2024/1799, 10.7.2024.

bility requirements ensure that it is technically feasible to repair a good over a longer period of time. Thus, they are a prerequisite for the effective exercise of the contractual right to repair over this period. This example illustrates the impact product design rules may have on the practical ability to exercise contractual rights. In the field of automated contracting, product design features could also impact the contractual actions positively, but also negatively. They could impact the level of user control over the system's actions, the risk of unexpected actions, and ultimately the parties' practical ability to conclude automated contracts in line with their actual intentions. The Model Law however refrains from touching upon product design rules.

Furthermore, while the Model Law can also be relevant for consumer contracts, it does not enter into the consumer law domain. This is understandable given the UNCITRAL focus on business-to-business transactions. Consumer law is nevertheless a relevant domain for automated contracting. While the uptake of automated systems in consumer contracts is not clear at this stage, it could have high potential in the future. A number of legal questions arise in the context of specific use of automated systems in consumer contracts. One viewpoint calls into question whether consumers still need specific protection when using automated systems. The argument is that the high capabilities of automated systems can level the playing field with business operators by removing existing information and power asymmetries in the contractual relationship. Moreover, a business dealing with a consumer's automated system may even end up being the weaker party. On the other hand, the approach reflected in the ELI DACC Rules suggests that specific rules on protection of consumers are warranted to deal with new issues and asymmetries that can arise from the use of automated systems.

The ELI DACC Rules include areas addressed by the Model Law, but also a range of other issues. They include product design requirements for the contract for the supply of the automated system, liability rules for the supplier, as well as additional safeguards, for instance from manipulation of digital assistants. While specific consumer rules could clearly cover a much wider range of issues, the substantive solutions on the same issues could be the same or diverge. For instance, on legal recognition, the ELI DACC Rules take the same approach as the Model Law.[79] However, as regards at-

79 European Law Institute, Article 17 of the Guiding Principles and Model Rules on Digital Assistants for Consumer Contracts, 19.3.2025.

tribution, the approach diverges.[80] The general rule on attribution takes the same approach (Article 22 paragraph 1). However, for the scenarios where the action of the automated system deviates from those which could be reasonably expected by the consumer, the opposite solution is put forward, namely that the action should not be attributed to the consumer. Moreover, it should not have legal effect (Article 22 paragraph 2).

Data protection albeit clearly outside the scope of the exercise, deserves a mention, in view of the potential interaction of contract law and specific data protection rules. There is no issue regarding the interaction of the Model Law with data protection rules in general, because it explicitly provides that data protection rules prevail (Article 2(2)). Furthermore, it affirms that the use of automated contracting cannot be an excuse for non-compliance with applicable mandatory rules (Article 10).[81] While there is no question about the applicability of the general data protection framework, there could be questions around specific rules. Of particular relevance to automated contracting is the right to object to solely automated decisions under Article 22 of the General Data Protection Regulation (GDPR).[82] It entitles data subjects not to be subjected to a decision based solely on automated processing if it produces legal effects in relation to that person or similarly significantly affects him or her. The European Data Protection Board recently clarified the relevance of this rule with respect to smart contracts. It confirmed that 'the execution of a smart contract may, in some cases, constitute an automated decision'.[83] It further clarified that the data controller in such cases should ensure that the relevant safeguards are satisfied, including the possibility of human intervention and contesting the decision. This is particularly relevant where a smart contract qualifies as a legal contract and performs contractual actions that fall in the scope of a decision under Article 22 of GDPR.

---

80 European Law Institute, Article 17 of the Guiding Principles and Model Rules on Digital Assistants for Consumer Contracts, 19.3.2025.

81 Guide to Enactment of the UNCITRAL Model Law on Automated Contracting, 2025, para 90.

82 Regulation (EU) 2016/679 of the European Parliament and of the Council of 27 April 2016 on the protection of natural persons with regard to the processing of personal data and on the free movement of such data, and repealing Directive 95/46/EC (General Data Protection Regulation) (Text with EEA relevance), OJ L 119, 4.5.2016.

83 The European Data Protection Board, Guidelines 02/2025 on processing of personal data through blockchain technologies, Version 1.1, of 08.04.2025, para 105.

IV. Conclusion

In conclusion, the Model Law takes a targeted approach and focuses on several key contractual issues generating legal uncertainty. It provides viable solutions that should facilitate risk assessment and mitigation for economic operators. By tackling legal uncertainty as an important obstacle that could discourage prospective users, it should facilitate uptake of automated systems in contracting.

It remains to be seen how the Model Law will be implemented. The respective UN General Assembly Resolution provides guidance, namely supplementing existing rules on e-commerce.[84] However, different jurisdictions could take different routes to implementation. Some may follow the 'wait and see' approach and first examine whether the courts can deal with the legal issues linked to automated contracting under the existing legal frameworks on contract law and e-commerce. Potential implementation of the Model Law could only come at a later stage, depending on the development of the case-law. Other jurisdictions may take a 'proactive approach' and implement the Model Law as a means to ensure more legal certainty for interested economic operators from the outset. The implementation of the Model Law in itself could trigger additional questions, notably whether the rules are sufficient or other areas of uncertainty should also be tackled. Therefore, both a targeted approach to implementation or more ambitious approaches in terms of scope are possible.

Whatever approach is chosen by various jurisdictions, the Model Law makes an important contribution to the international legal framework, albeit through a non-binding instrument. By harmonising core issues of automated contracting, it delivers on the objective to enhance legal certainty and commercial predictability for users of automated contracting, including for those operating cross-border. The Model Law may not have solutions to all questions, but it provides a solid basis to build on. Its adoption is a success, also because it is timely. It provides an international blueprint, at a time when automated contracting is increasingly used, but not yet widely spread across the economy. Therefore, it can serve as a basis to develop international practice and rules in a harmonised way. Respectively, it will facilitate the transition towards digital trade where automation, including innovative autonomous contracting systems, plays a growing role.

84 Resolution 79/119, adopted by the General Assembly on 4.12.2024 on the Model Law on Automated Contracting.

Conclusion of Contracts and Contracting Parties

What does it mean to have "the intention to contract" in an AI Contract?

*Henry Gabriel**

I. Introduction

The question may need to be viewed in the rear-view mirror. Today there are contracts constantly being formed by way of artificial intelligence (AI).[1] These contracts will continue to be created, they will be performed, and in some circumstances, the law will have to provide remedies for the breach or non-performance of these contracts. To the extent that the law insists on intent[2]as an element of a contract, the theory will have to follow the result. We must acknowledge these contracts and then determine what are the constituent parts of the contract.[3] How these contracts are created

---

* Henry Gabriel, Professor of Law, Elon University.

1 As discussed below, the subject of this paper is the use of AI to enter and perform a contract. The subject is not electronic contracting in general. Using electronic means to create and perform contracts has been widely accepted everywhere and the rules and laws governing electronic commerce are well developed and accepted. Thus, for example, the UNCITRAL Model Law on Electronic Commerce provided a set of general principles for the substitution of writings and signatures with electronic records and digital signatures that allowed parties to do electronically what was traditionally done with paper and ink. See UNCITRAL Model Law of Electronic Commerce, https://uncitral.un.org/sites/uncitral.un.org/files/media-documents/uncitral/en/19-04970_ebook.pdf. These general principles have been adopted in 87 countries. https://uncitral.un.org/en/texts/ecommerce/modellaw/electronic_commerce/status. It is important to distinguish between a party using an electronic agent and electronic means, the subject of general electronic commerce law, and the question of whether an electronic party by way of AI can be a party to a contract.

2 Or "assent". See e.g., American Law Institute Restatement of Contracts 2d, sec. 18: "Manifestation of mutual assent to an exchange requires that each party either make a promise or begin or render a performance."

3 The scholarship on this subject began decades ago. See e.g., Tom Allen and Robin Widdison, 'Can Computers Make Contracts', Harvard Journal of Law and Technology 1996, 25 (49) ('Since the program changes over time, without any human intervention, it would be very difficult to characterize it as the embodiment or expression of human intention. Hence, the doctrine as it now stands would deny validity to agreements generated by an autonomous computer.'). See also, Anthony J Bellia Jr, 'Contracting with

without specific human intervention to meet the requirement of the intent to contract is the subject of this paper.

II. AI Contracting Today

AI is used in the creation and performance of both commercial and consumer contracts. The global AI contract management system market size is expected to be valued around four billion US dollars by 2033, from 360 million USD in 2023, growing at an annual rate of over 27% over the next decade.[4] AI contracting includes automated contract drafting, real-time monitoring of contract obligations, and predictive analytics to forecast potential legal issues. AI automates contract creation, analysis, and compliance tracking. AI system users may request that their AI virtual assistants to purchase an object on the internet, or systems may be programmed with the purpose of autonomously forming contracts of a specific type, as is sometimes done with high-frequency stock transactions.[5]

Consumers are constantly confronted with these contracts by businesses that use dynamic pricing, such as ride sharing programs, airlines and online sellers. AI generated dynamic pricing is used to update prices and services to respond to market conditions, inventory and demand.[6] Irrespective of how the law responds, the world is currently full of and will continue to generate millions of contracts based on AI systems.

Electronic Agents', Emory Law Journal 2001, 1047 (2001). Regardless of the questions raised about the validity and enforceability of the contracts, the use of these automated contracts grew rapidly, and are now ubiquitous. It is too late to question their validity now.

4 https://market.us/report/ai-in-contract-management-system-market/#:~:text=Key%20Takeaways,technological%20advancements%20in%20contract%20management (last viewed April 29, 2025). Artificial Intelligence has projected to contribute $15.7 trillion to the global economy by 2030. https://www.nu.edu/blog/ai-statistics-trends/#:~:text=AI%20Adoption%20in%20Businesses,priority%20in%20their%20business%20plans (last viewed April 29, 2025).

5 Financial Industry Regulatory Authority, Artificial Intelligence (AI) in the securities industry (Report, June 2020). This type of high-speed trading is estimated to make up more than half of the securities transfers in the United States. Charles Korsmo, 'High-Frequency Trading: A Regulatory Strategy', University of Richmond Law Review 2014, 523 (574–5).

6 See e.g., Robert Weiss and Ajay Mehrotra, 'Online Dynamic Pricing: Efficiency, Equity and the Future of ECommerce' Virginia Journal of Law and Technology 2001, 11.

III. What is meant by artificial intelligence?

1. Artificial Intelligence

Artificial intelligence ('AI') does not have a standard or fixed definition. Some definitions refer to certain computing techniques or human intelligence,[7] but these definitions risk encompassing more traditional computer systems as well. For the purpose of this paper, I will use a more specific definition based on 'autonomy: AI systems are 'systems that display intelligent behavior by analyzing their environment and taking actions – with some degree of autonomy –to achieve specific goals.'[8] AI systems are often described as non-deterministic systems in that the results the system provides is not necessarily determined by the inputs received by the system.

A consequence of AI systems as discussed here is that the operation and results may be unpredictable for both the user and the developer of the system.[9] This autonomy of AI systems is what makes these systems more legally challenging than deterministic computer systems. AI systems do not

7 See e.g, Maura R. Grossman & Gordon V. Cormack, 'The Grossman-Cormack Glossary of Technology Assisted Review', Federal Courts Law Review 2014, 85; Ashley Deeks, 'The Judicial Demand for Explainable Artificial Intelligence Essays', Columbia Law Review 2019, 1832.

8 Communication from the Commission to the European Parliament, the European Council, the Council, the European Economic and Social Committee and the Committee of the Regions: Artificial Intelligence for Europe, 25 April 2018, <https://eur-lex.europa.eu/legal-content/ENG/TXT/HTML/?uri=CELEX:52018DC0237> (24 September 2023), paragraph 1.
Such an autonomy-centered definition helps emphasize the distinguishing features of modern AI systems. For example, take an AI system that utilizes machine learning. Such a system very aptly illustrates how relationships can be established independently between the input the system receives and the output it should generate. As a result, the way this type of system works differs fundamentally from more traditional computer algorithms in which the system's programmer imparts the connection between input and output directly. For example, we can think of a vending machine: the programmer of such a machine explicitly instructs the system what to do if a certain coin is inserted and a certain button is pressed. With machine learning, the programmer does not have to provide this instruction. The system derives the routine itself, for instance by being provide with a large number of examples.
Maarten Herbosch, 'Contracting with Artificial Intelligence', The Rabel Journal of Comparative and International Private Law 2023, 672 (674).

9 See e.g., Andrew D. Selbst, 'Negligence and AI's Human Users', Boston University Law Review 2020, 1315 (1332).

"reason" like a human, and for this reason it is inaccurate to attribute to an AI system the reasoning, motives and intentions of humans.[10]

It must be assumed that the use of AI systems creates enormous benefits for the users. Because AI systems do not have to anticipate and have pre-programed all system outputs, they can often exceed the speed and accuracy of humans in certain areas.[11]

These benefits of speed and efficiency must be weighed against the indeterminacy of the output. This unpredictability may be exacerbated because an AI system may adjust itself even during a specific operation. Furthermore, future data or the system's future 'experience' may continuously affect it making predictability of the output even more tenuous. In addition to the potentially unpredictable output, it may be difficult or impossible to understand why the AI system has arrived at a particular output.

a) Smart Contracts

This discussion excludes what may be called "smart contracts". 'Smart contract' is a term often subject to some considerable misunderstanding. 'Smart contract' is not a legal concept. The term refers to part of the process by which some or all contract performance is executed and enforced digitally and without the need for human intervention except at the level of writing code to automate contract performance. Smart contracts substitute algorithmic functions for human contract performance and enforcement. Smart contracts that use algorithmic functions operate effectively as tools for humans to achieve results that could otherwise be done by humans but

10 The AI system will have produced the output in question using a strictly mathematical process that often contains few conceptual clues. W. Nicholson Price II & Arti K. Rai, 'Clearing Opacity through Machine Learning', Iowa Law Review 2021, 775 (778–779). This makes the operation of AI systems fundamentally different from how we think. Conscious human thought proceeds conceptually, and therefore it may be difficult to understand the mathematical process behind AI.

11 See e.g., Ryan Calo, 'Singularity: AI and the Law', 41 Seattle University Law Review 2018, 1123 (1124); Tokio Matsuzaki, 'Ethical Issues of Artificial Intelligence in Medicine', California Western Law Review 2018, 255; Adam J. Kolber, 'Not-So-Smart Blockchain Contracts and Artificial Responsibility', Stanford Technology Law Review 2018, 198 (205); Michael Hatfield, 'Professionally Responsible Artificial Intelligence', Arizona State Law Journal 2019, 1057 (1060).

are done more efficiently by algorithmic programs.[12] A mechanical version of a smart contract is a vending machine.[13]

It is not these deterministic algorithmic functions that are the focus of this paper. The question posed here are AI programs that propose or negotiate the terms of contracts and then agree upon those terms autonomously.[14]

b) Artificial General Intelligence

For current AI systems, the scope of their autonomy is limited. These systems are said to be "weak", as their autonomy is limited to some specific application or applications for which they are created. "Strong" artificial in-

---

12 Lauren Henry Scholz, 'Algorithmic Contracts', Stanford Technology Law Review 2017, 128.

13 Nick Szabo is credited with inventing the term 'smart contract'. Kevin Werbach & Nicholas Cornell, Contracts Ex Machina, Duke L. J. 2017, 101 (107).
In the English case *Thornton v. Shoe Lane Parking Ltd.*, 1 All ER 686 (1971), the court found that a parking garage operator could enter into a contract with a customer by using an automatic ticket machine to issue tickets to drivers entering the garage. The court stated,
The customer pays his money and gets a ticket. ... It can be translated into offer and acceptance in this way. The offer is made when the proprietor of the machine holds it out as being ready to receive money. The acceptance takes place when the customer puts his money into the slot. The terms of the offer are contained in the notice placed on or near the machine stating what is offered for the money. *Ibid.* at 689.
Important for this discussion, the court did not find the ticket machine to be an agent of the company, but a tool used by the company to enter into the contract: The ticket machine is not "a booking clerk in disguise" with whom the driver can negotiate a contract. *Ibid.*

14 The law does not struggle with whether a contract exists through a mechanical vending machine. The answer is assumed. If we take this a step further, the invention of the mechanical cash register to tally up the amount owed for purchases in a store is just an extension of the vending machine hypothetical. The cash register mechanically calculates sums quicker and more efficiently than the store clerk, but the use of this mechanical device raises no real issues in contract law. Cash registers today are almost all automated by computer programs, and most allow the store to scan the items by way of a bar code to enter prices of the goods and to calculate the final sum, including taxes. Where along this spectrum from a mechanical vending machine to an automated cash register has any new contract issues been raised? It is hard to see any. But these examples are not the subject of this paper, for these examples are all examples of systems, mechanical or electronic that provide deterministic results that could have been provided by a human but slower and more inefficient. These are contracts that are not made by computers, but by humans that use computers to automate human tasks as part of the contracting process.

telligence, or artificial general intelligence, are AI systems that may behave autonomously in any situation.

At present, 'no machines with self-sustaining long-term goals and intent have been developed, nor are they likely to be developed in the near future.'[15] Some even doubt whether they are at all possible.[16]

Assuming artificial general intelligence develops to the point that it can be considered a legal person, at that time the law may recognize an AI as a legal person for purposes of contracting.[17] As we are a long way from that point now, we must necessarily find another way to justify and recognize contracts formed by artificial intelligence.

2. Why Might "Intent" Matter in the Law of Contract

Unlike areas of the law, such as tort and criminal law, where the application of the law is automatic and parties cannot choose to opt out of its requirements and sanctions, contract law requires the parties to agree to be bound. Does this require intent? It is often said so.[18]

Yet clearly, we do not specifically need a human being to be a party to a contract. Corporations, partnerships and other legal persons regularly enter into enforceable contracts; a legal result that is rarely questioned. These "legal persons" are held responsible for the consequences of their contracts.

It has been suggested that one can distinguish non-human legal persons from AI, which is not legal persons for purposes of contracts, for in one case legal personhood is recognized and in the other it is not.[19] As for the intent to contract, though, this is a false distinction, for in both cases there cannot be intent', actual or implied. Simply put, as with AI, a corporation cannot have intent.

---

15 Peter Stone, et al., Stanford University, Artificial Intelligence and Life in 2030, Palo Alto 2016.

16 John O. McGinnis, 'Accelerating AI', 104 Northwestern University Law Review Colloquy 2009, 366 (369); but see, John Linarelli, 'Advanced Artificial Intelligence and Contract', Uniform Law Review 2019, 330.

17 See e.g., John Linarelli, 'Advanced Artificial Intelligence and Contract', Uniform Law Review 2019, 330.

18 See e.g., Farnsworth, Contracts, § 3.7, Burlington, Mass, 1999.

19 John Linarelli, 'Advanced Artificial Intelligence and Contract', Uniform Law Review 2019, 330.

Legal persons such as corporations, though, can be distinguished from AI systems. Legal persons, such as a corporation, must be able to enter into contracts on their own behalf for this is essential to the function of the business entity. Corporations may be 'legal persons', but as such they have assets to back up their contractual obligations. Moreover, there are human beings that make the decisions that guide a corporation, including the decision to enter into a contract and presumably to understand the risk of entering into the contract. Thus, the intent of a corporation to enter into a contract arises from the authorized person who is making the decision on behalf of the corporation. It is therefore easy to find the 'intent' to contract by a corporation by assigning the intent to the person acting on behalf of the corporation or other legal person.[20]

The concept of intent itself needs some clarification before its place in an AI contract can be analyzed. Certainly, for example, under American law a party need not intend to be legally bound for there to be a binding contract: 'Neither real or apparent intention that a promise be legally binding is essential to the formation of a contract'.[21]

---

20 This is not to say that the individual is responsible for the contract; the corporation is. The point is that the "intent" to contract can be attributed to a human whereas the contract itself is attributed to the corporation or other non-human legal person.

21 American Law Institute Restatement 2d. § 21. It is this meaning of intent; the intent to be legally bound to a contract with which we are concerned. "Intent" is also used in relation to the interpretation of the contract when the parties are not disputing the existence of the contract itself: "[T]he intention of a party that is relevant to formation of a contract is the intention manifested by him rather than any different undisclosed intention .... The definitions of 'promise,' 'agreement.' and 'term' ... also refer to 'manifestation of intention.' It follows that the meaning of words or conduct of a party is not necessarily the meaning he expects or understands." American Law Institute Restatement 2d of Contracts § 200, Comment b. This rule of intent for the interpretation of contracts, at least under the American Law, was classically stated by Judge Learned Hand:

A contract has, strictly speaking, nothing to do with personal, or individual, intent of the parties. A contract is an obligation attached by the mere force of law to certain acts of the parties, usually words, which ordinarily accompany and represent a known intent. If, however, it were proved by twenty bishops that either party, when he used the words, intended something else than the usual meaning which the law imposes upon them, he would still be held, unless there was some mutual mistake, or something else of the sort.

Hotchkiss v. National City Bank, 200 F.287, 293 (S.D. N.Y. 1911).

But it is a mistake to take statements such as this as denying the necessity of intent[22] as an element of creating a contract. What is meant is that a party need not have subjective intent. A party need not have a subjective mental intent to enter into a contract; a party need only objectively appear to have that intent. This standard is often stated as what a 'reasonable person under the circumstances' would understand.[23]

It is also important to appreciate that the law requires not simply an abstract 'intent' to enter into a contract, but the intent to enter into a contract on the agreed upon terms.[24] It is this aspect of contract law that for some

22 American law states it as "assent". See, American Law Institute Restatement of Contracts 2nd, Chapter 3: Formation of Contracts: Mutual Assent. In American contract law, "intent" refers to a party's internal desire or subjective state of mind to enter into a contract, while "assent" refers to the outward expression of agreement or approval, which is judged by an objective standard. This means what a reasonable person would understand from the party's actions and words, not necessarily from their private thoughts. Essentially, "intent" is what someone is thinking, while "assent" is what they demonstrate through their behavior. Although the English Law does not reflect the language of mutual assent found in the American Law, the English Law is substantially similar in its approach to "intent" in contract law. See e.g., Edwin Peel, Trietel on the Law of Contract, §1-002, London 2015.

23 See e.g., UNIDROIT Principles of International Commercial Contracts (2016), art 4.1(2); United Nations Convention on Contracts for the International Sale of Goods, Art. 8(2). It should be noted that, '[a]n objective intention to be bound is an important feature ... in all legal systems.' Schwenzer, Hachem, and Kee, Global Sales and Contract Law, 136, Oxford 2012. This aspect of contract law is often referred to as a "meeting of the minds". This is an unfortunate phrase as it suggests that the parties must have subjective assent, when this is not the law.

24 Irrespective of any other questions about the creation and performance of contracts, contracts formed by AI, the contract must meet the requirement of definiteness. The two essential elements to form a contract are definiteness of terms and the intent to enter into a contract. See e.g., UNIDROIT Principles of International Commercial Contracts (2016), Art. 2.1.2. A good of thumb is that the terms have to be definite enough that a court could enforce the agreement. For a comparative discussion of the "definiteness" of contract terms, see Schwenzer, Hachem, and Kee, Global Sales and Contract Law, §§ 10.01-10.18, Oxford 2012.
Whether a contracting party is AI or the user of AI, the contract still needs to be definite in its terms. The concern in this paper is not the question of the definiteness of terms to an agreement but the intent to contract. I am assuming that the AI system allows the other party access to the terms being offered and agreed upon. For example, under contemporary online contracting it can be difficult to know whether an online offer has been read, and it can be legally difficult to know whether unread online contracts should be enforced. Browse-wrap contracts purport to bind purchasers to terms in agreements that are disclosed in a hyperlink. "click-wrap" or "scroll-wrap" contracts require purchasers to click 'I agree' and perhaps to scroll through the agreement before clicking. The debate on whether these types of con-

raises difficulty with AI systems that provide terms that may be unknown to the respective contracting parties at the time of contract formation.[25]

What is useful in the analysis of contractual intent is the understanding that conduct alone can show intent to enter into a contract.[26] Through the

---

tracts should be enforced has generally been settled in the affirmative as long as the party has reasonable access to the terms.

Individual contracts may have a variety of regulatory restrictions, such as information disclosure requirements, cancellation rights, and rules that govern amendments, renewals or extensions. These requirements or terms are beyond the scope of this paper.

25 It has been suggested that this problem exists under both a subjective theory of assent as well as the more commonly recognized objective theory of assent. The following hypothetical has been posed by one commentator to highlight this point, Matthew Oliver, 'Contracting by Artificial intelligence: Open Offers, Unilateral Mistakes and Why Algorithms are not Agents', Australian National University Journal of Law and Technology 2021, 45 (64-65):

Suppose that Annie runs an online antique store, 'Annie's Antiques.' To maximise her profits, she uses a sophisticated AI algorithm to set her prices and sell her antiques through a website. At a given moment, Annie does not know what antiques are being sold by her website, to whom, or for what price. Annie's activities are focused on sourcing antiques and maintaining the algorithm. The contracts negotiate and completed by Annie's algorithm purport to bind Annie. Yet, it seems that Annie does not manifest subjective or objective consent to be bound by the terms of these contracts.

Suppose that Annie's website offers to sell a rare antique widget for one dollar, and that a customer eagerly uses the website to buy the widget at that price. Does Annie intend to sell the widget to that customer for one dollar? Clearly, she does not. How could she, since she does not know what terms her website offers or whether they are accepted? There is thus no meeting of the minds between Annie and her customer. Annie lacks the specific intent—to enter into a contract to sell that widget at that price—required by a subjective theory of contracts.

The objective theory of contracts does not resolve this problem. According to the objective theory of contracts, it does not matter what Annie actually intends. What matters is whether she performs acts 'which ordinarily accompany and represent a known intent,' such that a reasonable counterparty would believe that she intends to sell the widget for one dollar. A reasonable customer (let us assume) would know that the website is operated by an algorithm and is not supervised in real time. No matter what words the website uses, a reasonable customer would not believe that Annie specifically intends to sell the widget to them for one dollar. For this reason, the words used by the website cannot constitute an objective manifestation of consent by Annie to the specific terms of the contract. Thus, it seems that Annie has manifested neither the subjective nor the objective intent necessary to enter into a legally binding agreement to exchange a rare antique widget for one dollar.

26 This is particularly pronounced in some Common Law jurisdictions. This has long been recognized in the United States by statute, see Uniform Commercial Code sec. 2-204(1) & (2), and by court decisions in Australia and the United Kingdom.

conduct of the parties, intent can be implied when the parties are acting upon and performing on what can only reasonably be interpreted as a contract. Once performance has begun or has been concluded in what is obviously an exchange, it would be ludicrous to deny the existence of a contract that the parties clearly intended. In this case, intent is implied as the law makes the obvious assumption that the parties intended to enter into the contract.[27]

That conduct can show the existence of a contract certainly provides the correct result when the formalities of offer and acceptance, particularly the time of acceptance, is not clear. But this rule may have a more expansive role in contract than merely patching up the questions of formation. For it also recognizes that certain formalities of contract are not necessary when hindsight shows that the parties expect there to be a contract and that the parties have also assumed the risks that attach to the contract.

If both parties are operating under the assumption that there is a contract and both parties have assumed the risks that the law will enforce the contract, why should this not be equally true when only one party is the AI contracting party and the other party is working under the assumption that a contract exists and that the contract should be performed according to its terms? If a party knows it is contracting with an AI system and assumes both the existence of a contract as well as the risk attendant to the contract, it is unclear why the law would deny the validity of the contract. This should particularly be the case when performance has been accepted by the non-AI contracting party.[28]

This, of course, becomes more attenuated if both sides of the contract are facilitated by AI systems. But even here, as I discuss below, the requirement of intent in the law of contract should not be a hindrance.

MacRobertson Miller Airline Services v. Commissioner of State Taxation, 133 CLR 125 (Western Australia, 1975); G Perry Trenthan v. Archital Luxfer 1 LLR 25. 1993 U.K. Court of Appeals. Conduct as a basis for contract enforcement has also been recognized in the UNIDROIT Principles of International Commercial Contracts, art 2.2.2, and the Principles of European Contract law, art 2101(1).

27 This is what the first sentence of this paper refers. It is not that intent is not an element of a contract; it is. Intent need not be shown, however, as a discreet element of the contract when the parties have, in the totality of their actions, shown they intend to have a contract.

28 The law is certainly capable of disengaging the exchange from contract law and applying the appropriate measure of mutual restitution, but this result is messy and denies the common expectations of the non-AI party.

3. How AI Systems Might Contract

There are three approaches that have been suggested as to how contracts with AI systems might be created. The question of the intent to contract differs with each approach.

First, the AI system might enjoy some level of legal personhood. In this case, we need to work in the requirement of intent to the contracting ability of the AI system.

Second, the AI system may be considered an agent of the system user. In this case, we need to examine the requirements of intent necessary for an agent and whether the AI system can meet that requirement.

Third, we may consider the AI system as a tool that is used by the person choosing to contract by using the AI system. In this case, it is the intent of the system use that will meet this contract requirement.

a) AI as an Autonomous Legal Person

If society gets to the point where it recognizes that AI systems have legal personhood, there will be the need for the regulation of AI systems just as we have the need to regulate other non-human legal persona. At that point in time the law of contract will have to adjust, if necessary, to the necessity of showing intent to contract by the AI system.

The recognition of legal personhood of AI systems has not been done anywhere to date, though, and is not likely to be done in the foreseeable future. The current and near future technology does not suggest the development of AI systems that can approximate the type of reasoning and understanding that would provide for the AI system to have an independent comprehension of its actions.

The recognition of an AI as a legal person will be more complex than the recognition of other legal persons, such as a corporation. As I noted above, other types of recognized legal persons, such as corporations, have a human that is making the decision on behalf of the legal person. Corporations cannot contract by themselves. They need human assistance.

Moreover, a legal person, such as a corporation, is contracting on behalf of the corporation. AI systems, at the present time, do not contract on their own behalf. It is therefore possible to find the requisite element of intent to contract stemming from the party for whom the AI system is contracting. This will not be the case, if in the future, AI systems contract on their own behalf. If that arises in the future, then the analogy between AI and other legal persons will no longer be relevant.

Since contracts are currently facilitated by AI systems and these contracts are recognized by the law, the obvious conclusion that must be drawn is that the law, to the extent that the law has actually confronted this question, must be allowing AI systems to function as part of the world of contracts without the AI system having legal personhood. How this is achieved in the law of contracts is examined below.

b) AI as Agents of the User

It has been suggested that AI systems can be considered 'agents' of the users of the AI system.[29] As I will discuss, this approach has several flaws.

Putting aside the obvious question of whether an AI system can have any 'intent' to negotiate or enter into a contract,[30] there is also the question of whether the AI system has a legal personality that fits within the legal notion of an 'agent'.[31]

These problems have been sidestepped by some. For example:

> When algorithms take on a role in contract formation analogous to that of human agents, they should be considered constructive agents for the purpose of contract formation. The company consenting to the contract can be said to have authorized or ratified the contract formed on its behalf by the algorithm. This approach explains easy cases while also showing why algorithmic contracts, even many black box algorithmic contracts, are enforceable.[32]

There is something attractive about considering the AI system as an agent, for the agent can bind the principal (the user of the AI system) and therefore the contract would be binding on the principal, which is of course,

29 See e.g., Lauren Scholz, 'Algorithmic Contracts', Stanford Technology Law Review 2017, 128; Samir Chopra and Laurence White, 'A Legal Theory for Autonomous Artificial Agents', Ann Arbor 2011.

30 John Linarelli, 'Advanced Artificial Intelligence and Contract', Uniform Law Review 2019, 330.

31 The scholarship gets a bit blurry here as the term "agent" is often used not in its legal sense, but as a synonym for an instrumentality used by the user of the AI system. See e.g., Martin-Bariteau & Scassa, 'AI and Contract Law', in: Artificial Intelligence and the Law in Canada 3, Toronto 2021.

32 Lauren Scholz, 'Algorithmic Contracts', Stanford Technology Law Review 2017, 128.

the party for whose benefit the contract is made. There are, however, both practical as well as theoretical problems with treating an AI system as an agent. [33]

First, there is the problem of applying agency law and the responsibilities of an agent to an entity that is neither a human nor a legal person. Generally, an agent must understand that the agent is an agent.[34] It would be quite a stretch to assume an AI system could have this understanding.

Moreover, if the AI system were an agent, it would have to independently intend to enter into the contract. AI systems cannot manifest 'intent', or even know that it is entering into a contract.

One might apply the law of apparent authority[35] to an AI system when a third party (which will presumably be the other contracting party) has justifiably relied that the user of the AI system has given the AI system the authority to act on the user's behalf.[36] This, though, only provides a connection in agency law, but does not address the question of how an AI system manifests the intent to enter into a contract.

33 It is generally the American position that a computer programs, including AI, is not an "agent" under the law of agency. See, American Law Institute Restatement (Third) of Agency § 1.04 comment: "Likewise a computer program is not capable of acting as a principal or an agent as defined by the common law. At present, computer programs are instrumentalities of the persons who use them. If a program malfunctions, even in ways unanticipated by its designer or user, the legal consequences for the person who uses it are no different than the consequences stemming from the malfunction of any other type of instrumentality. That a program may malfunction does not create capacity to act as a principal or an Agent." This position was stated at a specific point in time, and it alone should not be binding on either future American law or the law of other jurisdictions.

34 See e.g., American Law Institute Restatement (Third) of Agency § 3.01: "Actual authority ... is created by a principal's manifestation to an agent that, as reasonably understood by the agent, expresses the principal's assent that the agent take action on the principal's behalf."

35 This is what I assume is meant by "constructive agents". See, Lauren Scholz, Algorithmic Contracts Stanford Technology Law Review 2017, 128.

36 See e.g., American Law Institute Restatement (Third) of Agency § 2.03 comment (c): "Apparent authority holds a principal accountable for the results of third-party beliefs about an actor's authority to act as an agent when the belief is reasonable and is traceable to a manifestation of the principal. ... A third party's reasonable understanding of the principal's conduct will reflect general business custom as well as usage that is particular to the principal's industry and prior dealings between the parties."

A legal purist may question whether the AI system can ever be an agent:

> An AI program can only give people the reasonable belief that it intends to contract if it is reasonable to believe that an AI program can have intentions. Thus, for the agency solution to be plausible, the people who propose it must show that AI programs really can have intentions.[37]

I suspect this is legally correct, but I wonder whether the law may be able to accommodate this given the likelihood that reasonable businesspeople would not make these fine legal distinctions in their transactions.

It may be that although an AI system cannot have the subjective actual realization that it intends to enter into a contract, but since the standard in contract law is "objective intent", the AI system can appear to be manifesting the intent to enter into a contract by the merely performing the functions that exhibit the traits of contract formation and performance.

The limits of this analysis, though, are quickly obvious. It may be reasonable for a human contracting party that knows it is contracting with an AI system to assume the AI system is the agent of the AI system's user. But if both parties to the agreement are using AI systems, it is a far stretch to assume that the two AI systems know the other system is an agent of the user much less that the AI system itself recognizes that it is an agent itself.

Following further this question of possible agency, it must be remembered that an agent is only authorized to function within its scope of authority.[38] Because the scope of an AI program is to do what the AI is programmed to do, it is usually always functioning within the authority is has been granted. But this may not be so. With AI systems that are effectively "black boxes",[39]where it may be unclear how the AI arrived at the result, trying to unravel the process that led to the result to see if the result is within the scope of the 'agency' may be near impossible.

Moreover, without legal personhood, it is also unclear how to frame a system of liability for the AI operating as an agent that would be separate

---

37 Matthew Oliver, 'Contracting by Artificial intelligence: Open Offers, Unilateral Mistakes and Why Algorithms are not Agents, Australian National University Journal of Law and Technology 2021, 45 (70).

38 See e.g., UNIDROIT Principles of International Commercial Contracts (2016), Art. 2.2.2(2): "The agent has authority to perform all acts necessary in the circumstances to achieve the purposes for which the authority was granted."

39 Maarten Herbosch, 'Contracting with Artificial Intelligence', The Rabel Journal of Comparative and International Private Law 2023, 672 (677).

from the liability of the principal. Woe be the poor court that has to untangle this.

This problem is similar to the one confronted by the Singapore Court of Appeals in the now famous case *Quoine Pte Ltd v B2C2 Lt.*[40] Under Singaporean law, a contract can be void for unilateral mistake only if the non-mistaken party had 'actual knowledge' of the mistake. In this case, only the algorithms were aware of the disputed transactions at the time the transactions occurred. Quoine argued the algorithm's knowledge of the trades could be enough to void the contract, because the algorithm could be treated as a 'legal agent'.[41] After all, Quoine argued, if human traders 'had met on the floor of the exchange' and completed the contracts at issue, these contacts would be void for unilateral mistake.[42] The court, however, rejected the agency argument:

> They are, in effect, mere machines carrying out actions which in another age would have been carried out by a suitably trained human. They are no different to a robot assembling a car rather than a worker on the factory floor or a kitchen blender relieving a cook of the manual act of mixing ingredients. All of these are machines operating as they have been programmed to operate once activated'. The appellate court explicitly endorsed and ultimately upheld this reasoning stating 'We agree [that] it would be wholly artificial to recast the relevant matrix of fact, which was one where the contracting parties did not in fact know beforehand that they were going to enter into the Trading Contracts or their terms[.] ... We also agree with the Judge that it follows from this that in cases where contracts are made by way of deterministic algorithms, any analysis concerning knowledge of a mistake or unconscionably taking advantage of one must be done by reference to the state of mind of the programmers of the algorithms at the time of the programming.[43]

The *Quoine* case has staked its ground. However, it is but one court addressing the question, and it specifically limited its holding to determinative systems. It does not answer the question of whether an AI system might

40 Quoine Pte Ltd v B2C2 Ltd [2020] SGHC(I) 02.
41 These arguments are explained in the lower court's opinion, which was affirmed on appeal. Quoine Pte Ltd v B2C2 Ltd [2020] SGHC(I) 02, p. 86.
42 Quoine Pte Ltd v B2C2 Ltd [2020] SGHC(I) 02, p. 86.
43 Quoine Pte Ltd v B2C2 Ltd [2020] SGHC(I) 02, p. 46.

be considered an agent in a non-determinative system,[44] although for the reasons discussed above, neither does agency analysis work well for non-deterministic AI systems.

c) AI as a Tool to Create and Perform Contracts

The question whether an AI system should be treated as having a legal personality or should be treated as an agent of the user of the AI system may easily be avoided by concluding instead that, at least at this point in the development of technology, the AI system is simply considered a tool used by the user of the AI system to facilitate contracts.

Thirty years ago, the drafters of the 1994 UNIDROIT Principles of International Contracts provided that: "A contract may be concluded either by the acceptance of an offer or by conduct of the parties that is sufficient to show agreement"[45]. As an example of the application of this rule, the Principles provide:

> The language of this Article is sufficiently broad to cover also cases of so-called automated contracting, i.e. where the parties agree to use a system capable of setting in motion self-executing electronic actions leading to the conclusion of a contract without the intervention of a natural person.[46]

That this was included in the UNIDROIT principles thirty years ago is not remarkable, for even then automated contracting was common and well accepted. What is also not remarkable is that the UNIDROIT Principles assume that the automated system functions as the tool of humans that

---

44 The *Quoine* decision is probably correct in its holding that the algorithm is not an agent. The court's holding that one should look to the state of mind of programmer may lead to odd or incorrect results. For it may be that the focus in a given case should not be on the programmer but the user of the algorithm if the user is not the programmer. By determining that the algorithm was not an agent the court avoided the question of who the principal necessarily would have been.

45 UNIDROIT Principles of International Commercial Contracts (2016), Art. 2.1.1.

46 UNIDROIT Principles of International Commercial Contracts (2016), Art. 2.1.1. provides this illustration:
Automobile manufacturer A and components supplier B set up an electronic data interchange system which, as soon as A's stocks of components fall below a certain level, automatically generates orders for the components and executes such orders. The fact that A and B have agreed on the operation of such a system makes the orders and performances binding on A and B, even though they have been generated without the personal intervention of A and B.

choose to use the system and therefore derive both intent and responsibility for the contract from the people who choose to use the system.

Since all computer systems (at least today) are created and put into use by humans, it has become common to consider the systems as tools of the people who use these systems.[47] Certainly this has not been a problem with mechanical devices. The owner or operator of a vending machine is the contracting party behind the vending machine and the contracts that are created when the machine is used and dispenses the items the machine dispenses. It is an easy leap from this to automated contracting systems, particularly when it cannot seriously be questioned today whether automatic contracting over the internet creates binding contracts although the automated systems are not monitored by an individual.[48]

As noted above, without recognizing the AI system as an independent legal person, it can have no liability. But no legal system presently or in the near future is likely to recognize an AI system as an independent legal person.

To consider the AI system as an actual or apparent agent of the AI system user would thrust the potential liability on the AI system user as the principal under agency law. Since someone has to be responsible, under agency law it will be the principal.

Therefore, if we consider the AI system as a tool used by the user of the AI system, the system user would be the contracting party for any contracts facilitated by the AI system. This would effectively be the same result as if we treated the AI system as an agent, but without the problems we have seen if the AI system is considered an agent of the user.

This appears to be the correct result. The legal question of intent as an element of the contract formation is resolved. It is the intent of the system user that allows the contract to be formed.

The AI system cannot have an 'intent' to contract as that concept is recognized in the law. An AI system has neither any interest in whether a contract is formed, nor does it have any interest in the consequences of the contract. Conceptually, it is just a tool.

---

47 See e.g., State Farm Mutual Automobile Insurance Company v. Bockhost, 453 F.2d. 533 (U.S. Fed. Ct. App. 10th Cir. 1972).

48 Whether one wants to posit that the reason contracts are enforced is because society benefits from economic exchanges or because one is morally obligated to meet one's promissory obligations (or a combination of the two), the same result is reached once the AI system is attributed to a person who chooses to use the system.

One may question whether the move from an automated computer system where the result is preordained by the computer program- a determinative system- to an artificial intelligence system that creates non-determinative results is significant enough to question the underlying theory that assumes the AI system is simply a tool provided by the user. The suggestion is that whereas one may have the intent to contract using deterministic computer systems, one cannot have the intent to agree to all of the unknown results that may result from the use of an AI system.[49]

I suggest there should be no legal distinction between determinative and non-determinative systems. Whether the AI system is a deterministic or non-deterministic system, the AI system has no interest in the contract; the automated system is not contracting for itself. It is contracting for another party. This result might be different in the future when and if an AI program has real legal personhood, makes independent decisions for its own behalf, understands the consequences of its actions, and chooses to contract on its own behalf. Such a result is a long way in the future.

The concern that the system user cannot have the intent to contract under terms the user cannot know in advance appears to be wholly misplaced. The distinction between deterministic and non-deterministic AI systems appears to misunderstand the concept of intent as it applies with contracts made by AI systems. Certainly, it is not enough to have a general intent to contract; one must also intend to agree to the specific terms of the agreement. Yet, contract law clearly allows and needs to allow parties the opportunity to contract with open-ended terms. This can include, for example, an agreement to buy or sell certain goods at a future time at the then market price. (If this is done automatically by an electronic agent, this would of course be a deterministic system).

A simple example should suffice to show why this is so. Assume a contract today to buy and take delivery of a commodity six months from now at the market price of the commodity. Surely the contract is binding and enforceable now even though the future market price is unknown at the time the contract is formed. Contracts such as these are entered into every day. The validity of these agreements is not in question, and certainly the law of contract would not wish to invalidate standard, well-known and accepted

49 Maarten Herbosch, 'Contracting with Artificial Intelligence', The Rabel Journal of Comparative and International Private Law 2023, 672 (699-70). This is not the position of this author, and the author refutes this suggestion.

business practices, particularly those that serve important economic and social purposes.

Thus, the question not whether one can contract on terms that are not fully provided for at the time of contracting, but whether there is the possibility of an indeterministic result that extends the risk assumed by the contracting party such that the 'intent' to contract cannot be presumed.[50] It must be assumed that in some circumstances indeterminant AI system create the possibility of risks beyond those that we would impose upon the party using the AI system. It would appear, though, the issue is not whether there is a contract (with whatever element of 'intent' is necessary to create the contract) but who or what is responsible for the actions of the AI system.

For in these circumstances, the parties are relying on the existence of a contract, and absent some unexpected result from the AI system, the parties would consider the contract both existing and binding. The law of contract does not provide that there is a contract when the parties like the result from an automated system and there is not a contract when they do not like the result. The law of contracts has other remedies for performances that exceed the risks the parties have assumed, but the lack of the contract itself is not a remedy.

As already noted, a substantial percentage of securities transactions are handled by high-speed trading platforms where the trading parties do not know what has been bought or sold until long after the transactions have been concluded. Certainly, the trading partners assume they are the contracting parties; it is not assumed that the trading platforms themselves that shift the assets back and forth based based on an algorithmic program are the contracting parties.

One might suggest that these trading platforms are based on deterministic and not non-deterministic systems, and it is the indeterminacy that distinguishes the securities trading platforms from an AI system that is non-deterministic.[51] But this is not necessarily the case; trading platforms may use indeterministic AI systems. The difference between a deterministic and indeterministic system is only a question of risk.

50 Maarten Herbosch, 'Contracting with Artificial Intelligence', The Rabel Journal of Comparative and International Private Law 2023, 672 (699-70).

51 The *Quoine* case only considered deterministic systems. Quoine Pte Ltd v B2C2 Ltd. [2020] SGHC(I) 02.

Indeterministic systems may create a higher level of risk than deterministic systems, but this possibility should not necessarily result in the unenforceability of the contract. The law is not that short-sighted. These transactions occur and will continue to occur.

Potential risky behavior is not, in and of itself, a reason to prevent contracting. As one court has pointed out:

> While the contract law concepts of offer and acceptance do sit peculiarly when we are dealing with algorithms effectively negotiating with one another, we should also keep in mind another applicable common law precept – that the Courts will not intervene to save parties from a bad bargain, whether that bad bargain arose through an error of judgment or simple carelessness. In this case, the defendants had been careless in the coding of their algorithm, and the result was a bad bargain.[52]

IV. Is the Real Problem the Guardrails?

It seems the real question is not whether a party can intend (or consent) to a contract with indeterminate terms, but whether there is sufficient protection when an AI system responds with a result that is outside the boundaries for which the parties would reasonably agree. The question is whether the law provides sufficient guardrails when things go wrong.

AI contracting presents specific risks that are not normally associated with contracting in general. First, there is the possibility of rogue autonomous systems that, as they learn new solutions, may produce results outside the expected risks assumed by the contracting parties. This may include irrational pricing[53] or other terms. The AI system may also com-

52 Quoine Pte Ltd v B2C2 Ltd. [2020] SGHC(I) 02.

53 System failures may result in markets halting trading. See e.g., https://apnews.com/article/nyse-stock-exchange-halted-volatility-berkshire-hathaway-af4f1fe180a031000a8fd48e33a8d833.

mit fraud,[54]become racist,[55]or otherwise discriminate.[56] There is also the question of asymmetric information as well as the inability to determine how the AI gets the results it does.[57]

At a minimum, '[t]here is a theme running through all these examples of AI contracting. Whether they are contracting with retail consumers or trading on financial markets, companies can use innovations in AI technology to negotiate more profitable contracts for themselves while creating new and unpredictable risks for their counterparties and for the market as a whole'[58]

But the law already provides robust responses to contracts that go seriously awry. For example, the Supreme Court of Canada has affirmed that the doctrine of unconscionability prevents overbearing automated contracts.[59]

Unconscionability, hardship, mistake, and other contract defenses will be available to parties when the AI generated contract simply does not stand up to reasonable standards of enforcement. The law of contract knows how to cabin in the boundaries of unassumed risk.

Moreover, as pointed out decades ago, the risk of producing unpredicted results is placed on the person best able to control the risk. If the risks are allocated in this manner, a strong incentive is provided for those who

54 Laren Henry Scholz, 'Algorithmic Contracts', Stanford Tech. Law Review 2017, 128 (132). The AI system itself cannot commit fraud as an AI system is not capable of perceiving bad behavior and acting upon that perception. The potential "fraud" arises when what the AI system produces would be considered fraud if done by a human.

55 https://www.theguardian.com/technology/2016/mar/24/tay-microsofts-ai-chatbot-gets-a-crash-course-in-racism-from-twitter. The AI system itself cannot be racist as an AI system is not capable of perceiving bad behavior and acting upon that perception. The potential "racism" arises when what the AI system produces would be considered rcism if done by a human.

56 https://www.reuters.com/article/world/insight-amazon-scraps-secret-ai-recruiting-tool-that-showed-bias-against-women-idUSKCN1MK0AG/. The AI system itself cannot discriminate as an AI system is not capable of perceiving bad behavior and acting upon that perception. The potential "discrimination" arises when what the AI system produces would be considered discrimination if done by a human.

57 This may be mitigated somewhat by the European General Data Protection Regulation, E.U. Regulation 2016/679 that requires algorithmic transparency and accountability in automated decision making.

58 Matthew Oliver, 'Contracting by Artificial intelligence: Open Offers, Unilateral Mistakes and Why Algorithms are not Agents', Australian National University Journal of Law and Technology 2021, 45 (59).

59 Douez v. Facebook, 2017 Supreme Court of Canada 33; Uber Technologies inc. v. Uber, 2020 Supreme Court of Canada 16.

use electronic agents to ensure that they are properly programmed and frequently monitored.'[60]

V. The Question of Mistake and Misunderstandings

Before concluding, I would like to examine one area of the law to emphasize the difficulty of applying any notion of understanding, be it intent or otherwise on an AI system. Specifically, I would like to examine the law of mistake and misunderstanding as it applies in contract.

Starting with a common definition of mistake, I want to examine how a mistake might be handled when one or both contracting parties are AI. The UNIDROIT Principles of International Commercial Contracts defines a 'mistake' as "an erroneous assumption relating to facts or to law existing when the contract was concluded".[61] If both parties are human, it is possible to have a mutual mistake; a mistake shared by both parties; a mistaken belief that had the parties known the truth the parties would not have entered into the agreement under the same terms or entered into the agreement at all.[62]

Since AI systems does not have beliefs, much less mistaken beliefs, if both contracting parties are AI systems it is difficult to imagine how the doctrine of mistake could apply to the contract.[63] If only one contracting party is an AI party, one might assume the defense of a unilateral mistake might be available, but for many legal systems, the defense of unilateral

60 Ian R. Kerr, 'Spirit in the Material World: Intelligent Agents as Intermediaries in Electronic Commerce', Dalhousie Law Review 1999, 189 (233).

61 UNIDROIT Principles of International Commercial Contracts (2016), Art. 3.2.1. This discussion on mistake is limited to where the contracting parties have erroneous assumptions about facts or the law. A broader definition of "mistake" might include the failure of the AI system itself. These failures are discussed in the section below on guardrails.

62 Different legal systems will handle the effect of this type of mistake in different ways, but a common approach is shown in the UNIDROIT Principles of International Commercial Contracts (2016), Art. 3.2.2, "A party may only avoid a contract for mistake if, when the contract was concluded, the mistake was of such importance that a reasonable person in the same situation as the party in error would only have concluded."

63 This is not to say that AI systems do not make mistakes. They just make a qualitatively different type of mistake. AI systems may occasionally produce a system output that a human would define as incorrect. AI systems, through their mathematical processes, may arrive at results that are, from a human perspective, so manifestly incorrect that no human should have made the same mistake.

mistake is only available when the non-mistaken party knew or should have known of the mistake, a situation that could not exist when the non-mistaken party is an AI contracting party. Thus, for the latter two situations, mistake would not normally be a defense in contract. Some other solution will need to evolve, or we may simply conclude mistake is not a defense in AI contracting.

Likewise, with "misunderstanding" about the meaning of the terms to an agreement as a defense to a contract, traditional contract rules would not appear to apply. AI systems do not understand language and therefore AI systems cannot misunderstand the language used in an agreement. Thus, if both parties are AI contracting parties, 'misunderstanding' the terms of a agreement simply does not make sense. If one party to an agreement is an AI contracting party, it is also unclear how there could be a misunderstanding on the meaning of the terms of the agreement between the parties when one of the parties by definition has no understanding of the terms of the agreement.

These questions of mistake and misunderstanding disappear if we place humans at the core of the contracting and not the AI systems themselves. I point this out to emphasize the necessity of placing a responsible human behind the AI system. AI systems cannot stand alone in the world of contract.

VI. Conclusion

Today, two things are happening at once. First, transactions are occurring that are based on dynamic information processed by AI systems that may provide results that may not be known or anticipated by the users of the AI system but are clearly thought by the users of the AI systems to be binding contracts. Second, courts and legal scholars are trying to parse these transactions to see if the existing law of contracts provides adequate rules to govern these transactions. Until sometime in the far future when AI systems develop as independent legal persons, the current law of contracts appears to provide adequately for the requirement that parties need to intend to contract to create a binding contract by considering the AI systems as tools used by the parties that use the AI systems.

Legal Framework for AI Contracting: Key Rules on Validity, Attribution and Risk Allocation

Teresa Rodríguez de las Heras Ballell[*]

Abstract:

Automation in forming and performing contracts is proving to be a major revulsive for contract law. As contract law evolves with the transformation of our economy and society, today's economy is not only digital, but essentially and increasingly automated. The penetration of AI in contracting involves 'distancing humans from contracts' and challenging the notion of (human) autonomy and its meaning and significance for contract law. This Paper traces how contract law needs to face and can solve the key dilemma posed by automated contracting: 'human distance' from the contract lifecycle. This Paper explains the key policy decisions that have been adopted for the legal recognition of AI contracting in the UNCITRAL Model Law on Automated Contracting, the ELI Principles on Automated Decision-Making, and the ELI Model Rules on Digital Assistants for Consumer Contracts.

I. Contract law in a quandary: (AI) automated contracting or intuitu hominis contracts

With the pervasive expansion of AI in present economy, automation has become a hallmark of our society. As mechanization transformed our productive model and distanced humans from an increasingly number of tedious tasks and repetitive processes, algorithmic (and more intensely AI) automation is distancing humans from a growing array of decision-making, creative, and intellectual activities.

* Full Professor of Commercial Law, Universidad Carlos III de Madrid. ORCID: 0000-0001-8211-1801
Paper prepared in the framework of the Research Chair on *AI: Foundations and Frontiers*, of which the author is the Director.

Thus, automation poses a major challenge to legal systems, to classical concepts, and to the very conception of the activity that the law is expected to regulate. Automation 'distances' humans from decision-making. In contrast to previous technologies used throughout history, automation and, notably, AI-driven automation impact on the hitherto intrinsically human decision-making capabilities. Already decades ago there was a need for the recognition of the validity and enforceability for electronic contracting, this need reappears today for automated contracting (expression used to refer to AI contracting indistinctively). However and contrarily, automated contracting is not only posing a purely formal challenge, a change of the medium, as electronic contracting did, but actually a challenge of a substantive nature, how decisions are made. The question is then whether a decision, any decision in any field and for any purpose, can be valid and enforceable when it is taken by automated systems, on the sole ground that no human has reviewed it or ratified it. The answer, if affirmative, will be crucial to even start considering the automation of contracting.

Automation in forming and performing contracts is then proved to be a major revulsive for contract law, and a strong catalyst for an in-depth reflection on consumer protection paradigms.

The use of automated systems – including AI systems – to form and to perform contracts stokes a vivid debate on the notion of (human) autonomy and its meaning and significance for contract law, vis-à-vis the notion of AI agency.

Automated contracting raises novel and unprecedented challenges to contract law that add such a level of complexity so as to require revisiting legal terms, notions and categories.[1] Automated contracting is putting an unbearable strain on the very notion of contract, consent, (human) autonomy. Thus, automated contracting confronts an anthropocentric contract law with 'actions', 'outputs', 'code', 'design features', or 'failures' that may have legal relevance and contractual meaning.

Contract law can either embrace them, and accommodate them into the core notions of contract by frictionless assimilation ('contracts formed by automated systems are contracts') or, relegate them to a parallel regime of '(non-human) automated contracts' governed by AI agency, to preserve the purity of human-centric contract law. The dilemma is whether contract law is poised to embrace this evolution of contractual practice or will be

1 Alpa, 'Intervento conclusivo', in: Gatt (*a cura di*), *Il Contratto del Terzo Millennio. Dialogando con Guido Alpa*, Editoriale Scientifica 2018, pp. 75-106, p. 77.

indefectibly fractured into two regimes: automated contracting and *intuitu hominis* contracts.

In developing a legal framework enabling automated contracting, this Paper advocates that at least three main policy solutions must be implemented. First, a rule on legal recognition of both contracts formed or performed by automated systems, and actions performed by automated systems in connection with the formation or the performance of a contract (*infra* B). Second, rules on attribution of actions performed by automated systems (*infra* C). Third, rules on risk allocation, specifically, in relation to unexpected outcomes (*infra* C).

This Paper traces the proposed key solutions to the above-described main policy questions provided for by three main instruments dealing with automated contracting: the UNCITRAL Model Law on Automated Contracting, 2024 (hereinafter, MLAC);[2] the ELI Guiding Principles on Automated Decision-Making, 2022 (hereinafter, ELI PADM);[3] and the ELI Model Rules on Digital Assistants for Consumer Contracts, 2025 (hereinafter, ELI DACC).[4]

II. Legal recognition of automated contracting: the dilemma of 'human distance' in contracting

1. From electronic contracting to automated contracting: the principle of non-discrimination in UNCITRAL texts

Automated contracting embodies a new challenge to contract law that goes far beyond the challenges of electronic contracting that have been already overcome. In fact, electronic contracting, a few decades ago, posed a challenge to legacy contract-law rules.[5] Traditional contract-law rules had

2 UNCITRAL Model Law on Automated Contractings (2024) and Guide to Enactment, https://uncitral.un.org/en/mlac.

3 ELI Guiding Principles on Automated Decision-Making in the EU (2022), https://www.europeanlawinstitute.eu/fileadmin/user_upload/p_eli/Publications/ELI_Innovation_Paper_on_Guiding_Principles_for_ADM_in_the_EU.pdf.

4 ELI Guiding Principles and Model Rules on Digital Assistants for Consumer Law (2025), https://www.europeanlawinstitute.eu/projects-publications/publications/eli-guiding-principles-and-model-rules-on-digital-assistants-for-consumer-contracts/.

5 UNCITRAL texts in the 1996 Electronic Commerce Model Law (with Guide to Enactment) – hereinafter, MLEC; 2001 Electronic Signatures Model Law (hereinafter, MLES); 2005 UN Convention on the Use of Electronic Communications in Interna-

been ideated, formulated, and applied, paradigmatically, for face-to-face and in-writing distance transactions highly dependent upon the available medium, dominantly paper, and the means of communications for sending and receiving relevant declarations and other statements between the parties. Electronic contracting confronted then traditional contract law with the admissibility of the digital medium as a functional equivalent to writing in paper and the use of electronic communications[6] to express and convey declarations of will and other statements with pre-contractual, contractual or contract-performance relevance. It was essentially a formal dilemma, or a dilemma of form. In essence, substantive rules on contracts remained unchallenged.

Automated contracting posed a substantive dilemma instead: the need to rethinking contract law in 'non-human terms' insofar as human actions with legal relevance are now replaced by machine-driven actions in relation to and for the purposes of forming and performing contracts. For the sake of appreciating the criticality of the challenge, the radical perspective of automated contracting as 'contract without humans' is adopted. Even just in a metaphorical way, this radical and extreme approach is more effective so as to highlight that the challenge should not be understood in terms of deeming AI as a simple tool. Otherwise, the debate will be simplified and reductionist.

In developing an enabling legal regime for automated contracting, the initial assumption must be that the use of an automated system is not, solely on that grounds, an insurmountable impediment to recognizing the validity and effectiveness of the resulting actions, declarations and legal transactions.

This principle of recognition has traditionally been formulated in the texts of Uniform Law for International Trade as a rule of non-discrimination. Thus, both the UNCITRAL Model Law on Electronic Commerce, 1996 (hereinafter, MLEC) and the UN Convention on the Use of Electronic Communications in International Commerce, 2005 (hereinafter, CEC) expressly provide for such recognition with the formula 'shall not be de-

tional Commerce (hereinafter, CEC) approved by General Assembly Resolution 60/21, of 23 November 2005.

6 CEC – 'Electronic communication' is defined as "any communication that the parties make by means of data messages; while 'data message" is defined as "information generated, sent, received or stored by electronic, magnetic, optical or similar means, including, but not limited to, electronic data interchange, electronic mail, telegram, telex or telecopy".

nied legal effect, validity or effectiveness... on the sole ground that'. Thus, information in data messages,[7] declarations of the parties expressed in data messages or a contract formed[8] by or in the form of electronic communications[9] shall not be denied legal effect solely on such grounds. In the *acquis communautaire* and in national law, however, a positive formulation of this recognition has been chosen in the form of a conditional statement – 'contracts concluded by electronic means shall produce all the effects provided for by the legal system, when consent and the other requirements necessary for their validity are met'[10] - which is aimed precisely at ensuring their recognition and removing any obstacle that would deprive them of validity and effectiveness.[11]

This principle of recognition of electronic contracting is not, however, sufficient to give the same legal coverage to automated contracting. The functional equivalence that makes it possible to equate the legal effects of an electronic communication with those of a declaration of will expressed by other traditional means does not fully recognize the equivalence of actions, declarations and decisions that have been generated, executed and 'adopted' by AI systems, without human intervention (in each action). Ultimately, automated contracting deviates from classical contracting concepts

7 MLEC, Art. 5:
"Information shall not be denied legal effect, validity or enforceability solely on the grounds that it is in the form of a data message".

8 MLEC, Art. 1(1):
"In the formation of a contract, unless otherwise agreed by the parties, an offer and its acceptance may be expressed by means of a data message. A contract shall not be denied validity or enforceability solely on the ground that a data message was used in its formation".

9 CEC, Art. 8(1):
"A communication or a contract shall not be denied validity or enforceability solely on the ground that it is in the form of an electronic communication".

10 In the Spanish law on electronic commerce, Art. 23(1), Law 34/2002, of 11 July, on information society services and electronic commerce. BOE no. 166, of 12/07/2002 (hereinafter, LSSI).

11 Directive 2000/31/EC of the European Parliament and of the Council of 8 June 2000 on certain legal aspects of information society services, in particular electronic commerce, in the Internal Market (Directive on electronic commerce), OJ L 178, 17.7.2000, p. 1, Art. 9(1):
"Member States shall ensure that their legislation allows contracts to be concluded by electronic means. Member States shall ensure in particular that the legal regime applicable to the contractual process does not hinder the actual use of contracts by electronic means, nor lead to depriving such contracts of legal effect and validity by reason of their conclusion by electronic means".

in a manner fundamentally different from the challenges presented by electronic contracting. While in electronic commerce it is the medium, in automated contracting it is the 'autonomous' action of the system, performed without human intervention, in the very process of decision-making and execution of the action.

The assumption that AI systems operate with varying levels of autonomy is undoubtedly the fracture point in a continuing line of reasoning on the pure basis of functional equivalence.

In this respect, the remarks of the UNCITRAL Secretariat's Explanatory Note to Article 12 of the CEC[12] are particularly revealing. This provision provides an extremely valuable legal basis for automated contracting, but, as it can be seen from the explanatory comments to the text itself, not sufficient in the current state of scientific and technical progress. Article 12 contains very interesting and very useful elements for analysis. The provision is formulated with the classic formula of the principle of non-discrimination ('shall not be denied validity or enforceability') and refers, clearly and literally, to contracting resulting from the interaction with or between automated systems (Human-to-Machine, H2M, or M2M, Machine-to-Machine). Unlike electronic contracting, which dominates the provisions of the rest of the instrument, this article rightly draws attention to the 'lack of intervention by a natural person'. It is not the medium, not the fact of using electronic communications that are to be disabled as grounds for denying validity and effectiveness; the scope of application of Article 12 CEC is indeed automated contracting.[13] In the Explanatory Note, the commentary to the provision is, if possible, more revealing in stating that the increasingly frequent use of automated message systems, which it goes so far as to call 'electronic agents' (today normally named digital assistants, AI-driven assistants, or AI Agents) has invited a review in some legal systems of 'the

12 Art. 12 CEC:
"A contract formed by the interaction between an automated message system and a natural person, or by the interaction between automated message systems, shall not be denied validity or enforceability on the sole ground that no natural person has reviewed or participated in each of the various acts performed through the systems or the contract resulting from such acts".

13 Art. 4.g) CEC:
"'Automated message system' means a computer program or an electronic or other automated means used to initiate an action or to respond to transactions or data messages, which operates, in whole or in part, without intervention or review by a natural person each time an action is initiated or a response is generated by the system".

traditional legal doctrine on contract formation in order to determine its applicability to contracts that are concluded without the intervention of a natural person'. As explained in the commentaries, while there was no reason not to recognize the validity of contracting by means of automated message systems, even if they were not explicitly provided for in the existing texts (MLEC, Vienna Convention[14]), an express recognition would favor the use of automated systems and provide their use with greater legal certainty.

This provision is undoubtedly a fundamental anchor for the legal regime of automated contracting, but its scope is consciously limited when projected onto the current state of development of technology. In the Explanatory Note, it is noted that ('at present') the attribution of the actions of an automated message system to a natural or legal person is based on a deterministic conception of programming. In other words, Article 12 CEC is based on the assumption that the technical parameters by which an automated system is programmed determine its ability to function. And it recognizes that the possibility that new developments in AI allow the system to learn, to modify instructions or to set new objectives with certain levels of autonomy goes beyond the concept of automatism on which the principle of recognition underpinning the provision is based (Art. 12 CEC).

The differential characteristics of AI systems as learning systems with varying levels of autonomy overflow solution that integrates Article 12 CEC into the Uniform Law on International Trade.

Under the MLAC, automated contracting is meant to describe the use of automated system to form or to perform contracts (Art. 2.1 MLAC). As the Guide to Enactment explains, the expression 'to form or to perform contracts' is intended to cover any and all stages of the contract life cycle, including negotiations and precontractual dealings and termination of contracts.

The definition of 'automated system' pursuant to Article 1 MLAC reveals the key and distinctive features of automated contracting and the source or reason for the dilemma: 'computer system that is capable of carrying out actions without the necessary review or intervention of a natural person'. Despite the conciseness of the definition, it is aimed to embrace AI systems as described in internationally recognized notion such as the one

14 United Nations Convention on Contracts for the International Sale of Goods (Vienna, 1980). Date of adoption: 11 April 1980. Entry into force: 1 January 1988.

recommended by OECD[15], after its latest revision,[16] and incorporated in the European Regulation on AI (hereinafter, AI Act).[17]

2. Principle of non-discrimination and law-compliant Automated Decision-Making in the ELI Guiding Principles

Therefore, the ELI Guiding Principles for Automated Decision-Making[18] propose a principle of explicit recognition formulated as a principle of non-discrimination[19] of automated decision-making (ADM) on the sole ground of their automated nature. The material scope of application of these principles is broader than the notion of automated contracting. While it is largely overlapping as it includes decisions affecting or influencing the contractual position of the 'affected person',[20] their rights and interests, it also extends to other actions or decisions which may not be linked to a contractual process at one of its life-cycle stages (decision of a public authority in relation to an administrative file, notification in a judicial

15 OECD, AI terms & concepts, https://oecd.ai/en/ai-principles. OECD, *Recommendation of the Council on Artificial Intelligence*, OECD/LEGAL/0449, May 2019.

16 OECD, AI terms & concepts https://oecd.ai/en/ai-principles, OECD, *Recommendation of the Council on Artificial Intelligence*, OECD/LEGAL/0449, Revision 8 November 2023:
An AI system is a machine-based system that, for explicit or implicit objectives, infers, from the input it receives, how to generate outputs such as predictions, content, recommendations, or decisions that can influence physical or virtual environments. Different AI systems vary in their levels of autonomy and adaptiveness after deployment.

17 Regulation (EU) 2024/1689 of the European Parliament and of the Council of 13 June 2024 laying down harmonised rules on artificial intelligence and amending Regulations (EC) No 300/2008, (EU) No 167/2013, (EU) No 168/2013, (EU) 2018/858, (EU) 2018/1139 and (EU) 2019/2144 and Directives 2014/90/EU, (EU) 2016/797 and (EU) 2020/1828 (Artificial Intelligence Act) (Text with EEA relevance) PE/24/2024/REV/1. *OJ L, 2024/1689, 12.7.2024.*

18 ELI *Guiding Principles for Automated Decision-Making in the EU*, available at https://www.europeanlawinstitute.eu/fileadmin/user_upload/p_eli/Publications/ELI_Innovation_Paper_on_Guiding_Principles_for_ADM_in_the_EU.pdf.

19 Guiding Principle 2: Non-discrimination against WMD
As a general rule, ADM shall not be denied legal effect, validity or enforceability solely on the grounds that it is automated.

20 The term 'affected person' is used in the ELI *Guiding Principles for ADM* to describe (p. 10) 'the natural or legal person interacting with the ADM, either being the person affected by the final decision, or the person using or relying on, for subsequent purposes, including subsequent decision-making, the output of the ADM (prediction, recommendation, rating, ranking). The affected person can be a consumer or a professional user'.

procedure, infringement of an industrial property right). In view of this lack of full overlap in the scope of application, it is nevertheless interesting to use these principles in the analysis of automated contracting to the extent that they are applicable.

The principle of non-discrimination (Guiding Principle 2), which is an essential enabling element of automated contracting, does not, in principle, prevent the legislator from deciding to adopt specific or additional rules for the use of automated systems for certain purposes. These rules may range from design requirements to transparency requirements[21] or explainability requirements. Failure to comply with these requirements may entail legal consequences of various kinds, but it does not deviate from the principle of non-discrimination; rather, it preserves and builds on the non-discrimination principle. This strong statement is valid at least at this point of the analysis where the general principles on which to build the legal regime of automated contracting are being presented, but when more specific legal questions are raised, it will be necessary to return to this principle in order to contextualize and qualify it. Thus, for example, if it were regulated that AI systems for consumer digital assistants must be designed to allow the consumer to choose the main purchase criteria and deactivate the purchase functionality at any time without losing the other utilities of the system, non-compliance with this design requirement would result in administrative sanctions, a ban on supply in the European market or loss of certification.[22] This is the aspect that does not impact on automated

---

21 For example, the simple transparency requirements for automated rating and ranking systems imposed by Regulation (EU) 2019/1150 of the European Parliament and of the Council of 20 June 2019 on promoting fairness and transparency for professional users of online intermediation services (Text with EEA relevance) PE/56/2019/REV/1 OJ L 186, 11.7.2019, p. 57, Art. 5(1) and (2):
"1. Online intermediary service providers shall state in their general terms and conditions the main parameters governing the ranking and the reasons why those parameters have a higher relative importance than other parameters.
2. Online search engine providers shall set out the main parameters which, individually or collectively, are most significant in determining the ranking and relative importance of those main parameters, by providing a publicly and easily accessible description, written in a simple and comprehensible manner, in the online search engines they offer. The description should be kept up to date".

22 As in other sectors with a high regulatory burden and a strong technical component, certification also plays an important role in business management and the implementation of AI systems. Alongside previous certifications, ISO has approved ISO/IEC 42001, the first international management system standard for AI that is certifiable. The standards set out requirements for establishing, implementing, maintaining and

contracting in a pure private-law sense. However, non-compliance with this specific requirement may also have a direct or indirect impact on the rules are being developed for automated contracting. The absence of consumer control over the decisional criteria of the digital assistant could be a factor for non-attribution of the decision or for assuming/presuming a consent-invalidating error. It could also be relevant in a liability action for lack of conformity or on grounds of defective product. Suffice it here to reinforce the principle of non-discrimination as the basic rule of the legal system for automated contracting.

Similarly, but in the opposite sense, the principle of non-discrimination also does not imply or preclude the legislator from prohibiting or limiting the use of automated systems for certain purposes or in certain decisions. The EU regulatory framework for AI illustrates these scenarios very vividly. Article 5 AI Act prohibits certain AI practices on the basis of their use or purpose - subliminal techniques to alter a person's behavior with a risk of causing harm, systems based on inferring emotions in certain areas and for certain purposes. Designed as a regulatory framework, its infringement carries penalties (including administrative fines) - Art. 71 AI Act -. Beyond the AI Act, which provides the most obvious framework for identifying prohibitions or limitations on the basis of intended use or purpose, there are also other restrictions, notably on the full automation of certain activities or processes in the rules for digital services[23] - Art. 12(1)[24] DSA on the choice

---

continually improving an AI management system with the aim of ensuring that systems are developed and used responsibly. To this end, it is interesting to note how the certification criteria essentially embody the guiding principles for the development and use of AI systems that have crystallized in the various instruments studied: reliability, transparency and responsible use; respect for ethical principles and values such as fairness, non-discrimination and respect for privacy; mitigation of risks and implementation of appropriate preventive and mitigation measures; prioritization of human well-being, safety and user experience in the design and deployment of AI; compliance with applicable laws.

23 Regulation (EU) 2022/2065 of the European Parliament and of the Council of 19 October 2022 on a Single Market for Digital Services and amending Directive 2000/31/EC (Digital Services Act) OJ L 277, 27.10.2022, pp. 1–102.

24 Art. 12(1) DSA:
"Providers of intermediary services shall designate a single point of contact to enable recipients of the service to communicate directly and rapidly with them, by electronic means and in a user-friendly manner, including by allowing recipients of the service to choose the means of communication, which shall not solely rely on automated tools".

of means of communication between service providers and recipients or Art. 20(6) DSA on complaint-handling mechanisms.[25]

The validity and effectiveness of automated decision-making's non-discrimination is limited exclusively by the reason that no human has reviewed or ratified the decision. Hence, it does not remedy other grounds that may be invalidating or limiting, nor does it operate independently of the requirements and rules applicable to the legal situation in each case. Therefore, Guiding Principle 2 operates in conjunction with Guiding Principle 1 *(Law-compliant ADM)*[26] which establishes a rule of compliance with the rules applicable to the equivalent non-automated decision. One might think that this statement is too self-evident and, because it is obvious, useless. However, it has several ramifications or derivatives that allow for more far-reaching reflections.

First, it contains a warning against circumvention by the mere use of an automated system. The use of an automated system cannot be an excuse to avoid compliance with the applicable law. The applicable law must be determined by reference to the equivalent legal situation if an automated system had not been used. This perspective transforms such a basic rule into a useful design and implementation guideline. Ultimately, the use of automated systems does not require an express legal authorization. It relies on the binomial of non-discrimination and law compliance to ensure legal recognition and, from there, to attach to it the legal regime that corresponds by equivalence - thus, if it is a banking contract, it will comply with the regulations that are applicable to it regardless of its automation.

Second, in its positive variant as an active obligation to ensure law compliance, it raises some interesting questions. The internal and external complexity that defines the functioning of an AI system requires some considerations that refer us to the regulatory framework. Each operator of the AI value chain will be responsible for the compliance with the requirements corresponding to each activity - design requirements, transparency, explainability, auditing, risk management, etc.

25 Art. 20(6) DSA:
"Providers of online platforms shall ensure that the decisions, referred to in paragraph 5, are taken under the supervision of appropriately qualified staff, and not solely on the basis of automated means".

26 Guiding Principle 1: Law-compliant AMD
An operator that decides to use ADM for a particular purpose shall ensure that the design and the operation of the ADM are compliant with the laws applicable to an equivalent non- automated decision-making system.

This approach to the legal recognition and admissibility of automated systems in and for contracting under the formula of the principle of non-discrimination also leads to the assumption that a prior agreement between the parties is not necessary for the use of an automated system in any of the phases of the contractual cycle as a requirement for its validity and effectiveness. This very essential and basic statement takes us back to the early days of electronic contracting, where its full legal admissibility depended precisely on freeing it from its being made conditional to prior agreement between the parties.

Full recognition of the validity and effectiveness of actions with a (pre- and post-) contractual purpose executed by automated systems must necessarily include this fundamental premise of the absence of prior agreement. In sum, the principle of non-discrimination implies that these actions cannot be denied validity and legal effectiveness solely on the grounds of their automated nature, without human intervention, and, therefore, that prior agreement between the parties is not an additional requirement to be satisfied in order for automated contracting to be legally recognized.

The dilemma on automated contracting has been solved in its first part. Are automated contracts valid and enforceable under existing (human-centric) contract law and within the present contractual 'culture'? Even more, are these contracts negotiated, formed, and/or performed by automated systems actually 'contracts'? Do we need to reconcile automated contracting with the fiction of a dialogued, human-driven agreement based on a meeting of minds or, instead, to deem this classical conception already exhausted or overcome?

The principle of non-discrimination would be aimed to deactivate any legacy impediment. But the entire dilemma is not solved. Is automated contracting valid solely on the basis of party autonomy, as parties accept and agree on? Are we admitting instead a 'functional equivalence' between human autonomy and AI agency? Yet, could parties agree on banning, limiting or subjecting to certain conditions the use of AI systems in their transactions? If so, these practices would bring about to legal life the category of *intuitu hominis* contracts (*infra* D).

3. Legal recognition of automated contracting, technology neutrality, and right to use

Both the MLAC and the ELI DACC contains a provision explicitly providing for the legal recognition of contracts as well as actions in connection with the formation or the performance of a contract. The drafting of the provision is largely similar between the two instruments. Minor divergences respond to the need to align with the terminology used by each instrument.

As per Article 5 MLAC, '(a) contract formed using an automated system shall not be denied validity or enforceability on the sole ground that no natural person reviewed or intervened in any action carried out in connection with the formation of the contract'. Followed by the same statement referred to any action (offer, renegotiation, termination notice, performance): (3) 'An action carried out by an automated system in connection with the formation or performance of a contract shall not be denied legal effect, validity or enforceability on the sole ground that no natural person reviewed or intervened in the action'.

For the ELI DACC provide rules for contracts between a business and a consumer regarding the use of digital assistants by one or both parties for their contractual relations (Art. 1), the drafting is slightly adapted to the applicable terms (pursuant to Art. 2 Definitions). Thus, Article 17 ELI DACC states that (a)n algorithmic contract is not to be denied validity or enforceability solely because a digital assistant was used, irrespective of whether only one party or both parties used digital assistants. (2) 'Any action carried out by a digital assistant in respect of the contractual relations between a consumer and a business is not to be denied legal effect, validity or enforceability on the sole ground that a digital assistant was used'.

After sharing this fundamental policy solution, the two instruments separate each other again in how each of them approaches the use by the parties of automated system/digital assistants in contracting. The main consumer protection goal driving the ELI DACC explains the disparate approach.

In line with its tradition, the MLAC reaffirms in Article 4 the principle of technology neutrality. But in this provision, the principle is combined with a rule on the voluntary use of automated systems throughout the contract life cycle. It states that *(n)othing in this Law requires the use of an automated system or a particular method in automated systems to form or perform contracts*. Thus, in addition to reiterating the technology-neutrality approach, insofar as the MLAC does not mandate the use of a particular method, solution or model of automated system in automated contracting, the provision gives expression to the principle of private autonomy and, specifically, 'reaffirms the freedom of the parties not to use automated systems in their contractual relations (but rather to use other forms of electronic contracting or "traditional" paper-based or in-person contracting)'. Albeit it may be unnecessary to reaffirm this well-established principle, this explicit recognition was considered of value by some jurisdictions as regards automated contracting (par. 42 Guide to Enactment, MLAC).

Contrariwise, the assumption of an asymmetric relationship between consumers and traders together with a promising rebalancing potential of the use of digital assistants in consumer transactions are behind the different approach taken by the ELI DACC. In its Article 3,[27] the ELI DACC focus on the right of consumers to use a digital assistant in their contractual relationships with traders and provide for rules preventing traders from banning, limiting, or forcing the consumer to use a digital assistant in their contracting, unless there are legitimate grounds.

The question that triggers this approach is whether the use of automated systems for consumer decision-making can strengthen the consumer's position and improve bargaining power. If a consumer, assisted by a digital assistant, i.e. by an automated system that searches and processes information, selects and recommends options or even makes the final contracting decision with a prior review of the purchase conditions, is in a position to make better informed decisions, the use of automated systems in consumer

---

27 Art. 3: Use of Digital Assistants ELI DACC:
(1) Consumers have the right to use a digital assistant for their contractual relations with a business.
(2) A business must not use any contractual terms or conditions in a contract with a consumer which directly or indirectly waive or restrict this right. Any such terms are not binding on the consumer.
(3) A business must not design, organise, or operate their online interfaces in a way that prevents consumers from using digital assistants in their contractual relations with a business.
(4) A business must not require a consumer to use the consumer's digital assistant for contractual relations. The main functionality of a product which incorporates a digital assistant must not be restricted if a consumer declines to use that digital assistant.
(5) Paragraphs (1) - (4) do not apply where there are legitimate grounds recognised by the applicable law in respect of the matters addressed in these paragraphs. Furthermore, paragraphs (2) and (3) do not apply to businesses categorised as micro or small enterprises under the applicable law.

relations accompanies and makes the protective function of consumer law more effective.

If such a premise is assumed, the limitation or prohibition of their use will be avoided or prevented as far as possible because it empowers the consumer. Thus, whether the principle of non-discrimination of automated systems in contracting, reinforced by the premise that it also mitigates consumer's vulnerabilities and improves their bargaining position, is transformed into a right of use without limitations or barriers in consumer relations.

Without going deeper into this more complex debate, which deserves more nuanced attention, it suffices to spotlight one of the principles proposed in the ELI *Interim Report, EU Consumer Law and Automated Decision-Making (ADM): Is EU Consumer Law Ready for ADM.*[28] Of the eight principles tentatively proposed in the first phase of the project, principle 4 (*Non-discrimination and ADM-barrier free principle*) encapsulates the idea that consumers might benefit from the use of automated systems for trading and contracting. Moreover, automated systems in the form of digital assistants can most effectively and fully realize the ultimate ratio of the 'informed decision'[29] which the consumer makes in full knowledge of the facts and with full, adequate and sufficient information to ensure that it is in their best interests. This principle has crystallized in Article 3 ELI DACC.

---

28 The co-rapporteurs of the project are Christoph Busch, Teresa Rodríguez de las Heras Ballell, (Dariusz Szostek until October 2023), Christian Twigg-Flesner and Marie Jull Sørensen. The project consists of two phases. The first phase has been completed with the drafting, adoption and publication of a report analyzing the suitability/readiness of European consumer law for the use of automated systems and incorporating legislative recommendations to ensure that the *acquis* does not contain barriers to automated consumer contracting and that consumer protection is not undermined by automation. This report approved by the ELI Council on 27 November 2023 and published in the same year, *Interim Report, EU Consumer Law and Automated Decision-Making (ADM): Is EU Consumer Law Ready for ADM,* examines the adequacy of existing rules while already anticipating some of the principles that will guide the second phase of the project aimed at formulating a set of principles and model rules for automated contracting.

29 Art. 2(e), Directive 2005/29/EC of the European Parliament and of the Council of 11 May 2005 concerning unfair business-to-consumer commercial practices in the internal market and amending Council Directive 84/450/EEC, Directives 97/7/EC, 98/27/EC and 2002/65/EC of the European Parliament and of the Council and Regulation (EC) No 2006/2004 of the European Parliament and of the Council, (*Unfair Commercial Practices Directive*), OJEU L 149/22, 11.6.2005.

Both in their current state of development and in their expected future evolution, automated systems operating as digital assistants for consumers would act as powerful managers of transaction-relevant information. They can collect, contrast, compare and verify information provided by traders about the product, recommend the best combination of attributes, advise on the most appropriate contractual terms, negotiate certain terms, search for the best offer, reject proposals incorporating contractual terms that the consumer has marked as unacceptable, or dynamically review long-term relationships such as subscriptions or contracts for the supply of products or services. These functionalities and potential applications of digital assistants would seem to dilute the weakened position of a consumer unable to deal with scattered, overwhelming, biased or complex information. The digital assistant stands as a consumer protection net and a 'manager of consumer interests' with unparalleled collection, verification, integration and search capabilities.

On a first reading, automated contracting would seem to rebalance consumer relations, eliminating asymmetries and reducing the need for safeguards. But the context is much broader and more complex and cannot, and should not, be solved with the erroneous assumption that there are no more 'consumer relations' – maybe new types of contextual, relational, or systemic asymmetric relationships. Indeed, as a premise, the ELI *Interim Report, EU Consumer Law and Automated Decision-Making (ADM): Is EU Consumer Law Ready for ADM* starts from the principle (*Principle 2: Application of Consumer Law to Algorithmic Contracts*) that the actions of the digital assistant are attributed to the consumer and, as such, consumer protection rules apply. Perhaps this should only be an interim and transitory answer that will have to be discarded when (if) the transition to M2M transactions in all economic relations is completed. Then, focus shall need to be placed on 'technological asymmetries' and 'digital vulnerabilities'.[30]

The effective exercise of an eventual right to use automated systems for contracting by consumers would require, first, preventing the use of technological, operational or design measures that block, deter or disable the use of digital assistants (*blockers*); and, second, implementing contractual, technological and design solutions that facilitate the virtual assistant to perform the necessary actions under equivalent conditions. Nevertheless, the implementation of these technological and operational, design and

30 Crea/De Franceschi (eds.), *The New Shapes of Digital Vulnerability in European Private Law*, Baden-Baden: Nomos 2024.

programming measures involves costs and requires changes in communication channels, interfaces and contracting procedures. They could therefore become a burden for smaller companies, putting them at a disadvantage vis-à-vis established market players and large platforms. This disruptive effect on the market has to be taken into account in the final shaping of the principle of non-discrimination and *no barriers*. In addition, and from another perspective that applies equally to small and large entities, the use of automated systems can saturate the system, simultaneously block available offers without completing the transaction, alter prices or erroneously generate messages of lack of availability (*bots* for purchasing tickets, assistants who keep multiple transactions pending simultaneously, *bots* that saturate the system and block it, automated systems that multiply bookings). Therefore, there may be cases where legal restrictions (and legitimate and reasonable contractual prohibitions) may exist, or be imposed, on the use of automated systems to protect specific interests, such that their use becomes unlawful, inappropriate or unreasonable.

III. Attribution rules and the challenge of unexpected actions

1. The meaning and the relevance of attribution in automated contracting

The assumption that AI systems act with varying levels of autonomy[31] makes attribution a more complex and absolutely critical task. A system of attribution rules and factors is instrumental when the option of 'electronic persons'[32] is abandoned.

Attribution in AI systems must take into account two important considerations.

Firstly, it does not consist in determining the origin of a message or an action already completed and determined, which the automated system would simply transmit or generate according to predefined instructions and without any margin for unpredictability, but in attributing decisions

31 Some studies analyze the emergence of autonomous, interactive and reactive actions of certain AI systems, in particular large language models, to challenge a purely deterministic and instruction-based definition of algorithmic systems under human control. Chan A et al. (2023) Harms from Increasingly Agentic Algorithmic Systems, IEEE Computer Society 2022-March. https://arxiv.org/abs/2302.10329.

32 Pagallo, 'Vital, Sophia, and Co.-The Quest for the Legal Personhood of Robots', Information, MDPI, 2018.

or actions which, with a certain level of autonomy and in accordance with explicit or implicit objectives, the system adopts and executes.

Secondly, attribution is a prerequisite that underpins other solutions of the legal regime of automated contracting such as the treatment of error or the rules on allocation of risks due to malfunctioning or unexpected outcomes.

Thus, attribution serves for multiple purposes. As a first anchor on which to build a regime for mistakes in automated contracting. As a model to extrapolate to the question of the 'attribution of information' to ensure a conscious and informed decision of the person to whom the decision of the automated system is attributed. As a threshold, for example, with respect to decide whether the cases of absolutely unforeseeable and unexpected actions should be treated from the point of view of non-attribution, a defect of consent or as a scenario of liability. All these questions reveal that attribution, in general terms, has several layers that require separate treatment.

The debate on the attribution of the actions of automated systems has been marked and, to some extent, clouded by a complex and delicate debate, not always framed in the right terms, on 'electronic personality'.[33] This is neither a new nor an unprecedented proposal. The question of the personhood of AI systems has been raised for decades, from a variety of perspectives.[34] Sometimes with a strong ethical and philosophical flavour, on other occasions with pragmatism and a vision of personality as a useful and efficient mechanism for risk distribution and selective attribution of rights and/or obligations. In short, legal personality as a legal fiction[35] or technical-legal solution has already shown malleability and plasticity to

33 European Parliament resolution of 16 February 2017 with recommendations to the Commission on civil law rules on robotics (2015/2103(INL)), Civil law rules on robotics, P8_TA(2017)0051, para 59, "(p) urges the Commission, when carrying out an impact assessment of its future legislative instrument, to explore, analyse and consider the implications of all possible legal solutions, such as:
"to create in the long term a specific legal personality for robots, so that at least the most complex autonomous robots can be considered as electronic persons liable to repair any damage they may cause, and possibly to apply electronic personality to cases where robots make intelligent autonomous decisions or interact with third parties independently".

34 Solum, 'Legal Personhood for Artificial Intelligences', North Carolina Law Review 70, pp. 1231-1287, 1992.

35 On the evolution of the theory of legal personality, Galgano, 'El concepto de persona jurídica', Revista Derecho del Estado 16, pp. 13-28, 2004.

adapt to other situations without implying a full mimicry of the human condition, i.e. without entailing an anthropomorphic conception[36] in the recognition of personality.

However, the option of attributing legal personality to AI systems with certain levels of autonomy (as a unique solution or according to certain thresholds of autonomy) entails significant practical difficulties and shifts the problems to a second stage without solving them.[37] In addition to ethical concerns, it may have implications for the soundness and coherence of the liability system as a whole with practical obstacles to the compensatory purpose or with a counterproductive allocation of incentives to use AI systems as a shield for protection and diversion of liability. All this could ruin both the compensatory and the preventive purpose of liability.[38] Thus, the need for attribution formula becomes even more pressing.

2. Attribution rules and factors in the MLAC

MLAC sets out two consecutive rules for attribution of actions carried out by automated systems in Article 7. In tribute to the prevailing role of party autonomy, paragraph 1[39] refers to the parties' agreement on the procedure (and then the rules and relevant factors) to attribute the actions performed by the automated system. Thus, the primary rule is that the output of an automated system would be attributed in accordance with any procedure agreed to by the parties. Parties can establish this procedure in a preliminary agreement for negotiations, in a framework contract between the parties for repeated transactions, or in the terms and conditions of a platform operated by a third party to which both parties have joined and throughout which they conclude their contracts via an automated system.

---

36 Maneesha, 'Unsettling Anthropocentric Legal Systems: Reconciliation, Indigenous Laws, and Animal Personhood', Journal of Intercultural Studies 41(1), pp. 77-97, 2020, doi: 10.1080/07256868.2019.1704229; Salazar Ortiz/Láriz Durón, 'Una crítica al antropocentrismo desde la ética ambiental'. Euphyía 11(20), pp. 107-130, 2017, https://doi.org/10.33064/20euph1363.

37 *Expert Group on Liability and new Technologies,* in its two trainings: New Technologies formation and Product Liability formation.

38 Ghersi, Teoría General de la reparación de daños: análisis económico y sociológico del daño individual y social, Astrea, Buenos Aires 1997, at pp. 141-145; Díez Picazo, *Derecho de daños,* Civitas, Madrid 1999, at pp. 41 et seq.

39 Art. 7(1) MLAC:
'As between the parties to a contract, an action carried out by an automated system is attributed in accordance with a procedure agreed to by the parties'.

In the absence of parties' agreement, MLAC opts for a fall-back rule based on two components: use and purpose. Article 7 in its paragraph 2 states that 'an action carried out by an automated system is attributed to the person who uses the system for that purpose'. As explained in the Guide to Enactment, par. 66:

> It is intended to attribute the action to the person with the strongest link to that action, and for that attribution to be determined objectively, in the light of all the circumstances. Depending on those circumstances, a range of factors may be relevant in identifying that person, including: (a) the person deploying the automated system; (b) the control exercised over the operational parameters of the system and the action; (c) the benefit or value derived from the action; (d) the nature and purpose of the contract; and (e) trade usages and the practices established between the parties

This solution is neither replacing nor adopting agency law rules. The automated system is not treated as an agent acting on behalf of the principal. Instead, a set of factors are proposed to attribute the actions carried out by the automated system that pivot on a 'qualified' use and a purpose or aim that connects the factual use with the outcome in a transactional context. This is the first step in the process of attributing the legal consequences of that action that would depend upon each type of situation (contractual effects as a contracting party, liability for damages, relevant pre-contractual information in consumer contracts) (par. 71 Guide to Enactment, MLAC).

ELI DACC adopts an approach to attribution that initially seems to be simpler and broader as it is only based on the 'use'.

> Article 22(1): Attribution and its limits
> *A person who uses a digital assistant for contractual relations is bound by the actions taken by the digital assistant and all the actions of the digital assistant are attributed to that person.*

However, the limits of attribution, as discussed below, show that, given the consumer protection goal, the attribution solutions are largely different to those laid down in MLAC. Indeed, the default rule for attribution of unexpected outcomes (see *infra* C.III) is diametrically opposite.

3. Typology of risks and risk-allocation solutions in automated contracting

The rules and factors proposed for attributing to a person actions or decisions (output) of an AI system are crucial to deal with certain situations that we can classify as pathological: errors, system failures and unforeseen or unexpected outcomes.

A classification or typology of these relevant risk cases is proposed for the purposes of attribution.

The first category of risks refers to cases where the automated system malfunctions, fails or has technical problems in its operation. In these cases, the system does not perform the expected action, performs it late or incorrectly, or makes decisions that do not correspond to the operator's (or user's) expectations.

The second category of risks includes cases where third party interference, hacking attack or cybersecurity breaches lead to an omission (no action by the system), an action or a decision by the AI system that the operator (user) does not recognize, deviates substantially from its intention or is simply wrong for whatever reason.

The third category of risks comprises the assumptions most closely linked to the nature of AI systems as learning systems with a strong dependence on data: unexpected outcomes. Automated systems can give rise to unanticipated, unexpected outcomes that deviate substantially from what is expected, suffer *hallucinations,*[40] and evolve in their learning towards unanticipated tasks, extrapolate data, generate biases, or execute actions that exceeds the training scope.

In the face of these situations, which distinctive features of AI make particularly serious or at least intense (autonomy and learning capacity, opacity, complexity, vulnerability, data dependence), three legislative policy options can be considered, in general terms, which are not necessarily mutually exclusive. First, non-attribution. Second, liability rules. Third, the (adapted) application of existing rules on defects of consent, or other causes for invalidity or nullity. We propose to add a fourth possible solution to attribution of unexpected outcomes: the formulation of bespoken rules for unexpected outcomes of AI systems.

The proposed solution to the risk categories must be clear and predictable, provide certainty in commercial trade, and achieve an appropriate

40 Ziwei et al., 'Survey of Hallucination in Natural Language Generation', ACM Computing Surveys 55, 2023.

distribution of risks between the parties. Therefore, unjustified and abusive recourse to the legislative policy option of 'non-attribution' can significantly undermine confidence in trade while discouraging automated contracting and increasing transaction costs. Faced with the risk of non-attribution, prices and costs in automated contracts would move upwards to cover the risk, specific safeguards and insurance would be imposed, or the use of AI would be limited in particularly large transactions or transactions where frustration of the economic purpose of business due to non-attribution are unacceptable or difficult to reverse.

Hence, Article 7(3) MLAC enshrined as a primary rule of attribution aimed to provide legal certainty and predictability in (B2B, mainly) automated trade: *(a)ttribution of an action carried out by an automated system shall not be denied on the sole ground that the outcome was unexpected.*

On the contrary, the non-attribution option would mean that, in the event of failure, third party interference or deviation (alleged and/or acknowledged by the other party) from the expected operation, the action or decision is not attributable to the person to whom would otherwise be attributed the origin of the output result of the IA system. For the sake of legal certainty, non-attribution is an uncomfortable and, in certain cases, devastating solution because it undermines trust and frustrates expectations. Therefore, non-attribution as a general solution might not be optimal.

It may, however, be the preferred solution in consumer relations as a measure to protect the consumer who would not be bound by an action or decision resulting from a failure, interference by a third party or a deviation of the system towards unforeseen, surprising or unexpected results. In the ELI DACC this option has been considered and adopted as the primery rule. The action or decision would not be attributable to the consumer and would not have any legal effect. This avoids the situation of subsequent attribution to another actor in the supply chain. Where an action deviates from what the consumer could reasonably expect, that action will have no legal effect and are not attributed to the consumer. In assessing whether the actions of the digital assistant deviate from those a consumer could reasonably expect, paragraph 3, Article 22, laid down a non-exhaustive list of relevant factors.[41]

41 Art. 22(3) ELI DACC
"The relevant factors to be applied in determining whether the actions of the digital assistant deviated from those a consumer could reasonably expect, include:

Article 22(2): Attribution and its limits

Where the actions of a digital assistant used by a consumer for contractual relations deviate from those which could reasonably be expected by the consumer, the actions of the digital assistant have no legal effect and are not attributed to the consumer.

This non-attribution rule is combined with a liability solution, in the form of compensation of the damage caused to the other party (of the consumer) by the non-attribution at the expense of the operator who is liable - the provider of the AI system (digital assistant or AI) to the consumer.[42]

The major difficulty is to decide whether failures and errors, on the one hand, and unforeseen decisions, on the other, can and should be treated together as a single category in the case of automated contracting, or whether, on the contrary, they respond to different scenarios. In the latter case, the debate is whether automated outputs that could be qualified as 'unforeseen', 'unexpected' or 'unintended' require a different solution. This has been the debate that arose in the deliberations of UNCITRAL Working Group IV in the preparation of the provisions for automated contracting.[43]

(a) any information given to the consumer about the adaptive capability of the digital assistant;

(b) whether the operation of any adaptive functionality of the digital assistant was inconsistent with such information;

(c) external factors such as loss of access to third-party data supplies, errors in that data, or cybersecurity breaches; and

(d) whether in the specific circumstances, the consumer could not reasonably have expected that the action in question would be taken."

42 Art. 25 ELI DACC: *Liability of the supplier of a digital assistant to third parties*
"Where the actions of a digital assistant are not attributed to the consumer who deployed it under Article 22(2), the supplier of the digital assistant to that consumer is liable to the business with whom the consumer's digital assistant was dealing for losses the business has incurred as a result of the non-attribution. The conditions for awarding damages are governed by the applicable law.

43 A/79/17. Article 8. Unexpected actions carried out by automated systems".
"[1. Unless otherwise agreed by the parties, where an action carried out by an automated system is attributed to a party to a contract, the other party to the contract is not entitled to rely on that action if, in the light of all the circumstances:
(a) The party to which the action is attributed could not reasonably have expected the action; and
(b) The other party knew or could reasonably be expected to have known that the party to which the action is attributed did not expect the action.
2. Nothing in this article affects the application of any rule of law or agreement of the parties that may govern the legal consequences of an action carried out by an automated system.] "

Therefore, despite the decisive rule in Article 7(3), an additional Article 8 is included in the Model Law as an optional provision (in square brackets) with an accompanying footnote inviting States enacting the Model Law to consider incorporating the provision into their domestic law if they wish specifically to legislate the issue of unexpected actions carried out by automated systems (pars. 73 and 74 Guide to Enactment, MLAC). During the preparation of the Model Law, it was felt that a stand-alone provision specifically addressing the issue was unnecessary and could even be undesirable if it interfered with fundamental domestic law concepts and principles, as well as with established trade usages. Nevertheless, it was stated that a stand-alone provision could be useful for some jurisdictions to supplement existing solutions and so Article 8 was included as an optional provision.

The starting point for Article 8 is the principle that a party using an automated system as part of its trade-related activities bears the risk of the output of that system as per Article 7(3). In general terms, paragraph 1 mitigates that principle with regard to unexpected outputs by allowing a party to disavow the output in certain circumstances, and thus avoid the legal consequences of that output that may flow under other law.

The scope of the proposed provision refers exclusively to the second typology of actions performed by automated systems, i.e. unforeseen or unexpected actions. But it is also intended to deal with cases of 'programming error, or interference by a third party, or transmission error'. Its wording was originally based on Article 13(5) LMCE,[44] which does not focus on unforeseen results but on attribution of origin or transmission errors. Therefore, the need has arisen to look for other legal solutions to unforeseen results that are uniquely and specifically linked to AI systems and not to the problems of electronic means of communication of messages.

The assumption that the principle that should govern the use of AI systems is that the party using the system to form or perform a contract bears the risk involved[45] would invite to look for solutions in other texts. In the UNCITRAL system, Article 14 CEC and Articles 25 and 79 Vienna Convention might be considered. Both texts seek to strike a balance between the interests of the parties by applying the concepts of reasonable expectations and fair dealing. Despite these efforts, however, the solution is not clear and continues to raise doubts.

44 A/CN.9/WG.IV/WP.182, par. 43.
45 A/CN.9/WG.IV/WP.182, par. 42.

IV. AI contracting and intuitu hominis *contracts in human-machine hybrid societies*

The principle of non-discrimination against automated contracting neither ignores nor limits private (human) autonomy. While it is clear that not requiring prior agreement for the use of automated systems as a requirement for validity is a key consequence of the principle of non-discrimination, parties can agree on the use of (or on the conditions under which they will use) automated systems in their dealings. There are various possible scenarios.

First, parties can set the terms of use of automated systems in a transaction-specific and concrete manner. They could, for example, incorporate these terms in a preliminary agreement governing the negotiations between the parties, or it could simply be a pre-agreement that one party imposes on the other (with a first unilateral declaration that the other party accepts) if the latter wants to negotiate and contract with the former.

Second, parties may establish a contractual framework of collaboration to regulate long-term relationships or repeated and successive operations and include and detail the conditions for the use of automated systems between them at any stage of the contracting cycle.

Third, conditions for the use of automated systems may be contained in the *membership agreement*[46] which is concluded between the parties (platform users) and the platform operator and which regulates not only the interaction between each user and the operator, but also incorporates the rules (either directly or by reference) governing transactions between users. What is interesting in this scenario is that the pre-agreement is not concluded between the parties, but is concluded bilaterally between the user and the operator, but determines the use of automated systems in the contractual relations between users. The underlying approach is that accepting the terms of the membership agreement (and the platform policy it incorporates therein) is a prerequisite for accessing and contracting on and through the platform. Thus, parties accept and, when contracting on the platform, do so with the reasonable expectation that their automated contracting will be in accordance with the platform policy accepted by all parties.

46 Rodriguez de las Heras Ballell, 'Las condiciones de uso de los sitios web y los *brose-wrap agreements*', in: Calvo Caravaca/Oviedo Albán, *Nueva Lex Mercatoria y contratos internacionales,* Ibañez, Colombia, 2006, pp. 303-346.

Against such a backdrop of options and the wide variety of approaches that the agreement may take, it is necessary to address the most extreme scenario that would entail a banning on the use of automated systems for certain transactional purposes, in certain contexts or for one of the parties to the negotiation or contract. If we start from the principle of total and absolute recognition of the decisions taken or assisted decisions and actions executed by automated systems, this type of prohibitive agreement would reflect the will of the parties to restrict the means, the form and the conditions under which they decide to conduct their dealings or the contracts they conclude.

A first interpretation of these clauses, especially when they refer to the performance of contractual obligations, could be that they are aimed to govern service or work agreements concluded *intuitu personae.* Such contractual restrictions or prohibitions on the use of automated systems are likely to emerge strongly in the context of creative intellectual, or artistic works or even professional services. While in modern economies, the collective exercise of professions and the frequent need for subcontracting or assistance of the debtor by assistants endows the requirement of special 'qualities of the person' with another dimension, the current state of the debate on AI systems and in particular generative AI may lead to the emergence of prohibitive clauses in contexts with a high creative component. A trend could crystallize towards *intuitu hominis* relationships limiting the use of automated systems in the execution of works, the provision of services or the performance of any of the contractual obligations.

This trend, which I have coined as *intuitu hominis* contracting, could find not only a particularly fruitful environment but also and above all a more convincing justification in artistic, creative or intellectual activities (a novel, a weekly newspaper column, a scientific article for a magazine, a musical work, an advertisement). Without yet entering into the debate on the 'artificial authorship'[47] or the originality of work that have been generated

47 The traditional response in various jurisdictions to the concept of authorship, without expressly referring to or excluding creations by 'non-human' entities, reveals indications that the recognition of authorship and originality depends essentially on the intervention of a human being. Judgment of the Court (Fourth Chamber) of 16 July 2009. Infopaq International A/S v Danske Dagblades Forening. Case C-5/08. ECLI:EU:C:2009:465; U.S. Supreme Court, *Feist Publications, Inc. v Rural Tel. Serv. Co.,* 499 U.S. 340 (1991), March 27, 1991; Federal Court of Australia, *Acohs Pty Ltd v Ucorp Pty Ltd* [2012] FCAFC 16 (2 March 2012). Sánchez Merino, 'Artificial Intelligence and a new cornerstone for authorship', WIPO-WTO COLLOQUIUM

or created by AI systems and would therefore reflect the personality of a 'non-human entity' as author (or inventor)[48], the question is approached here solely from the perspective of the compliant performance of the contractual obligation. Then, whether, in the absence of any specification of the conditions under which a given contractual obligation must be performed, the principle of non-discrimination precludes a claim of non-conformity or non-conforming performance merely because an automated system has intervened or assisted in the performance. The possibilities are manifold, including the obligations to deliver, to make payment, and to enable access to a service, as well as to sort, to select, or to produce content. The automa-

---

PAPERS, Research Papers from the WIPO-WTO Colloquium for Teachers of Intellectual Property Law 2018, WIPO-WTO, 2019, pp. 26-41.

48 The debate on the authorship of works generated by AI systems has also extended to the protection of inventions with industrial property rights. Thus, for example, the *UK Supreme Court* upheld in a decision of 20 December 2023 the IPO's rejection of the designation of an AI system (called DABUS, Device for the Autonomous Bootstrapping of Unified Sentience) as an inventor in a patent application - *Thaler (Appellant) v Comptroller-General of Patents, Designs and Trade Marks (Respondent)* [2023] UKSC 49, on appeal from: [2021] EWCA Civ 1374 -. The office had insisted that only "persons" could be inventors in the invention protection scheme. The court confirms this restrictive interpretation of the requirement to designate a "person" as an inventor:
"(...) DABUS is not a person or persons and, for the reasons (...) given, it is not a tenable interpretation of the 1977 Act that a machine can be an inventor". (par. 94)
Previously, the patent application designating DABUS as inventor had also been rejected by the Australian patent authority (*Deputy Commissioner of Patents*) on the same interpretative grounds: the meaning of the term inventor in patent law is "inherently human". In the first instance before the Australian courts - *Thaler v Commissioner of Patents* [2021] FCA 879 - 30 July 2021 - however, the court decision reversed the patent authority's refusal to accept the application on the grounds, in effect, that it hindered innovation. This decision by Judge Beach is interesting because it not only addresses the issue from the perspective of the broad and modernizing interpretation of the term "inventor" but also raises the issue of attribution. According to Judge Beach's reasoning, neither legal personality is being attributed to DABUS nor recognition to the IA system of industrial property rights. It only requires an attribution formula based on the ownership and possession of the system by whoever would be the future holder of the patent rights. In other words, even if DABUS is designated as the inventor, the patent right will be recognized to the owner of the system. Specifically, the judge admits that it will be the patent holder who will be the owner of the rights to the DABUS source code and owner and possessor of the device in which it resides. This generous interpretation, however, is reversed on appeal by the *Full Court of the* Australian *Federal Court - Commissioner of Patents v Thaler* [2022] FCAFC 62 - on the basis of the line of jurisprudence set out by the *High Court of Australia*, which defines the axis of patentability as a 'human action'.

tion of these actions is not only frequent, but also convenient as it naturally materializes the benefits associated with automation in a particularly visible and intense way.

The answer is less conclusive when the action carried out involves an essential creative, intellectual or professional activity that is decisive for the full satisfaction of the other party's interest. If, in the absence of any explicit prohibition or reference in the contract, AI-assisted financial advice, an audit report produced by an automated system or a claim or a contract drawn up by a Generative AI system are, by the mere fact of automation, compliant with the contractual obligation assumed by the contracting party. Unlike the more mechanical or material actions of delivering, paying or providing access to a service, in which human intervention would not, at least in principle, appear to be decisive to ensure a particular expected quality, it could be questioned whether the provision of a service that requires or presupposes a certain professional qualification or license or authorization to be lawfully exercised in the market can be provided entirely by an automated system or with its aid or assistance. In this interesting scenario, and assuming that the parties have not specified anything to the contrary, a determined defense of the principle of non-discrimination leads not to question the conformity of performance, on the assumption that it is the diligence of the contracting party in the selection, maintenance and supervision of the executing or auxiliary automated systems that will determine conformity. Interestingly, the spotlight of the diligence is transferred or relocated, and its content is modulated so that it does not focus on the personal and direct execution, but on the selection, supervision and monitoring of the automated performance. The diligence is converted into a protocol that replaces direct execution with automated execution under certain requirements. But it is not clear who has to be the licensed/authorized/qualified/registered professional along the value chain. As it should be based or depend upon the attribution of the actions performed by the automated system.

While the most forceful defense of an unwavering principle of non-discrimination leads not to question functional equivalence in terms of conformity, a certain tendency towards what I have called *intuitu hominis* relationships and, above all, practical reasons of exposure to liability are generalizing the practice of disclosure. The obligation to report the use of AI in the generation of content by labelling the content thus generated has crystallized precisely as a legal obligation in the AI Act (Art. 50(2) AI Act). Similarly, transparency obligations apply for AI systems intended to interact with natural persons under certain conditions. But parties may go beyond and decide to report, as good practices, internal protocols of action or codes of conduct, or even to contractually impose, the use of AI systems in some of the tasks relevant for the negotiation, conclusion or execution of the contract or for the provision of the services. For example, law firms that inform their clients of the use of generative AI in certain tasks under strict supervision or with due review or advertising agencies that include in their contracts clauses prohibiting or, in this case, informing them of content generated by or with the assistance of AI systems. This practice requires a proper assessment of strategic, commercial and reputational considerations because it can have important and not subtle competitive implications.

AI contracting is catalyzing a necessary debate on traditional foundations of contract law and consumer protection paradigms in a new transactional environment. Contract law needs to face and decides how to solve the dilemma between automated contracting and *intuitiu hominis* contracting and re-imagine contracts in a human-machine hybrid society.

The Party to an AI Contract: Navigating Attribution in Autonomous Transactions

*Sebastian Schwamberger**

I. Introduction: The Enigmatic Nature of AI Contracts and Party Attribution

The rapid advancements in Artificial Intelligence (AI) have ushered in a new era of technological innovation, profoundly impacting various aspects of human interaction, including the realm of contract law. As AI systems become increasingly sophisticated and autonomous, they are now able to conclude contractual agreements independently.[1] This phenomenon gives rise to what can be termed an 'AI contract'—a contract formed not through direct human deliberation, but by the autonomous decision-making processes of an AI system.[2] This distinguishes AI contracts from mere auto-

---

* Assistant Professor (Tenure-Track) of Private Law and Digitalisation at the University of Graz. Former holder of the junior professorship for civil law, commercial law and digitalisation law at the University of Rostock.

1 See e.g. the often cited case *Quoine v B2C2* [2020] SGCA(I) 02, 14.10.2019, decided by the Supreme Court of Singapore. In April 2017, an unexpected event occurred on the QuoineExchange, a cryptocurrency trading platform operated by Quoine. B2C2 Ltd., a firm utilizing trading software, was involved in a series of highly unusual transactions. During these trades, B2C2 exchanged Bitcoin (BTC) for Ethereum (ETH) with two other platform users at an astonishing rate: approximately 10 BTC for 1 ETH. This price was roughly 250 times more favorable to B2C2 than the prevailing market rate. The root cause of this anomaly was Quoine's failure to implement essential modifications to crucial parts of its system. Upon discovering the error, Quoine, acting as the exchange operator, unilaterally reversed these transactions. Subsequently, B2C2 initiated legal action against Quoine, alleging breach of contract, among other claims. A central point of contention in this lawsuit was whether the parties on the other side of B2C2's trades could invoke the legal principle of unilateral mistake (under either common law or equity). The applicability of this doctrine would potentially have validated Quoine's decision to cancel the disputed transactions without B2C2's consent.

2 See further Article 2(4) of the ELI Guiding Principles and Model Rules on Digital Assistants for Consumer Contracts: '"Algorithmic contract" means a contract where one or both parties use a digital assistant to automate some or all aspects of their contractual relations.' Article 2(1)(b) of Wendehorst, Discussion Draft: Principles for AI in Contracting, Version 3.0: '"automated contracting" means the preparation, negotiation,

mated order assistants or 'if-then' functions that trigger predefined actions such as ordering new printer cartridges when ink levels are low.[3] In an AI contract, the AI system itself initiates and executes the contractual act based on its own assessment and algorithms, rather than simply executing a pre-programmed human command.[4] A paradigmatic example often cited is the 'smart fridge' that autonomously orders groceries based on its own sophisticated decision-making, potentially even considering current trends or attempting to 'surprise' its owner, rather than merely reordering depleted items.[5]

The emergence of AI contracts presents a significant challenge to established principles of contract law, particularly concerning the fundamental question of party attribution, especially when the AI leads to unexpected outcomes (e.g. the fridge wants to surprise the owner with 50kg of avocado, because they were discounted).[6] The process of identifying the cases in

conclusion or fulfilment of contracts or other aspect of contract management using electronic agents'. See also Art 7(1) UNCITRAL Model Law on Automated Contracting: 'As between the parties to a contract, an action carried out by an automated system is attributed in accordance with a procedure agreed to by the parties'.

3 Scholz, 'Algorithmic Contracts', Stan Tech L Rev 2017, 128 (135); Hennemann, *Interaktion und Partizipation* (Tübingen 2020), pp. 231 et seq.; Wendehorst/Grinzinger, 'Vertragsrechtliche Fragestellungen beim Einsatz intelligenter Agenten', in: Ebers et al. (eds.), *Künstliche Intelligenz und Robotik* (Munich 2020), pp. 141 (141 et seq.).

4 Clemens, 'Die elektronische Willenserklärung – Chancen und Gefahren', NJW 1985, 1998 (2002); Hennemann, p. 231, 238; Effer-Uhe, 'Erklärungen autonomer Softwareagenten in der Rechtsgeschäftslehre', RDi 2021, 169 (171); Kainer/Förster, ZfPW 2020, 275 (279); Dornis, Künstliche Intelligenz und Vertragsschluss, AcP 2023, 717 (721).

5 On this example see Pagallo, 'Killers, fridges, and slaves: A legal journey in robotics', AI & SOCIETY 2011, 347 (347); Floridi, 'Artificial companions and their philosophical challenges', E-mentor 2007, 84 (85). See also Bräutigam/Klindt, 'Industrie 4.0, das Internet der Dinge und das Recht', NJW 2015, 1137 (1138); Sosnitza, 'Das Internet der Dinge - Herausforderung oder gewohntes Terrain für das Zivilrecht?', CR 2016, 764 (766); Specht/Herold, 'Roboter als Vertragspartner? Gedanken zu Vertragsabschlüssen unter Einbeziehung automatisiert und autonom agierender Systeme', MMR 2018, 40 (41); Kainer/Förster, 'Autonome Systeme im Kontext des Vertragsrechts', ZfPW 2020, 275 (276); Kaulbach, 'Vertragsschluss ohne Willenserklärung?' JZ 2022, 1148 (1148 et seq.).

6 For an overview of international developments due to the challenges AI poses to contract law, see Wendehorst, 'Discussion Draft: Principles for AI in Contracting (Version 2.1)', EuCML 2024, 43 et seq.; see already Weitzenboeck, 'Electronic Agents and the Formation of Contracts', International Journal of Law and Information Technology, 2001, 204; It should be mentioned that there are also viewpoints that do not see a need for regulation in this regard, see e.g. Arbeitsgruppe „Digitaler Neustart" der

which an operator using the AI system, is the party to the contract becomes a complex endeavour when the AI system independently concludes a contract. This complexity is further compounded by the intricate ecosystem surrounding AI systems, which typically involves not only the direct human users (e.g., Alice and Bob in a bilateral AI-driven transaction) but also various other actors, such as the developer of the AI software, the provider of the AI system (which may also function as a platform for contract conclusion), and the entity on whose servers the AI operates. Each of these stakeholders could potentially be considered a party to the contract, leading to considerable legal uncertainty.

This paper aims to unravel the complexities surrounding party attribution in contracts autonomously concluded by Artificial Intelligence systems. It will first critically delineate the fundamental challenges in assigning legal responsibility to actions executed by AI, meticulously examining why potential candidates for contractual party status—specifically the AI itself, its developers, and its providers—prove incongruent with established legal principles and commercial realities. Building upon this foundational analysis, the subsequent sections will engage with the approaches to attribution taken by leading international and European initiatives. By systematically exploring their conceptual frameworks, this work seeks to distill not only the common denominators but also, and more crucially, the salient distinctions in their proposed solutions. This comparative inquiry will then serve as the basis for articulating a refined framework that clarifies the conditions under which an operator becomes a contractual party, or when such attribution is precluded, and further addresses the crucial question of liability in instances where a prospective contract fails to materialize.

II. The Unsuitability of AI, Developer, and Provider as Contractual Parties

The core difficulty in attributing an AI contract fundamentally arises from the inherent autonomy of the AI's decision-making process. Unlike conventional contracts, where human intent and volition are paramount, an AI system operates devoid of subjective legal personality or conscious intent

Konferenz der Justizministerinnen und Justizminister der Länder, 'Bericht vom 15. Mai 2017', 2017, pp. 102 et seq., available via https://www.justiz.nrw.de/sites/default/files/imported/files/2017-06/bericht_ag_dig_neustart.pdf.

in the human sense.[7] Before proposing the preferred solution for attribution of AI contracts to the operator, also for unexpected outcomes of AI actions,[8] it is imperative to methodically exclude other potential candidates for contractual party status together with their potential liability in cases of unexpected outcomes.

1. No legal personality to AI

The notion of an AI system itself possessing legal personality—and thereby being capable of independently entering into and being bound by contractual obligations—is currently, and indeed for the foreseeable future, legally untenable within established jurisprudential frameworks.[9] Contemporary legal systems are fundamentally predicated on the concept of legal personality being exclusively vested in natural persons and duly constituted legal entities, such as corporations or associations. Endowing an AI system with legal personality would necessitate a radical and unprecedented redefinition of legal subjecthood, raising profound philosophical, ethical, and practical quandaries that extend far beyond the current scope of existing

---

7 Clemens, NJW 1985, 1998 (2002); Scholz Stan. Tech. L. Rev. 2017, 128 (135); Hennemann, p. 232, 238; Wendehorst/Grinzinger, in: Ebers et al., pp. 139 (141 et seq.); Effer-Uhe RDi 2021, 169 (171); Kainer/Förster, ZfPW 2020, 275 (279); Dornis, AcP 2023, 717 (721); Schubert, in: Säcker et al. (eds.), Münchener Kommentar zum Bürgerlichen Gesetzbuch, 9th Edition (Munich 2025), BGB § 164 mn. 117.

8 On the different approaches under German Law see Hennemann, pp. 233 et seq.; Wendehorst/Grinzinger, in: Ebers et al., pp. 139 (149 et seq.); Dornis, AcP 2023, 717 (720 et seq.).

9 Teubner, 'Digitale Rechtssubjekte?', AcP 2018, 157 (163); Wendehorst/Grinzinger, in: Ebers et al., p. 139 (141); Dornis, AcP 2023, 717 (723). At the European level, discussions around a specific legal status for robots haven't moved beyond a recommendation. The European Parliament's Committee on Legal Affairs, in its draft report with recommendations to the Commission on Civil Law Rules in Robotics (2015/2103(INL) of May 31, 2016), suggested creating a dedicated legal status for robots (see pages 13 et seq.). However, this proposal was notably absent from the European Commission's subsequent communication to the European Parliament, the European Council, the Council, the European Economic and Social Committee, and the Committee of the Regions, titled 'Artificial Intelligence for Europe' (COM (2018) 237, of April 25, 2018). But see Calo, 'Robotics and the Lessons of Cyberlaw', Cal. L. Rev. 2015, 513 (549): '[W]e may be on the cusp of creating a new category of legal subject, halfway between person and object. And I believe the law will have to make room for this category.'; Balkin, 'The Path of Robotics Law', Cal. L. Rev. C. 2015, 45 (57): '... the assignment of status may be incomplete, contextual, unstable, and, above all, opportunistic'.

legal instruments and societal consensus.[10] Furthermore, allowing an AI to directly serve as a contractual party would inevitably create a significant accountability vacuum, given that AI systems do not have a liability fund or would first have to be provided with one for potential liability.[11]

2. The developer is too far away

Similarly, the developer of the core AI software is, by the very nature of their role, typically too far away from the specific, individual conclusion of a particular AI contract to be reasonably considered a direct contractual party. The developer's primary function is the creation and refinement of the underlying technological framework; they generally do not exercise real-time control over, nor do they initiate, the countless individual transactions executed by deployed AI systems. Attributing contracts directly to the developer would impose an unconscionable burden and fundamentally distort the commercial realities of AI deployment and liability allocation within the software development ecosystem.

Furthermore, the remoteness in time and space between the development phase and the actual contract conclusion is significant. An AI system might be deployed globally, years after its core algorithms were developed, and its behavior could be influenced by subsequent training data, user configurations, or third-party integrations, all beyond the original developer's immediate control. This chain of causation and intent is simply too attenuated to establish a direct contractual nexus. Attributing contracts directly to the developer would impose an untendable or disproportionate burden and fundamentally distort the commercial realities of AI deployment and liability allocation within the software development ecosystem.

The legal responsibilities of developers typically align with product liability for defects in the software itself[12] or general tortious conduct, rather than assuming contractual obligations for transactions they neither entered

10 But see, *inter alia*, Wettig/Zehendner, 'A legal analyses of human and electronic agents', Artificial Intelligence and Law 2004, 111 (127 et seq.); Matthias, *Automaten als Träger von Rechten* (Berlin 2008) pp. 253 et seq.; Chopra/White, pp. 153 et seq. See also Allen/Widdison, 'Can Computers Make Contracts?', Harv. J. Law & Tech. 1996, 9, who opt for a legal personality under future legislation.

11 Teubner, AcP 2018, 157 (163).

12 e.g. the new Product Liability Directive (EU) 2024/2853. See thereon the contributions in Lohsse/Schulze/Staudenmayer (eds.), Münster Colloquia on EU Law and the

nor directly facilitated on a per-instance basis. Holding developers liable as principals for every contract their AI tools generate would stifle innovation and render the commercialization of AI unfeasible. However, also tortious liability may fail in a lot of circumstances, since the damage caused by a defective AI is most likely a pure economic loss (e.g. because Alice bought goods above market price due to the defective AI) and tort law typically grants compensation for pure economic loss only in very limited circumstances.[13] In this vein, the new Product Liability Directive also only compensates damage to goods, persons and data, but not pure economic loss.[14]

3. The provider as the contractual partner?

Lastly, while the provider of the AI system, often functioning as a digital platform or service provider, undeniably facilitates the transaction, attributing the core contract for goods or services to them presents significant misalignments with the parties' intentions and commercial realities. The counterparty (Bob, for instance) typically intends to conclude a contract for specific goods or services with the AI's user, Alice, not with the provider or platform as the principal for the underlying transaction. The provider's role is predominantly that of a technological service facilitator, offering infrastructure, connectivity, or access to the AI's capabilities. Their business model usually revolves around service fees or commissions, not around acquiring or divesting the subject matter of the AI-driven contract itself.

Crucially, neither the provider nor the ultimate human counterparty (Bob) has a vested interest in the provider becoming the principal party to the contract for the actual goods or services. For Bob, the focus is on

---

Digital Economy VII – Liability for AI (Baden-Baden 2023); Wagner, 'Liability Rules for the Digital Age – Aiming for the Brussels Effect', JETL 2022, 191.

13 For an overview see Kadner/Graziano, in: Winiger et al., Digest European Tort Law Vol. III, 3b/30, mn. 9 et seq.; Winiger, in: Winiger et al., Digest European Tort Law Vol. II, 8/30 mn. 1 et seqq.

14 See Article 6(1) Directive (EU) 2024/2853: 'The right to compensation pursuant to Article 5 shall apply in respect of only the following types of damage: (a) death or personal injury, including medically recognised damage to psychological health; (b) damage to, or destruction of, any property, except: (i) the defective product itself; (ii) a product damaged by a defective component that is integrated into, or inter-connected with, that product by the manufacturer of that product or within that manufacturer's control; (iii) property used exclusively for professional purposes; (c) destruction or corruption of data that are not used for professional purposes.'

receiving the product or service from Alice or the entity Alice represents, and holding the provider accountable for the quality or delivery of those goods or services would be a misdirection of liability. Bob's contractual expectation is with Alice, the actual source or recipient of the goods/services. Similarly, the provider explicitly seeks to avoid becoming the direct principal in potentially countless transactions between their users. Imputing these contractual obligations for the primary transaction to the provider would fundamentally misrepresent their economic relationship and distort the allocation of risk inherent in such arrangements. While the provider will undoubtedly have distinct contractual relationships with both Alice and Bob concerning the terms of use of the platform or AI service itself, these are separate legal relationships entirely distinct from the specific AI-driven contract for the primary goods or services. To hold the provider liable as a direct party to every individual AI-generated contract would create an unmanageable burden and disincentivize the development and widespread deployment of AI systems, which would run counter to the very purpose of facilitating such autonomous interactions.

The only plausible scenario where the provider could become the contractual partner for the AI-generated transaction would be through the application of doctrines akin to apparent authority.[15] This would require the existence of an objective impression, reasonably created by the provider's conduct, that the AI system is acting directly on their behalf, or that the provider is the principal for the underlying goods or services, rather than merely providing the AI for a transaction between Alice and Bob. Such situations were already discussed with regard to online marketplace platforms[16] which typically structure their terms to ensure that the contracts for goods are concluded directly between the individual seller (Bob) and the buyer (Alice), with the platform merely acting as an intermediary. However, if the platform's presentation is ambiguous, or if it doesn't sufficiently clarify that the seller is a third party, and it's also common for the platform itself to sell goods directly, then Bob might reasonably believe he's contracting with the platform.[17] In such cases, despite the platform's underlying intent,

15 See Article 3:201(3) PECL with further references in the Notes.

16 See, with regard to the purchase of apps: Kremer, 'Vertragsgestaltung bei Entwicklung und Vertrieb von Apps für mobile Endgeräte', CR 2011, 769 (771); Peschel/Schwamberger, 'Der Vertragspartner beim App-Erwerb', ZIIR 2016, 411 (412); Klein/Datta, 'Der-App-Anbieter als Vertragspartner des Nutzers', CR 2016, 587 (588 et seq.).

17 Cf. Kremer, CR 2011, 769 (771); Peschel/Schwamberger, ZIIR 2016, 411 (412); Klein/Datta, CR 2016, 587 (589).

the principle of apparent authority would likely dictate that the contract is indeed formed between Bob and the platform, rather than between Bob and Alice. In the absence of such a clear and justifiable appearance that the AI (or the entity it represents) is acting for the provider, the default assumption should remain that the transaction is between the AI's user and the counterparty.

Under specific circumstances, a software provider might also be held liable to two parties: Alice, who uses the provider's AI, and Bob, a seller who enters into a contract with Alice through the AI. Typically, there's a contractual agreement governing Alice's use of the AI. If the AI doesn't meet the contractually agreed-upon specifications or its objective characteristics, the provider is held liable, e.g. for B2C-Contracts under the Digital Content and Digital Services Directive[18]. Furthermore, if a defect in the AI leads to Alice entering into unforeseen – but binding – contractual circumstances with Bob, Alice may be able to claim damages from the provider. The primary challenge here is to define what constitutes the actual damage. One option would be to consider the contract itself as the damage,[19] it would need to be a financial disadvantage suffered by Alice. For example, this could include purchasing items above market price or acquiring unneeded items that she then has to resell at a loss. In B2C-contracts, the consumer's right of withdrawal under the Consumer Rights Directive[20] often prevents significant damages. Since AI usage frequently involves distance selling, this right allows Alice to withdraw from the contract. In such cases, any potential damages would likely be limited to minor expenses like return shipping costs.

The situation is more difficult when it comes to the liability of the provider towards Bob, since these two generally don't have a contractual relationship. Bob interacts with Alice, who is using the AI, rather than

18 Directive (EU) 2019/770.

19 According to the German Supreme Court, in cases of intentional, immoral harm (§ 826 BGB), damages aren't limited to compensating for objective financial losses. They also extend to allowing the injured party to be relieved of an 'unwanted' obligation that arose from the immoral conduct, as such an obligation itself constitutes compensable damage. See German Supreme Court BGH 26.1.2021 – VI ZR 405/19, NJOZ 2021, 1327 (1329), (= mn. 21; BGH 30.7.2020 – VI ZR 367/19, NJW 2020, 2804 (2806), mn. 21. In this case, the injured party can for the cancellation of the purchase agreement, contingent upon the simultaneous return of the item and refund of the purchase price, as compensation.

20 Directive (EU) 2011/83.

directly with the AI provider. This means Bob typically can't pursue claims against the provider based on a contract. Bob's damage manifests when a prospective contract between Alice and Bob fails to materialize as a direct consequence of an unforeseen AI malfunction. Should Bob, in such an instance, be deprived of an anticipated profit, this foregone gain constitutes his damage. However, it is crucial to recognize that this form of detriment is generally categorized as pure economic loss. In the absence of a direct contractual nexus, the recoverability of such losses within extra-contractual frameworks is typically severely restricted, often precluding compensation under established legal principles. Acknowledging this lacuna in existing legal provisions, the ELI Guiding Principles and Model Rules on Digital Assistants for Consumer Contracts (ELI Guiding Principles)[21] have proposed the introduction of a specific regime of provider liability for precisely these circumstances. The intent is to bridge the current legal gap, ensuring that providers can be held accountable when a defective AI directly impedes a commercial transaction, thereby inflicting a quantifiable financial detriment upon a third party such as Bob, notwithstanding the absence of a direct contractual relationship with the AI provider:

> Article 25
> Liability of the supplier of a digital assistant to third parties Where the actions of a digital assistant are not attributed to the consumer [...] the supplier of the digital assistant to that consumer is liable to the business with whom the consumer's digital assistant was dealing for losses the business has incurred as a result of the non-attribution. The conditions for awarding damages are governed by the applicable law.

III. Current Legal and Academic Discourse on Attribution in Automated Contracting

Consequently, in the absence of a clear and effective framework agreement, the attribution of AI contracts becomes problematic. The AI itself, its developer, and the platform provider are inherently unsuitable as primary contractual parties. By logical necessity, responsibility must ultimately fall

21 ELI Guiding Principles and Model Rules on Digital Assistants for Consumer Contracts, 19.5.2025, https://www.europeanlawinstitute.eu/fileadmin/user_upload/p_eli/Projects/Algorithmic_Contracts/Guiding_Principles_and_Model_Rules_on_Digital_Assistants_for_Consumer_Contracts.pdf.

upon the human legal subject who initiates, configures, or controls the use of the AI system for contractual purposes. This compelling logical progression leads to the strong legal presumption that the contract should be attributed to the operator of the AI system.

Several prominent approaches are currently debated to resolve this complex attribution problem.[22] One significant line of argument advocates for the analogous application of existing rules on attribution of agents, thereby treating the AI as an agent acting on behalf of its human principal.[23] Another proposed solution invokes the principle of the 'blanket declaration' (*Grundsatz der Blanketterklärung*),[24] where the user is considered to have made a broad, pre-emptive declaration of intent, which the AI then merely fills in with specific details. These various approaches, while differing in their specific mechanisms, converge on the need to ultimately anchor the AI's autonomous contractual actions within the established framework of human legal responsibility.

The burgeoning field of AI contracts has prompted significant discussion within legal academia and international organizations regarding appropriate rules for attribution. While specific legislation and soft law already exists,[25] several prominent initiatives and proposals offer valuable insights

---

22 For an overview see Andrade et al., 'Contracting agents: legal personality and representation, Artificial Intelligence and Law', 2007, 357; Dahiyat, 'Law and software agents: Are they "Agents" by the way?', Artificial Intelligence and Law, 2020, 59; Hennemann, pp. 233 et seq.; Wendehorst/Grinzinger, in: Ebers et al., pp. 139 (149 et seq.); Dornis, AcP 2023, 717 (720 et seq.).

23 Fischer, 'Computers as agents: a proposed approach to revised U.C.C. Article 2', Indiana Law Journal 1997, 545; Smed, 'Intelligent software agents and agency law', Santa Clara Comput High Technol Law J 1998, 503; Kerr, 'Spirits in the material world: intelligent agents as intermediaries in electronic commerce', Dalhous Law J 1999, 189; Specht/Herold, MMR 2018, 40 (43); Schirmer, 'Rechtsfähige Roboter?', JZ 2016, 660 (664); but see Bräutigam/Klindt, NJW 2015, 1137 (1138).

24 Möslein, 'Smart Contracts im Zivil- und Handelsrecht', ZHR 2019, 254 (273); Paulus/Matzke, 'Smart Contracts und das BGB – Viel Lärm um nichts?', ZfPW 2018, 431 (444).

25 The US Uniform Electronic Transactions Act (UETA) (1999), widely adopted, declares contracts formed by electronic agents (alone or with human interaction) valid, treating electronic agents as tools for which the user is responsible, and foresightedly considers future autonomous agents. The Model Computer Information Transactions Act (MCITA) (1999/2002), though largely unsuccessful, introduced concepts like 'electronic mistake' for potential relief and detailed rules on attribution. A Draft UCC Article 2 (2003), not adopted, contained provisions on terms not binding if an electronic agent could not process them, and defined 'conspicuous' for agent interaction. The UN Convention on the Use of Electronic Communications in Inter-

into how legal systems might address the question of who is bound when an automated system or AI concludes a contract. This initiative focusses on the UNCITRAL Model Law on Automated Contracting (UNCITRAL Model Law),[26] the ELI Guiding Principles and the Wendehorst Discussion Draft: Principles for AI in Contracting (PAIC 3.0)[27].

1. UNCITRAL Model Law on Automated Contracting

The UNCITRAL Model Law represents a significant step towards harmonizing approaches to contracts formed by automated systems. Specifically, Article 7, 'Attribution of actions carried out by automated systems,' provides a foundational framework.

> Article 7. Attribution of actions carried out by automated systems
> 1. As between the parties to a contract, an action carried out by an automated system is attributed in accordance with a procedure agreed to by the parties.
> 2. If paragraph 1 does not apply, an action carried out by an automated system is attributed to the person who uses the system for that purpose.
> 3. Attribution of an action carried out by an automated system shall not be denied on the sole ground that the outcome was unexpected.
> 4. Nothing in this article affects the application of any rule of law that may govern the legal consequences of attributing an action carried out by an automated system to a person.

The provision prioritizes contractual freedom, stipulating that an action carried out by an automated system is attributed in accordance with a

national Contracts (2005) similarly validates contracts formed by 'automated message systems,' avoiding the term 'agent.' The Canadian Uniform Electronic Commerce Act (2011) echoes UETA, explicitly clarifying that electronic agents are tools and agency law does not apply. Lastly, the E-Commerce Law of the People's Republic of China (2018) concisely states that automated contract formation and fulfillment are legally binding on the system's user. For an overview, see Wendehorst, 'Discussion Draft: Principles for AI in Contracting (Version 2.1)', EuCML 2024, 43 (44 et seq.); see already Weitzenboeck Int. J. Law Inf. Technol, 2001, 204.

26 UNCITRAL Model Law on Automated Contracting (2024), 11.7.2024, available via https://uncitral.un.org/en/mlac.

27 The draft is contained in this volume pp. 274 et seq. The previous Version (Wendehorst, Discussion Draft: Principles for AI in Contracting (Version 2.1), 22.2.2024) is available via https://papers.ssrn.com/sol3/papers.cfm?abstract_id=4704081.

procedure agreed to by the parties. In the absence of a specific agreement, Article 7(2) provides a crucial default. This provision is pivotal as it explicitly identifies the user as the party responsible for the automated system's actions, aligning with the concept of the "operator" proposed in this paper. The phrase "for that purpose" implicitly acknowledges the user's intent to employ the system for contractual ends. Furthermore, Article 7(3) addresses a common concern in automated contracting, stating that attribution of an action carried out by an automated system shall not be denied on the sole ground of unexpected outcome. The attribution in case of unexpected actions is further delineated in the optional Article 8 UNCITRAL Model Law:

> Article 8. Unexpected actions carried out by automated systems
>
> 1. Unless otherwise agreed by the parties, where an action carried out by an automated system is attributed to a party to a contract, the other party to the contract is not entitled to rely on that action if, in the light of all the circumstances:
>
> (a) The party to which the action is attributed could not reasonably have expected the action; and
>
> (b) The other party knew or could reasonably be expected to have known that the party to which the action is attributed did not expect the action.
>
> 2. Nothing in this article affects the application of any rule of law or agreement of the parties that may govern the legal consequences of an action carried out by an automated system.

Consistent with the principle of non-discrimination, the UNCITRAL Model Law generally assumes that existing legal frameworks can resolve issues arising from unexpected outputs. However, recognizing that some jurisdictions may benefit from specific guidance, Article 8 is included as an optional provision. This article specifically addresses actions that might be considered unintended, primarily focusing on non-deterministic AI systems where unpredictability is a key characteristic. It also covers deterministic systems, encompassing situations where an automated system operates as designed but generates an unexpected output, as well as errors in programming, transmission, or third-party interference.

Paragraph 1's application is contingent on two conditions related to the knowledge and expectations of the parties, reflecting principles of reasonable expectations and fair dealing: Subparagraph (a) focuses on what the party to whom the action is attributed could 'reasonably' have expected.

This requires an objective assessment based on factors such as the contract's nature, the transaction type, and established trade usages. Subparagraph (b) concerns the knowledge of the party seeking to rely on the unexpected action. This can be a subjective or objective determination.

2. ELI Guiding Principles and Model Rules on Digital Assistants for Consumer Contracts

The European Law Institute (ELI) has developed Guiding Principles and Model Rules on Digital Assistants for Consumer Contracts, offering a more consumer-centric perspective on attribution. Article 22, 'Attribution and its limits,' outlines key principles.

> Article 22: Attribution and its limits
>
> (1) A person who uses a digital assistant for contractual relations is bound by the actions taken by the digital assistant and all the actions of the digital assistant are attributed to that person.
>
> (2) Where the actions of a digital assistant used by a consumer for contractual relations deviate from those which could reasonably be expected by the consumer, the actions of the digital assistant have no legal effect and are not attributed to the consumer.
>
> (3) The relevant factors to be applied in determining whether the actions of the digital assistant deviated from those a consumer could reasonably expect, include:
>
> > (a) any information given to the consumer about the adaptive capability of the digital assistant;
> >
> > (b) whether the operation of any adaptive functionality of the digital assistant was inconsistent with such information;
> >
> > (c) external factors such as loss of access to third-party data supplies, errors in that data, or cybersecurity breaches; and
> >
> > (d) whether in the specific circumstances, the consumer could not reasonably have expected that the action in question would be taken.
>
> (4) Any contractual term providing that the business will not be bound by the actions of the digital assistant used by the business for its contractual relations with the consumer is only effective insofar as the actions to which that term applies are so unexpected that a reasonable person would conclude there has been a serious failure in the operation of the digital assistant.

(5) In circumstances where the actions of a digital assistant are deemed to have no legal effect under paragraph (2) or by virtue of the contract terms referred to in paragraph (4), either party is entitled to receive back any performance that was rendered in consequence of such action.

Similar to UNCITRAL, ELI Guiding Principle's Article 22(1) establishes a general rule of attribution: a person who uses a digital assistant for contractual relations is bound by the actions taken by the digital assistant and all the actions of the digital assistant are attributed to that person. This reinforces the idea that the individual deploying the digital assistant for contractual purposes bears the contractual responsibility. A crucial consumer-protective limitation is introduced in ELI Guiding Principle's Article 22(2): where the actions of a digital assistant used by a consumer for contractual relations deviate from those which could reasonably be expected by the consumer, the actions of the digital assistant have no legal effect and are not attributed to the consumer. This principle acknowledges that consumers might be unfairly bound by actions of an autonomous system that go significantly beyond their reasonable expectations, introducing a valuable safeguard.

To provide clarity, ELI Guiding Principle's Article 22(3) lists relevant factors to be applied in determining whether the actions of the digital assistant deviated from those a consumer could reasonably expect. These factors include any information given to the consumer about the adaptive capability of the digital assistant, whether the operation of any adaptive functionality of the digital assistant was inconsistent with such information, external factors such as loss of access to third-party data supplies, errors in that data, or cybersecurity breaches, and whether in the specific circumstances, the consumer could not reasonably have expected that the action in question would be taken.

ELI Guiding Principle's Article 22(4) addresses the enforceability of contractual terms where a business attempts to disclaim being bound by its own digital assistant's actions: any contractual term providing that the business will not be bound by the actions of the digital assistant used by the business for its contractual relations with the consumer is only effective insofar as the actions to which that term applies are so unexpected that a reasonable person would conclude there has been a serious failure in the operation of the digital assistant. This provision places a high bar on businesses to disclaim responsibility, protecting consumers from unfair surprises.

Finally, ELI Guiding Principle's Article 22(5) outlines the consequences when actions have no legal effect: in circumstances where the actions of a digital assistant are deemed to have no legal effect under paragraph (2) or by virtue of the contract terms referred to in paragraph (4), either party is entitled to receive back any performance that was rendered in consequence of such action, ensuring restitution for performances rendered under non-attributed actions. The ELI principles provide a strong consumer-protective lens, focusing on the reasonableness of the consumer's expectations when interacting with digital assistants.

3. Wendehorst Discussion Draft: Principles for AI in Contracting, Version 3.0 (PAIC 3.0)

The PAIC 3.0 offers a comprehensive and nuanced approach, particularly regarding the concept of 'operator' and scenarios involving loss of control. Principle 7: 'Attribution of output to operator,' is highly pertinent.

> Principle 7: Attribution of output to operator
>
> (1) The output generated by an electronic agent is attributed to the operator of the electronic agent within the meaning of Principles 5 and 6, whether or not that operator had control over the electronic agent when the output was generated.
>
> (2) However, another party cannot rely on attribution to the operator where the operator has lost control and where
>
> > (a) that party or any electronic agent used by that party had caused the loss of control by the operator of the electronic agent; or
> >
> > (b) that party was aware, or ought to have been aware, at the time when the output generated by the electronic agent would potentially produce legal effect, that the operator had lost control; this includes situations where that party had used an electronic agent that appropriately detected the loss of control or ought to have detected it in accordance with the technical capabilities required under Principle 12.
>
> (3) Where a party learns about the loss of control by the operator after the time when the output generated by the electronic agent would potentially produce legal effect, that party should not be allowed to rely on attribution to the operator where it would, in the circumstances, appear to be clearly inappropriate to do so, considering, in particular, the degree to which

(a) attribution or its denial would cause detriment to either party; and
(b) the loss of control had its origin in a sphere close to one or both of the parties.
The operator must, in this case, indemnify the other party for the loss it may have suffered by relying on attribution.

(4) The burden of proving that the operator has lost control of the electronic agent and that a situation covered by paragraphs (2) or (3) exists should lie with the operator.

The PAIC 3.0 offers a comprehensive and particularly nuanced approach, structuring the question of attribution across a sophisticated three-level framework encapsulated in Principles 5, 6, and 7.[28] The framework begins at the first level with Principle 5, which is dedicated to the fundamental identification of the 'operator'. This principle clarifies who qualifies as the operator in situations with multiple potential parties, defining it as the person on whose behalf the agent generates output. Once the operator is identified, the second level, Principle 6, addresses the attribution of the electronic agent as such to that operator. This step ensures that the agent is genuinely connected to the operator and not, for instance, being used fraudulently or without authorization.

Only after these foundational questions are settled does the framework move to the third and final level, addressed in the highly pertinent Principle 7: 'Attribution of output to operator'. This principle deals with the attribution of the concrete output generated by an electronic agent that has already been correctly identified and attributed to its operator. Principle 7(1) firmly establishes the general rule: the output is attributed to the operator, whether or not that operator had granular control over the electronic agent when the output was generated. This aligns with the operator-centric view, reinforcing the idea that deploying an autonomous system implies accepting responsibility for its outputs.

However, Principle 7(2) introduces crucial limitations to this attribution, aiming to prevent unfair outcomes. Another party cannot rely on attribution where the operator has lost control and where that party (or its agent) either caused the loss of control or was (or ought to have been) aware of it. This includes situations where the other party's agent should have detected the loss of control in accordance with the technical capabilities required under Principle 12.

28 Wendehorst, in this volume, pp. 274 et seq.

Principle 7(3) addresses situations where a party learns about the loss of control after the output has potentially produced legal effect. In such cases, reliance on attribution should be denied if it would be 'clearly inappropriate to do so,' considering the potential detriment to either party and the origin of the loss of control. Crucially, where attribution is denied under this principle, the operator must indemnify the other party for any loss suffered by relying on attribution.

Finally, Principle 7(4) places the burden of proving the loss of control and the existence of a situation covered by paragraphs (2) or (3) squarely on the operator. This shifts the evidentiary burden to the party best positioned to provide information about the AI system's operation. By structuring the analysis in this way, the PAIC 3.0 offers a sophisticated framework that balances the need for clear attribution with considerations of fairness and risk allocation, particularly in scenarios where autonomous systems deviate from their intended operation.

IV. Syntheses and Attribution in AI Contracts

The evolving legal and academic discourse on attributing actions within automated contracting, particularly concerning AI, consistently points towards the human user or operator as the pivotal legal subject for establishing contractual liability, even where the outcome of the AI was unexpected, which means that the risk of malfunctions and unforeseen developments is on the operator.[29] This general rule ensures that legal subjecthood is maintained, as the contract is always attributed to a legal subject (the operator), thereby avoiding the problematic concept of an AI having legal personality[30]. It also ensures responsibility, meaning the party who benefits from the AI's autonomous contracting (the operator) also bears the responsibility for its actions.[31] Furthermore, it enhances predictability, allowing counterparties dealing with an AI system to generally assume that the contract is with the human or legal entity behind the AI. However, depart from

29 Wendehorst, EuCML 2024, 43 (53).

30 Teubner, AcP 2018, 157 (163); Wendehorst/Grinzinger, in: Ebers et al., p. 139 (141); Dornis, AcP 2023, 717 (723).

31 See, inter alia, Lerouge, 'The use of electronic agents questioned under contractual law. Suggested solutions on a European and American level', The John Marshall J Comp Inform Law 2000, 403 (421); Teubner, AcP 2018, 157 (181); Wendehorst/Grinzinger, in: Ebers et al., p. 139 (152).

this foundation, the various prominent initiatives—from the UNCITRAL Model Law to the ELI Guiding Principles and the PAIC 3.0 —reveal a nuanced understanding of this attribution, highlighting critical distinctions based on context, party involvement, and the inherent characteristics of AI.

A key distinction in these frameworks lies in their primary policy objectives and scope. The UNCITRAL Model Law, for example, prioritizes commercial certainty, establishing a robust default rule that holds the user accountable for an automated system's actions, even when outcomes are unexpected[32] and only leaves leeway to situations where the party to whom the action is attributed could 'reasonably' have expected the action[33] or the other party knew or could reasonably be expected to have known that the party to which the action is attributed did not expect the action.[34] Conversely, the ELI Guiding Principles adopt a strong consumer protection stance. They introduce a crucial safeguard that can negate attribution when an AI's actions deviate significantly from a consumer's reasonable expectations, aiming to mitigate power imbalances and protect less sophisticated parties from unforeseen contractual obligations. This consumer-centric view necessitates greater transparency from businesses regarding their AI's capabilities and places a higher burden on them to account for their AI's behavior.

Further significant differences arises in scenarios involving highly autonomous AI and potential loss of control, as meticulously addressed in the PAIC 3.0.[35] PAIC 3.0 introduces a clear, three-level structure (Principles 5, 6, and 7) that systematically addresses (i) the identification of the operator, (ii) the attribution of the agent as such, and (iii) the attribution of the concrete output.[36] While affirming the operator's general responsibility, even without granular control, this framework introduces carefully defined exceptions where attribution might be shifted or limited if the other party contributed to or was aware of the loss of control. It also provides for

32 UNCITRAL Model Law Article 7(3).

33 UNCITRAL Model Law Article 8(1)(a).

34 UNCITRAL Model Law Article 8(1)(b).

35 PAIC 3.0 Principle 7(2).

36 Additionally, the PAIC 3.0 are far more comprehensive. They delve into what concepts like "knowledge," "intent," or "reasonable expectations" mean in an AI-dominated environment and emphasize the role of an electronic agent's technical specifications. Also, the PAIC 3.0 recommend that legislators derogate from national doctrines of mistake, which are a primary source of legal uncertainty while the UNCITRAL Model Law allows for the full application of such doctrines in addition to its own rules, potentially undermining the goal of creating legal certainty.

indemnification where attribution is denied post-contract formation and strategically places the burden of proof for loss of control on the operator.

While it's true that distinctions exist among these three initiatives, it's crucial to understand that these differences don't render them incompatible.[37] Far from it, a deeper analysis reveals significant common ground. Beyond the clear identification of the operator as the primary contractual partner—a consistent theme across all three—a more fundamental shared principle emerges: attribution is never intended to be unlimited. Instead, there's a strong consensus that in specific, well-defined scenarios, attribution should not occur. This shared understanding forms a powerful basis for reconciliation.

Building on this, the next logical step is to attempt a robust synthesis of these individual drafts into a more unified framework. Such a synthesis would not only solidify the operator's role but also introduce crucial additional considerations. For instance, in defining the operator's responsibilities, we can draw valuable insights from the AI Act's[38] definition of a 'deployer,' thereby integrating contemporary regulatory thinking into the framework. Similarly, when outlining the exceptions to attribution, the concept of 'reasonable expectations' becomes paramount. This principle allows for a nuanced approach, ensuring that accountability is assigned fairly and pragmatically, avoiding overly broad or unjust attributions, and fostering an environment of predictable responsibility.

1. The Operator as the Attributable Party

The operator has been identified as the subject for the attribution of AI contracts, even where the outcome of the AI was unexpected, throughout the three initiatives. The operator is identified as the person that uses the AI.[39] The scope of 'use' should not be understood too broadly so as to avoid inadvertently making the AI provider the primary contractual party.[40] The provider's fundamental role is typically that of a technological enabler or infrastructure provider, not the principal in the underlying transaction initiated by the AI. The focus of the 'use' criterion should instead reside

37 Cf. Wendehorst, in this volume, pp. 274 et seq.
38 Regulation (EU) 2024/1689.
39 UNCITRAL Model Law Article 7(2); ELI Guiding Principles 22(1); PAIC 3.0 Principle 5(1).
40 See above p. 140.

on the party that deploys, configures, or actively enables the AI for the express purpose of concluding a specific type of contract. This implies a degree of intentionality and purposefulness on the part of the human actor in leveraging the AI for contractual outcomes.

Crucially, the definition of the operator for AI contract purposes should not necessarily require the explicit 'authority' criterion[41] as stipulated in the AI Act's definition of 'deployer':

> Article 3 Definitions
> For the purposes of this Regulation, the following definitions apply:[...]
> (4) 'deployer' means a natural or legal person, public authority, agency or other body using an AI system under its authority except where the AI system is used in the course of a personal non-professional activity;[...]

While the AI Act's definition of 'deployer' aligns more closely with the concept needed for contract attribution than its more technical definition of 'operator' which is more akin to a system provider, it is still not entirely suitable without modification for the specific exigencies of AI contract law. A new, dedicated definition of the 'operator' tailored for AI contract attribution is therefore preferable, albeit one that can draw inspiration from the AI Act's foundational concepts. For the specific purpose of AI contract attribution, the central criterion for defining the operator should unequivocally be the use of the AI system for contractual purposes. This concept of 'use' must be meticulously circumscribed to preempt unintended and potentially problematic implications.

This distinction is paramount because modern AI systems are increasingly hosted and operated on the servers of third-party providers, cloud services, or external platforms.[42] In such scenarios, the immediate human user, who we term the 'operator' for contractual purposes, may not possess direct technical or administrative authority over the underlying system's infrastructure or code. What truly matters is the initiation of the contractual process by the user, regardless of where the AI physically resides or who maintains its technical operations. Rather, it should be considered sufficient that the operator initiates the conclusion of the AI contract through the AI system. This means the operator performs the fundamental act of setting

41 See on this criterion: Wendehorst, in: Martini/Wendehorst (eds.), KI-VO, Künstliche Intelligenz-Verordnung (Munich 2024), Art. 3 AI Act mn. 84 seq.

42 Regarding the complexities of identifying the 'operator' under the AI Act in outsourcing and Software-as-a-Service (SaaS) contexts, see Wendehorst, in: Martini/Wendehorst Art. 3 AI Act mn. 88 et seq.

the parameters, activating the AI for a particular transactional objective, for example, procuring specific goods, engaging in certain services, or otherwise placing the AI in a position where it can autonomously conclude contracts on their behalf. It is not necessary for the operator to exercise granular, real-time control over every single functionality or specific decision of the AI system during the contractual process; indeed, the very essence of an AI contract lies in the AI's capacity for autonomy within pre-defined boundaries. The decisive factor for attribution is the volitional act of setting the AI in motion for a clearly identifiable contractual purpose, even if the precise details or unforeseen outcomes of the subsequent contract are left to the AI's autonomous decision-making algorithms.

In essence, the 'operator' is the identifiable human or legal person who intentionally deploys, configures, or enables an AI system to enter into contractual relations, thereby accepting the ultimate responsibility for the AI's autonomous contractual acts within the scope of that deployment. This definition aligns with the principle that legal responsibility ultimately resides with human actors, while pragmatically accommodating the unique characteristics of AI's autonomous capabilities.

2. Limitations on Attribution: Reasonable Expectations

While the general rule attributes an AI contract to its operator, the principle of fairness dictates crucial limitations to this attribution, particularly when the AI's actions diverge from what can a third party can reasonably and in good faith believe that the action is carried by the will of the operator. The notion that an operator implicitly accepts the inherent variability and potential for unforeseen actions within an AI's operational parameters is foundational. Thus, attribution to the operator should not be denied *solely* because the AI's contractual output was unexpected, as this fosters legal certainty and prevents operators from disclaiming responsibility for mere surprises. However, this general rule is critically tempered by more specific limitations that account for the nature of the parties and the circumstances of the AI's operation. Thus, and similar with the wording of the optional provision of the UNCITRAL Model Law[43], if the third party may not reasonably expect this outcome and is not good faith, attribution to the operator may be limited or denied.

43 UNICTRAL Model Law Article 8(1).

What a third party may reasonably expect should be treated differently depending on the contracting context. In consumer contracts, consistent with the ELI Guiding Principles[44], if an AI's actions used by a consumer fundamentally diverge from their reasonable expectations, those actions should generally not be attributed to the consumer or should have limited legal effect. Assessing 'reasonable expectation' involves considering circumstances that render the action genuinely unpredictable. For business operators in B2B contexts, the standard of 'reasonable expectation' is naturally higher, reflecting their commercial sophistication.

A major difference between the three initiatives lies in their consideration of the counterparty's expectations. The ELI Guiding Principles notably exclude the expectations of the contracting partner when determining the legal effect of an unexpected output. In contrast, both the optional rule within the UNCITRAL Model Law and the PAIC 3.0 adopt a different approach. These frameworks do consider the counterparty's knowledge and expectations, often requiring that the party relying on the unexpected action either knew, or reasonably should have known, that the other party did not intend or expect the output. For example, a third party may not be able to rely on attribution to the operator where the other party was, or ought to have been, aware of the operator's loss of control at the time the AI's output produced legal effect (introducing an objective standard of knowledge).[45] The same holds true, where the other party used an AI that appropriately detected, or ought to have detected, the loss of control based on agreed technical specifications, thereby encouraging vigilant AI systems.[46]

Beyond the considerations of counterparty expectations, another significant divergence among the various drafts lies in their treatment of the broader liability consequences stemming from non-attribution. Only the ELI Guiding Principles explicitly address these further legal repercussions. Specifically, ELI Guiding Principle Article 25 provides a dedicated basis for liability for the potential contractual partner of a consumer, where no contract materialized due to the unpredictability of an automated system's output. This provision empowers the potential partner to claim lost profits from the system operator, serving as a counter-balance to the otherwise highly consumer-friendly non-attribution rules. The question of liability in

44 ELI Guiding Principles Article 22(2).
45 See also UNCITRAL Model Law Article 8(1)(b). PAIC 3.0 Principle 7(2)(b).
46 PAIC 3.0 Principle 7(2)(b).

cases of non-attribution is a particularly controversial and important issue in the evolving landscape of automated contracting.[47]

3. The Role of Agreed Procedures (Party Autonomy)

It is stated under the UNCITRAL Model Law, that parties should retain the primary right to agree on specific attribution procedures through framework agreements.[48] The same holds true for the PAIC 3.0 under which the framework arrangement within the meaning of Part III PAIC 3.0 take precedence over default rules.[49] The dominant role of framework agreements has already been highlighted on other places. A prominent opinion suggests that a legally sound solution for AI deployment can be achieved through pre-transactional agreements.[50] This perspective argues that a legally binding relationship, effective from the outset, can even emerge from technically autonomous AI behavior. This might be facilitated by a framework agreement between parties, which would grant legal effect to algorithmic actions, for example, by treating silence as a declaration of intent in line with the agreement.[51]

For framework agreements to be a universally effective solution, however, their practical application must successfully navigate two central challenges that are particularly demanding for traditional contract law. The first is timing:[52] A framework agreement, by its very definitional nature, necessitates conclusion prior to the specific AI contract it purports to govern. However, in a substantial portion of the emerging AI-driven transac-

47 See on this issue already above p. 137.

48 UNCITRAL Model Law Article 7(1).

49 PAIC 3.0 Principle 4(1)(b). However, as also set out by Wendehorst (pp. 274 et seq.), framework arrangements would only exceptionally deal with the issues addressed in Part II, i.e. in Principles 5, 6 and 7, in practice. The ELI Guiding Principles Article 22(4) of course take a more cautious approach, since its focus is on consumer contracts.'

50 Dornis, AcP 2023, 717 (743 et seq.).

51 Dornis, AcP 2023, 717 (743 et seq.).

52 This hurdle is addressed by PAIC 3.0 Principle 9(1) regarding 'automated ad hoc framework arrangements,' which stipulates: 'framework arrangements may also be established for and on the occasion of a single automated transaction through electronic agents, where (a) this would not be inconsistent with an existing framework arrangement established through other means; and (b) there is sufficient evidence that the provisions reflect the intentions of the relevant operators at the relevant time.'

tional landscape, the expectation of a pre-existing or enduring relationship between the potential contracting parties is often unrealistic. Instead, it is increasingly plausible that two previously unacquainted parties might engage in their inaugural transaction precisely through their respective AI systems. In such novel scenarios, the fundamental prerequisite of a prior framework agreement simply cannot be met, rendering this solution inoperative for a significant and growing segment of AI contracts. The second hurdle is personality or privity:[53] A substantial and growing volume of AI contracts is projected to be concluded facilitated by, or directly through, digital platforms or online marketplaces. In these multi-party environments, a framework agreement might indeed exist between Alice and the platform, and similarly, a distinct agreement between Bob and the same or another platform. However, a framework agreement strictly between Alice and the platform does not inherently establish privity of contract or directly attribute legal effects for the specific contract ultimately concluded between Alice and Bob, or more precisely, their respective AIs. The platform's role is typically that of an intermediary facilitating the interaction, rather than assuming the mantle of a direct contractual party to the underlying transaction for goods or services between Alice and Bob. Thus, while framework agreements are the key in established relationships, their effectiveness as a universal solution depends on developing mechanisms to bridge the contractual gap in scenarios that lack a direct, pre-existing nexus between the human principals.

The existence of these challenges, particularly in scenarios where no explicit contractual agreement for attribution is realistically feasible or in place, underscores the compelling and undeniable need for a robust and coherent default rule of attribution. Conversely, this perspective doesn't preclude the utility of framework agreements in certain *ex post* scenarios, where they can potentially offer fitting solutions.[54] If a preceding agreement wasn't feasible, parties might find it beneficial to enter into subsequent

53 PAIC 3.0 Principle 8(1)(b) provides a solution by allowing a framework agreement to be formed from third-party terms (e.g., from a platform provider) that both parties have accepted. The full text states that such an agreement may arise from 'conditions of future automated contracting which each of the contracting parties separately have accepted or can reasonably be expected to have accepted and that are defined by a third party, such as (i) the provider of a platform or similar infrastructure on which automated contracting occurs; (ii) the provider of an electronic agent used for automated contracting; or (iii) the body providing a standard or any other harmonized technical specifications for electronic agents.'

54 Dornis, AcP 2023, 717 (744).

agreements to clarify contentious rights or obligations. For instance, if an AI system has already engaged in a transaction and ambiguity arises regarding attribution, the parties could consider retrospectively establishing a framework that grants legal effect to the AI's actions. This might involve formalizing an understanding of which human principal is bound, or how liability for the AI's behavior should be allocated. While this approach can be useful for resolving specific post-transactional uncertainties, it's important to recognize it as a reactive measure for dispute resolution rather than a universally applicable solution for the broader challenges of AI contract attribution.

V. Conclusion

The profound advancements in Artificial Intelligence and its burgeoning capacity for autonomous contractual engagement present a fundamental re-evaluation for established tenets of contract law, particularly concerning the pivotal question of party attribution. As AI systems increasingly act as independent agents in commercial transactions, the traditional reliance on human intent and legal personality undergoes rigorous scrutiny, underscoring an urgent imperative for clear and adaptable frameworks to delineate contractual bindingness.

This discourse has systematically delineated the inherent complexities surrounding party attribution in the emergent domain of 'AI contracts', distinguishing them from mere automated processing systems. The analysis has revealed the inherent unsuitability of the AI system itself, its developers, and platform providers as primary contractual subjects. Endowing AI with legal personality currently remains jurisprudentially untenable, threatening to create an unconscionable accountability vacuum. Developers, owing to their foundational yet remote role in specific transactions, are ill-suited to bear direct contractual responsibility, their liabilities more appropriately confined to product defects or pure economic loss in tort. Similarly, while AI providers indisputably facilitate these transactions, attributing the core contract for goods or services to them would fundamentally misalign with prevailing commercial realities and the parties' genuine intentions. Their function is predominantly that of technological enablers, with their liabilities typically circumscribed by their service agreements, absent compelling instances of apparent authority.

Consequently, the compelling logical trajectory points to the human user or operator as the indispensable legal subject to whom contractual liability must ultimately be attributed, even when the AI's output proves unexpected. This approach steadfastly preserves legal subjecthood within existing jurisprudential constructs, rigorously ensures accountability for those who derive commercial benefit from AI's autonomous contracting capabilities, and significantly enhances predictability for counterparties engaging with AI systems. The 'operator' is most precisely defined as the identifiable natural or legal person who intentionally deploys, configures, or enables an AI system for specific contractual purposes, thereby implicitly assuming ultimate responsibility for its autonomous contractual acts within the parameters of that deployment. This definition, while drawing conceptual inspiration from contemporary regulatory instruments such as the AI Act's notion of a 'deployer,' necessitates meticulous tailoring to the exacting requirements of contract attribution, focusing on the volitional act of initiating the AI for a transactional objective.

While the operator's role is established as the general rule of attribution, a comprehensive examination of prominent international and European initiatives—including the UNCITRAL Model Law on Automated Contracting, the ELI Guiding Principles and Model Rules on Digital Assistants for Consumer Contracts, and the PAIC 3.0 —unveils a sophisticated understanding that attribution is never intended to be boundless. These frameworks, despite their divergent underlying policy objectives, share a fundamental consensus: attribution ought to be delimited in specific, rigorously defined circumstances. The UNCITRAL Model Law, for instance, prioritizes commercial certainty, anchoring user accountability unless particular conditions regarding reasonable expectations or awareness of an unexpected outcome are demonstrably met. In sharp contrast, the ELI Guiding Principles adopt a robustly consumer-protective posture, potentially negating attribution when an AI's actions diverge significantly from a consumer's reasonable expectations, thereby demanding heightened transparency from businesses. The PAIC 3.0 further refines these limitations, particularly in scenarios involving loss of control, introducing nuanced exceptions where attribution might shift or be restricted if the counterparty either contributed to or was cognisant of the loss of control, often placing the burden of proof squarely on the operator and mandating indemnification. Pertinently, the question of liability for non-attribution remains a particularly controversial and critically important issue in this evolving legal landscape, with the ELI Guiding Principles uniquely providing a specific basis for such claims, including for lost profits, thereby acting as a counterpoise to their otherwise highly consumer-favorable non-attribution rules.

Finally, while the principle of party autonomy, realized through framework agreements, retains undeniable utility—especially within established commercial relationships—its practical efficacy for comprehensive AI contract attribution is substantially curtailed by inherent timing constraints (the frequent absence of a pre-existing relational nexus) and fundamental privity issues (the often-intermediary function of digital platforms). This compellingly underscores the imperative for robust and meticulously crafted default rules of attribution to effectively address the vast and expanding domain of AI-driven transactions where explicit, pre-contractual agreements prove unfeasible.

In summation, navigating the intricate question of "the party to an AI contract" mandates a sophisticated and adaptive legal methodology that judiciously balances technological innovation with the foundational principles of certainty, fairness, and accountability. By firmly positing the operator as the primary attributable party while scrupulously delineating justifiable limitations to this attribution based on reasonable expectations, loss of control, and specific contextual factors, legal systems can effectively accommodate the transformative potential of autonomous contracting, thereby ensuring that the promise of AI innovation is realized within a predictable, equitable, and coherent legal framework.

Enabling Innovation and Protecting Consumers in the Agentic Economy: Why the Digital Fairness Act Should Regulate Agentic AI

*Christoph Busch**

I. Introduction

Agentic AI is widely seen as the next major advancement in artificial intelligence.[1] After an initial focus on generative AI chatbots, more recently agentic AI systems (or AI agents) have become the centre of attention. Unlike chatbots, agentic AI systems are not limited to generating text, images or other content. AI agents are able to browse the web and autonomously perform multi-step tasks on behalf of users such as buying goods online, booking train tickets or making restaurant reservations. As a consequence, consumers could soon be able to delegate a growing share of their daily purchasing decisions to AI agents. This could have a transformational impact on the structure and functioning of digital markets.[2] In this sense, the coming wave of agentic AI is a platform shift similar to the transition from desktop computing to the mobile internet and has the potential to fundamentally change how we interact with digital services.

* Professor of Law, University of Osnabrück & Affiliated Fellow, Information Society Project, Yale Law School. This research has been carried out within the scope of the project „Granular Society – Granular Law? Individuality and Normative Models in the Data Society“ funded by the Volkswagen Stiftung under a Momentum Grant.

1 See e.g. Lareina Yee, Michael Chui and Roger Roberts, Why agents are the next frontier of generative AI, McKinsey Quarterly (24 July 2024), https://www.mckinsey.com/capabilities/mckinsey-digital/our-insights/why-agents-are-the-next-frontier-of-generative-ai#/ (all web pages last visited 20 July 2025).

2 David M. Rothschild et al., The Agentic Economy (29 May 2025), p. 3, https://arxiv.org/pdf/2505.15799v2 (arguing that the use of agentic AI could could reorganize markets, redistribute power, and catalyze the creation of new products and services); see also Christoph Busch, Consumer Law for AI Agents, German Law Journal 2025 (forthcoming).

The rise of AI agents coincides with a policy debate about the future of EU consumer law.[3] Following the publication of the final report[4] on the Digital Fairness Fitness Check in October 2024, the European Commission is currently preparing an update of the existing consumer laws to ensure effective consumer protection in digital markets. A legislative proposal for a Digital Fairness Act is expected for the third quarter of 2026. Considering the rapid developments in the field of agentic AI and its potentially transformative impact on digital markets, one would expect that AI agents take centre stage in the policy debate about the future of EU consumer law. However, this is not the case. It rather seems that agentic AI is the blind spot in the policy debate leading to the Digital Fairness Act. There is a significant risk that the upcoming reform of consumer law will ignore one of the key developments in digital markets. As a consequence, the Digital Fairness Act could be outdated before it enters into force.

Against this background, this Chapter argues that the Digital Fairness Act should regulate agentic AI. To be clear, this is not a simplistic plea for layering new rules on top of the existing regulatory framework. The task for the EU legislator is rather to adapt the existing rules so that they do not lose their effectiveness in the emerging agentic economy. It would be a serious shortcoming if the envisaged reform of EU consumer law were to ignore the coming wave of agentic AI. Updating the existing regulatory framework for agentic commerce is essential for two reasons: enabling innovative agent-based business models and protecting consumer autonomy in tomorrow's agentic economy. In this sense, ensuring that EU consumer law is "agent-ready" is necessary for creating the legal infrastructure for the future of the Digital Single Market.

The rest of the Chapter is organized as follows. Section 2 provides some technical background on AI agents and explains how agentic AI systems will transform online shopping. Section 3 briefly outlines the Commission's

3 See e.g. Emilia Mišćenić and Piotr Tereszkiewicz, Towards a New Digital Fairness Act, Journal of European Consumer and Market Law 2024, 229; Monika Namyslowska, The Silent Death of EU Consumer Law and Its Resilient Revival: Reinventing Consumer Protection Against Unfair Digital Commercial Practices, Journal of Consumer Policy 2025, 317; Hans-W. Micklitz, Natali Helberger, Betül Kas, Monika Namysłowska, Laurens Naudts, Peter Rott, Marijn Sax, Michael Veale, Towards Digital Fairness, Journal of European Consumer and Market Law 2024, 24; Christoph Busch and Amelia Fletcher, Shaping the Future of European Consumer Protection, Towards a Digital Fairness Act?, CERRE Issue Paper, December 2024.

4 European Commission, Fitness Check of EU consumer law on digital Fairness (3 October 2024) SWD (2024) 230 final.

plans for a Digital Fairness Act and explores how consumer law should adapt to the rise of AI agents. Section 4 concludes by stressing the importance of balancing innovation and consumer protection in the agentic economy.

II. The Agentic Economy

Since the public release of ChatGPT in November 2022, generative AI has taken the world by storm.[5] It is hard to keep track of the fast-changing landscape of AI-driven tools and business models ranging from AI chatbots, AI browsers and AI search engines to AI agents. One cannot help feeling that a new AI-powered business model is launched every week. This section can therefore only offer a snapshot of current developments in the field of agentic AI. More specifically, it provides a working definition of AI agents that serves as basis for the following policy considerations. In addition, it offers a brief overview of how agentic AI will transform the online retail landscape.

1. Defining AI Agents

There is not yet a generally agreed and definitive definition of AI agents.[6] In computer science, the concept of "agent" has been used for decades. According to a leading textbook on AI, an agent is, in a very general sense, "anything that can be viewed as perceiving its environment through sensors and acting upon that environment through actuators".[7] However, for the purposes of this Chapter, which focuses on issues of consumer policy, this definition (which would include a thermostat) is too broad. A more suitable working definition can be borrowed from a recent report on AI regulation by the UK Department for Science, Innovation and Technology: AI agents are "autonomous AI systems that perform multiple sequential steps – sometimes including actions like browsing the internet, sending

5 Catherine Thorbecke, A year after ChatGPT's release, the AI revolution is just beginning (CNN Business, 30 November 2023), https://edition.cnn.com/2023/11/30/tech/chatgpt-openai-revolution-one-year/index.html.

6 For an overview see Melissa Heikkilä, What Are AI Agents?, MIT Tech. Rev. (5 July 2024), https://www.technologyreview.com/2024/07/05/1094711/what-are-ai-agents/.

7 Stuart Russell and Peter Norvig, Artificial Intelligence, 4th ed. 2021, p. 54.

emails, or sending instructions to physical equipment—to try and complete a high-level task or goal."[8] Similar definitions for AI agents have been proposed by industry stakeholders, such as IBM[9] ("a system or program that is capable of autonomously performing tasks on behalf of a user or another system by designing its workflow and utilizing available tools"), or OpenAI[10] ("AI systems that can pursue complex goals with limited direct supervision").[11]

From a technology perspective, AI agents are to be distinguished from generative AI models, such as Large Language Models (LLMs) or other foundation models (FMs), although AI agents make use of such AI models to perform their tasks.[12] AI agents are essentially an extra layer of software built on top of foundation models such as OpenAI's GPT models or Anthropic's Claude which allows them to interact with other systems, apply reasoning and work according to goals and priorities set by the user.[13]

Agentic AI systems can be deployed at various layers of the tech stack. Some of the first AI agents have been deployed at the application layer either as separate apps (e.g. OpenAI Operator) or as a new feature of existing AI chatbots (e.g. PerplexityAI „Buy with Pro"). In the near future, AI browsers such as Dia and Comet, which integrate agentic features into web browsing, could become the next gateway to the Internet.[14] OpenAI is also expected to launch an AI browser later this year.[15] Another variant is

8 UK Department for Science, Innovation and Technology, A pro-innovation approach to AI regulation: government response (6 February 2024), https://www.gov.uk/government/consultations/ai-regulation-a-pro-innovation-approach-policy-proposals/outcome/a-pro-innovation-approach-to-ai-regulation-government-response; see also Friso Bostoen and Jan Krämer, AI Agents and ecosystem contestability (November 2024), p. 5.

9 Anna Gutowska, What are AI agents?, IBM (3 July 2024), https://www.ibm.com/think/topics/ai-agents.

10 OpenAI, Practices for Governing Agentic AI Systems (14 December 2023) https://openai.com/index/practices-for-governing-agentic-ai-systems/.

11 Friso Bostoen and Jan Krämer, *supra* note 8, p. 5.

12 Ibid.

13 Blair Levin and Larry Downes, Can AI Agents Be Trusted, Harvard Business Review 2025, https://hbr.org/2025/05/can-ai-agents-be-trusted.

14 Brian X. Chen, Is A.I. the Future of Web Browsing?, New York Times (11 July 2025), https://www.nytimes.com/2025/07/11/technology/personaltech/ai-internet-browser-dia.html.

15 Kendick Cai, Krystal Hu and Anna Tong, OpenAI to release web browser in challenge to Google Chrome, Reuters (10 July 2025), https://www.reuters.com/business/media-telecom/openai-release-web-browser-challenge-google-chrome-2025-07-09/

the deep integration of agentic AI features with the operating systems (OS) of digital devices such as smartphones (e.g. Apple Intelligence).

2. The Rise of Agentic Commerce

AI agents have the potential to significantly transform how users access digital services and interact with technology.[16] More specifically, in the context of online commerce, agentic AI could fundamentally change how consumers shop online and engage with online marketplaces.

From today's perspective, it is still unclear who will win the race for the agentic reconfiguration of online retail. One possibility is that AI agents provided by AI-first players like OpenAI or PerplexityAI could replace today's dominant online marketplaces or develop into a new kind of "virtual marketplace". In November 2024, the AI-powered search engine Perplexity launched a shopping feature that lets users make purchases directly within the search platform.[17] In April 2025, OpenAI rolled out a similar shopping capability inside the ChatGPT app.[18] AI-powered shopping agents could become the new access point for online commerce and change the way consumers search for products. As a result, many shoppers may soon start their customer journeys in apps like ChatGPT or PerplexityAI – rather than on Google or Amazon.

However, it is also conceivable that today's market leaders will use their financial clout and large user bases to dominate the market for AI agents themselves.[19] The leading Big Tech companies are indeed not sitting idle. In

(arguing that OpenAI's browser is designed to keep some user interactions within a ChatGPT-like native chat interface instead of clicking through to websites).

16 Bill Gates, AI is about to completely change how you use computers, Gates Notes (9 November 2023), https://www.gatesnotes.com/ai-agents.

17 Emma Roth, Perplexity's AI search engine can now buy products for you (18 November 2024), https://www.theverge.com/2024/11/18/24299574/perplexity-ai-search-engine-buy-products.

18 Reece Rogers, OpenAI Adds Shopping to ChatGPT in a Challenge to Google, Wired (28 April 2025), https://www.wired.com/story/openai-adds-shopping-to-chatgpt/.

19 See Sayash Kapoor, Noam Kolt and Seth Lazar, Resist Platform-Controlled AI Agents and Champion User Centric Agent Advocates (8 May 2025), https://arxiv.org/pdf/2505.04345 (arguing that AI agents controlled by large platform companies could intensify surveillance and exacerbate user lock-in); see also David M. Rothschild et al., *supra* note 2, p. 3, https://arxiv.org/pdf/2505.15799v2 (arguing that companies like Apple, Google, Microsoft or Meta are well positioned to extend their current marketplaces to include AI agents).

April 2025, Amazon began testing "Buy for me", a new AI shopping agent that enables customers to shop on third-party websites.[20] In May 2025, Google rolled out "Project Mariner", an experimental AI agent that browses websites and can make purchases on behalf of consumers.[21]

Agentic AI technology is still in its early days and many of the above initiatives are still at an experimental stage. But at the current pace of technological developments, AI agents could soon become the standard when it comes to online shopping. Currently, many consumers may still be reluctant to delegate their purchases to AI agents. But over the next few years, agentic commerce could be normalized as AI agents become more reliable. This could lead to a profound structural change in digital markets. One possible scenario is that today's increasingly centralized "web of platforms" is transformed into a more decentralized and interoperable "web of agents," in which agents freely connect and interact with each other.[22] Another scenario is that the agentic economy, much like the platform economy, tends towards concentration with only few agents remaining which could use their demand-steering powers to become the new "gatekeepers".[23]

However, if built with the right legal and technical safeguards, AI agents could also become a tool for consumer empowerment. Agentic AI systems could reduce transaction costs for consumers and facilitate comparison shopping across a wide range of products helping consumers to find the best offer. Moreover, the use of AI agents could reduce the vulnerability of consumers to dark patterns or harmful online architectures that are designed to exploit human weaknesses. Therefore, from a regulatory perspective, the question is not only how the design and functioning of online shops has to change when AI agents do most of the browsing and shopping for us. The "agentic turn" in online commerce also raises the question how consumer law has to adapt to ensure a high level of consumer protection in the emerging agentic economy.

---

20 Maxwell Zeff, Amazon's new AI agent will shop third-party sites for you, TechCrunch (3 April 2025), https://techcrunch.com/2025/04/03/amazons-new-ai-agent-will-shop-third-party-stores-for-you/.

21 Maxwell Zeff, Google rolls out Project Mariner, its web-browsing agent, TechCrunch (20 May 2025), https://techcrunch.com/2025/05/20/google-rolls-out-project-mariner-its-web-browsing-ai-agent/.

22 David M. Rothschild et al., *supra* note 2, p. 2.

23 Friso Bostoen & Jan Krämer, Is the DMA Ready for Agentic AI?, CERRE Report, July 2025, p. 6.

III. Agentic AI and Digital Fairness

Against the background of the dynamic technological developments which are transforming consumer markets, the EU Commission has recently launched a process to reform EU consumer law. However, the Commission‘s reform plans do not yet seem to reflect the profound changes brought about by agentic AI. To make this point, this section first briefly outlines the key steps in the reform process leading towards the envisaged Digital Fairness Act. So far, AI agents have played virtually no role in this process. In a second step, we explain why the rise of agentic AI requires a reorientation of the regulatory design of EU consumer law.

1. Towards a Digital Fairness Act

On 3 October 2024, the European Commission released its eagerly anticipated final report on the Digital Fairness Fitness Check.[24] The report provides the findings of an in-depth evaluation of three key directives that form the core of EU consumer law: the Unfair Commercial Practices Directive (UCPD), the Consumer Rights Directive (CRD) and the Unfair Contract Terms Directive (UCTD). The evaluation focused on the question of whether these Directives provide an adequate level of consumer protection in the digital environment.

The Commission's answer to this question is somewhat ambivalent.[25] On the one hand, the Fitness Check Report concludes that the three Directives under review have provided the necessary minimum regulatory certainty and consumer trust.[26] On the other hand, the Commission identifies a rather long list of problematic practices including dark patterns, addictive design, influencer marketing, harmful personalisation practices and digital subscriptions that may require further regulatory action.[27]

Building on the results of the Fitness Check, in September 2024 President von der Leyen asked Commissioner McGrath to develop a Digital Fairness Act "to tackle the unethical techniques and commercial practices

24 Fitness Check Report, *supra* note 4.

25 See Christoph Busch and Amelia Fletcher, Shaping the Future of European Consumer Protection: Towards a Digital Fairness Act, CERRE Issue Paper (November 2024), p. 5.

26 Fitness Check Report, *supra* note 4, p. 36.

27 Fitness Check Report, *supra* note 4, pp. 146-203.

related to dark patterns, marketing by social media influencers, the addictive design of digital products and online profiling, especially when consumer vulnerabilities are exploited for commercial purposes".[28] According to Commissioner McGrath the Digital Fairness Act, which shall complement the Digital Services Act and the Digital Markets Act, can be seen as the "missing piece of the puzzle in the EU's digital rulebook".[29]

At the time of writing, it is not yet clear what the exact shape and content of the planned Digital Fairness Act will be. A legislative proposal from the Commission is not expected before the third quarter of 2026. It is also unclear whether the Commission will propose a Directive or a Regulation (as the term "Act" might suggest). A likely scenario is that the Commission will limit itself to a few targeted amendments to existing Directives following the model of the Modernisation Directive[30] adopted in 2019.

The future of the Commission's plans is currently uncertain. Unsurprisingly, several business associations have rejected the plan to introduce new consumer law rules. They call for cutting red tape in order to increase the competitiveness of the European businesses and argue that the shortcomings identified in the Fitness Check "are not evidence of a lack of rules but point to ineffective enforcement."[31] It is certainly true that the effectiveness of enforcement of EU consumer law rules needs to be improved. But enforcement is only as good as the rules to be enforced. The best way to increase the effectiveness of enforcement is to increase the enforceability of the rules. This not only requires increasing the clarity of the the regulatory framework and removing unnecessary overlaps between existing rules. It also means ensuring that existing rules can be applied effectively to new technologies such as AI agents. Rather surprisingly, this aspect has hardly played a role in the policy debate to date.

The Fitness Check Report only briefly addresses issues around automated contracting.[32] As part of the analysis of problematic practices that may

---

28 European Commission, Mission Letter by Ursula von der Leyen (President of the European Commission) to Michael McGrath (Commissioner-designate for Democracy, Justice, and the Rule of Law (17 September 2024).

29 Michael McGrath, Written answer to the questions from the European Parliament's Committee on Internal Market and Consumer Protection (October 2024), p. 4.

30 Directive (EU) 2019/2161.

31 Joint Industry Statement on the Digital Fairness Act: A call for competitivenes-driven policy (4 June 2025), https://doteurope.eu/wp-content/uploads/2025/06/Joint-industry-statement-on-the-Digital-Fairness-Act.pdf.

32 Fitness Check Report, *supra* note 4, pp. 195-199.

require additional regulation, the Report mentions automation tools that "can assist the consumer in navigating traders' offers and making purchases".[33] As potential problems relating to automated contracting the Report mentions that the use of automation tools implies consumers giving up to certain degree the control over the transaction. Other problems may be related to a lack of transparency regarding key features of the automation tools.

However, these considerations from the Fitness Check Report are not taken up again in the public consultation launched on 17 July 2025, nor in the Call for Evidence for an Impact Assessment published on the same day.[34] Similarly, the European Commission's call for tenders for a Study to Support the Impact Assessment only mentions contracts concluded via digital assistants in passing (in connection with a possible reduction of information obligations).[35] In the Call for Evidence, the Commission emphasizes that "the Digital Fairness Act will focus on addressing the identified gaps and areas of legal uncertainty concerning consumer protection online."[36] As expected, the consultation questionnaire focuses on the following topics: dark patterns, addictive design, specific features of digital products (e.g., video games), unfair personalization practices, harmful practices by social media influencers, unfair marketing practices related to pricing (e.g., drip pricing), problems with digital contracts (e.g., regarding the termination or renewal of subscriptions). In addition, the questionnaire addresses possible legislative changes to simplify the regulatory environment. These are certainly all very important issues. However, it is striking that agentic AI systems are not mentioned at all.

33 Fitness Check Report, *supra* note 4, p. 195. In this context the Fitness Check Report refers to the Interim Report on Algorithmic Contracts published in December 2023 by the European Law Institute (ELI), see ELI, EU Consumer Law and Automated Decision-Making (ADM): Is EU Consumer Law Ready for ADM?, Interim Report (18 December 2023).

34 European Commission, Call for evidence for an impact assessment (17 July 2025), Ref. Ares (2025) 5829481, p. 2.

35 Technical Specifications for a Study to support the Impact Assessment for the Digital Fairness Act, 12 June 2025, Ref. Ares (2025) 4698035, p. 14 (on file with author).

36 European Commission, *supra* note 34, p. 2.

2. Updating EU Consumer Law for Agentic AI

Before we examine in more detail how EU consumer law needs to be adapted to respond to the challenges of the agentic economy, it is important to emphasize that agentic AI systems are not simply another iteration of technological progress, but rather a paradigm shift for consumer law. To understand the transformative impact of AI agents on EU consumer law, it is necessary to consider a fundamental premise of consumer law that seems so self-evident that it is usually not even stated. EU consumer law in its current form is human-centric, i.e. it is designed with the needs and weaknesses of human consumers in mind. Put differently, the design of consumer law rules is based on the premise that purchasing decisions are made by humans. Therefore, EU consumer law aims to protect human consumers and ensure their autonomy.

But this premise no longer holds in the agentic economy. Let me be clear, to avoid any misunderstanding: the consumer law of the future will still serve the purpose of protecting human consumers. In this sense, it will remain a consumer law *for humans.* However, in many cases, these humans will no longer be the ones who interact directly with traders and make transactional decisions on websites. Increasingly, these tasks will be delegated to AI agents, i.e. intelligent machines. In this sense, the consumer law of the future must also be a consumer law *for machines.*

In view of this paradigm shift, it is not sufficient to argue that many provisions of the existing EU consumer law are technology-neutral and that everything will therefore be fine. In a sense, the new agentic economy will be more complex and diverse than today's consumer markets. In the future, old-school human consumers will coexist with "augmented consumers" (who are assisted by generative AI tools such as ChatGPT) and AI agents acting as "algorithmic consumers".[37] The next generation of EU consumer law must reflect this new reality. The following subsections aim to provide some initial thoughts on what this may entail for the regulatory design of consumer law.

37 See Michal S. Gal and Niva Elkin Koren, Algorithmic Consumers 30 Harvard Journal of Law & Technology 309 (2017).

a) Rethinking Consumer Protection by Design: From Buttons to APIs

As stated above, EU consumer law is based on the premise that humans visit online shops and make their purchasing decisions there. That is why EU law stipulates a broad range of "design requirements" for web shops. For example, Article 8(2)(1) CRD requires online traders to provide consumers with several key items of information (e.g. main characteristics of the goods or services, total price, duration of the contract, and conditions for terminating the contract). This information must be provided "in a clear and prominent manner, and directly before the consumer places his order." In practical terms, this means that the core information items must be clearly distinguishable from the rest of the text displayed on the website and other design elements.[38] Article 8(2)(2) CRD further requires the trader to ensure that consumers, when placing their order, "explicitly acknowledge" that the order implies an obligation to pay. If the order is placed by activating a button, the button must be labelled in an easily legible manner only with the words "order with obligation to pay" or a corresponding unambiguous formulation. In the context of online marketplaces, these provisions are complemented by Art. 31(1) DSA which requires marketplace operators to design their online interfaces in a way that enables traders to comply with their obligations under EU consumer law.

The question arises as to whether these design-based regulations will continue to fulfill their function in the future agentic economy. How can labelling requirements for buttons ensure consumer protection if consumers will no longer press the buttons themselves but delegate this task to their AI agents? What does it mean that a consumer must "explicitly acknowledge" an obligation to pay if the purchase is made via an agentic AI system? Will it be sufficient if the AI agent provides such an "explicit acknowledgment"? Or should the AI agent be required to ask for the consumer's express consent by means of a "confirmation prompt"? This could help to ensure that the consumer remains in control of the transaction, but it would interrupt the agentic workflow and reduce the benefits of automation.

When considering the above questions, it may also be necessary to differentiate between different types of agentic AI systems. So-called "web brows-

38 BT-Drs. 17/7745, 11; Barbara Leier, Die Buttonlösung gegen Kostenfallen im Internet, CR 2012, 378 at 382; see also Benjamin Raue, „Kostenpflichtig bestellen" – die neuen Informations- und Formpflichten im Internethandel (§ 312g BGB), MMR 2012, 438 at 440 (arguing that this can be achieved by choosing an appropriate font size, font type and color).

ing agents" (e.g. OpenAI Operator) mimic human behaviour and click their way through an online shop. However, other types of AI agents may use a specific application programming interface (API) for agent-to-agent (A2A) communication and no longer click any buttons at all. The considerations show that the current design-based approach of EU consumer law could reach its limits in the context of agentic commerce.

The questions outlined above do not only arise in relation to the conclusion of contracts. Similar problems could also arise when AI agents are used to exercise a right of withdrawal or for cancelling a subscription contract. Similarly, one could ask whether the recently introduced "withdrawal button" (Art. 11e CRD) or "cancellation buttons" (as required and German[39] and French[40] law) provide an "agent-friendly" design that allows consumers to delegate these tasks to their AI agents. Maybe, it will be necessary in the future to provide a "cancellation API" in addition to a "cancellation button" to facilitate agentic workflows in the subscription economy.[41]

b) Digital Vulnerability 2.0: Manipulation by and of AI Agents

A key challenge in the brave new world of agentic commerce will be managing emerging risks of manipulation and addressing new vulnerabilities arising from the use AI agents. The risks related to agentic AI systems fall into two distinct categories: manipulation *by* and *of* AI agents. First, there is the danger that agentic AI systems are used to manipulate consumers. Second, AI agents themselves could fall victim to manipulation by third parties (e.g. rogue traders and hackers). Such attacks on agentic AI systems could eventually cause harm to the consumer on whose behalf the AI agent has been deployed.

Much has already been written about the first category of risk (manipulation *by* AI agents), mostly under the heading "algorithmic manipulation" and "algorithmic harm".[42] The use of AI agents could take the already

39 Section 312k German Civil Code.

40 Article L-215-1-1 (2) French Consumer Code.

41 See also Christoph Busch and Christian Twigg-Flesner, A Roadmap for Regulating Subscriptions in the Digital Fairness Act, Journal of European Consumer and Market Law 2024, 234-241.

42 See e.g. Gerhard Wagner and Horst Eidenmüller, Down by Algorithms? Siphoning Rents, Exploiting Biases, and Shaping Preferences: Regulating the Dark Side of Per-

existing possibilities for algorithmic manipulation to a whole new level. AI agents will become more powerful the more they know about consumers. Access to the consumer's purchasing history, calendar, or e-mail account will enable the AI agent to make increasingly targeted recommendations or to make purchases according to the consumer's stated and revealed preferences. This can yield many benefits for consumers. At the same time, giving AI agents access to personal data increases the risk of manipulation. AI agents could exploit information asymmetries and behavioural biases on the part of consumers. It will be a key task of consumer law to ensure that AI agents act in the best interests of consumers and do not become "manipulation engines".[43]

Some protection against manipulation could be provided by the existing transparency rules for rankings and recommender systems. The number of such rules aimed at algorithmic transparency has increased significantly in recent years.[44] However, it remains to be clarified whether the existing rules, which have been written with web shops and online platforms in mind, are applicable to AI agents. This is probably not the case for Articles 27 and 38 DSA, as these provisions only apply to online platforms (Art. 3(i) DSA). Conversely, Art. 6a(1)(a) CRD and Art. 7(4a) UCPD are likely to be applicable, as these provisions are formulated in a technology-neutral manner.

It remains to be seen whether these transparency requirements will be sufficient to protect consumers from more subtle manipulation techniques. A supplementing role could be played by the (rather vaguely formulated) prohibition of manipulation in Article 5(1)(a) of the AI Act. Additional

---

sonalized Transactions, 86 University of Chicago Law Review 581 (2019); Philipp Hacker, Manipulation by algorithms. Exploring the triangle of unfair commercial practice, data protection, and privacy law, 29 European Law Journal 2023, 142-175; Oren Bar-Gill, Cass R. Sunstein and Inbal Talgam-Cohen, Algorithmic Harm in Consumer Markets, 15 Journal of Legal Analysis 2023, 1-47; see also Oren Bar-Gill and Cass R. Sunstein, Algorithmic Harm: Protecting People in the Age of Artificial Intelligence, OUP 2025.

43 Kate Crawford, AI Agents Will Be Manipulation Engines, Wired (December 2023, 2024), https://www.wired.com/story/ai-agents-personal-assistants-manipulation-engines/.

44 See, e.g. Art. 7(4a) UCPD, Art. 6a(1)(a) CRD, Arts. 27, 38 DSA, Art. 5 P2B Regulation; see also Christoph Busch, From Algorithmic Transparency to Algorithmic Choice: European Perspectives on Recommender Systems and Platform Regulation, in: Genovesi, Kaesling & Robbins (eds.), Recommender Systems: Legal and Ethical Issues (Springer 2023) pp. 31-54.

legal requirements will apply if the supplier of the agentic AI system is a designated "gatekeeper" under the DMA.[45] In this scenario, Article 6(5) DMA applies, which prohibits the practice of self-preferencing.

The picture would be incomplete without mentioning that AI agents can also help to mitigate existing consumer vulnerabilities. In particular, the use of AI agents could reduce the vulnerability of consumers to digital choice architectures that are designed to exploit human weaknesses. In this sense, AI agents could help protect consumers from dark patterns. Unlike humans, AI agents are probably less likely to suffer from "click fatigue" if they are forced to click through too many steps to be able to make the desired choice. Perhaps AI agents are also more resistant to "nagging" (i.e. repeatedly urging consumers to make a particular choice) or "pressuring" (e.g. countdown timers and scarcity notifications). AI agents are also likely to be less influenced by "confirm shaming," emotional messages, and the colour of buttons.

However, even if AI agents are more resilient regarding dark patterns, this does not mean that they are invulnerable against any type of manipulation. The threat scenario could change in the agentic economy from dark patterns aimed at humans to "agentic dark patterns". Instead of manipulating human consumers, rogue raiders could seek to manipulate AI agents by exploiting their technical vulnerabilities.[46] In particular, agentic AI systems could be vulnerable to cybersecurity exploits and adversarial attacks that trick AI agents into a transaction. Examples of such vulnerabilities includes prompt injections (i.e. embedding malicious commands to alter the behaviour of AI agents) and adversarial image perturbations (i.e. subtle image-specific modulations of individual pixels that are designed to alter image categorization). These techniques could be used to hijack AI agents in order to trigger harmful actions (e.g. unauthorized transfers of funds or disclosure of personal data).[47]

45 It is unclear, however, whether the category of "virtual assistants" (Art. 2(2)(h) DMA) covers today's digital assistants that autonomously access apps, use browers and act on behalf of consumers, see Friso Bostoen and Jan Krämer, Is the DMA Ready for Agentic AI, CERRE Report, July 2025, pp. 22-31.

46 See Rory van Loo, Digital Market Perfection, 117 Michigan Law Review 815, 841 (2019) (arguing that sellers might "adopt misperception tactics against AIs similar to those they deploy for consumers").

47 Ibid.

In summary, it may be necessary to redefine the concept of "digital vulnerability" [48] in the agentic economy. On the one hand, new vulnerabilities could emerge (manipulation of and by AI agents), while on the other hand, AI agents could also mitigate existing vulnerabilities, particularly in the context of dark patterns.

c) Shifting Focus: From Contract Law to Design Requirements for AI Agents

Beyond the adjustments to consumer contract law and unfair competition law outlined above, a more fundamental shift in the regulatory focus may be necessary to ensure effective consumer protection in the agentic economy. EU consumer law currently puts its focus primarily on the "magical moment" of contract formation.[49] The full arsenal of consumer protection instruments is deployed at this time or, more precisely, shortly before and after the conclusion of the contract. This is when pre-contractual information duties, documentation requirements, specific form requirements for the conclusion of consumer contracts, and withdrawal rights come into play. Collectively, these instruments are designed to safeguard the consumer's ability to make a free and informed decision.

In the agentic economy, however, it may well be that no human consumer is directly involved when the contract is concluded, but only an AI agent acting on behalf of the consumer. The "human in the loop" is only

48 For an overview, see Camilla Crea and Alberto De Franceschi (eds.), The New Shapes of Digital Vulnerability in: European Private Law (Nomos 2024); see also Natali Helberger, Betül Kas, Hans-W. Micklitz, Monika Namysłowska, Laurens Naudts, Peter Rott, Marijn Sax, Michael Veale, Digital Fairness for Consumers, BEUC Report, (May 2024), p. 12 (arguing that the concept of digital vulnerability is characterised by three aspects, "its relational nature, its architectural nature, and the erosion of privacy"). Other authors refer to "systemic vulnerability", see e.g. Christine Riefa, Protecting vulnerable consumers in the digital single market, (2022), European Business Law Review, 33, 607-634 (arguing that consumer vulnerability is created by the system design, in particular the design of online choice architectures).

49 See Thomas Pfeiffer, New Mechanisms for Concluding Contracts, in: Reiner Schulze (Ed.) New Features in Contract Law (Sellier 2007) pp. 161-168 at 167(discussing whether such a „magical moment" exists in EU contract law); see also Hans Schulte-Nölke, EC Law on the Formation of Contract – from the Common Frame of Reference to the 'Blue Button', 3(3) European Review of Contract Law, 332-349 (2007) (arguing that EU law exhibits a high level of regulatory density before and after the conclusion of contract while the moment of conclusion, the "magical moment" when the contract becomes binding, is almost not regulated at all).

involved at the beginning of the process, when the consumer deploys the AI agent, sets parameters, and specifies preferences for the purchase (e.g. defining the maximum amount for the transaction). In order to ensure effective consumer protection, consumer law must step in already at this stage and formulate requirements for the design of agentic AI systems. In other words, the focus of consumer law might shift away from consumer contract law towards consumer protection "by design", i.e. a form of product safety law for AI agents. The recently adopted ELI Guiding Principles and Model Rules on Digital Assistants for Consumer Contracts illustrate how this approach could work by combining design requirements for AI agents with contract law rules. This regulatory model is based on the idea that „the objective of ensuring high levels of consumer protection in respect of digital assistants is best achieved through a combination of *ex ante* requirements and *ex post* rights."[50]

d) Towards an Average Consumer Test for AI Agents?

On a conceptual level, the rise of agentic AI systems could also have an impact on the model of the "average consumer". This consumer image or *Verbraucherleitbild* serves as normative standard for the application of consumer law rules. For example, in order to determine whether a particular commercial practice is considered unfair it is necessary to assess whether it materially distorts or is likely to materially distort the economic behaviour of an average consumer.[51] According to the case law of the Court of Justice of the European Union (CJEU), the relevant benchmark is the perspective of a average consumer who is "reasonably well-informed, reasonably ob-

---

50 European Law Institute, Guiding Principles and Model Rules on Digital Assistants for Consumer Contracts, Introduction (May 2025). The full text and explanatory commentary can be accessed at, https://www.europeanlawinstitute.eu/projects-publications/publications/guiding-principles-and-model-rules-on-digital-assistants-for-consumer-contracts/; see also Christoph Busch, Marie Jull Sørensen, Teresa Rodriguez de las Heras Ballell and Christian Twigg-Flesner, Towards the Next Generation of Consumer Law: the ELI Guiding Principles and Model Rules on Digital Assistants for Consumer Contracts, Journal of European Consumer and Market Law 2025, 89; Christoph Busch and Christian Twigg-Flesner, Towards an AI-ready consumer law – the model of the ELI Guiding Principles and Model Rules on Digital Assistants for Consumer Contracts (forthcoming).

51 See Art. 5(2) UCPD.

servant and circumspect".[52] In the recent *Compass Banca* case the CJEU underlined that the average consumer test is not "supposed to be merely a theoretical exercise" and that "considerations that are more realistic must also be taken into account".[53] More specifically, the Court held that in applying the average consumer test, it is possible to take into account the influence of cognitive biases on that average consumer.[54]

But how can such a behaviourally informed average consumer test be applied in cases where the transactional decision was not taken by a human but an AI agent? How does the decision-making of AI agents differ from that of humans? Will the behaviour of AI agents come closer to the elusive ideal of the reasonably well-informed, reasonably observant and circumspect consumer? Or do AI agents show similar heuristics and biases than humans?[55]

At this stage, it is an open question whether AI agents will be more "rational" than human consumers. Research in the emerging fields of „machine psychology"[56] and "AI psychometrics",[57] which study the behaviour of large language models (LLMs), is still at an early stage. We currently still know too little about the behaviour of AI agents to be able to give a definite answer as to whether the "average consumer test" developed for humans can also be applied to AI agents, or whether an "average AI agent test" needs to be developed.[58]

52 CJEU, Case C-210/96 Gut Springenheide and Rudolf Tusky v Oberkreisdirektor des Kreises Steinfurt [1998] ECR I – 4657, paras 30-31.

53 CJEU, Case C-646/22 Compass Banca SpA v Autorità Garante della Concorrenza e del Mercato (14 November 2024), para. 51.

54 Id. at para. 53.

55 For a more detailed analysis see Christoph Busch, *supra* note 2.

56 Thilo Hagendorff, Ishita Dasgupta, Marcel Binz, Stephanie C.Y. Chan, Andrew Lampinen, Jane X. Wang, Zeynep Akata, Eric Schulz, Machine Psychology, https://doi.org/10.48550/arXiv.2303.13988.

57 Max Pellert, Clemens M. Lechner, Claudia Wagner, Beatrice Rammstedt & Markus Strohmaier, 19(5) AI Psychometrics: Assessing the Psychological Profiles of Large Language Models Through Psychometric Inventories, Perspectives on Psychological Science, 808-826 (2024).

58 Id. („In any case the significant variability observed between models in our study indicates that a definitive answer to the question of whether LLMs exhibit cognitivie limitations and biases cannot be drawn").

IV. Conclusions

EU consumer law is not prepared for the agentic AI revolution. The analysis has shown that the rise of the agentic economy raises a broad range of new questions to which existing consumer law does not yet provide adequate answers. With the right safeguards, AI agents can become a tool for consumer empowerment. But we have to build the necessary legal infrastructure to make this happen. Innovative business models building on AI agents need legal certainty. Making EU consumer law "agent-ready" is therefore not only a matter of consumer policy but also key element of the strategy to strengthen the competitiveness of the EU. Adapting consumer law rules to the coming wave of agentic AI will require a nuanced approach balancing innovation and consumer protection. Policymakers should not wait for the next "iPhone moment"[59] to address these challenges; they should start now creating a consumer law that works for both humans and machines. The Digital Services Act and the Modernisation Directive have updated EU consumer law for the platform economy. The Digital Fairness Act should take the next step and prepare EU consumer law for the agentic economy.

59 Cf. Bernard Marr, Is this AI's iPhone moment?, Forbes (8 July 2024), https://www.forbes.com/sites/bernardmarr/2024/07/08/is-this-ais-iphone-moment/.

Attribution of Knowledge and Pre-Contractual Information Duties

AI Contracting and Contract Law (Default) Rules

*Florian Möslein**

I. The Rise of AI Contracting

The digital transformation of commercial and legal practices has brought about a paradigm shift in the creation, negotiation and management of contracts. One of the most significant develop-ments is the increasing use of artificial intelligence (AI) in contracting processes, a phenomenon often referred to as „AI contracting".[1] This chapter opens by examining the technological trajectory and emerging landscape of AI-assisted contract management, drafting and reviewing contracts, and contracting through autonomous AI agents. In view of this context, the subsequent analysis will then address the manifold legal implications of this progression. In order to assess the need to adapt contract law and potential implications for its normative foundations, however, it is vital to analyse and comprehend the rise of AI contracting first.

1. Contract Automation: From Simple Digital Tools to Autonomous Contracting

Automated contracting has evolved from relatively simple digital tools for contract formation and contract management – such as DocuSign (offering e-signatures and basic contract templates) and OneFlow (enabling real-time collaboration and lifecycle tracking)[2] – into highly sophisticated

* Professor of Law and Director of the Institute for Law and Regulation of Digitalisation (www.irdi.institute) at the Philipps-University Marburg.

1 See, for instance, *M. Ebers,* Artificial Intelligence, Contracting and Contract Law: An Introduction, in: M. Ebers, C. Poncibò & M. Zou (eds.), Contracting and Contract Law in the Age of Artificial Intelligence (Hart Publishing, 2022), p. 19; cf. also *M. Herbosch*, Contracting with Artificial Intelligence, RabelsZ 87 (2023), 672; *id.*, To err is human: Managing the risks of contracting AI systems, Computer Law & Security Review 56 (2025), 106110, available at https://doi.org/10.1016/j.clsr.2025.106110.

2 In more detail: http://www.docusign.com and https://oneflow.com/; for a broader overview see *J. Green*, Legaltech and the Future of Startup Lawyering, in: A. Masson &

technical systems that assist with, and increasingly replace, human involvement in the contracting process. The boosting use of AI in this area reflects a wider trend towards automating contractual practices and related legal services,[3] as part of a global push towards digitalisation, datafication and the adoption of algorithmic decision-making across economic sectors.[4]

Early applications of AI in legal practice focused on improving the efficiency of managing and retrieving documents. Contract lifecycle management (CLM) platforms introduced functionalities such as clause recognition, risk flagging and metadata extraction.[5] Today, these tools are enhanced by natural language processing (NLP) and machine learning (ML) algorithms, enabling the identification and semantic analysis of contractual provisions to facilitate intelligent contract classification and performance monitoring.[6] These technologies have the potential to transform traditional CLM platforms from passive repositories into intelligent systems capable of reading, interpreting, and even suggesting contractual clauses. Law firms and in-house counsel are increasingly relying on AI-enhanced systems not only to manage contracts, but also to generate, revise, and optimise them, often in real time.[7]

G. Robinson (eds.) Mapping Legal Innovation: Trends & Perspectives (Springer, 2021), p. 189.

3 One example concerns the transformation of standard contract terms; in more detail *F. Möslein*, Digitized Terms: The Regulation of Standard Contract Terms in the Digital Age, European Review of Contract Law 19 (2023), 300.

4 *F. Möslein*, Contract Governance in the Network Economy, European Business Law Review 35 (2024), 383 (focussing on contractual implications of these developments).

5 On these earlier forms of contract automation see, for instance, *L. di Matteo*, International Contracting: Law and Practice (WoltersKluwer, 5th ed., 2022), § 14.16 [D][3].

6 *M. Ebers* (n. 1), p. 21.

7 A recent survey reports that 70.8% of in-house legal teams anticipate AI-driven transformation in contract management over the next three years, moving beyond simple administration to strategic use—signalling usage in generation, revision, optimization, often in real time: *SpotDraft*, 2025 AI Impact on In-House Legal Teams Survey Report, available at https://www.spotdraft.com/ai-impact-report-2025.

2. AI-Assisted Contract Drafting and Review

Using AI for contract drafting and review offers a new level of autonomy.[8] AI systems now routinely assist with the creation of contract templates, tailoring clauses according to transaction type, jurisdiction and risk preferences.[9] They increasingly draw on large databases of precedent contracts and use probabilistic models to identify common clause patterns and suggest appropriate language.

Kira Systems is one such example, using machine learning (ML) to extract and analyse key contract clauses across large document sets, thereby aiding due diligence and compliance efforts.[10] ROSS Intelligence previously offered AI-assisted legal research to inform contract preparation (prior to ceasing operations).[11] Juro and Lexion offer end-to-end contract automation platforms where contracts can be created, reviewed, approved and stored with minimal human intervention.[12] Notably, systems such as Spellbook (developed by Rally) integrate with word processors to provide real-time drafting assistance, drawing on large language models such as GPT-4 to offer suggestions and flag inconsistencies as the text is written.[13]

These technologies offer clear economic advantages by increasing drafting speed, reducing transaction costs, improving consistency, and mitigating legal risks.[14] AI can highlight deviations from standard terms, enforce company playbooks and explain potential legal risks in plain language,

---

8 On the distinction between autonomy and automation see *E. Mik*, From Automation to Autonomy: Some Non-Existent Problems in Contract Law, Journal of Contract Law 36 (2020), 205.

9 Similar *A. Zhang Yang*, AI in Contract Drafting: Transforming Legal Practice, Richmond Journal of Law and Technology, October 2024, available at https://jolt.richmond.edu/2024/10/22/ai-in-contract-drafting-transforming-legal-practice/.

10 For an early account see *K. Betts & K. Jaep*, The Dawn of Fully Automated Contract Drafting, Duke Law & Technology Law Review 15 (2017), 216, at 225.

11 Details are discussed in a video interview with *Noah Waisberg*, Co-Founder & CEO, Kira Systems and *Andrew Arruda*, Co-Founder & CEO, Ross Intelligence, available at https://beyondinnovation.tv/artificial-intelligence/how-ai-is-revolutionizing-contract-law-with-kira-systems-and-ross-intelligence/.

12 See www.juro.com and https://www.lexion.ai/.

13 www.spellbook.legal; see also *Law Tech Daily Briefing*, Revolutionizing Contract Drafting with AI, 26 May 2023, available at https://www.lawtechdaily.com/may-26-2023/.

14 Similar *K. Werbach & N. Cornell*, Contracts Ex Machina, Duke Law Journal 67 (2017), 313, 317 (noting that firms can achieve significant cost savings and efficiency gains when using computers to automate contracting); see also *A. Gambino & A. Stazi*, Contract Automation from Telematic Agreements to Smart Contracts, The

making contract review accessible also to non-lawyers, marking a significant shift in the distribution of legal expertise.

3. Contracting Through AI Agents

One of the most significant developments in the field of AI contracting is the emergence of autonomous contracting agents, i.e. AI systems that form or perform contracts with limited or no human oversight.[15] These agents range from e-commerce bots executing dynamic pricing strategies to algorithmic traders in financial markets that enter into binding agreements in milliseconds based on predefined parameters.[16] Similar agents are already being used extensively in the field of programmatic advertising, for example. In this area, automated systems purchase and sell digital ad space in real time based on user data, budget constraints and performance goals.[17] In the field of logistics and supply chain management, AI agents have been developed to negotiate shipping terms and allocate procurement contracts across vendors.[18] These transactions occur without direct human participation in the negotiation, yet they could result in legally enforceable obligations.

A particularly illustrative example of AI contracting is the use of digital personal assistants or intelligent agents that engage in contract-like be-

---

Italian Law Journal 7 (2021), 97, 101 ("reducing the time delay due to distance, limiting communication risks, automating responses and reducing transaction costs").

15 On AI agents in general *N. Kolt*, Governing AI Agents, Notre Dame Law Review 101 (2025), forthcoming; for more specific considerations from a contract perspective see the blogpost by *P. Cramer, J. Mollod & C. Rimmer*, Contract Law in the Age of Agentic AI: Who's Really Clicking "Accept"?, April 9, 2025, available at https://newmedialaw.proskauer.com/2025/04/09/contract-law-in-the-age-of-agentic-ai-whos-really-clicking-accept/.

16 For a broad overview, covering various fields such as banking, insurance and healthcare, cf. the contributions, in: *K. Huang* (ed.), Agentic AI: Theories and Practices (Springer, 2025). More specifically on the latter example: *International Organization of Securities Commissions (IOSCO)*, Artificial Intelligence in Capital Markets: Use Cases, Risks, and Challenges (March 2025), pp. 51 et seq.

17 *V. Kumar, A. Ashraf & W. Nadeem*, AI-powered marketing: What, where, and how?, International Journal of Information Management 77 (2024), 102783.

18 Cf. the experimental studies conducted by *S. Kirshner, Y. Pan, J. Wu & A. Gould*, Talking Terms: Agent Information in LLM Supply Chain Bargaining (June 2025), available at https://papers.ssrn.com/sol3/papers.cfm?abstract_id=5273609.

haviour on behalf of consumers.[19] For instance, a voice assistant could place a grocery order, accept delivery terms, and authorise payment – all within a framework that closely resembles contractual formation. Similarly, enterprise AI agents in B2B environments have the potential to autonomously negotiate service-level agreements based on real-time performance metrics, risk thresholds, or inventory data.[20]

These examples highlight a transition from AI-assisted to entirely AI-driven contracting. The human role is evolving to focus more on configuration and oversight, such as defining the parameters within which AI systems operate. This shift implies that human individuals are no longer directly involved in contract negotiation or execution. As a result, complex questions regarding legal capacity, attribution, consent, and mistake in contracts concluded without contemporaneous human intention arise.

4. Broader Technological and Economic Context

The rise of AI contracting must be understood within a broader technological and economic framework that makes such developments not only possible but commercially necessary. From a technological standpoint, the widespread adoption of cloud computing, application programming interfaces (APIs) and modular software architecture has facilitated the seamless integration of AI tools into larger enterprise systems. These integrations facilitate continuous monitoring and optimisation of contract performance, dynamic adjustment of terms, and real-time data analytics that inform contract design.[21] Concurrently, the emergence of large language models (LLMs) — such as OpenAI's GPT-4, Meta's LLaMA, or Anthropic's Claude — has led to a substantial enhancement in the expressive and interpretive capabilities of AI. These models can now engage with legal texts not merely as strings of characters, but as structured arguments and normative state-

19 *C. Busch*, Consumer Law for AI Agents, German Law Journal 25 (2025), forthcoming (sub B.I.).

20 *N. Kolt*, Governing AI Agents, Notre Dame Law Review 101 (2025), forthcoming (atp. 4 in the preprint version, available at https://papers.ssrn.com/sol3/papers.cfm?abstract_id=4772956).

21 On the relevance of APIs (and their legal framework) in particular. *F. Teuguia*, Navigating the Legal Landscape of APIs: Innovations, Strategies for Sustainable, Inclusive, and Secure Digital Ecosystems, World Futures 81 (2025), 255–290, available at https://doi.org/10.1080/02604027.2025.2499205.

ments.[22] Their capacity to reason over legal content, generate persuasive language, and adapt to evolving linguistic and jurisdictional contexts signifies a substantial advancement in computational legal practice.[23]

From an economic perspective, these technological developments are highly relevant in terms of addressing current concerns in the legal industry and in other sectors. In the present business climate, companies are under mounting pressure to reduce legal expenditure, accelerate deal velocity, and manage compliance risk within a global and complex regulatory environment.[24] AI contracting offers compelling solutions to these challenges: automated tools enable rapid scaling of legal operations without proportional increases in cost, while providing governance features that enhance auditability and reduce human error. Concurrently, the platformisation of legal services — offering "legal tech as a service" — has resulted in the emergence of new market participants and competitive dynamics.[25] Legal knowledge is becoming more modular and monetised, accessible through APIs or embedded software features, rather than being confined to bespoke legal advice. In this context, AI is not merely augmenting legal practice; it is reshaping the structure of legal services and redistributing the boundaries of legal expertise.

5. Towards a New Contract Paradigm

The convergence of these technological, economic, and institutional dynamics developments indicates that AI contracting is more than a passing

22 In more detail: *E. Horner, C. Mateis, G. Governatori & A. Ciabattoni*, From Legal Texts to Defeasible Deontic Logic via LLMs: A Study in Automated Semantic Analysis (2025), preprint available at https://arxiv.org/abs/2506.08899.

23 An example of the increasing ability of LLMs to produce persuasive legal discourse is their capacity to categorise traditional legal interpretation techniques: *G. Dugac & T. Altwicker*, Classifying legal interpretations using large language models, Artificial Intelligence and Law (2025), available at https://doi.org/10.1007/s10506-025-09447-9.

24 On the effects of legal risk and compliance costs on firm behaviour, underscoring pressures on businesses to manage legal expenditure and compliance risk in a complex regulatory environment: *D. Ryu*, The Pricing and Economic Impact of Legal Risk (2025), working paper available at https://ssrn.com/abstract=4967369.

25 For some early accounts cf. *M. Hartung, M.-M. Bues & G. Halbleib* (eds.), Legal Tech – Die Digitalisierung des Rechtsmarkts, 2018; *K. Möslein/Leimeister/F. Möslein/Reichwald* (eds.), Recht als Dienstleistung – Strategischer Produktivitätsfaktor unternehmerischer Innovation?, 2012; *J. Taeger* (Ed.), Law as a Service (LaaS) – Recht im Internet- und Cloud-Zeitalter, 2013.

trend. It rather signifies a far-reaching and probably fundamental transformation in the nature of contractual relationships. As AI systems evolve from mere tools to agents, and from assisting to autonomously performing tasks, fundamental questions of contract law become increasingly important. In the event of errors made by autonomous AI agents, who is responsible for their actions? In the context of transactions between AI-driven machines, what is the definition of consent? In what manner should courts interpret contracts whose terms have been negotiated or generated by algorithms?

Before exploring some initial regulatory responses to these issues, it is important to emphasise that AI has the potential to transform the fundamentals and functions of contract law. Contracts are evolving beyond mere instruments of human interaction to become increasingly driven by digital technologies and embedded in a broader ecosystem of algorithms, data flows, and automated decision-making processes. The challenge for legal policy and for legal scholarship is to develop a normative framework that can accommodate this reality while upholding the core values of autonomy, fairness and legal certainty.

II. The Emerging Regulatory Framework

The rules governing AI contracting lie at the intersection of emerging technologies and traditional contract law, raising complex questions concerning responsibility, transparency and enforceability. This chapter examines the emergence of new, supranational rules regarding AI contracting by comparing the EU Artificial Intelligence Act — a pioneering, albeit limited attempt to regulate AI usage — with instruments that focus specifically on contracts, such as the UNCITRAL Model Law on Automated Contracting and the ELI DACC Model Rules. Together, these instruments highlight the challenges and limitations of the current regulatory approaches to AI-driven contracting.

1. EU AI Act

The European Union's Artificial Intelligence Act (AI Act) is a significant regulatory milestone, establishing a harmonised legal framework for the development, deployment and use of AI systems within the internal market.[26] As part of the EU's broader digital strategy, the Act ensures that AI systems are safe, transparent, reliable and accountable. However, its relevance to AI contracting is limited, particularly from a contract law perspective.

a) Regulatory Architecture

Structurally, the AI Act follows a risk-based regulatory logic.[27] It begins with general provisions defining the scope of the regulation and introducing key concepts such as AI system, provider, and deployer. One particularly relevant definition in this context is that of the 'deployer' in Art. 3 para. 4 of the AI Act, which includes any natural or legal person, public authority, agency or other body using an AI system under its authority except where the AI system is used in the course of a personal non-professional activity. In particular, it should be noted that this term differs substantially from the 'end user' definition employed in Article 3(21) of the Market Surveillance Regulation,[28] which demonstrates the limited protective nature of the AI Act for consumers.[29] The core of the regulation lies in its classification of AI systems by risk level.[30] Systems that are deemed to pose an unacceptable risk, such as those involving manipulative or exploitative techniques, are prohibited outright. High-risk systems, including AI applications in areas such as critical infrastructure, law enforcement and employment, are permitted but subject to strict regulatory requirements. These include obligations relating to risk management, data governance, technical documentation and human oversight, primarily aimed at the providers or developers of the AI systems. For lower-risk systems, the AI Act imposes

26 Regulation (EU) 2024/1689 of the European Parliament and of the Council of 13 June 2024 laying down harmonised rules on Artificial Intelligence, OJ L 2024/1689.

27 For an in-depth discussion of this regulatory approach see *M. Ebers*, Truly Risk-based Regulation of Artificial Intelligence: How to Implement the EU's AI Act, European Journal of Risk Regulation 16 (2025), 684; cf. also *M. Kaminski*, Regulating the Risks of AI, Boston University Law Review 103 (2023), 1346.

28 Regulation (EU) 2019/1020 of the European Parliament and of the Council of 20 June 2019 on market surveillance and compliance of products, OJ L 2019/169.

29 Similar *Ch. Wendehorst*, The Proposal for an Artificial Intelligence Act COM (2021) 206 from a Consumer Policy Perspective, Study commissioned by the Austrian Federal Ministry of Social Affairs, Health, Care and Consumer Protection (2021), pp. 11 et seq.

30 In more detail *P. Bronner*, Risikoklassifizierung, Risikobewertung und Risikominimierung nach der KI-Verordnung, Künstliche Intelligenz und Recht (KIR) 2024, 55.

transparency obligations, particularly in cases where humans interact with AI tools such as chatbots, in order to ensure that users are aware that they are communicating with an automated agent. Moreover, Art. 4 of the AI Act requires all providers and deployers to ensure that all personnel involved with AI systems possess sufficient AI literacy, encompassing both technical understanding and regulatory compliance, across all organisational levels operating within or impacting the EU market.[31]

b) Relevance to AI Contracting

Despite its comprehensive nature, the AI Act's regulatory impact on AI contracting is limited at best.[32] Firstly, the AI tools that are commonly used in contract-related processes, such as legal drafting assistants, document review systems and negotiation bots, do not usually fall into the category of high-risk AI systems under Art. 6 AI Act. These tools are rarely used in the sensitive sectors targeted by the Act and therefore usually avoid the more onerous compliance obligations.[33] Even when used in commercial or legal settings, they are generally classified as low risk, with minimal associated transparency obligations. Nevertheless, providers must conduct and document a risk assessment to confirm this classification and ensure ongoing compliance.[34]

Moreover, the regulatory focus of the AI Act is almost entirely on the providers and developers of AI systems rather than on those who use them to facilitate everyday legal or commercial tasks.[35] In the context of contracts, this means that law firms, businesses or public bodies using

31 *Ph. Hacker, A. Engel, S. Hammer & Brent Mittelstadt*, Introduction to the Foundations and Regulation of Generative AI, forthcoming, in: ids. (eds.), The Oxford Handbook of the Foundation and Regulation of Generative AI (Oxford University Press, in preparation), preprint available at https://academic.oup.com/edited-volume/59908 [sub IV.1.a].

32 Similar *M. Herbosch*, To err is human: Managing the risks of contracting AI systems, Computer Law & Security Review 56 (2025), 106110, available at https://doi.org/10.1016/j.clsr.2025.106110.

33 More specifically, they are unlikely to be included in Annex III of the AI Act and typically serve narrow, assistive functions without independently affecting fundamental rights; in more detail on the classification concept: *H. Ruschemeier*, Art. 6, in: Ch. Wendehorst & M. Martini (eds.), KI-Verordnung, (C. H. Beck, 2024), para. 27-33.

34 In more detail: *H. Ruschemeier*, Art. 6, in: Ch. Wendehorst & M. Martini (eds.), KI-Verordnung, (C. H. Beck, 2024), para. 96-100.

35 See above, reference n. 28 et seq.

AI tools to generate or perform contracts are not the primary subjects of the AI Act's regulatory attention, unless they have developed the system themselves or are using it in a particularly sensitive domain. For end users of AI systems in contract formation, the obligations are minimal and largely procedural. There is no specific recognition of contract law concerns, such as consent, attribution of actions or the enforceability of algorithmically generated contract terms. In this sense, the AI Act fails to address the fundamental issues of contract law raised by AI contracting practices.[36]

The limited intersection between the AI Act and AI contracting reveals a deeper structural gap. Although the AI Act covers the technical and ethical aspects of AI deployment, it does not address the legal aspects of contracts created, negotiated or reviewed by AI systems. For example, it does not address the question of whether an AI-generated contract clause can be attributed to a party, how transparency and fairness in automated negotiations should be assessed, or what should happen when an AI assistant misinterprets contractual intent. These questions are left to conventional contract law and to emerging soft-law frameworks, such as the UNCITRAL Model Law on Automated Contracting and the ELI's Model Rules on Algorithmic Contracts, which will be discussed below. In the context of ongoing legal transformation, the AI Act may be seen as a necessary but insufficient step toward a comprehensive legal framework for AI contracting. It sets important guardrails for the safe operation of AI systems but does not yet address the normative shifts occurring in private law due to the increasing use of AI in contract formation and execution. As AI systems become more autonomous and integrated into legal processes, a broader legal response will be needed—one that not only regulates the technology itself but also adapts contract law doctrines to reflect the realities of AI-generated legal relationships. This includes clarifying the role of default rules, adapting doctrines of intent and interpretation, and perhaps rethinking the very notion of contractual agency in the age of machine-assisted contracting.

36 Cf. again *M. Herbosch*, To err is human: Managing the risks of contracting AI systems, Computer Law & Security Review 56 (2025), 106110, available at https://doi.org/10.1016/j.clsr.2025.106110 ("its provisions do no directly target contract-supporting AI systems").

2. UNCITRAL Model Law on Automated Contracting

Unlike the EU AI Act, which focuses on regulating the risks associated with AI systems and imposes obligations on providers of high-risk AI systems in particular, the UNCITRAL Model Law on Automated Contracting takes a more enabling, contract-centric approach. Rather than addressing the design or ethical governance of AI, it aims to promote the legal recognition and use of automated systems in contracting by emphasising legal certainty, technological neutrality and party autonomy. This approach reflects the Model Law's alignment with the principles of contract law rather than with the regulatory oversight of AI systems.

a) Background and Rationale

The UNCITRAL Model Law on Automated Contracting (Model Law or MLAC)[37] represents a significant development in the harmonization and modernization of international contract law in response to the increasing use of automated systems in commercial contracting. Its genesis lies in the broader digital transformation of trade, and in particular, the shift from traditional to electronic and now automated modes of contract formation and performance.[38] Following exploratory work by the UNCITRAL Secretariat starting in 2018, and the formal inclusion of the topic in UNCITRAL's work programme in 2021, the Model Law was adopted at the Commission's 57th session on 4 December 2024, following consensus on its key provisions and drafting principles.[39]

The core motivation behind the Model Law is to address the legal uncertainty surrounding the use of automated systems—including (but not limited to) those using AI techniques—in the creation, performance, and modification of contracts.[40] While earlier UNCITRAL instruments, such as the Model Law on Electronic Commerce (1996) and the Electronic Communications Convention (2005), provided for the legal validity of

37 The text of the UNCITRAL Model Law and the Guide to Enactment are available at https://uncitral.un.org/en/mlac.

38 In this sense *United Nations General Assembly*, Resolution adopted on 4 December 2024 on the Model Law on Automated Contracting, A/RES/79/119, also available at https://uncitral.un.org/en/mlac, at p. 1.

39 In more detail on the drafting history: *UNCITRAL*, Guide to Enactment, 2025, p. 10.

40 *UNCITRAL*, Guide to Enactment, 2025, p. 6.

electronic communications and contracts, they were not expressly designed to accommodate systems operating with little or no human oversight. The Model Law thus closes a significant normative gap and builds upon existing texts by offering tailored provisions that explicitly legitimize and regulate contracting processes carried out by autonomous or semi-autonomous systems.[41] Unlike these earlier texts, however, the Model Law acknowledges the unique characteristics of AI- and automation-based contracting. Consequently, it diverges from the fundamental approach of functional equivalence.[42] Instead, it establishes the validity and enforceability of such contracts independently of traditional legal analogies, enabling greater adaptability to technological evolution.

b) Scope of Application

The Model Law is deliberately broad in scope, applying to the use of any automated system—defined in Art. 1 para. 1 lit. a) as a "computer system that is capable of carrying out actions without the necessary review or intervention of a natural person"—in the formation and performance of contracts (cf. Art. 2). According to Art. 1 para. 2, this includes both deterministic (i.e. rule-based) and non-deterministic (i.e. AI-based) systems, and it covers a wide range of commercial use cases such as smart contracting via distributed ledger technologies, automated negotiation through chatbots, and algorithmic procurement platforms.[43]

Importantly, the law is not confined to consumer contracts or low-value transactions.[44] Instead, it encompasses both B2B and B2C environments. Moreover, it is technologically neutral in design (cf. Art. 4).[45] Technology

41 Cf. again *UNCITRAL*, Guide to Enactment, 2025, p. 6 ("intended to complement and supplement laws on electronic transactions, in particular those based on other UNCITRAL texts on electronic commerce").

42 For an in-depth examination of this principle, see C. Twigg-Flessner, Contract Automation -Is Functional Equivalence Enough?, in: B. Zeller & C. Baasch Andersen (eds.), Routledge Handbook on Transnational Commercial Law (Routledge, 2025), p. 474.

43 Similar *UNCITRAL*, Guide to Enactment, 2025, p. 8.

44 Cf. *UNCITRAL*, Guide to Enactment, 2025, p. 18 ("Article 2 does not delimit the types of contracts or transactions to which the Model Law applies").

45 *UNCITRAL*, Guide to Enactment, 2025, p. 9: "The principle of technology neutrality dictates that the law should not mandate or favour the use of any specific technology or method, thus making the law compatible with technologies that are not yet foreseen".

neutrality ensures that the law is adaptable to evolving technical standards and business practices. It also does not prescribe any specific form of automation, leaving scope for dynamic market innovation. Moreover, the Model Law is not intended to displace existing legal requirements relating to consumer protection, data governance, or ethical AI use. As clarified in Art. 2 para. 2, other legal provisions governing the design, commissioning, operation, or use of automated systems remain unaffected.[46]

By drawing a distinction between the formation and performance of contracts (Art. 2 para. 1 lit. a and lit. b), the Model Law recognizes that automation may occur at various stages of the contract lifecycle. This modular approach is consistent with the approach taken in the Electronic Communications Convention.[47] It is also compatible with national legal doctrines that differentiate between the consensual and executory dimensions of contract law, as found for example in German or French private law.[48]

c) Substantive Provisions

aa) Legal Recognition of Automated Systems

At the heart of the Model Law are Articles 5 and 6, which establish the legal validity and enforceability of contracts formed or executed using automated systems. These provisions ensure that a contract cannot be denied legal effect simply because no human reviewed or intervened in the process. Article 6 extends this recognition to contracts expressed in computer code, as well as to those incorporating dynamic, real-time data. This provision explicitly acknowledges emerging use cases, such as smart contracts deployed on blockchain infrastructures or contracts whose terms adjust based on

---

46 See also *UNCITRAL*, Guide to Enactment, 2025, pp. 18 et seq.

47 *UNCITRAL*, Guide to Enactment, 2025, p. 17.

48 The German Civil Code (Bürgerliches Gesetzbuch, BGB) is structurally divided into two parts: Book I (General Part, §§ 145–156) covers contract formation, including offers, acceptance and interpretation, and Book II (Law of Obligations, §§ 241–853) covers the performance of obligations, breach of contract and remedies. For a similar approach in French law, see for example *J. Sénéchal*, Contract Formation and Non-performance in French Law, in: R. Schulze & F. Zoll (eds.), The Law of Obligations in Europe (de Gruyter, 2013), p. 343 (separately examining "la formation du contrat" and "l'inexécution").

market feeds or sensor input.[49] In this regard, the Model Law aligns with the provision in Art. 36 of the EU Data Act[50] which introduces specific requirements for smart contracts used in data sharing.[51] Taken together, the two provisions highlight an increasing legislative trend towards accommodating automated and self-executing contractual mechanisms.

This regulatory posture stands in marked contrast to the EU AI Act, which focuses on the *ex ante* regulation of AI system design and use based on risk classifications, particularly for high-risk applications.[52] While the AI Act places the burden of compliance primarily on developers and deployers of AI systems, the UNCITRAL Model Law maintains a facilitative approach, seeking only to remove legal uncertainty in the use of automated systems in contracting, irrespective of risk profiles or technical architecture. Compared to other international and European initiatives—most notably the European Law Institute's (ELI) Guiding Principles and Model Rules on Digital Assistants for Consumer Contracts—the Model Law refrains from detailing obligations related to transparency, fairness, or data governance.[53] Instead, it focuses narrowly on functional legal recognition, consistent with the enabling traditions of earlier UNCITRAL texts. National lawmakers in jurisdictions aligned with EU law, particularly those implementing or interpreting the AI Act and related digital regulations, may thus need to reconcile the procedural permissiveness of the Model Law with the more protective orientation of European consumer and AI law.

49 *UNCITRAL*, Guide to Enactment, 2025, pp. 25 et seq.

50 Regulation (EU) 2023/2854 of the European Parliament and of the Council of 13 December 2023 on harmonised rules on fair access to and use of data (Data Act), OJ L 2023/2854.

51 For a detailed analysis, see *F. Möslein*, Commentary on Art. 36, in: C. Czychowski, T. Lettl & B. Steinrötter (eds.), Data Act (C. H. Beck, 2025), pp. 701 et seq.; cf. also *S. Omlor*, Intelligente Verträge im Data Act, Juristenzeitung (JZ) 2025, 236.

52 See above, section II.1.

53 In more detail on the ELI Guiding Principles below, section II.3. For an overview of further AI-specific laws around the world (in particular those enacted in South Korea, Brazil, Canada, and the Vatican), see *Ph. Hacker, A. Engel, S. Hammer & Brent Mittelstadt*, Introduction to the Foundations and Regulation of Generative AI, forthcoming, in: ids. (eds.), The Oxford Handbook of the Foundation and Regulation of Generative AI (Oxford University Press, in preparation), preprint available at https://academic.oup.com/edited-volume/59908 [sub IV.1.b].

bb) Attribution and Legal Effects

Articles 7 and 8 address the attribution of legal acts carried out by automated systems, thereby establishing a connection between the output of an automated system and a person, excluding the system itself.[54] Article 7 introduces a dual mechanism: parties may allocate attribution by agreement, but in the absence of such agreement, the action of the automated system is attributed to the person using it.[55] Notably, attribution cannot be denied solely because the result was unexpected.[56] This mechanism reinforces legal certainty in systems that operate independently, including those using AI techniques with stochastic elements that generate "an output that may not be predicted in a particular case but within a range of probabilities".[57]

Article 8 provides an important safety valve: under defined conditions, reliance on an automated action may be disallowed if one party could not have reasonably expected the action and the other party knew or should have known of that. This legal construct establishes a connection to doctrines of mistake and misrepresentation, thereby providing protection against "black box" anomalies without compromising the overarching principle of enforceability.[58] It should be noted, however, that this particular provision has been designated as optional, as evidenced by its inclusion in square brackets. The accompanying footnote invites states that have enacted the Model Law to consider incorporating the provision into their domestic legislation if they wish to legislate on the issue of unexpected actions carried out by automated systems.[59]

From a comparative perspective, the approach of Article 8 only aligns to a limited extent with current legal systems that already accept machine-generated communications in contract law. In the context of German law,

54 See *UNCITRAL*, Guide to Enactment, 2025, p. 27 ("linking the output of an automated system to a person to the exclusion of the system itself").

55 Cf. *UNCITRAL*, Guide to Enactment, 2025, pp. 28 et seq. (differentiating between the "primary rule" in para. 1 and the "fallback rule" in para. 2).

56 Art. 7 para. 3 Model Law; see also *UNCITRAL*, Guide to Enactment, 2025, p. 29.

57 *UNCITRAL*, Guide to Enactment, 2025, p. 15.

58 See also *UNCITRAL*, Guide to Enactment, 2025, p. 31.

59 On the "black box" phenomenon in general see *C. Tschider*, Beyond the Black Box, Denv. L. Review 98 (2021), 683; more specifically with regard to AI contracting: *M. Ebers*, Artificial Intelligence, Contracting and Contract Law: An Introduction, in: M. Ebers, C. Poncibò & M. Zou (eds.), Contracting and Contract Law in the Age of Artificial Intelligence (Hart Publishing, 2022), p. 19, 25; *M. Herbosch*, Contracting with Artificial Intelligence, RabelsZ 87 (2023), 672, 677.

for instance, declarations of intent (Willenserklärungen) can be attributed through agency and organisational structures. However, this framework presupposes a determinable human or organisational origin of intent. Conversely, the attribution of autonomous declarations, such as those generated by AI systems, remains problematic under current law because of their unpredictable nature.[60] Consequently, conventional doctrines of agency or representation are insufficient to accommodate autonomous AI decisions.[61] In common law jurisdictions such as England and the United States, courts and legislators have increasingly acknowledged that automated systems can perform legally binding actions, particularly in the context of contract formation.[62] Although these systems are not formally recognized as legal agents, their outputs may be attributed to the party that deployed them under doctrines similar to agency, principal liability, or estoppel, provided the circumstances give rise to a reasonable inference of authority or reliance.[63] However, these systems lack consistent statutory recognition, making the Model Law a potential benchmark for legislative reform.

---

60 In more detail *L. Specht & S. Herold*, Roboter als Vertragspartner?, Zeitschrift für IT-Recht und Recht der Digitalisierung (MMR), 2018, 40, 42-44.

61 Current scholarly discourse explores possible doctrinal extensions, including the analogical application of rules on representation of minors, further development of the concept of 'Botenschaft' (bot agency), or the introduction of new legal constructs to address attribution in the context of autonomous systems: Cf. *G. Borges*, Rechtliche Rahmenbedingungen für autonome Systeme, Neue Juristische Wochenschrift (NJW) 2018, 977, 979; *F. Kainer & L. Förster*, Autonome Systeme im Kontext des Vertragsrechts, Zeitschrift für die gesamte Privatrechtswissenschaft (ZfPW) 2020, 275, 294 et seq. and 303; extensively *S. Herold*, Vertragsschlüsse unter Einbeziehung automatisiert und autonom agierender Systeme (Carl Heymans, 2020), in particular pp. 239 et seq.

62 Cf. in particular: *Quoine Pte Ltd* v *B2C2 Ltd* [2020] SGCA(I) 02 (affirming that that contracts can be formed automatically between trading algorithms); *R (Software Solutions Partners Ltd)* v *HM Customs & Excise* [2007] EWHC 971 (where the court upheld contracts formed via insurance software without human intervention, treating the system as the medium of offer and acceptance).

63 See, for instance, *I. Ayres & J. Balkin*, The Law of AI Is the Law of Risky Agents Without Intentions, University of Chicago Law Review Online (2024), available at https://lawreview.uchicago.edu/online-archive/law-ai-law-risky-agents-without-intentions (framing AI contracting under broad agency principles, even without formal legal personhood).

cc) Transparency and Disclosure

Article 9 of the Model Law preserves the application of any other laws that impose obligations to disclose information regarding the design, use, or effects of automated systems. Although this provision may seem limited in scope, it operates as a crucial compatibility clause: It enables national legal systems to retain sector-specific or mandatory rules, particularly those relating to consumer protection, data privacy, or AI ethics, without having to modify or override the Model Law.[64]

This minimalist approach enables the Model Law to function as a neutral procedural framework that coexists with national or supranational instruments imposing substantive safeguards. For example, in EU Member State jurisdictions implementing the Consumer Rights Directive, the Digital Services Act or also the AI Act, these more demanding instruments will continue to apply to consumer-facing automation and AI tools. States considering enactment will thus need to evaluate how the Model Law interacts with existing national contract law, data regulation, and AI governance regimes.

dd) General Principles

Finally, Articles 3 and 4 of the Model Law set out fundamental interpretative principles to guide the application of the Law in a rapidly changing technological landscape. The provision in Art. 3 emphasises the international origin of the Model Law and highlights the importance of promoting uniformity in its interpretation, alongside the observance of good faith. It also states that any issues not expressly resolved by the text should be settled in accordance with the general principles underlying the Model Law, most notably international harmonisation, technological neutrality and party autonomy.[65] These provisions align with the broader policy objective of insulating the legal framework from the risks of doctrinal inflexibility or obsolescence in the face of technological innovation.

---

64 See also *UNCITRAL*, Guide to Enactment, 2025, pp. 35 et seq. (highlighting that the rule is based on provisions from related UNCITRAL instruments, and that the Model Law does not affect or determine the consequences of not complying with these external disclosure requirements).

65 See *UNCITRAL*, Guide to Enactment, 2025, p. 19 and, more extensively on the fundamental principles themselves, pp. 8 et seq.

In a similar vein, Art. 4 codifies the principle of technological neutrality, explicitly stating that the Model Law does not require the use of automated systems or prescribe specific technological methods for contractual formation or fulfilment.[66] The provision reflects a conscious effort to avoid favouring specific technologies, such as blockchain, artificial intelligence, or smart contracts, in favour of functionally defined terms such as 'automated systems' and 'data messages'. By avoiding technological determinism, the Model Law ensures its applicability across diverse sectors and systems, thus preserving its relevance over time. At the same time, the emphasis on party autonomy empowers contracting parties to customise the application of automation in their transactions, including through bespoke attribution arrangements or also by contracting around default rules, provided these agreements do not contravene mandatory legal norms.

3. ELI DACC Model Rules

The Guiding Principles and Model Rules on Digital Assistants for Consumer Contracts (ELI DACC Model Rules), adopted by the European Law Institute in 2025 as a soft-law instrument,[67] in contrast, take a more normative approach, especially in B2C scenarios, imposing disclosure duties, addressing algorithmic bias, and contemplating the cognitive state of algorithmic agents. To provide a full picture, these provisions will only be outlined briefly here, in comparison with the UNCITRAL Model Rules.[68]

66 See already fn. 45 above; for a more detailed discussion of the principle in previous digital trade regulation cf. S. *Shadikhodjaev*, Technological Neutrality and Regulation of Digital Trade: How Far Can We Go?, European Journal of International Law 32 (2021), 1221.

67 The document is available at https://www.europeanlawinstitute.eu/projects-publications/publications/eli-guiding-principles-and-model-rules-on-digital-assistants-for-consumer-contracts/.

68 For a more comprehensive account, see *C. Busch, M. J. Sørensen, T. Rodriguez de las Heras & C. Twigg-Flesner*, Towards the Next Generation of Consumer Law: the ELI Guiding Principles and Model Rules on Digital Assistants for Consumer Contracts, Journal of European Consumer and Market Law (EuCML) 2025, 89.

a) Consumer-focused, Risk-based Approach

The ELI DACC Model Rules aim at providing a framework for the use of algorithmic systems, particularly digital assistants, in consumer contracting. Unlike the UNCITRAL Model Law with its broad scope covering commercial transactions and its emphasis of the legal recognition of actions by automated systems, these rules target business-to-consumer (B2C) relations and integrate consumer protection considerations into the legal and technical aspects of digital assistants.[69]

Another defining feature of the ELI DACC Model Rules is their approach to risk allocation.[70] The deployment of digital assistants, whether by consumers or businesses, generally places operational risk on the party deploying them. However, in circumstances where consumers engage with digital assistants in the context of contractual relations, the Model Rules limit attribution in instances where the digital assistant exhibits behaviour that deviates from the expectations of the consumer.[71] Moreover, Chapter 2 sets out detailed design requirements aimed at enhancing consumer protection by assigning legal responsibility to the digital assistant supplier, while providing developers with clear guidance on functionalities such as parameter setting, consent mechanisms and system deactivation.[72] In contrast, the UNCITRAL Model Law does not prescribe how automated systems should be designed or operated, and remains technologically neutral.[73]

b) Dual Contractual Focus: Supply and Use

The ELI DACC Model Rules govern two distinct yet interconnected contractual relationships: the contract for supplying a digital assistant to the consumer and the contracts concluded through its use.[74] The former rela-

69 On this scope and purpose, see Art. 1 ELI DACC Model Rules.

70 Similar: ELI DACC Model Rules, p. 9.

71 In more detail below at II.3.c).

72 Similar *C. Busch, M. J. Sørensen, T. Rodriguez de las Heras & C. Twigg-Flesner*, Towards the Next Generation of Consumer Law: the ELI Guiding Principles and Model Rules on Digital Assistants for Consumer Contracts, Journal of European Consumer and Market Law (EuCML) 2025, 89, 91 (design requirements „balance the benefit of automation with the need to give some control to the consumer to manage the risk that contract automation invariably creates").

73 See above, at II.2.c)dd).

74 In this sense ELI DACC Model Rules, p. 10: "The use of digital assistants will usually involve two separate contracts: first, a contract for the supply of a digital assistant

tionship is covered by provisions relating to information obligations, supplier liability and the disclosure of conflicts of interest (Chapter 2), while the latter covers issues relating to attribution, legal effect and enforceability (Chapter 3). Unlike the UNCITRAL Model Law, which is limited to the operation of automated systems in the formation and performance of contracts, the ELI DACC Model Rules therefore have a dual focus. Conversely, the UNCITRAL Model Law does not address the contractual or regulatory status of such systems, nor their supply or integration into consumer goods.

c) Attribution and Legal Effects

The attribution of legal acts performed by digital assistants constitutes a central issue (also) in the ELI DACC Model Rules. In accordance with Art. 22 para. 2, the attribution to the consumer is subject to a reasonableness standard: Actions of the digital assistant that deviate significantly from what the consumer could reasonably expect, due to system errors, adaptive behaviour or external failures, are not legally binding on the consumer.[75] In such cases, the onus may shift to the supplier, who may be held accountable for any losses incurred by third parties.[76] In contrast, the UNCITRAL Model Law employs a more straightforward attribution model, under which actions of automated systems are generally attributed to the user, subject only to a limited provision concerning 'unexpected outcomes'.[77] Moreover, the ELI DACC Rules impose limitations on the utilisation of contractual disclaimers, stipulating that clauses which seek to exclude liability shall be deemed ineffective unless the digital assistant's behaviour could be deemed so unforeseeable as to constitute a substantial malfunction (cf. Art. 22 para. 4). This is also in contrast to the more permissive approach to liability exclusions under the UNCITRAL framework.[78]

[...]; secondly, a contract concluded between a consumer and a business through the consumer's use of a digital assistant and frequently also by the business [...]. In the ELI DACC Model Rules, these two contracts are dealt with in two separate chapters".

75 In more detail on this standard, and with illustrations: ELI DACC Model Rules, p. 57.

76 See also *C. Busch, M. J. Sørensen, T. Rodriguez de las Heras & C. Twigg-Flesner*, Towards the Next Generation of Consumer Law: the ELI Guiding Principles and Model Rules on Digital Assistants for Consumer Contracts, Journal of European Consumer and Market Law (EuCML) 2025, 89, 91.

77 See above, at II.2.c)bb).

78 See again above, at II.2.c)dd).

d) Regulatory Alignment

The ELI DACC Model Rules are intended to supplement existing frameworks for consumer and contract law.[79] Designed to be compatible with broader digital regulation, including the General Data Protection Regulation (GDPR), the AI Act and the Data Act, they also take into account related instruments such as the Digital Services Act and the Digital Markets Act. This integrative approach enables the ELI DACC Model Rules to function within a layered regulatory environment, thereby strengthening consumer protection in the context of automated contracting.[80] In contrast, the UNCITRAL Model Law deliberately avoids addressing specific regulatory domains such as data protection, cybersecurity and algorithmic accountability. Its main aim is to ensure the legal recognition of automated contracting processes across jurisdictions without addressing the vulnerabilities particular to consumer transactions or the normative implications of system design.

III. The Blind Spot: Rethinking Default Rules

In this emerging legal framework for AI contracting, regulatory attention has been primarily focused on the procedural mechanics of AI-driven contract formation, notably by addressing questions of legal capacity, attribution, and transparency. In contrast, however, no consideration has been given to the substantive effects of AI contracting on the default rule architecture that underpins conventional contract law. It has been overlooked that the increasing use of AI systems in contracting undermines the traditional role and function of default rules. This blind spot is significant. As AI systems become increasingly sophisticated, with capabilities such as automated drafting, dynamic negotiation, and predictive analytics, there is an increasing risk that they may displace the regulatory function and behavioural anchoring traditionally fulfilled by default rules.[81] The regulatory challenge extends beyond a mere adjustment of doctrinal principles;

79 Similar at the very beginning of its preliminary observations: ELI DACC Model Rules, p. 9.

80 Cf. ELI DACC Model Rules, p. 10 (underlining "the objective of ensuring high level of consumer protection in respect of digital assistants").

81 For a broader discussion on the impact of digitalisation on default rules see, however, *F. Möslein*, Digitizing Defaults: Methods and Mechanisms of Generating Default

rather, it pertains to the legal design and the institutional function of contemporary contract law.

1. The Transition from Gap-Filling to Code-Filling

At their core, default rules operate as the legal infrastructure of private autonomy. They fill contractual gaps, reduce transaction costs, and nudge parties toward socially desirable outcomes without restricting freedom of contract.[82] Their design has long oscillated between mimicking the hypothetical will of the parties and embedding heteronomous regulatory content.[83] However, AI contracting threatens to erode both of these rationales.

On the one hand, AI systems—especially those leveraging large language models and probabilistic inference—can generate highly tailored contractual terms that anticipate contingencies with unprecedented granularity. Optimistic projections suggest that such systems might produce more complete contracts, rendering default rules redundant as gap-fillers.[84] While

Rules in the Digital Age, in: B. Häcker & J. Ungerer (eds.), Default Rules in Private Law (Oxford University Press, 2025), 53.

82 For broader discussions see, for instance, *I. Ayres & R. Gertner*, Filling Gaps in Incomplete Contracts: An Economic Theory of Default Rules, Yale Law Journal 99 (1989) 87; *C.J. Goetz & R.E. Scott*, The Limits of Expanded Choice: An Analysis of the Interactions Between Express and Implied Contract Terms, California Law Review 73 (1985), 261.

83 In more detail: *F. Möslein*, Dispositives Recht (Mohr Siebeck, 2011), p. 120-150, 281; see also *F. Möslein*, Governance by Default: Innovation und Koordination durch dispositives Recht, in: S. Grundmann, B. Haar & H. Merkt (eds.), Festschrift für Klaus J. Hopt (de Gruyter, 2010), p. 2861. In US literature, it is often argued that rule-makers need to orientate themselves towards the hypothetical intentions of private parties, simply because the latter will otherwise deviate from the default rules in question; see, for instance, *R. E. Scott*, Rethinking the Default Rule Project, Virginia Journal 6 (2003) 84, 94 („Choosing a default rule on the basis of some normative conception of fairness would be wrong, in the sense that it would not increase the amount of fair contracts in the world, but it would increase the amount of contracting costs in the world, as parties contracted out of the codes").

84 In this sense *H. Thompson*, AI and the law, Working Paper 2024, available at https://papers.ssrn.com/sol3/papers.cfm?abstract_id=5045069 (arguing that generative AI will help attorneys write more complete contracts, weakening the demand for courts). From the opposite perspective *D. Hadfield-Menell & G. Hadfield*, Incomplete Contracting and AI Alignment, Working Paper 2018, available at https://papers.ssrn.com/sol3/papers.cfm?abstract_id=3165793 (proposing to use the framework of incomplete contracting as a lens for understanding and addressing the AI alignment problem, particularly by teaching AI systems to leverage external institutions, cultural

such views may verge on legal science fiction, they underscore the decreasing reliance on traditional default mechanisms when AI can produce bespoke clauses at scale and at minimal cost. Even if such perfection remains elusive, the predictive and generative capacities of AI systems challenge the economic justification for default rules as transaction cost reducers.[85] When drafting, negotiation, and review can be performed by machine agents in real time and at near-zero marginal cost, the traditional barriers to contracting around defaults all but disappear.

On the other hand, the utilisation of AI systems has the potential to disrupt the information asymmetries that underpin numerous regulatory defaults. The operation of so-called penalty default rules is based on the incentivisation of the disclosure of information that would otherwise be private.[86] However, should AI systems be capable of extracting, inferring, or simulating such information autonomously, drawing upon extensive repositories of both structured and unstructured data, the informational basis for these defaults would be compromised.[87] The prevailing regulatory structure may be rendered obsolete by the informational and computational capacities of contractual parties utilising AI.

2. De-Stickying of Defaults Rules: Eroding the Nudging Effect

A further dimension of this blind spot relates to the behavioural stickiness of default rules. Traditionally, defaults derive normative force from behavioural phenomena such as the status quo bias, endowment effects,

---

norms, and implied terms in the way humans do when contracts are necessarily under-specified).

85 More extensively, *F. Möslein*, The Regulation of Automated Contracting, in: Y. Atamer & A. Hellgardt (eds.), Oxford Handbook of Regulatory Contract Law (Oxford University Press, in preparation for 2025).

86 In the law and economics literature, the term 'penalty default rules' is often being used, see *I. Ayres & R. Gertner*, Filling Gaps in Incomplete Contracts: An Economic Theory of Default Rules, Yale Law Journal 99 (1989) 87, at 91; more extensively: *I. Ayres & R. Gertner* , Strategic Contractual Inefficiency and the Optimal Choice of Legal Rules, Yale Law Journal 101 (1992) 729; *I. Ayres & E. Talley*, Solomonic Bargaining: Dividing a Legal Entitlement to Facilitate Cosean Trade, Yale Law Journal 104 (1995) 1027.

87 *F. Möslein*, Digitizing Defaults: Methods and Mechanisms of Generating Default Rules in the Digital Age, in: B. Häcker & J. Ungerer (eds.), Default Rules in Private Law (Oxford University Press, 2025), 53, 63-65.

and bounded rationality.[88] These psychological factors explain why default rules often 'stick', even when deviation would be rational from an economic perspective.[89] They operate as a subtle form of libertarian paternalism, structuring choice architectures in a way that guides parties without coercing them.[90]

AI contracting disrupts this architecture. Machine agents are not susceptible to behavioural biases in the same way as humans. They do not internalise defaults through social learning, nor do they exhibit status quo adherence or satisficing tendencies.[91] Instead, AI systems are programmed — or learn — to optimise according to objective functions specified by their developers or users. When such agents engage in contract drafting or negotiation, they are likely to bypass legal default rules altogether, selecting clauses based on statistical prevalence, inferred utility or prescriptive frameworks embedded in corporate playbooks. This means that the default rules lose their stickiness, not because they are formally repealed, but because they are systematically circumvented. More fundamentally, as AI systems can easily compare and implement alternative terms, the implicit cost of contracting around default rules diminishes significantly.[92] The traditional frictions that gave default rules their traction, i.e. informational deficits, drafting complexity, and negotiation inertia, are neutralised in AI contracting environments. The result is a significant reduction in the effectiveness of default rules as nudging instruments.

88 Extensively *F. Möslein*, Dispositives Recht (Mohr Siebeck, 2011), pp. 316 et seq.

89 *O. Ben-Shahar & J. Pottow*, On the Stickiness of Default Rules, Florida State University Law Review 33 (2006), 651.

90 Similar: *P. Schlag*, Nudge, Choice Architecture, and Libertarian Paternalism, Michigan Law Review 108 (2010) 913, 915 (describing default rules as "the mother of all nudges"); more generally on the concept itself: *R.H. Thaler, C.R. Sunstein & J.P. Balz*, Choice Architecture, in E. Shafir (Ed.), The Behavioral Foundations of Public Policy (Princeton University Press, 2012), 428.

91 *A. Gulati, M. Angel Lozano, B. Lepri & N. Oliver*, Bringing Irrationality into Automated System Design, Working Paper 2022, available at https://arxiv.org/abs/2210.01122 (emphasizing that AI systems remain bias-free by default, and human-like biases only appear if intentionally designed in).

92 Similar *H. Thompson*, AI and the law, Working Paper 2024, available at https://papers.ssrn.com/sol3/papers.cfm?abstract_id=5045069, pp. 8-10.

3. From Benchmarks to Black Boxes: Eroding the Yardstick Function of Default Rules

Default rules also serve as benchmarks for fairness and reasonableness, particularly in judicial contexts: They act as yardsticks against which contractual practices are assessed, including in areas such as standard terms regulation, consumer protection, and judicial interpretation of ambiguous clauses.[93] For example, default rules play an important role in the European Court of Justice's case law on general terms and conditions: "When assessing whether a contract term 'causes a significant imbalance in the parties' rights and obligations, to the detriment of the consumer, national courts have to carry out, in the first place, a comparison of the relevant contract term with any rules of national law which would apply in the absence of the contract term".[94] Yet this interpretive function is increasingly undermined when contracts are generated and executed by opaque AI systems. If neither party can fully explain how a given clause was selected due to the 'black box' phenomenon (i.e. because it was produced by a self-learning model based on latent statistical correlations),[95] courts may find it difficult to apply traditional fairness, equity or expectation doctrines.[96]

Moreover, the possibility of AI-generated 'majoritarian' clauses — drafting patterns that emerge from large-scale data analysis rather than deliberate legal decision-making — raises normative concerns[97] While such clauses may reflect common practices, they may also perpetuate market biases or exploitative norms.[98] There is a risk that AI will mimic rather than improve contractual practice, thereby reinforcing existing inequalities or informational asymmetries under the guise of optimisation. In such a

93 *F. Möslein*, Dispositives Recht (Mohr Siebeck, 2011), pp. 318 et seq.

94 CJEU, C-415/11 *Aziz* ECLI:EU:C:2013:164, para 68; see also C-226/12 *Constructora Principado* ECLI:EU:C:2014:10 , para 21; C-421/14 *Banco Primus* ECLI:EU:C:2017:60, para 59; C-186/16 *Andriciuc* ECLI:EU:C:2017:703, para 59; C-229/19 and C-289/19 *Dexia* ECLI:EU:C:2021:68 , para 48.

95 On that phenomenon, see already above at n. 58.

96 Similar *F. Möslein*, Digitizing Defaults: Methods and Mechanisms of Generating Default Rules in the Digital Age, in: B. Häcker & J. Ungerer (eds.), Default Rules in Private Law (Oxford University Press, 2025), 53, 71 et seq.

97 For a critical examination of traditional majoritarian theory in contract law, see *M. Grochowski*, The Majoritarian Concept of Default Rules: Towards a Shift in Paradigms?, Studies in Private Law / Studia Prawa Prywatnego 15 (2020), 63.

98 Similar concerns have already been raised with regard to conventional (majoritarian) default rules, cf. *R. Korobkin*, The Status Quo Bias and Contract Default Rules, Cornell Law Review 83 (1998), 608.

world, the distinction between market mimicry and regulatory defaults becomes both more important and more difficult to maintain.

If AI displaces the conventional justificatory functions of default rules, then the need for deliberate legal articulation of model rules becomes more pressing. Lawmakers and legal institutions may need to recalibrate default rules not only in terms of substance, but also in terms of their interface with technological systems. This could include embedding default rule logic into legal APIs, structuring default rules as modular clauses available to contracting agents, or establishing formal repositories of legally validated clause sets. In this sense, default rules may need to be "digitally legible" to remain functionally relevant.

IV. Conclusion: Towards AI-Responsive Default Rules

The growing reliance on AI systems for contract formation, performance and interpretation signals a pivotal moment for the future of contract law, particularly with regard to default rules. The current rulemaking in this field reveals a legal blind spot: a growing mismatch between the procedural focus of AI contracting regulation and the substantive erosion of the default infrastructure of contract law. If this blind spot is not addressed, it could undermine one of the most effective tools of private law: its ability to balance autonomy and regulation through defaults.

The way forward requires a dual response.[99] First, lawmakers should reconsider the normative role of default rules in contractual environments characterised by high automation and low transaction costs. This may include a renewed emphasis on regulatory defaults, especially in asymmetrical contexts such as consumer contracting or digital platform governance. Second, legal institutions must begin to translate default rules into machine-readable formats, enabling their integration into the systems that now draft and perform contracts. Such translation may involve not only technical standardisation, but also normative decisions about which values and assumptions ought to guide automated contracting.

Ultimately, AI contracting requires legal scholarship and rule-making to address the limitations of traditional legal instruments in digital environ-

99 For similar considerations, but with regard also to additional phenomena of digitalisation, cf. *F. Möslein*, Digitizing Defaults: Methods and Mechanisms of Generating Default Rules in the Digital Age, in: B. Häcker & J. Ungerer (eds.), Default Rules in Private Law (Oxford University Press, forthcoming in 2025), 53, 72-80.

ments. The default rules of contract law — long the quiet workhorses of private autonomy — must be reimagined if they are to remain relevant in the age of artificial intelligence.

Attribution of Pre-contractual Information and Knowledge: the ELI Model Rules on Digital Assistants for Consumer Contracts and beyond

Christian Twigg-Flesner[*]

I. Introduction

The potential of using artificial intelligence (AI) systems to automate some or all of the stages of a typical contracting lifecycle has been much debated, both in scholarly literature[1] and in the development of model rules and principles.[2] In these discussions, much attention has been paid to how one should categorise an AI system used for contract automation, and to what extent the actions of an AI system should be attributed to the person who has used it to automated their contracting activities. A consensus has emerged that such systems should be treated as a "tool" used for contracting, rather than as something distinct from the person using it, and that the

* Professor of Contract and Consumer Law, University of Warwick, United Kingdom; Co-reporter for the ELI *Guiding Principles and Model Rules on Digital Assistants for Consumer Contracts.*

1 See e.g., Tom Allen and Robin Widdison, "Can computers make contracts?" (1996) 9 *Harvard Journal of Law & Technology* 26; Lauren Heny Scholz, "Algorithmic Contracts" (2017) 20 *Stanford Technology Law Review* 128; Samir Chopra and Laurence White, "Artificial Agents and the Contracting Problem: A solution via an agency analysis" (2009) *University of Illinois Journal of Law, Technology and Policy* 363; Friedemann Kainer and Lydia Förster, "Autonome Systeme im Kontext des Vertragsrechts" (2020) 6 *Zeitschrift für die gesamte Privatrechtswissenschaft* 275; or Christian Twigg-Flesner, "Consumers, digital delegates, contract formation and consumer law", in: Larry Di-Matteo, Cristina Poncibò, and Geraint Howells (eds.), *The Cambridge Handbook of AI and Consumer Law : Comparative Perspectives* (Cambridge University Press, 2024).

2 Three, in particular: the UNCITRAL *Model Law on Automated Contracting* (2024), the *Principles of AI in Contracting* drafted by Christiane Wendehorst, the latest version of which, Version 3.0, was published in Vincent Sagaert and Joeri Vananroye (eds.), *Privaatrecht plenis coloribus. Liber Amicorum Mathis Storme* (Mechelen: Kluwer, 2024); and, most recently, the ELI *Guiding Principles and Model Rules on Algorithmic Contracting for Consumer Contracts* (May 2025).

actions of such a system should be attributed to that person, i.e., that person bears the legal consequences of the system's actions.[3]

A related, but distinct, question concerns whether, and to what extent, any information or "knowledge" received by an AI system should be attributed to the person using it for its contracting activities. This might be significant insofar as the knowledge of a contracting person might be relevant to the application of some doctrines of contract law, as well as because the law frequently imposes an obligation on one (prospective) contracting party to disclose information, or to give information, to the other party. This is particularly common in the case of consumer contracts, where extensive pre-contractual information duties are imposed on traders, with the objective of ensuring that the informational disadvantage of consumers is reduced. The effectiveness of these pre-contractual information duties has been much debated,[4] particularly in light of behavioural economics findings,[5] but legal duties to provide information before a consumer concludes a contract remain a firm part of consumer law.[6]

Once AI systems are deployed by either or both parties to a contract, both the distribution of contract-relevant knowledge and compliance with specific disclosure and pre-contractual information obligations may need to be addressed where the AI system might have received the relevant information from the other party, and, depending on its capabilities, where the AI system might have obtained relevant information from other sources such as external databases or internet searches as part of its decision-making processes. Building on the view that AI systems are generally treated as tools and the legal effects of its actions attributed to the relevant contracting

3 See Article 7(2) UNICTRAL Model Law; Article 5(2) of the Principles on AI Contracting, and Article 22(1) of the ELI Model Rules. See also Eliza Mik, "Much ado about artificial intelligence: or the automation of contract formation" (2022) 30 *International Journal of Law and Information Technology,* 484.

4 Michael J Trebilcock and S Elliot, "The Scope and Limits of Legal Paternalism", in: Peter Benson (ed.), *The Theory of Contract Law* (Cambridge: Cambridge University Press, 2001); Geraint Howells, "The Potential and Limits of Consumer Empowerment by Information" (2005) *Journal of Law and Society,* 349; Omri Ben-Shahar and Carl E Schneider, *More than you wanted to know – the failure of mandated disclosure* (Princeton, 2014).

5 E.g., Anne-Lise Sibony and Genevieve Helleringer, "EU Consumer Protection and Behavioural Sciences: Revolution or Reform?", in: Alessandro Alemanno and Anne-Lise Sibony, *Nudge and the Law* (Bloomsbury, 2015).

6 Cf. Geraint Howells, Christian Twigg-Flesner and Thomas Wilhelmsson, *Rethinking EU Consumer Law* (Routledge, 2017), ch.3.

party, one might further ask whether any information obtained by an AI system should also be attributed to the relevant contracting party. If this is given a positive answer, then a related question is whether any legal duties to provide information[7] can be satisfied by making the relevant information available to the AI system. It must immediately be noted that there cannot be a simple brightline answer to these questions; rather, much will depend on the technological capabilities of the particular AI system that has been deployed by a contracting party.

The purpose of this contribution is to unpack these questions and to examine how the European Law Institute tackled this question in its *Guiding Principles and Model Rules on Digital Assistants for Consumer Contracts* (DACC). The DACC are the first set of model rules that specifically focus on contract automation in a consumer context. As legal information duties are particularly prevalent in consumer law, focusing on the DACC is instructive, although there will also be a comparison with the other two key texts, UNCITRAL's *Model Law on Automated Contracts* (MLAC) and the *Principles for AI in Contracting* (PAIC).

II. Knowledge, Information, and AI systems

Before analysing the approach taken in the ELI DACC, it is necessary to clarify why the question of attribution of knowledge and information is important. From a legal perspective, there are two aspects for which this question is significant. First, there are some rules of any Contract Law system which are framed in a way that considers the mental state of one of the contracting parties, i.e., it assumes a human with distinctly human abilities. It is generally accepted, although not necessarily inevitable,[8] that automated transactions, whether by means of AI systems or other digital technologies, are still treated as legal contracts within the scope of Contract Law. This has the advantage that there is no doubt over the legal effectiveness of such transactions as contracts and that there is sufficient legal certainty through the application of familiar rules of Contract Law. That said, there will be

7 Such as those in EU consumer law under Article 6 of the Consumer Rights Directive (2011/83/EU).

8 Cf. Roger Brownsword, "Teaching the law of contract in a world of new transactional technologies", in: Warren Swain and David Campbell, *Reimagining Contract Law Pedagogy* (Routledge, 2019), esp. pp. 115-8.

some rules which are less obviously applicable to automatically concluded contracts, notwithstanding the fact that such contracts are legally effective. Once a rule of Contract Law requires consideration of what a contracting party intended, what it might have known or at least have been aware of, whether it had notice of something or how something was perceived by that party, the continued application of such rules in circumstances when an AI system is used will require close examination. After all, these are all rules that have evolved from, and are designed for, contracting with humans-in-the-loop. Once a human contracting party has been taken out of that loop, it is necessary to ask whether these rules are still fit for purpose.[9] If, as is usually the case, the actions of an AI system are attributed to the person whose actions have been taken over by the AI system, then the Contract Law rules in issue would focus on the mental state of that person. As that person was not involved in the relevant decision, this would entail working out whether any of the actions of the AI system or any data it has could be said to be part of the contracting party's mental state. Any such attempt will invariably entail a degree of artificiality in determining what the contracting party using an AI system did, or should have, known.[10]

The second aspect is compliance with information duties. This is of particular relevance to consumer contract law, where the mandatory provision of detailed pre-contractual information is a common tool to reduce the informational disadvantage of consumers.[11] This requires that a business provides specific items of information to a consumer before a contract is made, and, sometimes, also during the performance of a contract. In some instance, such information has to be made available, in others, it must be given to the designated recipient, i.e., the consumer.[12] Where information has to be made available, or provided, it might be displayed on a website, which would usually suffice if a consumer is browsing the website themselves in order to select the product(s) they wish to purchase. Would this change if the consumer was replaced by an AI system? One might suggest that there would be no change because the purpose for providing information in this way is to ensure that a consumer can make

9 Roger Brownsword, "Law Disrupted, Law Re-Imagined, Law Re-Invented" (2019) *Technology and Regulation* 10, pp. 11,12.

10 Compare the contorted reasoning of the majority of the Singapore Court of Appeal, in: *Quoine Pte Ltd v B2C2 Ltd* [2020] SGCA(I) 2 in considering the application of the doctrine of unilateral mistake in the case of contracting by deterministic algorithms.

11 See e.g, Article 6 of the Consumer Rights Directive (2011/83/EU).

12 E.g., Article 7(1) of the Consumer Rights Directive (2011/83/EU).

a fully-informed decision. If the AI system is making that decision instead and is technically capable of reading this information, then it should be treated as if the information was available to the consumer.

However, what if the law requires that information is given to a consumer, i.e., there has to be an active step to ensure that a consumer has got the relevant information[13] (even if there is no obligation on a consumer to then read this information)? Where such information is provided by email and the AI system has provided the consumer's email to the business, the business would comply in its usual way. However, what if the AI system has provided an email address that is linked to the system itself? In that situation, it would be more difficult to argue that the information has been given to the *consumer*, even if it has been given to the AI system. If this issue were to come before a court, there is a reasonable prospect that a court could interpret any such requirement in light of the fact that the consumer had chosen to replace their role in the decision leading up to a contract with the AI system. A plausible approach might be to consider whether the business has taken the steps it would ordinarily take to give the information to a consumer. If so, the business should be treated as having complied with its obligations. This would certainly be a pragmatic approach where it is not obvious to the business that the consumer had been substituted with an AI system. However, if the business knows it is interacting with an AI system instead of a human consumer, it is less obvious that providing information to the AI system would satisfy a legal obligation to provide this to a consumer. A solution might depend on the purpose for which the information is required. If it is simply a repetition of pre-contractual information to confirm this in more durable form, providing it to the AI system should be regarded as sufficient. But if it is required for a consumer to make a decision during the performance of the contract,[14] it might be more difficult to say that providing it to the AI system is sufficient, unless it is clear that the AI system is technically capable of forwarding the relevant information to the consumer.

---

13 Cf. C-49/11 *Content Services Ltd v Bundesarbeitskammer* ECLI:EU:C:2012:419.

14 E.g., the obligation under s. 258 of the United Kingdom's Digital Markets, Competition and Consumers Act 2024, requiring that a consumer is given a reminder notice before a subscription contract renews automatically. Cf. Christoph Busch and Christian Twigg-Flesner, "A roadmap for regulating subscriptions in the Digital Fairness Act" (2024) 13 *Journal of European Consumer and Markets Law (EuCML)*, 234.

What the foregoing shows, therefore, is that the continued application of contract law to transactions concluded through the use of AI systems raises questions beyond the legal effectiveness and validity of such transactions (as contracts) and the attribution of an AI system's actions to the person who deployed it to automate the conclusion of the contract. Once it becomes necessary to consider whether a party had actual or constructive knowledge of elements of the transaction, or whether that party has received required information, things get more complicated. At this point, the question of whether contract law as a whole remains fit for purpose in an age of AI-mediated contracting becomes more stark, and a more open-minded attitude towards finding new solutions is needed.[15]

In very simple terms, knowledge is based on information about particular facts and an understanding of the meaning and implications of that information. Facts alone do not constitute knowledge, although access to facts is a precondition to knowledge.[16] Knowledge is also connected to „truth", i.e., the verifiability of the fact – otherwise, something is no more than a supposition, belief or opinion.[17] It is awareness of the truth of a particular claim that makes something part of someone's knowledge. It is important to recall that knowledge is not merely there for its own sake; humans rely on knowledge for all sorts of reasons including the ability to tackle novel and unfamiliar circumstances (as we are often doing in the context of digitalisation). For contracting, knowledge is important to understand what has been agreed and which obligations have been assumed by either party, and thus to identify the financial and other implications of that commitment.

Therefore, asking whether and when to attribute *knowledge*, rather than mere information (i.e., facts) might be starting in the wrong place, bearing in mind the technical capabilities of an AI system. Whilst it might be possible to say that an AI system has information in that is has been provided with lots of facts (i.e., data), that does not entail knowledge because AI cannot verify the truth of such information nor understand its implications, or meaning. Many AI systems are based on deep-learning algorithms,

---

15 Cf. Christian Twigg-Flesner and Geraint Howells, "Adapting consumer law to new technologies", in: Roger Brownsword and Larry Di Matteo (eds.) *The Cambridge Handbook of the Governance of Technology: Discontent, Disconnect and Disruption* (Cambridge University Press, 2026).

16 Jennifer Nagel, *Knowledge* (Oxford University Press, 2014), pp. 2, 3.

17 *Ibid*, p. 9.

which rely on very large amounts of data as part of its training process. In simple terms, data, such as words or images, is broken down and converted into tokens.[18] Each token has a large number of weights attached to it which are adjusted as more data is processed by the algorithm during its training phase. Because of this, an AI system does not see language in the way humans do; instead, each word, or word fragment, is converted into a token, connected through large numbers of vectors and weights. Its responses to particular prompts involve calculations as to the statistical probability that one token will be followed by another one, based on the many weights that were attached and modified during the training phase.[19] This allows an AI system to generate responses based on its training data and the way each token has been connected to other tokens. However, it is well-known that the most probable output based on statistical calculations does not mean that the output will be correct, and AI systems cannot verify the correctness of their outputs. Whilst an AI system might develop a form of meaning based on how different tokens connect to one another, this seems to be different from meaning in the human context.[20] This limitation would suggest that AI systems do not have *knowledge* at all, nor the capacity to develop it.[21] Furthermore, notwithstanding the arrival of so-called "reasoning models", AI systems do not reason in the way that humans do, because human reasoning and critical thinking, essential to the acquisition of knowledge,[22] require more than information and statistical connections between tokens.[23] The absence of full reasoning skills and the ability to use knowledge in a way that leads to new and creative inferences

18 For a practical illustration of how words are converted into tokens, see OpenAI, "Tokenizer", available at https://platform.openai.com/tokenizer [accessed 20 June 2025]. For example, the present authors name is broken down into 6 tokens.

19 Cf. Arvind Narayanan and Sayash Kapoor, *AI Snake Oil* (Princeton University Press, 2024), pp. 129-132.

20 For an interesting discussion, see Steven T. Piantadosi and Felix Hill, "Meaning without reference in large language models" (2022) arXiv:2208.02957v2.

21 See e.g., Melanie Mitchell, *Artificial Intelligence - A guide for thinking humans* (Penguin, 2019), ch.15.

22 See e.g. Michael Gerlich, "AI Tools in Society: Impacts on Cognitive Offloading and the Future of Critical Thinking" (2025) 15 *Societies*; https:// doi.org/10.3390/soc15010006.

23 For a related discussion, see Kyle Mahowald, Anna A. Ivanova, Idan A. Blank, Nancy Kanwisher, Joshua B. Tenenbaum and Evelina Fedorenko, "Dissociating language and thought in Large Language Models" (2024), https://arxiv.org/abs/2301.06627v3.

to unfamiliar situations is a further limitation.[24] On this basis, one cannot say that AI systems have knowledge in a way that might be even comparable to humans.

This would mean that one cannot attribute knowledge from an AI system to the relevant contracting party because the AI system does not have any *knowledge*. At best, one can consider whether the data (or facts or information) received by an AI system might be something that could be attributed to a contracting party, but that would raise tricky questions about how this would affect the application of existing rules of contract law, particularly those that require that a contracting party has knowledge and therefore the information that is a constituent of that knowledge).

The remainder of this contribution will focus on how the challenge of attributing information and "knowledge" has been tackled in the various model rules on automated contracting already available, focusing primarily on the ELI DACC.

III. The ELI DACC and information duties

It will by now be clear that there is no easy answer to dealing with the attribution of knowledge and information. In the remainder of this paper, the focus will be on how the various model rules developed recently seek to address this question, if at all. The first set of model rules deals specifically with consumer contracts, where information provision is frequently mandated in consumer law.

In May 2025, the European Law Institute (ELI) published the *Guiding Principles and Model Rules on Digital Assistants for Consumer Contracts* (DACC). The DACC are the first consumer-focused set of model rules on contract automation, particularly, but not exclusively, through the use of systems based on AI technologies. A brief overview of the scope and structure of the DACC is given here, followed by a closer look at the provisions directly relevant to the attribution of information. The DACC focus

24 Cf the discussion in a paper on AI thinking that has caught the eyes of many recently: Parshin Shojaee, Iman Mirzadeh, Keivan Alizadeh, Maxwell Horton, Samy Bengio, and Mehrdad Farajtabar, "The Illusion of Thinking: Understanding the Strengths and Limitations of Reasoning Models via the Lens of Problem Complexity" (2025), available at https://ml-site.cdn-apple.com/papers/the-illusion-of-thinking.pdf [accessed 20 June 2025].

on what has been termed "digital assistants", defined as "an application utilising algorithmic systems that, based on pre-set parameters, user inputs and data obtained from a range of sources, is designed to take actions to accomplish a set of pre-defined objectives for contractual relations".[25] In effect, digital assistants are conceived as a particular form of AI Agent. The term "agent" was deliberately not chosen for the DACC to avoid conflating AI agents with agents in the legal sense. Whilst it might be possible to draw some inspiration from principles of agency law in developing model rules on digital assistants,[26] there are also differences between the situations commonly addressed by the law of agency and any form of AI agent,[27] making any analogies with agency law of limited value.

A digital assistant is a type of application that might be provided on a standalone basis (i.e., as an app downloaded onto a smartphone), as an integrated feature of a smart product, or integrated on an online platform or e-commerce website. A digital assistant would be supplied to a consumer under one contract (a contract for the supply of a digital assistant, addressed by chapter 3 of the DACC) and be used by the consumer for contractual relations with businesses (algorithmic contracts, addressed by chapter 4 DACC).

The DACC are based on 8 guiding principles (GPs) and contain 25 Articles in total, divided into 5 chapters. Chapter 1 sets out the scope and key definitions,[28] as well as the right to use digital assistants.[29] The most significant novelty of the DACC is in chapter 2, which sets out several design requirements which must be met by digital assistants to be supplied to consumers. These cover the ability to set parameters both before and during deployment;[30] the mechanism for preventing the conclusion of a contract by allowing a consumer either to require that they must confirm that an order can be placed by a digital assistant,[31] or to object to the

25 Article 2(2) DACC.

26 See Lauren Heny Scholz, "Algorithmic Contracts" (2017) 20 *Stanford Technology Law Review* 128.

27 Noam Kolt, "Governing AI Agents" (2026) 101 *Notre Dame Law Review* 000 (forthcoming).

28 Articles 1 and 2 DACC.

29 Article 3 DACC.

30 Article 5 DACC.

31 Article 6(2)(a) DACC.

placing of an order before this happens; during a limited period of time;[32] and the temporary or permanent deactivation of a digital assistant.[33] Other design requirements address the need to disclose that a digital assistant is used,[34] a general obligation that digital assistants must not manipulate consumers,[35] including through the design of the user interface, and the possibility to document the decision-making process.[36]

Chapter 3 provides a number of rules in respect of the contract for the supply of a digital assistant. Such contracts would be categorised as contracts involving the supply of digital content or a digital service,[37] or software, and the DACC provisions enhance any already existing rules. The chapter requires several additional items of information to be provided to consumers before concluding a contract for the supply of digital assistant,[38] as well as the disclosure of any conflicts of interest between those of the consumer and another party.[39] Other provisions[40] address the consequences of temporary or permanent deactivation of a digital assistant for the contract for the supply of the digital assistant,[41] as well as the inclusion of the design requirements as an element of conformity with the contract and the supplier's liability for non-conformity,[42] including an obligation to pay damages for any losses incurred through the use of a digital assistant.[43]

Various aspects regarding contracts concluded through a digital assistants (referred to as an "algorithmic contract") are covered by chapter 4, including the legal validity and effectiveness of such contracts[44] and the continued application of consumer law,[45] as well as the duty of disclosure.[46]

---

32 Article 6(2)(b) DACC. Note the possibility of dispensing with either option for some contracts in Article 6(3) DACC.
33 Article 7 DACC.
34 Article 8 DACC.
35 Article 9 DACC.
36 Article 10 DACC.
37 E.g., under the Digital Content and Digital Services Directive (2019/770/EU), or the UK's Consumer Rights Act 2015, Part 1, chapter 3.
38 Article 11 DACC.
39 Article 12 DACC.
40 Note also Article 15 DACC on a very narrow duty to warn.
41 Article 13 DACC.
42 Article 14 DACC.
43 Article 16 DACC.
44 Article 17 DACC.
45 Article 18 DACC.
46 Article 19 DACC.

Further provisions deal with the provision of information,[47] and the attribution of a digital assistant's action to the person using it for its contractual relations and any limitations thereof,[48] and a prohibition on manipulating digital assistants.[49] Finally, Article 25 DACC, the sole article of chapter 5, provides a right of recourse for any business that has suffered a loss due to non-attribution of a contract under Article 22(2) DACC.

This short overview of the DACC provides the necessary context for a discussion of the provisions relevant to the question for this contribution, the attribution of information. First, it is necessary to take a closer look at several relevant provisions of the DACC. Among the guiding principles, three are particularly pertinent to explaining how the DACC deal with information: GP2 confirms that consumer law extends to any contract concluded through the use of a digital assistant, supplemented by GP3 according to which any obligations to provide pre-contractual information to a consumer remains relevant. This is given effect through Article 18 DACC, which states that "Consumer law applies to any contract concluded between a consumer and a business, irrespective of whether the consumer, the business or both parties use a digital assistant for their contractual relations." Both of these guiding principles reflect the position underpinning the DACC that the use of digital assistants should not affect the fundamental premises of consumer law, i.e., that a consumer is generally in a weaker position vis-à-vis a business in terms of bargaining strength and relevant information. Whilst a digital assistant could substitute for the consumer's own decision-making process, this does not mean that consumers could henceforth be ignorant of relevant information. The consumer-centric approach of the DACC which allows consumers to retain residual control entails that consumers have the relevant information available to them to exercise these controls.

It might be arguable that this very rationale for consumer law would be rendered irrelevant if digital assistants capable of independently sourcing information were to become widespread,[50] but one might note that

47 Articles 20 and 21 DACC, discussed below.

48 Article 22 DACC; see also Article 24 DACC.

49 Article 23 DACC.

50 For a discussion, see Christoph Busch, "Consumer Law for AI Agents" (2025) *German Law Journal* (forthcoming, preprint available on SSRN). See also Mateusz Grochowski, Agnieszka Jablonowska, Francesca Lagioia and Giovanni Sartor, 'Algorithmic Transparency and Explainability for EU Consumer Protection: Unwrapping the Regulatory Premises' (2021) 8 *Critical Analysis L* 43.

consumer law, particularly in the EU, has generally not put any weight on the actual knowledge or experience of a particular consumer, but instead worked with a generalisation that all consumers are an at informational disadvantage.[51] If this is the approach taken in the case of consumers with a high level of relevant expertise, than it would seem consistent to take the same view in the case of consumers who have used a digital assistant to take their contracting decisions for them. Whether there will ever be a strong case for reevaluating this consumer law rationale will depend on several factors, including the widespread availability and adoption of digital assistants by consumers, as well as the capabilities and reliabilities of an AI system and its underpinning AI technology.

Furthermore, GP7, the third relevant guiding principle, embodies the consumer-centric approach of the DACC and states that "A consumer must remain in control of a digital assistant through the ability to set, review and amend all the parameters used by a digital assistant; through the ability to prevent the conclusion of a contract through the digital assistant; and by deactivating the digital assistant." This guiding principle is then fleshed out in several of the design requirements noted earlier. Among the abilities mentioned in GP7, the fact that a consumer should be able to prevent the conclusion of a contract (through the functionalities offered in accordance with Article 6), in particular, requires that the consumer has access to any relevant information about the transaction. At the very least, this must be the pre-contractual information which a business is required to provide under the applicable consumer law rules. One way of providing such information is to make this available to a consumer directly, e.g., by e-mailing this to the consumer. However, in many situations, the relevant information is presented on the business's webpage or app, and so assumes that a consumer sees the information before placing an order. This would suffice for a digital assistant to access the information as part of its decision-making process, but it would not enable a consumer to see this information because it would be the digital assistant rather than the consumer browsing the website and accessing the information provided there.

51 See e.g., case C-110/14 *Horațiu Ovidiu Costea vSC Volksbank România SA* ECLI:EU:C:2015:538, para 21; case C-498/16 *Schrems v Facebook Ireland Ltd.* ECLI:EU:C:2018:37, para 39, case C-423/97 *Travel Vac SL v Sanchis* [1999] ECR I-2195.

The DACC offer one possible solution to this particular issue. First, Article 20 DACC on "contractual disclosures" provides that any obligation on a business to provide information to a consumer in a way that a (human) consumer can read this, whether before the conclusion of a contract or during its performance, such information "must also be provided in a structured, commonly used and machine-readable format".[52] The primary reason for this provision is to ensure that digital assistants can, indeed, access all the relevant information and use it as part of the decision-making process. Businesses would have to find a way of providing information in such a format in a way that this could be accessed by digital assistants and for digital assistants to have the functionality of identifying such information. Much of this could be solved through appropriate coding. As noted above, the way an algorithm processes information will differ from the way a human consumer would process information, and its presentation in a machine-readable format would not make it human-readable. It would therefore be difficult to suggest that such information should be attributed to the consumer if it has only been provided to a digital assistant in machine-readable format. This is the implicit position taken in the DACC.

However, the DACC address one situation that would clarify that when information received by a digital assistant could be made available to consumers, it can be regarded as having been given to consumers and therefore attributed to them. If a digital assistant can record information it has received in a format that could also be read by human consumers, Articles 6(5) and 21 DACC set out how such information should be made available to consumers. First, Article 6(5) DACC, which deals with the functionality to enable a consumer to prevent the conclusion of a contract, states that a digital assistant which can receive legally-required information and transmit this, or an accurate summary thereof, to the consumer, then the information must be made available to the consumer before an order is placed. This would allow the consumer to check the information before deciding whether to confirm or object to, as the case may be, the placing of an order. Importantly, this provision assumes that the information provided by the business can be transmitted directly to the consumer (or, where the technology has the relevant capability, to turn information from the machine-readable format into a human-readable one). It only applies to information that was provided by the business in the first place, i.e., it does

52 Article 20(1) DACC. Article 20(2) DACC provides a "carve-out" from this provision for micro and small enterprises.

not extend to any other information which the digital assistant might draw on as part of its decision-making process (although this is, to some extent, covered by the functionality to document decision-making under Article 10 DACC), and only at the point when the consumer has to decide whether to prevent the placing of an order. However, it would then be arguable that the consumer has been given the relevant information, and thus that information could be attributed to the consumer.

A broader rule is provided by Article 21 DACC. Paragraph (2) applies to the situation where all the information a business is required by law to give to a consumer before a contract is concluded is displayed on the business's online interface (i.e., their website). The information so displayed is available to the digital assistant as part of its decision-making process, and as result, the information is deemed to have been given to the consumer. In essence, this means that a business which currently complies with any pre-contractual information duties by providing all the required information on its website, or other online interface, can continue to do so where the consumer uses a digital assistant. Here, the DACC employ a legal fiction, because the consumer will almost certainly not have seen the informationbut often this will be so even when a consumer is active rather than their digital assistant. The fact that the information is displayed on the online interface and would be available to a consumer interacting with the business through this interface usually satisfies pre-contractual obligations to provide information.

This provision only deals with some of the instances when information must be given. It is not uncommon for the obligation to provide information to extend beyond displaying information on an online interface. In some instances, information must be confirmed in writing in a way that it remains accessible to a consumer; in others, information only has to be given during the performance of a contract.[53] Generally, this would mean that the information has to be provided directly to the consumer. However, once a consumer deploys a digital assistant, it might be more difficult to do so in practice; for instance, the contact details provided by the business might not include the consumer's personal email address but rather an email address linked to the digital assistant. Here, Article 21(1) offers a solution to ensure that businesses can comply with such information duties. This paragraph applies to information that must be provided at any point

53 E.g., Article 7(1) of the Consumer Rights Directive (2011/83/EU).

during the contractual relations between a business and a consumer, and only where the use of the digital assistant has been disclosed (required by Article 19 DACC, and usually done through the functionality mandated by Article 7 DACC). Furthermore, the digital assistant must have the functionality to receive this information, and either be capable of transmitting the information, or an accurate summary of this information, to the consumer, or, alternatively, be capable of storing this information in such a way that it can be made available to the consumer permanently through the digital assistant's user interface.[54] Additionally, this functionality must have been disclosed to the business, whether by technical or other means.[55] If all these requirements have been met, then Article 21(1) DACC treats the business as having complied with its obligation to provide information to the consumer.

It will be apparent from this discussion that the DACC focus only on the *de facto* attribution of some information to a consumer, i.e., the information that a business must provide under the applicable consumer law. The DACC do not extend to any information which a digital assistant might be programmed to obtain independently from other sources than the business's online interface. One of the reasons why this broader situation was not addressed is that, at the time of drafting the DACC, it was too uncertain whether digital assistant would include such wider information seeking functions, or whether they would be programmed to rely primarily, or exclusively, on the information that has to be provided by a business. Should such wider functionality become a standard feature of digital assistants, a new provision could be consider that would address whether and when other types of information might be attributable to a consumer.

It has been shown that, whilst the primary objective of Article 21 DACC is to facilitate compliance by a business with its information duties where a consumer utilises a digital assistant, it is possible to argue that where Article 21 is engaged, the information can be attributed to the consumer. Crucially, this would depend on the technical capacity of the digital assistant to transmit this information to the consumer, or at least to make it available to the consumer via the digital assistant's user interface. The mere fact that information is available to the digital assistant would not suffice. More importantly, the DACC would not attribute any information obtained by a digital assistant to a consumer where the digital assistant is not capable

54 Article 21(1)(a) DACC.
55 Article 21(1)(b) DACC.

of transmitting that information to the consumer or making it available in its user interface. The one exception is information displayed on the business's online interface, although there is often a legal requirement for such information to be confirmed in writing at some stage in any case. A clear distinction is therefore drawn between the attribution of *actions* taken by a digital assistant to the consumer or business using it for its contractual relations, and of any *information* acquired during this. In the case of the former, attribution flows from the decision to deploy a digital assistant, whereas in the latter case, the attribution of information depends on the technical capabilities of a digital assistant to make this information available to a consumer.

There are important implications of this approach where a digital assistant is used not only for the conclusion of contracts but also for actions that might need to be taken during the performance of the contract. For instance, a digital assistant might be capable of managing subscription-style contracts on behalf of a consumer. The law might require that a consumer is sent regular reminders about upcoming renewals and the possibility of terminating a subscription contract before it renews.[56] Unless the digital assistant has the technical capability of providing relevant information and reminder notices to consumers when received by the digital assistant, a business might not have complied with its legal obligations unless everything has been sent directly to the consumer. A lot will therefore come down to the design of such digital assistants. Building on the general provision in Article 18 DACC that consumer law continues to apply to such contracts even where a digital assistant is used by the consumer, the onus would be on the supplier (or, rather, the designer) of the digital assistant to include the relevant functionalities for transmitting such information or, alternatively, to ensure that a business has the consumer's contact details to provide the required reminder notices and then to allow the consumer to manage the subscription through the digital assistant's user interface.[57]

Overall, the default position in the DACC is that information received by a digital assistant would not be attributed to a consumer. The exception to the default is engaged where the digital assistant has the technical capability to transmit or make available such information to the consumer. Nothing in the DACC would go beyond the attribution of information, and none

56 Cf. section 258 of the Digital Markets, Competition and Consumers Act 2024 (UK).

57 This would be similar to the way in which subscriptions can already be managed through systems such as Google Play Store.

of its provisions suggest an attribution of *knowledge*. This approach seems consistent with the state of current AI technologies.

IV. Attribution in other model rules

In the previous section, the DACC's approach to information "attribution" was explored. For comparison, it is instructive to consider how the PAIC and the MLAC deal with knowledge and information. Starting with the PAIC, Principle 14(1) PAIC provides that "Where the law refers to elements such as 'awareness', 'knowledge', or 'notice', which imply that a party has received information on particular facts in a way enabling this party to draw correct conclusions about these facts, these elements should be deemed to be present in the operator if ... (b) the information has reached the electronic agent and the electronic agent is able to duly process information of the relevant kind." This is enhanced by a presumptive rule in Principle 14(2) PAIC that "where the electronic agent ought to be able to duly process information of the relevant kind according to the technical capabilities required in accordance with Principle 12, the requirements of point (b) of paragraph (1) should be presumed to be fulfilled.". Principle 12 PAIC lays down a requirement that an electronic agent must have the technical specifications and capabilities required by law or which the other party could reasonably expect. As a baseline, Article 12(1)(b)(iii) PAIC states that the other party can reasonably expect the capabilities which it would expect from a human performing the same task as the electronic agent", unless either of the more precise instances in Art.12(1)(b)(i) or (ii) applies.

In a similar vein to the DACC, the PAIC therefore look to the technical capabilities of an AI system to determine whether the person using the system (i.e., the operator) has the relevant knowledge or information. However, there is one important difference between the DACC and the PAIC: the DACC require that the information must be either transmitted or made available to the consumer using a digital assistant. The PAIC provides for a much broader attribution rule which focuses solely on the ability of the electronic agent to process the information and uses that as the basis for determining whether knowledge or information should be attributed to the party who is using the electronic agent. The approach taken in the PAIC would certainly facilitate the application of Contract Law rules to contracts concluded through the use of electronic agents. However, it also presupposes that these rules would continue to be fit for purpose for this form of contracting, but this will not invariably so in respect of legal rules which have a strong human component. Such rules might not easily translate into a context where a human is mostly no longer in the loop.

However, one needs to bear in mind the wider context of the PAIC. In particular, Article 11 PAIC makes it clear that whilst contract law can generally apply to contracts concluded through an electronic agent, there may be limits to this where specific contract law rules depend on a human's "cognitive, volitional or emotional states";[58] here, a different approach is suggested that would substitute the technical capabilities of an electronic agent for the human elements.[59] Article 14(1)(b) PAIC deems the operator to have the relevant information as long as the information has reached the AI system (the electronic agent, in the PAIC) and the system is capable of processing information of that kind. This is subject to the important qualification in the final paragraph of Article 14(1) PAIC. This provides that it would not be sufficient to rely on the electronic agent's capability to process the information it has received where this would be "inconsistent with the purpose of the rule of contract law in question or would result in a stricter attribution than for a human...". Although the exact scope of this proviso is not entirely clear, it does indicate that the use of AI systems cannot always be smoothly absorbed within existing rules of Contract Law. Once particular human elements are central to a specific rule, one might need to develop a different approach. Such an approach might need to reflect the fundamental difference regarding the way information is received and processed by humans on the one hand, and AI systems on the other.

A provision on attribution of knowledge was also considered for the MLAC, but ultimately not included. At the draft stage, the then draft Article 7, which was not adopted for the MLAC, provided that "[f]or the purposes of determining satisfaction of a legal requirement for the presence of intention, knowledge or awareness of a person in respect of an action carried out by an automated system, and unless otherwise required by law, regard may be had to the design, commissioning and operation of the system, as appropriate." However, this provision was not adopted in the final text.

Importantly, both the PAIC and the MLAC would have had in common that they start from the technical features and capabilities of the relevant system to determine when a legal requirement that a person should be

58 Article 11(1)(b) PAIC.
59 Article 11(2) PAIC.

deemed to have the information or knowledge is met where that person relies on an automated, or AI, system for its contracting activities. In this respect, there is alignment with the DACC position. All three sets of model rules take a more cautious approach than they do in respect of attribution of actions by or outputs from the AI system. The attribution of knowledge or information requires that the AI system has the technical capability of receiving and processing such information. Much will therefore turn on the design and technical capabilities of AI systems to be used for contracting, whether they be electronic agents in the PAIC sense, or digital assistant-style applications.

V. Conclusions

This contribution has focused on the vexed question of whether, and how, information and knowledge that might be said to have been acquired by an AI system could be attributed to the contracting party who utilised such a system for its contracting actions. Unlike the attribution of actions taken by an AI system, this question is far less straightforward to answer. First, one needs to separate the notion of *knowledge* from belief or opinion, and recognise that knowledge goes beyond having information. Beyond this, several factors must be considered, including the purpose of the relevant legal rule, the reason why one might ask whether information received by an AI system can be attributed to a contracting party, and, above all, the technical capability of an AI system.

The various model rules on contract automation considered here, particularly the DACC, all focus on the technical capabilities as a relevant factor for addressing the attribution of information and, in the case of the PAIC, knowledge. The DACC take a narrow approach, focusing primarily on facilitating compliance by a business with the information duties imposed on it by consumer law. The PAIC are broader in their approach, but recognise that there will be difficulties where the legal rule in question focuses on a human's "cognitive, volitional or emotional states".[60]

Indeed, the very question of whether it is sufficient to find a way of plugging transactions through AI systems into familiar systems of Contract Law becomes difficult to answer in a straightforward manner in respect of

60 Article 11(1)(b) PAIC.

rules which focus on the "human element". Whether simply substituting an AI system's technical capabilities (as suggested in the PAIC) would be sufficient is not clear cut, particularly in view of how knowledge should be understood. It might become necessary to recognise that the use of AI systems in contracting is more disruptive[61] and would therefore require more substantive intervention in contract law to address the particular challenges of AI contracting, even if this would lead to some degree of bifurcation within Contract Law. What is clear is that the implications of contracting through AI system will continue to require close analysis.

61 Cf. Roger Brownsword, "Law Disrupted, Law Re-Imagined, Law Re-Invented" (2019) *Technology and Regulation* 10; Christian Twigg-Flesner, "Disruptive Technology - Disrupted Law? How the Digital Revolution affects (Contract) Law", in: Alberto De Franceschi (ed.), *European Contract Law and the Digital Single Market* (Intersentia, 2016).

Contract Law in the Middle of an AI Summer

Eliza Mik[*]

I. Introduction

Technological progress and the growing number of automated processes has always been accompanied by a pressure to 'adapt' or 'modernize' contract law.[1] The popular assumption is that legal frameworks are outdated, inadequate or otherwise incapable to accommodate technological developments, especially as drastic as AI.[2] Before proceding with any form of regulation, it is worth reflecting on the seemingly simple question whether the principles of contract law require adaptations or whether they are sufficiently malleable to "adapt themselves." Before subscribing to the theory that contract law is directly affected by and should respond to technological change, we must be reminded that we are in the middle of an AI summer, a period of rapid advancements, significant investments and countless headlines proclaiming the dawn of a new AI era, spurred by the rather unexpected introduction of ChatGPT into the consumer mainstream in November, 2022. In this hot climate of indiscriminate fascination with innovation and a blind belief into everything that is proclaimed by the big technology companies (which are trying to sell products!), it is easy to forget that AI has a long history and that interest in this field has been cyclical. The technologies – or some aspects thereof - may be new, the legal debates are not. Legal scholarship has a long history of intermittent "enchantments" with various technologies that, after a period of theoretical turmoil and hype, often dissipated due to lack of market uptake or the simple realization that they do not create any significant new legal problems. Alternatively, technologies that seem groundbreaking and revolutionary at first, become

---

* The Chinese University of Hong Kong (CUHK) - Faculty of Law.

1 Rolf H. Weber, 'Contractual Duties and Allocation of Liability in Automated Digital Contracts', in: R. Schulze and D. Staudenmayer (eds.), *Digital Revolution: Challenges for Contract Law in Practice* (Oxford: Hart Publishing), p. 184.

2 Reiner Schulze, Dirk Staudenmayer, 'Digital Revolution – Challenges for Contract Law', in: R. Schulze and D. Staudenmayer (eds.), *Digital Revolution: Challenges for Contract Law in Practice* (Oxford: Hart Publishing), p. 19.

integrated into mainstream commerce and quickly lose their "groundbreaking" character. The pressure to regulate, modernize or adapt legal principles is understandable but must be resisted. We are not only in the middle of an AI summer but, as it seems, in the middle of an AI bubble. Floridi sees a "striking similarities between the current AI Hype Cycle and previous tech bubbles" and suggest "[w]hile this does not negate the profoundly transformative potential of AI technology, "it calls for caution and critical thinking."[3] It also calls for a cool head, if only to ensure that the devised solutions (if any) are not premature, address actual problems and do not create additional uncertainty. After all, as observed by Twigg-Flesner, the disruptive effect of technological development "can be gauged by considering whether a specific issue can be dealt with by applying existing legal rules to the particular questions which have been identified in respect of that issue. Thus, if it is possible to maintain existing rules but to clarify how these should be applied in the context of a new development, then the disruptive effect to the law is minimal."[4] Twigg-Flesner warns against rushing towards the introduction of new rules without careful consideration of the specific issues created by the relevant technologies. "In the rush to provide a legal response, more problems might be created than solved."[5] Before rushing legal responses, there should be absolute clarity as to what is new or – which technological factor warrants legal attention. As in the above quote, we need to identify "particular questions" and strive to "maintain existing rules," especially if such rules have worked so far. We must also be clear about the specific technological developments. Narratives filled with constant references to "disruption" and "revolution,"[6] interspersed with the latest technological term *du jour*, may lead to incorrect points of departure and untested assumptions that "something" must be done need to be done – especially if such terms are not well understood. When identifying legal challenges of technological origin, it is best to think of evolution instead of revolution and of adaptation instead of disruption. It must be remembered

3 Luciano Floridi, 'Why the AI Hype is Another Tech Bubble', (2024) 37 Philos. Technol., 128, https://doi.org/10.1007/s13347-024-00817-w; see also: Mark Buchanan, 'The laws of inflating the AI bubble', Nature Physics (2024), 1362.

4 Christian Twigg-Flesner, 'Disruptive Technology - Disrupted Law? How the digital revolution affects (Contract) law', in: A. De Franceschi, *European Contract Law and the Digital Single Market* (Intersentia, 2016).

5 Id.

6 Reiner Schulze, Dirk Staudenmayer, 'Digital Revolution – Challenges for Contract Law', in: R. Schulze and D. Staudenmayer (eds.), *Digital Revolution: Challenges for Contract Law in Practice* (Oxford: Hart Publishing), p. 19.

that the last decades have witnessed a gradual progression towards increasingly automated transactions and frictionless computation facilitating all stages of commercial interactions. Technological change is nothing new. Moreover, technological change has not only been gradual but also imperceptible to the average human, occurring in the background, behind the screens of our computers, at remote data centres housing powerful computing and communications infrastructure. Which of those gradual and often imperceptible changes necessitate a legal reaction – and why now? Which of the recent events warrants an adaptation of contractual principles given that online commerce and automated trading have been a constant feature of commercial interactions for not less than 25 years? It can hardly be assumed that a contract law must be adapted when - or whenever - Amazon upgrades its pricing engine or recommender system.

The present chapter briefly investigates the terminological turmoil that pervades legal discussions. It also reviews the core principles of contract law and, after providing some practical examples of the futility of tying changes to legal principles to changes in technology, it critically examines the core concepts behind the recently enacted UNCITRAL "Model Law on Automated Contracting" (MLAC or Model Law).[7] The discussion is confined to the common law of contract and makes no claims as to the relevant principles in civil law jurisdictions.

II. Terminological Turmoil

Theories proclaiming the purported need to modernize contract law and the widespread assumption that, in its present state, its principles cannot accommodate technological progress may derive from an undisciplined use of technical terms. Constant refrences to "AI," "autonomy" or "agentic," often seem to serve as self-explanatory justifications that "something must be done," often without an indication why a particular concept or technology warrants legal scrutiny and how exactly it changes existing practices. For we must not forget that no technology existist as an isolated, abstract concept and that its legal implications, if any, can only be evaluated through the lens of commercial reality. It is not about AI *per se* but about the specific use of one of the technologies falling under the ambit of AI in contracting practices.

7 See United Nations Report of the United Nations Commission on International Trade Law Fifty-seventh session (24 June–12 July 2024) A/79/17.

1. AI

The recent bestseller, "AI Snake Oil,"[8] commences with a hypothetical that adequately describes the current state of many legal debates surrounding AI. Readers are asked to imagine an alternate world in which the collective noun "vehicle" is used to describe many different forms of transportation. The word is used to refer to cars, buses, bikes, spacecraft, ships etc. Academic debates in this world are confusing. Scholars argue "about whether or not vehicles are environmentally friendly, even though no one realizes that one side of the debate is talking about bikes and the other side is talking about trucks. There is a breakthrough in rocketry, but the media focuses on how vehicles have gotten faster-so people call their car dealer (oops, vehicle dealer) to ask when faster models will be available. Meanwhile, fraudsters have capitalized on the fact that consumers don't know what to believe when it comes to vehicle technology, so scams are rampant in the vehicle sector. Now replace the word "vehicle" with "artificial intelligence," and we have a pretty good description of the world we live in. Artificial intelligence, Al for short, is an umbrella term for a set of loosely related technologies. ChatGPT has little in common with, say, software that banks use to evaluate loan applicants. Both are referred to as Al, but in all the ways that matter—how they work, what they're used for and by whom, and how they fail —they couldn't be more different."[9] A similar trend can be observed in legal scholarship, where the term AI is used as a Minsky-style "suitcase word"[10] that can be filled with multiple meanings in support of various arguments. Little attention is devoted to the fact that AI is a multifaceted concept that encompasses a wide research field as well as a range of diverse technologies. The result is a general confusion as to what exactly is meant by AI. Historically, AI has evolved along two paradigms: symbolic AI and sub-symbolic AI (also known as connectionist or neural approaches). Symbolic AI, often called "good old-fashioned AI," relies on explicit symbolic representations, logical deduction and hand-crafted rules for reasoning. Sub-symbolic AI, by contrast, uses

8 Arvind Narayanan, Sayash Kapoor, *AI Snake Oil: What Artificial Intelligence Can Do, What It Can't, and How to Tell the Difference*, (Princeton 2024), p. 1.

9 Arvind Narayanan, Sayash Kapoor, *AI Snake Oil: What Artificial Intelligence Can Do, What It Can't, and How to Tell the Difference*, (Princeton 2024), pp. 1-2.

10 A "suitcase word" is a term for a word that contains a variety of different ideas and meanings packed into it; see Marvin Minsky, *The Emotional Machine.*

numerical representations and statistical learning (e.g. neural networks) to model intelligence without explicit human-defined rules. At a basic level, symbolic AI uses *symbols and discrete structures* (e.g. logic statements) that have clear semantic meaning, whereas sub-symbolic AI uses *numeric representations* (vectors of features, weights) devoid of inherent semantic content. The 2022 ISO standard on AI concepts and terminology confirms that AI encompasses both approaches[11] and, more importantly, emphasizes that AI denotes a broad range of technologies, *and* a vast research field.[12] While both types of AI have been present – and integrated in commercial dealings - for decades,[13] the most recent wave of academic excitement seems to derive from advances in sub-symbolic AI, which is commonly associated with machine learning, generative AI and, more specifically, large language models ("LLMs"). If AI has been present for a long time and if it encompasses a multitude of technologies, then *which aspect* or *type* of AI justifies the need for legal change or regulatory intervention? Why now? What exactly has changed in contracting practices? After all, all AIs are computer programs and computer programs of varying complexity have been pervading commercial life for decades. Needless to say, scholarly debates about the use of computer programs in contracting seem less exciting – and publishable – than debates about legal responses to the AI revolution.

2. Automation & Autonomy

Similar confusion accompanies the term „autonomy". Purportedly, if "something" is autonomous, then it is independent from humans, operates without human control, makes "its own" decisions and produces "its own" output. Purportedly, autonomous AI (or similar) must be separated from their human operators and, in order to be directly attributed with the outputs of their operations, recognized as separate legal entitites.[14] The

11 ISO/IEC 22989 International Standard Artificial intelligence concepts and terminology (2022-07) ("ISO 22989"), 3.1.33, 3.1.34.

12 ISO 22989, Introduction.

13 J. McCarthy et al., 'A Proposal for the Dartmouth Summer Research Project on Artificial Intelligence 2' (Aug. 31, 1955) (unpublished research proposal, on file with Stanford University).

14 Laurence B Solum, 'Legal Personhood for Artificial Intelligences' (1992) 70 NCL Review 1231; Ignacio N Cofone, 'Servers and Waiters: What Matters in the Law of AI' (2018) 21 Stan Tech L Review 167.

attribution of the operations of an AI – or autonomous system - *to* the AI usually derives from the perceived need to redirect liability for unexpected outputs or malfunctions away from whoever created, operated or interacted with the AI.[15] While theories surrounding autonomous systems abound, the term itself is often left undefined. In the legal context, autonomy can be regarded as instrumental in determining and *justifying* moral as well as causal responsibility.[16] It is naturally associated with humans and their legal capacity to act. When "autonomy" is used to describe computer systems or programs, the tendency is to assume that the system is *like* a human, *independent* from humans or operating "by itself." Nothing can be further from the truth. In a technical context, autonomy denotes quantifiable relationships of control between biological or mechanical systems and their environments.[17] The term "control" is context dependent[18] and requires an examination of the system being controlled.[19] What is crucial in the present discussion, is that control can be indirect, exercised remotely and with varying degrees of delay. Each action of a computer program or AI system, no matter how autonomous, depends on and is always preceded by human input or instructions.[20] Even in autonomous systems, people are always present - "they just exist in a different place and time."[21] In principle, an autonomous system *could* operate for extended periods of time without direct human intervention. Nonetheless, all autonomous systems are created by humans and "operate based on algorithms and otherwise obey the commands of operators."[22] It is also easy to overlook that autonomy is an advanced form of automation, i.e. the application of technology or

15 See: Iria Giuffrida, 'Liability for AI Decision-Making: Some Legal and Ethical Considerations' (2019) 88 Fordham L Review 439, 440, 443-445; Bert-Jaap Koops and Mireille Hildebrandt, 'Bridging the Accountability Gap: Rights for New Entities in the Information Society?' (2010) 11 Minn J L Sci & Tech 2.

16 Roger Brownsword, 'Agents in Autonomic Computing Environments', in: Mireille Hildebrandt, Antoinette Rouvroy (eds.), *Law, Human Agency and Autonomic Computing — The Philosophy of Law meets the Philosophy of Technology*, (Routledge 2011), p. 68.

17 Stuart J Russell, Peter Norvig, *Artificial Intelligence: A Modern Approach*, 4th ed. (Pearson, 2021) ("Russel & Norvig"), p. 38.

18 James Ron Leigh, *Control Theory, A Guided Tour* (IET 3rd ed., 2012).

19 System definition 4 OECD.com.

20 Nick Bostrom, 'Superintelligence', Oxford University Press (2014); David Mindell, *Our Robots, Ourselves* (Random House, 2015), p. 196.

21 Mindell (n. 20), p. 204.

22 ISO para 5.13 explanatory note, p. 26.

processes to assist humans in the performance of various tasks,[23] including physical and cognitive.[24] Automation comes in different degrees depending on the amount of control that humans *chose to retain* over the performance of a task.[25] The degree of automation and hence the division of labour between human and machine depends on the type of task – and whether it can be performed more efficiently by a human or by a computer.[26] Consequently, while both "automation" and "autonomy" are technology neutral, the technologies deployed differ depending on the type and complexity of the task. The more complex the task, the more complex the technology. [27] In the context of contracting, automation concerns various aspects of information processing, such as collecting market information, calculating prices, as well as various forms of action implementation, such as placing bids on the stock market or oprocessing orders on e-commerce websites. The question arises: should the progressive refinement of our tools lead to legal differentiations? Should legal principles change depending on complexity of the computer program used to automate a particular task? Admittedly, even simple vending machines are autonomous because they require neither continuous human supervision nor the provision of ongoing instructions.

23 The International Society of Automation (ISA) defines automation as "the creation and application of technology to monitor and control the production and delivery of products and services."
https://www.isa.org/about-isa/what-is-automation; see also Thomas B Sheridan, 'Telerobotics, Automation and Human Supervisory Control ', MIT Press (1992).

24 Stephen Wolfram, 'Artificial Intelligence and the Future of Civilization', in: John Brockman (ed.), *Possible Minds, 25 Ways of Looking at AI*, Penguin Press, London (2019), p. 268.

25 See generally Parasuraman Raja, Thomas B Sheridan, and Christopher D Wickens, 'A Model for Types and Levels of Human Interaction with Automation' (2000) 30 IEEE Transactions on Systems, Man, and Cybernetics - Part A: Systems and Humans, 286.

26 Carl Benedict Frey, 'The Technology Trap: Capital, Labor, and Power in the Age of Automation', Princeton University Press (2019), 228.

27 Stuart J Russell, *Human Compatible*, Penguin (2019), p. 119; see also James Lighthill, 'Artificial Intelligence: A General Survey', Artificial Intelligence: A paper symposium (1973). UK: Science Research Council, where AI was associated with advanced automation and the replacement of human beings with machines for arrange of pragmatic purposes.

3. Agents

The technical meaning of the term "agent," which frequently appears alongside the concept of autonomy and AI, differs from its legal meaning. In law, an agent is a person or legal entity entity authorized to act on behalf of another person, the principal.[28] The agent's primary function is to create or change the legal rights, duties, or relationships of the principal with a third party. Crucially, agents are *persons* who have the legal authority to represent other persons.[29] In the technical context, however, the term "agent," denotes a wide array of technologies, ranging from word processors, browsers, and mail servers to trading algorithms and satellites. In principle, an 'agent' is a *device* or a *process* that responds to stimuli from its environment or, when designed to do so, to learn from its environment.[30] The canonical example of an autonomous agent is the Roomba vacuum cleaner, which is described as "a robotic vacuum-cleaning agent in a world consisting of squares that can be either dirty or clean."[31] It is also emphasized that such vacuuming agents lack autonomy if they rely exclusively on the prior knowledge of their designers (i.e. their initial instructions). They gradually learn the characteristics of their operating environment and thus evolve into more autonomous systems. Roomba's creators cannot, after all, know the configuration of each living room their robots will clean in the future![32] Autonomy is driven by the need to operate in unpredictable, future environments that cannot be known at the time the system is created. When examined up-close, the concept turns out to be less exciting than commonly believed. Once we realize that, from a technical perspective, a cordless vacuum cleaner is an autonomous agent, legal theories proclaiming the need to adapt contract law to "autonomous AI" sound less convincing.

28 Treitel, *Law of Contract*, 16th ed., Edwin Peel (OUP, 2025) 16-001.
29 Treitel, *Law of Contract*, 16th ed., Edwin Peel (OUP, 2025) 16-015.
30 Russel & Norvig, pp. 54-59; for a different definition see David L. Poole, Alan K Mackworth, 'Artificial Intelligence, Foundations of Computational Agents', Cambridge University Press (2017), who define an agent as 'something that acts in an environment,' which includes dogs, worms, robots and humans and a 'computational agent' as 'an agent whose decisions about its actions can be explained in terms of computation'; Samir Chopra, Laurence F White, 'A Legal Theory for Autonomous Artificial Agents', The University of Michigan Press (Ann Arbor, 2011).
31 Russel & Norvig, p. 55.
32 Russel & Norvig, pp. 59-60.

III. Objectivity and Technology Neutrality of Contract Law

While the technical terminology is somewhat confusing, the principles of the common law of contract are clear. Formulated in broad terms derived from centuries of cases that address actual contracting scenarios, the principles of contract law are permissive and technology neutral.[33] Contract law is also form agnostic, as it does not prescribe the manner contracts should be formed.[34] With very few exceptions,[35] the parties are allowed to express their agreement in any manner and to communicate their intentions by means of any technology.[36] As I have described elsewhere,[37] to be legally enforceable, contracts require intention and consideration. While consideration reflects the need for reciprocity, intention reflects the consensual underpinnings of contract law. The need for intention (or any mental states for that matter) is far less pronounced, however, than commonly assumed. In practice, the presence of intention is tempered by the objective theory of contract, which forms a cornerstone of commercial certainty, and ascribes legal consequences to *outward manifestations* of intention.[38] As famously observed by Oliver Wendell Holmes, Jr. "the law has nothing to do with the actual state of the parties' minds. In contract, as elsewhere, it must go by externals, and judge parties by their conduct."[39] When establishing the existence and contents of contracts, courts examine what was said,

33 Chris Reed, 'Online and Offline Equivalence: Aspiration and Achievement' (2010) 18 (3) IJ L & IT 249.

34 Hugh Beale, *Chitty on Contracts*, 35th ed., (Sweet Maxwell 2024) 1-065.

35 Law of Property Act 1925; Consumer Credit Act 1974; Bills of Exchange Act 1882; Copyright, Designs and Patents Act 1988, ss 90 (assignment) and 91 (licences) of copyright; s 222(3) (design rights); Patents Act 1977, s 30(6) (patents); Trade Marks Act 1994, ss 24(3) (assignments) and 28 (licences).

36 Treitel, *Law of Contract*, 16th ed., Edwin Peel (OUP, 2025) 2-004, citing Hart v Mills (1846) 15 L.J. Ex. 200; para.2-018; cf. Steven v Bromley & Son (1919) 2 K.B. 722; Glencore Energy UK Ltd v OMV Supply & Trading Ltd [2018] EWHC 895 (Comm); (2018) 2Lloyd's Rep. 223.

37 Eliza Mik, 'Much Ado About Artificial Intelligence or The Automation of Contract Formation' (2022) 30 *IJILT* 484.

38 Michael Furmston, 'Cheshire, Fifoot & Furmston's Law of Contract', 16th ed., Oxford University Press (2012), pp. 41-42.

39 Oliver Wendell Holmes, Jr., 'The Common Law', Dover Publ'ns, Inc. 1991 (1881), 309; see also Wayne Barnes, 'The Objective Theory of Contracts' (2008) 76 U. Cin. L. Review 1119 "The objective theory of contracts furthers the ideal of individual autonomy. Limiting contract terms to what is externally manifested gives promisees much more control over their own affairs. When the promisee is entitled to rely on gestures that can be objectively verified-versus having to discern the promisor's

written, or done, not what the parties privately thought or intended. The subjective intention or the motivations of the persons making a statement are not apparent from its contents thus legally irrelevant.[40] Contract law is, in principle, oblivious to the 'meeting of minds'[41] and "demands that we attend to what has happened out in the world."[42] Agreement, we are told, "is not a mental state but an act, an inference from conduct."[43] This approach not only protects the reliance of those who see, hear or otherwise observe the actions and utternaces of others and but also ensures legal certainty as well as commercial predictability. In practice - and in the majority of situations – the appearances of agreement correspond with the fact of agreement.[44] Consequently, contract law places less emphasis on the exceptional situations where this is not the case. The practical implications of the objective theory of contract may be not immediately apparent, especially with regards to its relationship with AI or the technical aspects of contracting. The most important implication is that a statement is evaluated from the perspective of a reasonable addressee,[45] who is confined to what he or she sees or hears and has no insight into the decision-making process, or actual intentions, of the other party and, more importantly, cannot determine whether – or to what extent - the other party relied on any technological tools in his or her decision-making. The reasonable addressee cannot distinguish between statements made by humans and statements made by humans *assisted by* the latest version of OpenAI's large langue model, or between statements made by (i.e. generated) a simple hand-coded computer program and statements made by a program that

internal cognition, which may vary from what is externally manifested-the promisee can better process information and order affairs accordingly." at 1129, 1130.

40 They acquire some relevance in the context of vitiating factors, see generally: Rick Bigwood, 'Exploitative Contracts', Oxford University Press (2003).

41 There is minimal room for subjective enquiry, see: Nick Sage, 'Reconciling Contract Law's Objective and Subjective Standards', (2023) 86 Mod Law Review 1422-1446; Clare Dalton, 'An Essay in the Deconstruction of Contract Doctrine' (1985) 94 Yale L J 997, 1042.

42 Aditi Bagchi, 'Contract as Exchange', (February 01, 2024), Fordham Law Legal Studies Research Paper No. 4949890, 113 California Law Review (forthcoming 2025), Available at SSRN: https://ssrn.com/abstract=4949890 or http://dx.doi.org/10.2139/ssrn.4949890 at 3.

43 Hugh Beale, *Chitty on Contracts*, 35th ed. (2024 Sweet Maxwell) 1-066.

44 Treitel, *Law of Contract*, 16th ed., Edwin Peel (OUP, 2025) 01-002.

45 Maple Leaf Macro Volatility Master Fund v Rouvroy [2009] EWCA Civ 1334; [2010] 2 All E.R. (Comm) 788 at [10], [17].

relies on a neural network trained on a vast amount of data. An email or a message displayed in the chat function on an e-commerce website may, after all, look identical despite being generated by completely different technologies. The objective theory of contract focuses on what is displayed on the computer screen, what can be seen by the reasonable addressee. It does not concern itself what happens behind the screen, in remote data centers housing complex technological stacks consisting of hundreds of GPUs running the latest instance of Amazon's web services. In sum, combined with the simple principle that intention can be manifested in any manner and by any means, the objective theory of contract can be said to make contract law "technology neutral" or even "technology resistant." It need not react to every technological breakthrough or to every latest machine learning model integrated into Amazon's pricing engine. The common law of contract need not *be* adapted, adjusted or otherwise modified to accommodate technological change. Judging by the last 200 years cases decided against the backdrop of relentless technological progress, the principles of contract law seem capable of accommodating even dramatic changes to the manner the parties form and perform contracts. This is not because such principles are static or unresponsive but because they are formulated in a manner that insulates them from most aspects of technological change.[46] Three additional observations are apposite.

First, in common law juridictions, contracts have never been regulated on the basis of the technology used to form or perform them. Historically, any regulation of contractual relationships has been limited to the rectification of systemic deficiencies or to the codification of existing practices.[47] No adaptations of contract law were needed to accommodate contracts made over the telephone and on the internet. No changes were required when the transacting parties moved from Ethernet to 5G and from desktops to smart phones, further accelerating the contracting process and confining the negotiation of multi-million-dollar transactions to even smaller screens.

46 Several "disturbances" concerned the electronic form of online communications, raising doubts as to whether they could be considered "in writing" or otherwise providing "a written memorandum" of the relevant contract, as well as the question whether an emailed acceptance should be effective on dispatch or open receipt, see Electronic Commerce: Formal Requirements in Commercial Transactions: Advice from the Law Commission December 2001.

47 E.g. Contracts (Rights of Third Parties) Act 1999; Sale of Goods Act 1979, Misrepresentation Act 1967; Law Reform (Frustrated Contracts) Act 1943, Unfair Contract Terms Act 1977.

To date, technological change has been gradually integrated into the law of contract by means of judicial decisions.[48]

Second, the primary function of contract law is to give effect to the parties' intentions and to facilitate bargains, not to regulate the digital economy or to protect consumers. Of course, it is often difficult to neatly separate contract law from consumer law,[49] especially in the European Union.[50] An extensive debate of these issues exceeds to scope of this chapter, though. After all, the question of whether a contract has been formed falls within the scope of the common law, and "much of the consumer-specific legislation presupposes the existence of a contract."[51] For present purposes, contract law is metephorically placed in a petri dish and examined in isolation, if only to illustrate the continued resilience of its core principles.

---

48 Entores Ltd v Miles Far East Corporation [1955] 2 QB 327; Brinkibon v Stahag und Stahlwarenhandelsgesellschaft mbH [1983] 2 AC 34; David Baxter Edward Thomas and Peter Sandford Gander v BPE Solicitors [2010] EWHC 306 (Ch); Newcastle Upon Tyne NHS Foundation Trust v Sandi Haywood [2017] EWCA Civ 153; Bernuth Lines Limited v High Seas Shipping Ltd [2006] 1 Lloyds Rep 537; J Pereira Fernandes SA v Mehta [2006] EWHC 813, [2006] 1 All ER (Comm) 885; Parker-Grennan v Camelot UK Lotteries Ltd [2024] EWCA Civ 185.

49 Hanoh Dagan, 'Between Regulatory and Autonomy-Based Private Law', European Law Journal 22 (2016), 644; Mateusz Grochowski, 'European Consumer Law after the New Deal: A Tryptich,' (2020) 39 Yearbook of European Law, p. 387; Bar-Gill, Oren, Ben-Shahar, Omri and Marotta-Wurgler, Florencia, 'A Companion Guide to the Restatement of Consumer Contracts' (2025), Coase-Sandor Working Paper Series in Law and Economics, 25-08, https://chicagounbound.uchicago.edu/law_and_economics/1042.

50 Mateusz Grochowski, 'European Consumer Law after the New Deal: A Tryptich,' (2020) 39 *Yearbook of European Law*, p. 387; 'The role of the common law of contract in the regulation has been reduced to such an extent that it would now be appropriate to treat consumer contract law as an almost entirely discrete body of law. Retaining contract law within the regulatory repertoire for consumer contracts becomes increasingly difficult because of their different approaches and underlying values'; Christian Twigg-Flesner, 'United Kingdom consumer law: incomplete transformation', in: H-W. Micklitz and C. Twigg-Flesner (eds.), *The transformation of consumer law and policy in Europe*, London: Bloomsbury Press (2023), p. 339; Brownsword has argued that "the regulation of consumer transactions has nothing to do with contract law," see R. Brownsword, 'Regulating Transactions: Good Faith and Fair Dealing', in: G. Howells and R. Schulze (eds.), *Modernising and Harmonising Consumer Contract Law*, Sellier (2009), pp. 87-88.

51 Twigg-Flesner (n. 50), p. 340.

Third, questions of contract law must be distinguished from questions of AI regulation.[52] The use of AI in many contexts raises significant concerns that may require urgent regulatory intervention,[53] facilitate price discrimination,[54] enable behavioral manipulation,[55] distort markets[56] and, quite possibly, threaten human existence.[57] These concerns have been thoroughly explored in legal literature[58] but do not fall within the ambit of contract law.

IV. Vending Machines as Examples of Technological Progress

The difficulty of tying legal principles to ongoing technological progress is best exemplified by vending machines. From a legal perspective, vending machines are offers directed to the world at large, made by those who display their goods by making the machine available to the public.[59] A contract is formed with whoever accepts such offer by providing payment and selecting the product. What is important in the present context is that

52 Brian Judge, Mark Nitzberg, Stuart Russell, 'When code isn't law: rethinking regulation for artificial intelligence', *Policy and Society*, Volume 44, Issue 1, January 2025, pp. 85–97, https://doi.org/10.1093/polsoc/puae020.

53 For a discussion of the concerns that automation and AI pose in the public sector, including law enforcement and privacy, see: Monika Zalnieriute, Lyria Bennett Moses, George Williams, 'The Rule of Law and Automation of Government Decision-Making' (2019) 82 MLR 425; M. Hildebrandt, 'Law as Computation in the Era of Artificial Legal Intelligence: Speaking Law to the Power of Statistics' (2018) 68 U Toronto L J 12; D. Hogan-Doran, 'Computer Says 'No': Automation, Algorithms and Artificial Intelligence in Government Decision-Making' (2017) 13 Judicial Review 345.

54 Robert M. Weiss, Ajay K. Mehrotra, 'Online Dynamic Pricing: Efficiency, Equity and the Future of E-Commerce' (2001) 6 Virginia J Law & Tech 11.

55 See also: Montreal Declaration for a Responsible Development of Artificial Intelligence (2018), which mentions the risks of creating dependencies through attention-capturing techniques or the imitation of human characteristics, at 5, 7.

56 Yesha Yadav, 'The Failure of Liability in Modern Markets' (2016) 102 Virginia L Review 1031 at 1063; Tom CW Lin, 'The New Financial Industry' (2014) 65 Ala L Review 567; Andrew J Keller, 'Robocops: Regulating High Frequency Trading After the Flash Crash of 2010' (2012) 73 Ohio State L J 1457 at 1461-1464.

57 Brundage, Miles et al. "The Malicious Use of Artificial Intelligence: Forecasting, Prevention, and Mitigation." ArXiv abs/1802.07228 (2018): n. pag.

58 Rory Van Loo, 'Helping Buyers Beware: The Need for Supervision of Big Retail' (2015) 163 U Penn L Review 1311 at 1330; M. Grochowski, A. Jabłonowska, F. Lagioia & G. Sartor, (2022). Algorithmic Price Discrimination and Consumer Protection: A Digital Arms Race?. Technology and Regulation, 2022, 36-47.

59 Thornton v Shoe Lane Parking Ltd [1971] 2 QB 163; Carlill v Carbolic Smoke Ball Co [1893] 1 QB 256 at 262 Lexmead (Basingstoke) Ltd v Lewis [1982] AC 225.

vending machines automate both contract formation and, as they automatically dispense products upon payment, contractual performance. The first known commercial use of vending machines came early in the 18th century in England, where coin-actuated "honour boxes" were used to sell snuff and tobacco.[60] In the United States, vending machines were commercially used from 1888, dispensing chewing gum, cigarettes and softdrinks.[61] During the 1970s, vending machines have been progressively equipped with microcomputer controls. Throughout the 1990s, the number of microcomputer components grew, and so did their computational power. In the 2000s vending machines became connected to the internet and equipped with sophisticated user interfaces: buttons were replaced with touch screens, coin slots with card readers. Many vending machines became capable of monitoring their inventory, observing purchasing patterns and adjusting their offering or prices accordingly. Apart from standard maintenance, trouble-shooting and re-stocking, vending machines operate autonomously and do not require ongoing human intervention or supervision in order to form and perform contracts. What matters in the present context is that for over a hundred years, millions of transactions have been made "with" (or: by means of) vending machines. And yet, despite their prevalence in both civil and common law jurisdictions, there is no *single* case questioning the validity or enforceability of the resulting contracts on the ground that such machines operate without human intervention, are incapable of agreeing to anything and occasionally produce unexpected output. There is also no single case that addresses their increasing technological sophistication. Were we to subscribe to the theory that contract law is directly affected by and should respond to technological progress then, given that vending machines have been equipped with progressively more sophisticated components (including AI!), there must have been a moment where contracts with vending machines ceased to be enforceable or valid. In other words, at some stage of their technological evolution, the purchases "from" such machines must have become "doctrinally suspect." When was this moment? Was it when vending machines started accepting cashless and

60 Britannica, The Editors of Encyclopaedia. 'vending machine', *Encyclopedia Britannica,* (27 May 2024), https://www.britannica.com/money/vending-machine. Accessed 8 June 2025.

61 It is rarely known that vending machines date back to ancient Egypt, notably a temple in Alexandria in 215 BC, where they were used to dispense "sacrificial water, see Kerry Segrave, *Vending Machines, An American Social History* (McFarland 2002).

mobile payments or the moment they became integrated with the vendor's stock monitoring systems? If increases in computation (or more powerful processors?) directly affect legal principles, then this watershed event must have been the integration of vending machines with machine learning technologies[62] or the moment when the low-end microcontrollers (which lack computing capabilities and connectivity) powering the machines' control boards were replaced with procesor based controllers.[63] While these suggestions may seem frivolous or extreme, they demostrate that any claims that the principles of contract law are technology-sensitive and require *adaptation* to technological change lead into dangerous territory. Any technology-specific approach and the introduction of legal distinctions based on the type of computer program or processor used to automate the contracting process, requires a clear indication of the technological features that render a given contract *potentially* invalid or unenforceable. Given the wide range of technologies falling under the ambit of AI and the fact that AI has been present in commercial life for decades, a broad reference to AI *in general* seems insufficient to ensure legal certainty. As indicated, we are in dangerous territory – a territory that demands a high level of IT literacy from those who embark on the endeavour of adapting contract law as well as a careful consideration of the practical implications of any technology-specific "adjustments." After all, it can hardly be assumed that contracts made with (i.e. by means of) vending machines cease to be valid or enforceable once such machines become equipped with more computing power or more sophisticated control boards. It seems equally unreasonable to assume that contracts formed through the chat function on websites should cease to be valid or enforceable once chats are powered by large language models – which are technically a type of AI - instead of simpler programs based on express instructions. To what extent, we must ask, should the technology matter given that it is hidden from the view of the reasonable addressee? To what extent, if any, are technological distinctions conducive to legal certainty?

62 C.-J. Chen et al., 'Smart Vending Machine System Prototyped with Deep- and Machine-Learning Technologies', *IEEE International Conference on Consumer Electronics - Taiwan (ICCE-Taiwan)*, Taoyuan, Taiwan (2020), pp. 1-2, doi: 10.1109/ICCE-Taiwan49838.2020.9258152.

63 Eriyeti Murena et al., 'Design of a Control System for a Vending Machine', (2020) 91 Procedia CIRP 758.

As an aside it is worth mentioning that the latest edition of Chitty, a pre-eminent reference work on contract law in the common law world, states that websites enabling the purchase of digital products, resemble "virtual vending machines."[64] The latter "are generally regarded as offers because there is no expectation or opportunity to negotiate, and no practical scope for withdrawal because the product or service is delivered immediately and cannot be easily returned. In the usual course of such transactions, the customer selects the digital content, provides payment details and confirms the order, whereupon the digital content will immediately download onto the customer's device (e.g. computer, smartphone or tablet)."[65] The fact that contracts with such "virtual vending machines" are formed and performed without direct human involvement and often rely on computer programs falling into the category of AI passes without mention.[66] Similarly, in the recently decided appellate case *Parker-Grennan v Camelot UK Lotteries Ltd*,[67] which involved a contract formed through the interaction with a computer system, the Court ignored the fact that the contract was formed and performed by automated means, without any human involvement on the side of the provider. The focus was, almost exclusively, placed on what the customer could see on her screen.[68]

V. The Model Law on Automated Contracting

The challenges of adapting contract law by means of "external interventions" as well as the potential to create additional uncertainty by providing solutions to non-existent problems are illustrated by the recently adopted UNCITRAL "Model Law on Automated Contracting" (MLAC or Model Law).[69] The MLAC claims to establish a legal framework to facilitate automated contracting, to provide legal recognition to automated contracts and actions carried out by automated systems and to overcome potential

64 Hugh Beale, *Chitty on Contracts,* 35th ed. (2024 Sweet Maxwell) 4-097.
65 Hugh Beale, *Chitty on Contracts,* 35th ed. (2024 Sweet Maxwell) 4-097.
66 Pertinently, the latest edition of Treitel's "The Law of Contract", published in April 2025 mentions neither artificial intelligence nor automation, see Treitel, *Law of Contract*, 16th ed., Edwin Peel (OUP, 2025).
67 [2024] EWCA Civ 185 [1].
68 [2024] EWCA Civ 185 [11], [12], [48], [59].
69 See United Nations Report of the United Nations Commission on International Trade Law Fifty-seventh session (24 June–12 July 2024) A/79/17.

obstacles to applying existing law to such contracts.[70] It does not aim to be a complete code for automated contracting but, we are told, assumes that existing law, including general contract law and electronic transaction laws, applies to automated contracting. It is also intended to supplement laws on electronic transactions, particularly those based on other UNCITRAL texts such as the Model Law on Electronic Commerce (MLEC) and the Electronic Communications Convention (ECC).[71] The latter instruments have addressed the use of electronic means to communicate intention, to conclude contracts in electronic form, and to carry out other actions throughout the contract life cycle.[72] Although space constraints preclude a detail analysis of the entire instrument, it is important to critically review some of its core articles and to address several misconceptions that guided its creation.

At a basic level, it is unclear why automated contracting requires "facilitation," "legal recognition" or what specific obstacles must be overcome to enable automated contracting, at least in common law jurisdictions. If contract law already applies to automated contracting,[73] and if its principles do not contain any impediments to this practice, then the entire *raison d'etre* of the Model Law seems questionable. The purported need to *supplement* existing principles with additional rules may result in unnecessary interference, if not uncertainty. At least if "to supplement" is understood as "a thing added to something else in order to complete or enhance it." Seemingly, despite evidence to the contrary, the drafters assumed that the principles of contract law were incapable of dealing with automated transactions. Moreover, the ECC already covers automated contracting as it specifically mentions the use of "automated message systems" and the lack of human involvement.[74] Yet, UNICTRAL insisted that the automation of

70 Guide to Enactment para 21.

71 Guide to Enactment para 6.

72 Draft Guide to Enactment para 5; see also Rolf H. Weber, "Contractual Duties and Allocation of Liability in Automated Digital Contracts", in: R. Schulze and D. Staudenmayer (eds.), *Digital Revolution: Challenges for Contract Law in Practice* (Oxford: Hart Publishing), p. 184.

73 Guide to Enactment para 90.

74 Art. 12 UN Convention on the Use of Electronic Communications in International Contracts 2005: "A contract formed by the interaction of an automated message system and a natural person, or by the interaction of automated message systems, shall not be denied validity or enforceability on the sole ground that *no natural person reviewed or intervened* in each of the individual actions carried out by the automated message systems or the resulting contract." (my emphasis).

the contracting process introduces "something of a 'disconnect' between the parties and their contractual actions, which is amplified with the increased sophistication and complexity of automated systems.[75] Purportedly, this was the case for systems deploying AI techniques programmed to operate "autonomously."[76] It was also observed that automation was particularly relevant to commercial contracting, which "is increasingly deploying techniques associated with artificial intelligence ("AI"), such as "machine learning" or "rules-based" approaches."[77] Automated contracting was also associated with the absence of human involvement (or intervention) and the lack of predictability.[78] Article 5, titled 'Legal recognition of automated contracting,' provides that a contract formed using an automated system shall not be denied validity or enforceability solely because no natural person reviewed or intervened in any action related to its formation.[79] An optional provision extends this principle to contracts *performed* using an automated system. It is explained that the provision aimes "at overcoming obstacles to applying existing legal requirements to contracts formed and performed using an automated system."[80] These statements are unconvincing. As demonstrated by e-commerce websites and automated trading systems (amongst others), contracts can be formed and performed with the assistance of automated systems of varying complexity. Given that "automated contracting" has pervaded commercial tansactions for not less than 50 years,[81] the provision seems redundant. While it could serve as a confirmation of existing law, it may also introduce unnecessary confusion by implying that the validity of automated transactions could be retrospectively questioned.

Further confusion derives from the definition of "automated systems," that is: computer systems that are capable of carrying out actions "without the necessary human review or intervention."[82] As automation, by defini-

75 Draft Guide to Enactment para 6.
76 Draft Guide to Enactment para 6.
77 United Nations Commission on International Trade Law Working Group IV (Electronic Commerce) Sixty-seventh session Vienna, 18–22 November 2024, Draft guide to enactment of the Model Law on Automated Contracting Note by the Secretariat.
78 MLAC Art. 1 (a); see also: UNCITRAL A/79/17, para 178.
79 MLAC Art. 5 (Legal Recognition of Automated Contracting).
80 MLAC Guide to Enactment para 29.
81 D. Dimov, "Conceptual Model of Automated Trading Systems Implementation" (2022) 3 ROBONOMICS: The Journal of the Automated Economy, 25.
82 MLAC Art. 5.

tion, renders continuous human review or intervention *unnecessary*, the word "necessary" seems redundant.[83] Regrettably, Article 1 (2) introduces further complications by stating that "an automated system may be programmed to operate in a deterministic or non-deterministic manner." The term "deterministic" is intended to denote a system that always generates the same output given the same input,[84] which may also be referred to as a "rule-based system."[85] It is unclear why a mention of deterministic and non-deterministic operation was considered necessary, particularly given the technology neutral character of the MLAC.[86] The accompanying materials indicate that non-deterministic systems are generally associated with AI and unpredictability,[87] a crucial detail that elucidates later provisions concerning unexpected operations. It is true that, from a technical perspective, the term "deterministic" denotes systems or processes in which the outcome is determined by the initial conditions and the governing rules, with no randomness involved. In a deterministic system, given a specific set of inputs, the output will always be the same. Theoretically, the operation of a deterministic system can be predicted with certainty.[88] Theoretical proclamations are, however, less relevant in practice. Theoretically, computer programs can be seen as deterministic: given the same input, they can be expected to produce the same output. Nonetheless, multiple factors can make their operations difficult to predict and hence non-deterministic, even in the case of rule-based programs that do not involve sub-symbolic AI. In practice, predictability is a function of complexity: the more complex the program, the less predictable it becomes.[89] Logically, complexity

83 The MLAC Guide to Enactment para 28 observes that "the requirement in the definition for such review or intervention to be "necessary" is intended to avoid the implication that an automated system ceases to fall within the definition on the sole ground that the system is subject to human oversight."

84 MLAC Guide to Enactment para 75.

85 MLAC Guide to Enactment para 29.

86 MLAC Art. 4 and MLAC Guide to Enactment para 12.

87 MLAC Guide to Enactment para 75.

88 https://www.wolframalpha.com/input?input=definition+of+deterministic.

89 These challenges derive from the principles of computational irreducibility, which states that operations of complex programs cannot be predicted without actually running those programs. This means that while some programs exhibit simple, predictable behavior that can be described by mathematical formulae (such programs are "computationally reducible"), many systems, especially those with complex behavior, are computationally irreducible so that their future states and outputs cannot be predicted without performing the full computation; see generally: Stephen Wolfram, *A new kind of science,* Vol. 5.,Champaign, IL: Wolfram Media (2002), pp. 737-742, 747;

will further increase when automated *systems* consist of and/or interact with multiple computer programs. We are no longer dealing with a single computer program, which *might* operate in a deterministic fashion, but with multiple computer programs of varying complexity operating *together*. Moreover, the operations of computer programs (or automated systems in general) can also be affected by unpredictable external conditions (i.e. the environment they operate in), such as inputs of an unexpected size or type, a shortage of system resources, like memory, connectivity or processing power. The predictability of computer programs also depends on the quality of their code and the amount of resources committed to their testing. As it is impossible to test a program for all possible inputs and interactions that could occur in its future operating environment,[90] it is practically infeasible to predict how it would operate in situations that have not been tested.[91] Moreover, even deterministic systems may be impossible to predict, whenever their operations are sensitive to initial conditions,[92] i.e. factors affecting the state of a system at a specific point in time.[93] A

Rowland Todd. "Computational Irreducibility." From MathWorld-A Wolfram Web Resource, created by Eric W. Weisstein. https://mathworld.wolfram.com/ComputationalIrreducibility.html; Hervé Zwirn, and Jean-Paul Delahaye, 'Unpredictability and computational irreducibility', in: *Irreducibility and Computational Equivalence* (Springer, Berlin, Heidelberg 2013), pp. 273-276; given the space constraints, I intentionally avoid the Decidability Theory and the Rice Theorem, which are also of practical relevance.

90 The problem is known as "combinatorial explosion", see Edward Tsang, *Combinational Explosion*, U. ESSEX (May 12, 2005), http://cswww.essex.ac.uk/CSP/ComputationalFinanceTeaching/ CombinatorialExplosion.html [https://perma.cc/R7KE-4BJD]; Richard E Fairley, 'Tutorial: Static analysis and dynamic testing of computer software' (1978) Computer 11.4, 15-16; Axel Halin, et al., 'Test them all, is it worth it? Assessing configuration sampling on the JHipster Web development stack' (2019) Empirical Software Engineering 24.2, pp. 674-717; Joshua A Kroll and others, 'Accountable Algorithms' (2017) 165 U Penn L Review 633, 645; Carlo Ghezzi et al., *Fundamentals of Software Engineering* (2d ed. Pearson 2002), pp. 269-273.

91 see Michael Sipser, 'Introduction to the Theory of Computation', 201(2006), A.M. Turing, *On Computable Numbers, with an Application to the Entscheidungsproblem. A Correction*, 43 PROC. LONDON MATHEMATICAL SOC'Y (1937), pp 544-46.

92 This concept, famously known as the *butterfly effect*, metaphorically suggests that a butterfly flapping its wings in Brazil could eventually lead to large-scale changes, like causing a tornado in Texas; see Edward N. Lorenz, 'Deterministic Nonperiodic Flow', *Journal of Atmospheric Sciences* 20.2 (1963), pp. 130-141, https://doi.org/10.1175/1520-0469(1963)020<0130:DNF>2.0.CO;2.

93 For example, it is technically infeasible to provide a complete snapshot of the state of financial markets at any given time given the number of variables involved and the difficulty of their measurement! Even a slight change in market sentiment can have

minuscule difference in such state can thus lead to dramatically different results.[94] Counterintuitively, a computer program can be both deterministic *and* unpredictable. This apparent contradiction derives from the practical ability to detemine its initial state and foresee its behavior, especially in the case of complex systems operating in unpredictable environments or over extended periods of time.[95] The above problems are aggravated in the case of systems encompassing sub-symbolic AI, which is inherently probabilistic and hence difficult to test.[96] It follows that, in practice, it is technically impossible to *program* a system "to operate in a deterministic manner" if it is to operate in an environment which is not fully known and predictable.

Leaving aside the questionable need to "recognise" automated contracting and the unfortunate mention of deterministic and non-deterministic systems, it is worth briefly discussing Article 7, which contains basic rules of attribution. The primary rule is that: "as between the parties to a contract, an action carried out by an automated system is attributed in accordance with a procedure agreed to by the parties."[97] Absent such procedure, the action is attributed to the person who uses the system for that purpose.[98] Attribution is to be determined objectively, based on circumstances.[99] It is emphsized that Article 7 does not affect the application of any exsiting rules governing the consequences of attribution or address questions of liability.[100] The proposed solutions may seem straightforward at first: whoever uses the system, is attributed with the consequences of its operation. Yet, UNCITRAL's preparatory works reveal the challenges of identifying the "person who uses the system." Factors that could be considered are "the

grave consequences further down the line; see also M. Hilbert and D. Darmo, 'How Complexity and Uncertainty Grew with Algorithmic Trading' (2020) Entropy, 22(5), 499, https://doi.org/10.3390/e2205049.

94 For accessible explanations, see: Melanie Mitchell, *Complexity, A Guided Tour* (OUP 2009), p. 20; Stuart Russel, *Human Compatible* (Penguin 2019), p. 96.

95 To complicate matters, some deterministic programs are intentionally designed to be unpredictable, e.g. a card-shuffling program for a poker game. The algorithm is deterministic, but it uses a pseudorandom number generator to produce a shuffle that players cannot predict!

96 See generally R. V. Yampolsky, "Unpredictability of AI: on the impossibility of accurately predicting all actions of a Smarter Agent" (2020) 7 Journal of Artificial Intelligence and Consciousness, 109.

97 MLAC Art. 7 (1).

98 MLAC Art. 7 (2).

99 Guide to Enactment para 66.

100 Guide to Enactment para 60, 71.

strongest link with a specific action," "the degree of control over the operational parameters of the system and the specific action" or "the material benefit or value received from the specific action."[101] It is also acknowledged that users may have limited *control over* or *understanding of* the system's operation especially if they did not create or commission its creation.[102] On one hand, the provision can be applauded for highlighting the urgency to address attribution by agreement. On the other, it can be regarded as superfluous because attribution is always case-specific and thus difficult to address in a more detailed and prescriptive manner. Apart from stating the default principle, it is extremely difficult to list all the relevant criteria that should be taken into account when deciding who should bear the consequences of an action of an automated system.[103] Given that attribution "shall not be denied on the sole ground that the outcome was unexpected,"[104] parties using automated system are incentivized to invest in their reliablity and discouraged from deploying systems they cannot control or do not fully understand. No one should be permitted to disavow an action on the basis that he or she did not expect its occurrence – especially if he or she decided to use an automated system the operations of which they do not understand. Why would anyone be protected from their own ignorance or unreasonable risk-taking? Unfortunately, absent agreement, the default risk allocation for "unexpected output" is described in the optional Article 8, which addresses automated contracting with the use of unpredictable "AI systems"[105] as well as "unpredicted or unintended outputs" deriving from "errors in programming, errors in transmission and third-party interference.[106] Article 8 states that "unless otherwise agreed by the parties, where an action carried out by an automated system is attributed to a party to a contract, the other party to the contract is not entitled to rely on that action if, in the light of all the circumstances:

(a) The party to which the action is attributed could not reasonably have expected the action;
and

101 Guide to Enactment para 66.
102 Guide to Enactment para 66.
103 The control problem comes to mind!
104 MLAC Art. 7 (3).
105 UNCITRAL A/79/17, para 219.
106 Guide to Enactment para 75.

(b) The other party knew or could reasonably be expected to have known that the party to which the action is attributed did not expect the action."

Article 8 focuses on what is best described as "unintended actions"[107] and covers both non-deterministic systems deploying AI techniques, for which unpredictability is a distinguishing feature and deterministic systems.[108] It applies to situations in which an automated system is operating as designed but generates an unexpected output, as well as to situations where the output is affected by the aforementioned errors in programming, errors in transmission and third-party interference.[109] As indicated, these factors alone do not convey the difficulty – if not impossibility – of ensuring that a system operates in a deterministic and hence predictable manner. Article 8 does not acknowledge the inherent inability to guarantee the predictability of complex systems operating over extended periods of time. Subparagraph (a) concerns "reasonable expectations" and calls for an objective determination of expectations, in light of all the circumstances of the particular action at the time it occurred.[110] Different factors may be relevant, including (a) the nature and purpose of the contract; (b) the type of transaction for which the action is carried out; and (c) trade usages and practices between the parties. Purportedly, information concerning the design, operation and use of the automated system may also be relevant, although such information might not be readily understood by the party so as to be a decisive factor in such determination.[111] This last statement is somewhat surprising given that the reasonableness of a person's expectations largely depends on his or her knowledge.[112] As indicated, no one should be protected from their own technical ignorance. The problems do not end here.

How can the relying party know what the other party (i.e. the party using the automated system) was expecting – or should have reasonably expected – given the lack of insight into his or her objectives, not to mention the technical aspects of the other party's automated system? What if the unexpected action derived from a bad business decision embodied in the

107 Guide to Enactment para 75.
108 Guide to Enactment para 75.
109 Guide to Enactment para 75.
110 (A/79/17, para. 224).
111 Guide to Enactment para 81.
112 Guide to Enactment para 80.

system's trading parameters? What if the action derived from incorrect programming or bad system design? Why should a person who *chose* to deploy an unpredictable and unexplainable be protected from the consequences of its operation? Contract law rewards risk taking but it does not protect the contracting parties from their technological choices. If "unpredictability is a distinguishing feature" of AI techniques,[113] then the operations of automated systems may *frequently* and *significantly* diverge from the expectations of those who use them for the very reason that they are difficult to predict! In practice, whether an action could or should have been expected depends on the technical literacy and business acumen of both parties. Determining the reasonableness of the parties' expectations requires a fine-grained and case-specific exmination of each purportedly unexpected action. The potential for legal uncertainty is immediately apparent: either party might attempt to disavow a particular action (i.e. transaction) on the basis that it was not or could not have been reasonably expected. Logically, attempts to deny attribution will only be made if the resulting transaction resulted in financial detriment to the party using the automated system. Only those who suffer negative financial consequences will retrospectively question attribution and claim that they could not have reasonably expected the particular action and that the other party knew or must've known that they did not expect the action. We could logically assume that unexpected actions will not be questioned if they result in financially beneficial outcomes. More importantly, in many contracting scenarios both parties may use automated systems so that neither party will be able to know or investigate the other's expectations – not to mention to monitor the operations of the systems and its individual actions.[114] After all, automaton is inherently associated with the absence of direct and continuous human supervision and involvement. UNCITRAL's suggestion that expectations should be evaluated "at the time the action is carried out"[115] is unconvincing because *at that moment* neither party may be present. To efficiently supervise automated processes and to evaluate whether their outputs were or could have been reasonably expected by the other party, these processes would have to be monitored in real-time and decelerated to human-speed.[116] This, however, would defeat the very purpose of automation. Admittedly, the above suggestion refers to

113 Guide to Enactment para 75.
114 Lisanne Bainbridge, 'Ironies of Automation' (1983) 19 Automatica, 775.
115 MLAC Guide to Enactment para 81.
116 Bainbridge (n. 114) 776.

a retrospective evaluation of what should have been expected at the time the action *was* carried out. The lack of human involement at that moment necessitates the construction of complex legal fictions as to what *should or could* have been expected. It was suggested that, to ensure objectivity, the unexpected action should also "significantly deviate from what was expected."[117] This could, for example, be established by comparing the unexpected output with the prevailing market prices. Such appraoch, however, requires a *retrospectie* evaluation of the expectations of *future* market movements. Establishing objectively reasonable expectations will only be possible in clear-cut or extreme scenarios where, for example, the offered price will be out of all proportion to the prevailing market rates. The retrospective evaluation of what one party should have expected about the expectations of the other is bound to imbue the law with unnecesary uncertainty. Implicitly, given the emphasis on objectivity, it assumes that both parties are commercially rational and familiar with the technical foundations of their systems. In practice, however, most problems will derive from the unpredictable nature of these systems (or any of their components) and the technical incompetence of their users. In short, Article 8 does not provide clear solutions but introduces an additional layer of uncertainty.

To clarify: problems of unexpected output differ from the challenges of retrospectively explaining or interpreting the operations of a particular program. The problems of explainability and interpretability of complex computer programs are worthy of regulatory attention, especially when they are used to "make decisions" direcly affecting human dignity and prosperity.[118] They are, however, of no direct concern in the area of contract law.

VI. Final Observations

As I have described elsewhere, contract law is 'forward compatible'.[119] Those claiming otherwise fail to appreciate the power of analogy and

117 UNCITRAL A/79/17, para 229.

118 Sandra Wachter, Brent Daniel Mittelstadt and Chris Russell, "Why Fairness Cannot Be Automated: Bridging the Gap Between EU Non-Discrimination Law and AI" (2021) 41 *CLSR* 105567; Philipp Hacker, Ralf Krestel, Stefan Grundmann and Felix Naumann, "Explainable AI under contract and tort law: legal incentives and technical challenges" (2020) 28 Artificial Intelligence and Law, 415.

119 Foloc 112.

the flexibility of the *ratio decidendi.* Contract law is generally capable of addressing most problems pertaining to technological change.[120] It does not need to be adapted or updated. In common law, the idea of introducing detailed rules of governing automated contracting seems radical given that the common law of contract has traditionally dealt with specific, clearly identified problems *post factum*, generally refraining from prescribing detailed rules concerning the technological aspects of the transacting process. Neither courts, nor regulators have the foresight and, admittedly, the competence to anticipate how a given technology will be integrated into commercial practice and what concrete problems, if any, it will cause. In an area like contract law, which seems generally indifferent to the way intention is manifested, the introduction of technology-specific rules runs counter to the fundamental principles governing this area. The automation of various aspects – and stages - of the contracting process does not raise any legal concerns. Quite the opposite: vending machines illustrate the difficulty of introducing legal differentiations based on technological developments. The letter is generally gradual, often imperceptible and difficult to pinpoint.

We must remember that, at present, we are in the middle of a very hot AI summer and that our views on any technology-related legal topic are easily framed[121] by the terminology used. Narratives laden with persistent references to AI, "self-learning algorithms" or "deep learning" create the impression – and force the seemingly unavoidable conclusion - that contracts concluded *by means of* such technologies must be doctrinally questionable or, at least, impossible to accommodate by existing principles. Legal analyses would be more balanced if discussions concerning the deployment of AI in the contracting process used less sensationalistic language. They would also benefit from a more informed use of technical terms.

Technological factors unquestionably render legal analyses more complex. Nonetheless, before contemplating any adaptations or adjustments, it is necessary to identify the *specific* technology and the *specific* problem(s) it purportedly creates. It is also necessary to have absolute certainty that existing principles cannot bear the weight of technological change.

---

120 Lyria Bennet Moses, 'Recurring Dilemmas: The Law's Race To Keep Up With Technological Change' (2007) U Ill J. L. Tech & Pol'y 239, 244.

121 I am referring to a term popularized by the Nobel-prize winner, Daniel Kahneman, which refers to the exploitation of a cognitive bias created by the manner certain problems are presented.

Defects of Consent and Unexpected Outcomes

When things go wrong – dealing with unexpected outcomes in automated contracting

Christiane Wendehorst[*]

Abstract

The increasing reliance on automated systems in contracting has introduced new challenges, particularly when these systems produce unexpected outcomes. This article explores the legal frameworks and principles designed to address such scenarios, focusing on the UNCITRAL Model Law on Automated Contracting (MLAC), the ELI Model Rules on Digital Assistants for Consumer Contracts (ELI DACC Model Rules) and the Principles for AI in Contracting (PAIC). By comparing these instruments, the article highlights their approaches to attribution, unexpected outcomes, and the role of technical capabilities. It concludes with recommendations for future legislative developments, particularly at the EU level, to ensure clarity and consistency in automated contracting.

I. Introduction

Members of the legal profession are not always seen as particularly likable. This may be because many people encounter lawyers only in rather unpleasant situations, such as in court. It may be due to the fees on legal invoices. But it could also stem from the fact that lawyers tend to focus on one thing above all else: What if something goes wrong? This inherently pessimistic outlook on the world, which always considers the worst-case scenario first, has earned lawyers a reputation as killjoys. This perception is no less relevant in the context of using artificial intelligence (AI) in contracting.

And yet, it is precisely the cases where things do not go smoothly that lawyers and legislators must focus on first and foremost. When a transaction proceeds without issues and both parties are happy and satisfied,

* Institute for Civil Law, Vienna, Deputy Director of the Institute for Digitalisation and Law, Scientific Director of the European Law Institute.

neither party will later invoke the law or bring a case to court. However, when something goes wrong, it typically benefits one party at the expense of the other, and the benefitted party will often not agree to an amicable resolution. This is the moment when contract law must prove its worth—even in the age of AI, where the entire lifecycle of a contract—from contract initiation and negotiation to contract formation, performance, and the fulfillment of post-contractual obligations—is often managed by software of various types, without direct human intervention.

II. National law on automated contracting

The immense practical significance and widespread use of software, without direct human intervention, throughout the lifecycle of a contract stands in stark contrast to the scant attention this phenomenon has received in national laws worldwide. This is true not only for the use of advanced AI—which might be somewhat understandable—but even for automation in the contractual context as such.

1. Legislation – different degrees of silence

The surprising silence of contract law when it comes to automation, let alone the use of sophisticated AI, certainly holds true for legislation as well as legislative proposals. Laws typically limit themselves to stating that automated contract formation is possible and that a contract cannot be denied legal recognition solely because it was concluded without a human being directly involved. Rules addressing what should happen when something goes wrong are scarce, and if they exist, they seem mostly focused on traditional input and transmission errors.

a) US Uniform Electronic Transactions Act (UETA) 1999

Already at the end of the last century, the US Uniform Electronic Transactions Act (UETA)[1] declared automated transactions to be effective. UETA is

1 Uniform Electronic Transactions Act 1999 (UETA), *National Conference of Commissioners on Uniform State Laws.*

a model law that has been adopted in its essential parts in all states except New York.

Sec. 14 UETA contains a central statement on the validity of a contract which is concluded either through the co-operation of electronic agents of all contracting parties or through the co-operation of the electronic agent of one party and a human actor. UETA also contains definitions for the terms "automated transaction" and "electronic agent". The official comments make it unmistakably clear that electronic agents are tools. Furthermore, the principle of full attribution is emphasised:

> "An electronic agent, such as a computer program or other automated means employed by a person, is a tool of that person. As a general rule, the employer of a tool is responsible for the results obtained by the use of that tool since the tool has no independent volition of its own. However, an electronic agent, by definition, is capable within the parameters of its programming, of initiating, responding or interacting with other parties or their electronic agents once it has been activated by a party, without further attention of that party. ..."

Although UETA was primarily designed for traditional software, the official explanations already take into account the development towards "autonomous" software agents:

> "...While this Act proceeds on the paradigm that an electronic agent is capable of performing only within the technical strictures of its preset programming, it is conceivable that, within the useful life of this Act, electronic agents may be created with the ability to act autonomously, and not just automatically. That is, through developments in artificial intelligence, a computer may be able to 'learn through experience, modify the instructions in their own programs, and even devise new instructions. Allen and Widdison, 'Can Computers Make Contracts?' 9 Harv. J.L &Tech 25 (Winter, 1996). If such developments occur, courts may construe the definition of electronic agent accordingly, in order to recognise such new capabilities."

There are very few rules on what happens "when things go wrong" in the sense of, e.g., an AI system producing unexpected outcomes. Indirectly, however, Sec. 9 on attribution, and even more so Sec. 10 on "change or error" contains a number of relevant provisions:

SECTION 9. ATTRIBUTION AND EFFECT OF ELECTRONIC RECORD AND ELECTRONIC SIGNATURE.

(a) An electronic record or electronic signature is attributable to a person if it was the act of the person. The act of the person may be shown in any manner, including a showing of the efficacy of any security procedure applied to determine the person to which the electronic record or electronic signature was attributable.

(b) The effect of an electronic record or electronic signature attributed to a person under subsection (a) is determined from the context and surrounding circumstances at the time of its creation, execution, or adoption, including the parties' agreement, if any, and otherwise as provided by law.

SECTION 10. EFFECT OF CHANGE OR ERROR.

If a change or error in an electronic record occurs in a transmission between parties to a transaction, the following rules apply:

(1) If the parties have agreed to use a security procedure to detect changes or errors and one party has conformed to the procedure, but the other party has not, and the nonconforming party would have detected the change or error had that party also conformed, the conforming party may avoid the effect of the changed or erroneous electronic record.

(2) In an automated transaction involving an individual, the individual may avoid the effect of an electronic record that resulted from an error made by the individual in dealing with the electronic agent of another person if the electronic agent did not provide an opportunity for the prevention or correction of the error and, at the time the individual learns of the error, the individual:

(A) promptly notifies the other person of the error and that the individual did not intend to be bound by the electronic record received by the other person;

(B) takes reasonable steps, including steps that conform to the other person's reasonable instructions, to return to the other person or, if instructed by the other person, to destroy the consideration received, if any, as a result of the erroneous electronic record; and

(C) has not used or received any benefit or value from the consideration, if any, received from the other person.

(3) If neither paragraph (1) nor paragraph (2) applies, the change or error has the effect provided by other law, including the law of mistake, and the parties' contract, if any.
(4) Paragraphs (2) and (3) may not be varied by agreement.

In the present context, it is particularly paragraph 1 of Sec. 10 that provides interesting insights that could be relevant also for the use of sophisticated AI.

b) Electronic Signatures in Global and National Commerce Act (ESIGN) 2000

The Electronic Signatures in Global and National Commerce Act (ESIGN)[2] is a United States federal law, passed by the U.S. Congress to facilitate the use of electronic records and electronic signatures in interstate and foreign commerce. The ESIGN can also be a source of inspiration for the courts of New York, as New York has not adopted UETA and the New York counterpart, the NY Electronic Signatures and Records Act (ESRA)[3], does not contain any "electronic agent" provision. ESIGN includes both a definition of "electronic agent" in Sec. 106(3) as well as a provision on the recognition of electronic transactions in Sec. 101(h). The latter provision of ESIGN also mentions attribution specifically in the context of electronic agents, albeit without much further explanation:

SEC. 101. GENERAL RULE OF VALIDITY.
(h) ELECTRONIC AGENTS—A contract or other record relating to a transaction in or affecting interstate or foreign commerce may not be denied legal effect, validity, or enforceability solely because its formation, creation, or delivery involved the action of one or more electronic agents so long as the action of any such electronic agent is legally attributable to the person to be bound.

2 Pub. L. 106–229, 114 Stat. 464, enacted June 30, 2000, 15 U.S.C. ch. 96.
3 <https://www.nysenate.gov/legislation/laws/STT/A3> accessed 15 October 2025.

c) Model Computer Information Transactions Act (MCITA) 1999/2002

The Model Computer Information Transactions Act (MCITA) of 1999 and 2002,[4] which was originally discussed under the name US Uniform Computer Information Transactions Act (UCITA), has only been adopted in two States[5] and can be described as having largely failed. As controversial as MCITA may be overall, it contains some surprisingly progressive approaches including a rule on how to address issues such as fraud and mistake. Sec. 206 introduces the term "electronic mistake" (albeit without defining it) and allows a court to grant "appropriate relief" in such cases, as well as in the case of trickery or the like:

> SECTION 206. OFFER AND ACCEPTANCE: ELECTRONIC AGENTS.
>
> (a) [Formation by interaction of electronic agents.] A contract may be formed by the interaction of electronic agents. If the interaction results in the electronic agents' engaging in operations that under the circumstances indicate acceptance of an offer, a contract is formed, but a court may grant appropriate relief if the operations resulted from fraud, electronic mistake, or the like. ....

Sec. 212 contains ideas on attribution, including some remarks on the burden of proof that are not found in the majority of other regulations.

> SECTION 212. DETERMINING ATTRIBUTION.
>
> (a) [When attribution established.] An electronic authentication, display, message, record, or performance is attributed to a person if it was the act of the person or its electronic agent, or if the person is bound by it under agency or other law. The party relying on attribution of an electronic authentication, display, message, record, or performance to another person has the burden of establishing attribution.

---

4 Uniform Computer Information Transactions Act 2002 (Last Revisions or Amendments Completed Year). Renamed the Model Computer Information Transactions Act (MCITA) in 2014.

5 In the states of Virginia and Maryland, see ULC, 'Computer Information Transactions Act' <https://www.uniformlaws.org/committees/community-home?CommunityKey=92b2978d-585f-4ab6-b8a1-53860fbb43b5#LegBillTrackingAnchor> accessed 15 October 2025.

d) Draft Article 2 Uniform Commercial Code (UCC) 2003

The draft of an amended Article 2 UCC[6] from 2003, which was not adopted by the States and was later withdrawn, has been similarly hapless as MCITA. However, it contains extremely interesting provisions that go well beyond what can be found in other regulations. In particular, the draft of Sec. 2-211 contains a provision according to which contractual provisions introduced by the contractual partner of the user of the electronic agent do not become part of the contract if the contractual partner should have known that the agent is technically incapable of adequately processing the corresponding information:

> SECTION 2-211. LEGAL RECOGNITION OF ELECTRONIC CONTRACTS, RECORDS, AND SIGNATURES.
> ... (4) A contract formed by the interaction of an individual and an electronic agent under Section 2-204(4)(b) does not include terms provided by the individual if the individual had reason to know that the agent could not react to the terms as provided.

The provision in the draft of Sec. 2-103, which actually deals with the definition of "conspicuous", is also interesting. With respect to electronic agents, this is said to apply to a provision if a "reasonably configured" electronic agent would have adequately processed the information. This is particularly the case if the software agent cannot take the next technical step without having reacted to the corresponding contractual provision.

> SECTION 2-103. DEFINITIONS AND INDEX OF DEFINITIONS.
> ... (b) "Conspicuous", with reference to a term, means so written, displayed, or presented that a reasonable person against which it is to operate ought to have noticed it. A term in an electronic record intended to evoke a response by an electronic agent is conspicuous if it is presented in a form that would enable a reasonably configured electronic agent to take it into account or react to it without review of the record by an individual. Whether a term is 'conspicuous' or not is a decision for the court. Conspicuous terms include the following:
> (i) for a person: ...

---

6 Proposed Amendments to Uniform Commercial Code Article 2 – Sales, *The American Law Institute/National Conference of Commissioners on Uniform State Laws* (2002).

(ii) for a person or an electronic agent, a term that is so placed in a record or display that the person or electronic agent may not proceed without taking action with respect to the particular term. ...

e) Canadian Uniform Electronic Commerce Act (Consolidation) 2011

Unsurprisingly, very similar provisions as have been discussed so far can also be found in the Canadian counterpart to UETA, the 2011 consolidated version of the Canadian Uniform Electronic Commerce Act.[7] There is both a definition of "electronic agent" and clarification that a contract may be formed by the interaction of an electronic agent and a natural person or by the interaction of electronic agents.

What is remarkable about the Canadian act in comparison to UETA is that, although the applicability to "autonomous" as opposed to merely "automated" contracting is not addressed, the commentary expressly points out that agency law cannot be applied either directly or by analogy.

Comment:
... Businesses and individuals use 'electronic agents', which are software programs, sometimes embedded in hardware, that can seek out information and respond to it or to incoming messages. This part deals with some of the legal effects of using such tools. The use of the term 'electronic agent' is widespread. The law of agency however plays no part in this discussion. An electronic agent is a tool, not an agent in law.

f) E-Commerce Law of the People's Republic of China 2018

The E-Commerce Law of the People's Republic of China of 2018[8] states much more briefly and concisely in Art. 48 that automated acts of contract conclusion as well as contract fulfilment are effective and work for and against the party using the system in question:

Article 48
Establishment or performance of the contract by a party to the e-commerce activities using an automatic transaction information system shall

7 Uniform Electronic Commerce Act 2011 (Consolidation), *Uniform Law Conference of Canada.*

8 Law on E-Commerce of the People's Republic of China 2018, CLI.1.321035.

> be legally binding upon the party that uses such automatic transaction information system. ...

Again, no differentiation is made between "automated" and "autonomous" contract conclusions, although here too there is no indication that the latter would be treated differently.

g) Guernsey Electronic Transactions (Electronic Agents) Ordinance 2019

Last but not least, the Electronic Transactions (Electronic Agents) Ordinance 2019[9] of the Island of Guernsey provides for relatively detailed provisions. Section 2 goes to great lengths to explain, in no less than five paragraphs, that all sorts of activities in a contractual context are not denied legal effect solely because of the use of electronic agents. What is new is the clarification that an electronic agent may act on behalf of one or more parties to the same transaction, and the broad definition of "contract". An innovative element is Section 3 according to which there is a presumption of an intention to create a legally binding contract:

> 3. Where an electronic agent has acted on behalf of a person for the purposes of the making, formation or creation of a contract, there is a rebuttable presumption that that person intended to create a legally binding contract.

2. Case law – two illustrations

It is impossible to give an exhaustive overview of existing case law with regard to situations where things went wrong with automated contracting. This is why, by way of illustration, only two judgments will be explained in more detail, one from a civil law and one from a common law jurisdiction.

a) German Federal Supreme Court on mistake in computer declarations

In a case decided by the German Federal Supreme Court in 2005[10] the plaintiff was a business selling computers and accessories via an online website. In January 2003, the plaintiff wanted to sell notebooks at the

9 Ordinance No. II of 2019.
10 Bundesgerichtshof (BGH), 26 January 2005, VIII ZR 79/04.

price of EUR 2,650, and the plaintiff's employee entered the correct price into the website's content management system. However, the input had to be processed by several software components, and as a result of the failure of one of the components, the website ultimately displayed the price of EUR 245. In February 2003, the defendant ordered a notebook at the stated sales price, and the plaintiff confirmed receipt and acceptance of the defendant's order at this price by means of an automated messaging system. The notebook was even delivered to the defendant with the plaintiff's invoice showing a sales price of EUR 245. Only a few days later, the plaintiff became aware of the issue and contested the purchase on the basis of mistake.

The German Federal Supreme Court ruled in favour of the plaintiff. The court argued that the plaintiff's intention was to sell the notebook at EUR 2,650, and that the subsequent error in the data transfer by the software component was to be considered as an error during transmission within the meaning of § 120 of the German Civil Code (BGB). The court considered all subsequent steps to be affected by that initial error and granted the plaintiff a right to cancel the transaction. Interestingly, the court did not even bother to discuss the fact that, quite apart from the display on the website, the plaintiff's automated sales system had expressly confirmed the transaction and that the notebook was also delivered with an invoice showing the lower price. While the scenario underlying this case is certainly very far from the kind of scenario we are concerned about in the context of advanced AI agents, it is nevertheless instructive insofar as the court was inclined to focus exclusively on the state of mind and instructions given by the system's operator.

b) Singapore Court of Appeal: Quoine v B2C2

One of the few really instructive court decisions worldwide is certainly *Quoine v B2C2*,[11] decided by the Singapore Court of Appeal. Quoine operated the QuoineExchange cryptocurrency exchange, on which B2C2 Ltd traded using trading software. One day in April 2017, a series of entirely unforeseen transactions took place, in which B2C2 exchanged Bitcoin (BTC) for Ethereum (ETH) with two other users of the platform at a price of around 10 BTC for 1 ETH, which was around 250 times higher than the market price in B2C2's favour. The cause was a failure by Quoine to make

11 *Quoine Pte Ltd v B2C2 Ltd* (2020) SGCA(I) 02.

necessary changes to critical system components. When Quoine noticed the error, it unilaterally cancelled the transactions as the system operator. B2C2 then sued Quoine for, among other things, breach of contract. One of the key issues was whether B2C2's counterparties could rely on the doctrine of unilateral mistake (either unilateral mistake at common law or unilateral mistake in equity), which might have justified Quoine's unilateral cancellation of the disputed transactions.

The majority of the judges held that there was no unilateral mistake at common law because the disputed transactions were the direct result of the deterministic algorithms deployed by B2C2 and that these algorithms functioned exactly as they were programmed to. The actual error was in the contracting parties' mistaken assumption about how the platform software operated, i.e. the wider circumstances of the transactions. The court also found that there was no unilateral mistake in equity. As to the question of actual or constructive knowledge the court held that what counts is the knowledge of the software's programmer at the time of the programming.[12] The programmer of B2C2's algorithm would have needed to foresee a "perfect storm of events", and there was no evidence to suggest that this was the case, nor any evidence of any sinister intent behind the programming of the trading software.

However, one of the five judges, International Judge Jonathan Mance, dissented and held that the law should not enforce contracts where both parties know as soon as they become aware of the transactions that they are based on a fundamental error.[13]

III. International and supranational soft law

1. UNCITRAL's work on automated contracting

a) UNCITRAL work before 2024

aa) The 2005 UN Convention on the Use of Electronic Communications in International Contracts

With its resolution 60/21 of 23 November 2005, the United Nations (UN) adopted the UN Convention on the Use of Electronic Communications

12 *Quoine Pte Ltd v B2C2 Ltd* (n. 11) at 97.
13 *Quoine Pte Ltd v B2C2 Ltd* (n. 11) at 152 ff.

in International Contracts (ECC) and called upon all governments to consider becoming party to the Convention. The 2005 ECC Convention, which is in force in 19 countries around the world, had been prepared by the UN Commission on International Trade Law (UNCITRAL). It takes a very similar approach to UETA. Article 12 clarifies the validity of contracts concluded by automated means, and Article 13 addresses the attribution of data messages:

> Article 13. Attribution of data messages
> ... (2) As between the originator and the addressee, a data message is deemed to be that of the originator if it was sent:
> ... (b) by an information system programmed by, or on behalf of, the originator to operate automatically.
> (3) As between the originator and the addressee, an addressee is entitled to regard a data message as being that of the originator, and to act on that assumption, if:
>
> > (a) in order to ascertain whether the data message was that of the originator, the addressee properly applied a procedure previously agreed to by the originator for that purpose; or
> > (b) the data message as received by the addressee resulted from the actions of a person whose relationship with the originator or with any agent of the originator enabled that person to gain access to a method used by the originator to identify data messages as its own.
>
> (4) Paragraph (3) does not apply:
>
> > (a) as of the time when the addressee has both received notice from the originator that the data message is not that of the originator, and had reasonable time to act accordingly; or
> > (b) in a case within paragraph (3)(b), at any time when the addressee knew or should have known, had it exercised reasonable care or used any agreed procedure, that the data message was not that of the originator.
>
> (5) Where a data message is that of the originator or is deemed to be that of the originator, or the addressee is entitled to act on that assumption, then, as between the originator and the addressee, the addressee is entitled to regard the data message as received as being what the originator intended to send, and to act on that assumption. The addressee is not so entitled when it knew or should have known, had it exercised reasonable

> care or used any agreed procedure, that the transmission resulted in any error in the data message as received.
> (6) The addressee is entitled to regard each data message received as a separate data message and to act on that assumption, except to the extent that it duplicates another data message and the addressee knew or should have known, had it exercised reasonable care or used any agreed procedure, that the data message was a duplicate.

Although the ECC focuses on the conclusion of contracts, the definition also refers to the use of automation in the fulfilment of contracts. The term "agent" is avoided in favour of "message system":

> Article 4 Definitions
> ... (g) 'Automated message system' means a computer programme or an electronic or other automated means used to initiate an action or respond to data messages or performances in whole or in part, without review or intervention by a natural person each time an action is initiated or a response is generated by the system; ...

bb) Further UNCITRAL work in the field

As to areas related to automation in contracting, it may also be worth drawing attention to the UN's resolutions 51/162 of 16 December 1996, 56/80 of 12 December 2001, 72/114 of 7 December 2017 and 77/101 of 7 December 2022, in which it recommended that all States give favourable consideration to the Model Law on Electronic Commerce (MLEC), the Model Law on Electronic Signatures (MLES), the Model Law on Electronic Transferable Records (MLETR) and the Model Law on the Use and Cross-border Recognition of Identity Management and Trust Services (MLIT) of UNCITRAL, respectively.

b) The 2024 Model Law on Automated Contracting (MLAC)

aa) Background and general aspects

In its resolution 79/119 of 4 December 2024, the UN General Assembly adopted UNCITRAL's Model Law on Automated Contracting (MLAC), approved in principle the accompanying Guide to Enactment and recommended that all States give favourable consideration to the MLAC when revising or adopting legislation relevant to electronic contracting.

The drafting of the MLAC was a collaborative effort led by UNCITRAL Working Group IV since 2021, with input from experts, stakeholders, and intersessional events. The mandate of Working Group IV related to the revision and further development of provisions on automated contracting. The Commission originally instructed the Working Group to compile, as a first step, the provisions of those UNCITRAL texts that relate to automated contracting (notably the MLEC of 1996, the ECC of 2005, the MLES of 2002, the MLETR of 2017 and the MLIT of 2022) and to revise these provisions where necessary. In a second step, possible new provisions dealing with a broader range of issues would be identified and developed. Finalisation of the Model Law took place during the 57th session of the Commission in June/July 2024 in New York, and the Guide to Enactment was finalised during the 67th session of Working Group IV in November 2024.

The MLAC is designed to complement existing laws on electronic transactions while addressing the unique challenges posed by automated systems. It addresses the use of automated systems throughout the contract lifecycle, including the formation, performance, modification, and termination of contracts. The MLAC is fully in line with the hallmarks of UNCITRAL work in the field, notably the principles of non-discrimination, technological neutrality and functional equivalence. In terms of non-discrimination, it explicitly ensures that contracts cannot be denied validity or enforceability solely because no human reviewed or intervened in the process. This is enshrined, in particular, in Articles 5 and 6, both of which deal with different aspects of legal recognition. In terms of technology neutrality, the MLAC avoids an explicit focus on specific technologies, such as AI or distributed ledger technologies (DLT), in order to ensure compatibility with future innovations. This neutrality is reflected in the deliberate choice of broad and inclusive terminology like "automated systems" or "contract automation" and is explicitly stated in Article 4.

bb) Attribution

A key feature of the MLAC is its approach to the attribution of actions carried out by automated systems, laid down Article 7. For UNCITRAL, this is a somewhat sensitive exercise, given that there is already a rather elaborate rule on attribution in Article 13 ECC, which Working Group IV did not intend to explicitly deviate from.

Looking more closely at the explanatory remarks, it is therefore not entirely clear what exactly Article 7 is about. We read remarks such as that Article 13 ECC should remain untouched but was "concerned with linking a data message to a person to the exclusion of another person", while Article 7 MLAC is concerned with "linking the output of an automated system to a person to the exclusion of the system itself". However, there is also the remark that Article 7 MLAC is concerned with "identifying the person 'behind' the output" and that Article 7 is "not intended to deal with matters of substantive law".[14] Furthermore, the explanatory remarks clarify that "Article 7 is thus of limited scope", mainly reaffirming "that automated systems are tools with no independent will or legal personality and that the output of automated systems should be attributed to persons and not to the system itself". The first two paragraphs of Article 7 read:

> Article 7. Attribution of actions carried out by automated systems
>
> 1. As between the parties to a contract, an action carried out by an automated system is attributed in accordance with a procedure agreed to by the parties.
> 2. If paragraph 1 does not apply, an action carried out by an automated system is attributed to the person who uses the system for that purpose.
>
> ...

Article 7 MLAC clarifies that, primarily, the issue of attribution should be subject to party autonomy, i.e. as between the parties to a contract, an action carried out by an automated system is attributed in accordance with a procedure agreed to by the parties. Such an agreement could, e.g., be expressed in a framework contract between the parties or in the rules of a platform operated by a third party to which both parties have assented for the use of an automated system operated via the platform.

If the parties have not specifically agreed on a procedure, an action carried out by an automated system is attributed to the person who (actually) uses the system for that purpose. According to the explanatory remarks, it is intended to attribute the action to "the person with the strongest link to that action". This strongest link is to be determined objectively, based on

14 UNCITRAL Model Law on Automated Contracting (2024) Part Two. Guide to Enactment of the UNCITRAL Model Law on Automated Contracting para. 60.

factors such as "(a) the person deploying the automated system; (b) the control exercised over the operational parameters of the system and the action; (c) the benefit or value derived from the action; (d) the nature and purpose of the contract; and (e) trade usages and the practices established between the parties".[15] On the other hand, it is emphasised that Article 7 is "not concerned with whether a person is characterized as an operator of the system".[16]

cc) Unexpected outcomes

The MLAC also tackles the issue of unexpected outputs from automated systems, particularly those deploying AI techniques. These outputs may arise from errors in programming, transmission, or third-party interference, or from the inherent unpredictability of non-deterministic systems.

Primarily, the issue is addressed by the last two paragraphs of Article 7 MLAC, which read:

> Article 7. Attribution of actions carried out by automated systems
>
> ... 3. Attribution of an action carried out by an automated system shall not be denied on the sole ground that the outcome was unexpected.
>
> 4. Nothing in this article affects the application of any rule of law that may govern the legal consequences of attributing an action carried out by an automated system to a person.

Again, it is not so easy to find out what these provisions are really about. The key to understanding the concept may be found in the explanatory remarks on paragraph 4, which explains that the provision "reinforces the distinction between attribution and liability and confirms that the rules on attribution are not concerned with allocating liability for the output of automated systems. ... However, it does not deny the connection between attribution and liability, as the application of the rules on attribution in

15 UNCITRAL Model Law on Automated Contracting (2024) Part Two. Guide to Enactment of the UNCITRAL Model Law on Automated Contracting para. 66.

16 UNCITRAL Model Law on Automated Contracting (2024) Part Two. Guide to Enactment of the UNCITRAL Model Law on Automated Contracting para. 67.

article 7 will ordinarily be a preliminary step to applying rules on liability under other law".[17]

Rules on mistake and the like under national contract law therefore seem to be qualified as rules on "liability" and remain unaffected to their full extent, i.e. it remains for the applicable national law on mistake etc. to decide how to apply existing doctrines to automated systems. In the light of this, however, paragraph 3 appears to be almost overreaching as it seems to meddle with very doctrinal questions that should typically be left to national law to decide. For example, the explanatory remarks on paragraph 3 explain that the provision "reaffirms the principle that attribution is not concerned with a person's state of mind. ... it clarifies that claims of unexpected outcomes are not to be settled by rules on attribution but rather by other law, in particular rules of contract law that may affect the legal consequences of unintended events, such as rules to avoid a contract in case of mistake or to excuse non-performance, ...".[18] One is left wondering why a UN text should be concerned primarily with how exactly States arrange concepts and doctrines under their national contract laws.

In the light of the explanatory remarks, the provisions on unexpected outcomes in Article 7 MLAC boil down to basically stating that MLAC does not introduce any additional rules on attribution, in particular not any rules on the relevance of a person's state of mind, but that a person's state of mind, including the fact that a person was taken by surprise by a particular output, should be relevant to the degree that it is considered relevant under existing law on mistake and the like.

However, there is also Article 8, which is remarkable in several respects. Already at first glance, the provision stands out as being presented in square brackets and with a footnote stating: "This provision is included for States wishing to enact one or more specific provisions addressing unexpected actions carried out by automated systems". It is thus a provision flagged as "optional", which seems somewhat odd as a Model Law is optional for States anyway. The provision reads:

> [Article 8. Unexpected actions carried out by automated systems
>
> 1. Unless otherwise agreed by the parties, where an action carried out by an automated system is attributed to a party to a contract, the other party

17 UNCITRAL Model Law on Automated Contracting (2024) Part Two. Guide to Enactment of the UNCITRAL Model Law on Automated Contracting para. 71.

18 UNCITRAL Model Law on Automated Contracting (2024) Part Two. Guide to Enactment of the UNCITRAL Model Law on Automated Contracting para. 68.

to the contract is not entitled to rely on that action if, in the light of all the circumstances:

(a) The party to which the action is attributed could not reasonably have expected the action; and
(b) The other party knew or could reasonably be expected to have known that the party to which the action is attributed did not expect the action.

2. Nothing in this article affects the application of any rule of law or agreement of the parties that may govern the legal consequences of an action carried out by an automated system.]

This optional provision addresses the legal treatment of unexpected actions by automated systems, particularly those deploying AI. Emphasis is put on the fact that the provision is "medium-specific" in that it only applies in the context of automated contracting and not in other contractual settings.[19] The explanatory remarks further stress the supplementary nature of Article 8, which is intended to preserve solutions under existing law that already address unexpected outcomes, such as rules to avoid a contract in case of mistake or to excuse non-performance in case of force majeure.[20]

While it is acknowledged that "systems deploying AI techniques present potential obstacles to applying these laws",[21] no effort is made to better reconcile the new additional rule and existing laws. At the end of the day, the idea of the MLAC seems to be that, in States that opt for the provision in Article 8, anyone wishing to challenge a transaction can rely both on Article 8 and on existing law of mistake and similar.

2. ELI's work on automated contracting

a) The 2023 Interim Report on "ADM readiness"

The European Law Institute (ELI) has equally been working on automated contracting since 2022.

19 UNCITRAL Model Law on Automated Contracting (2024) Part Two. Guide to Enactment of the UNCITRAL Model Law on Automated Contracting para. 76.
20 UNCITRAL Model Law on Automated Contracting (2024) Part Two. Guide to Enactment of the UNCITRAL Model Law on Automated Contracting para. 83.
21 UNCITRAL Model Law on Automated Contracting (2024) Part Two. Guide to Enactment of the UNCITRAL Model Law on Automated Contracting para. 83.

Initial work focused on principles and model rules for "algorithmic contracts", with a specific focus on consumer contracts. During the first project phase, emphasis was put on the use of algorithmic decision making (ADM), and in particular AI-driven systems, in the different stages of the life cycle of a contract. The project aimed to first assess the adequacy of existing EU consumer law for the use of ADM in contracts and then identify the gaps to be closed and the necessary legal steps required to facilitate algorithmic contracting in B2B, B2C, P2P and M2M transactions.

The main output of the first phase was published in December 2023 as an Interim Report and includes a critical commentary on key EU consumer law directives, which demonstrates the appropriateness of these provisions for the use of ADM in consumer contracts ("ADM readiness").[22] The Interim Report published after the first project phase already contained eight guiding principles.

b) The 2025 Model Rules on Digital Assistants for Consumer Contracts (ELI DACC Model Rules)

aa) Background and general aspects

The European Law Institute's Guiding Principles and Model Rules on Digital Assistants for Consumer Contracts ("ELI DACC Model Rules")[23] focus on the use of "digital assistants" in all the stages of the lifecycle of a consumer contract.

The ELI DACC Model Rules are designed to supplement existing rules on (consumer) contract law. They address three key challenges: (1) specific design requirements for digital assistants, i.e. draft regulation according to which particular functionalities must be incorporated into digital assistants or their user interfaces; (2) draft regulation for the contract for the supply of a digital assistant to a consumer; and (3) draft regulation for the contracts concluded and performed through the use of digital assistants,

22 *ELI*, EU Consumer Law and Automated Decision-Making (ADM): Is EU Consumer Law Ready for ADM? (Interim Report, 2023) <https://www.europeanlawinstitute.eu/projects-publications/current-projects/current-projects/algorithmic-contracts/> accessed 15 October 2025.

23 *ELI*, Guiding Principles and Model Rules on Digital Assistants for Consumer Contracts (May 2025) <https://www.europeanlawinstitute.eu/fileadmin/user_upload/p_eli/Projects/Algorithmic_Contracts/Guiding_Principles_and_Model_Rules_on_Digital_Assistants_for_Consumer_Contracts.pdf> accessed 15 October 2025.

the latter being referred to as "algorithmic contracts". The hallmark of the ELI DACC Model Rules, in particular when compared with the MLAC, is therefore that they take a holistic and regulatory approach which only a national legislator or supranational legislator (such as the EU legislator) can realistically take.

bb) Attribution and unexpected outcomes

With regard to attribution and unexpected outcomes, there is a conspicuous solution in Article 22 of the ELI DACC Model Rules, which deals both with the situation where a consumer uses a digital assistant in algorithmic contracts and with the situation where use of a digital assistant is made by the business:

> Article 22: Attribution and its limits
>
> (1) A person who uses a digital assistant for contractual relations is bound by the actions taken by the digital assistant and all the actions of the digital assistant are attributed to that person.
> (2) Where the actions of a digital assistant used by a consumer for contractual relations deviate from those which could reasonably be expected by the consumer, the actions of the digital assistant have no legal effect and are not attributed to the consumer.
> (3) The relevant factors to be applied in determining whether the actions of the digital assistant deviated from those a consumer could reasonably expect, include:
>
> > (a) any information given to the consumer about the adaptive capability of the digital assistant;
> > (b) whether the operation of any adaptive functionality of the digital assistant was inconsistent with such information;
> > (c) external factors such as loss of access to third-party data supplies, errors in that data, or cybersecurity breaches; and
> > (d) whether in the specific circumstances, the consumer could not reasonably have expected that the action in question would be taken.
>
> (4) Any contractual term providing that the business will not be bound by the actions of the digital assistant used by the business for its contractual relations with the consumer is only effective insofar as the actions to which that term applies are so unexpected that a reasonable person

would conclude there has been a serious failure in the operation of the digital assistant.

(5) In circumstances where the actions of a digital assistant are deemed to have no legal effect under paragraph (2) or by virtue of the contract terms referred to in paragraph (4), either party is entitled to receive back any performance that was rendered in consequence of such action

Where attribution to the consumer fails because the actions of the digital assistant were beyond what the consumer could reasonably expect, the supplier of the digital assistant will be liable to the third party that suffers damage because of the non-attribution.

Article 25: Liability of the supplier of a digital assistant to third parties

Where the actions of a digital assistant are not attributed to the consumer who deployed it under Article 22(2), the supplier of the digital assistant to that consumer is liable to the business with whom the consumer's digital assistant was dealing for losses the business has incurred as a result of the non-attribution. The conditions for awarding damages are governed by the applicable law.

Again, this somewhat unique approach, when compared with existing national law and UNCITRAL texts in the field, is easily explained by the fact that the ELI DACC Model Rules are specifically focused on consumer contracts and are addressed to a legislator that has the power to regulate and override existing private law regimes.

3. Academic work: "Principles for AI in Contracting" (PAIC)

The "Principles for AI in Contracting" (PAIC) are a purely academic draft set of proposed legal principles to guide the application of existing law and the development of new law in relation to automated contracting. They may serve as a source of inspiration for legislators and courts, for those involved in preparing industry standards, codes of conduct, or terms of use, as well as for contracting parties themselves. The PAIC are a reaction to the expected mass rollout of advanced AI in the context of contracting. This is in particular against the backdrop of the ongoing "contractualization" of the digital environment, as illustrated by the Data Act and other recent EU legislation for the digital economy.

a) Background and relationship with UNCITRAL and ELI work

The PAIC were drafted by the author in the summer of 2022 (version 1.0)[24] and further developed in 2023 (version 2.0),[25] early 2024 (version 2.1 – Discussion Draft)[26] and summer of 2024 (version 3.0)[27]. Version 3.0 is also attached as an Annex to this contribution. Version 4.0 is currently being prepared and will probably be published in late 2025 or early 2026. It might come with rather significant changes, including a re-arrangement and re-numbering of Parts and Principles, but the details are still in a flux.

The PAIC show a considerable number of similarities with the MLAC, which is unsurprising given that work on the PAIC began in parallel with the UNCITRAL project, and that the author participated as an observer in UNCITRAL sessions and also shared version 1.0 and subsequent drafts of the PAIC with the UNCITRAL Secretariat. Also, both MLAC and PAIC have been formulated against the backdrop of existing provisions, notably the 2005 ECC Convention. The most relevant similarities are technological neutrality of scope, the principle of legal recognition of contracts concluded by automated systems, attribution to the person using a system, and primary reliance on procedures agreed between the parties. However, even with regard to these overlaps, most provisions are distinctly different.

As to the PAIC's relationship with ELI work, there was equally mutual sharing of interim drafts, but probably very limited mutual influence. Version 3.0 of PAIC was published before the ELI DACC Model Rules and may have inspired or confirmed one or the other solution but given that PAIC is not designed for consumer contracts, at least not primarily so, influence remained rather marginal.

24 Not published, but only shared informally.

25 Annex to Christiane Wendehorst, Softwareagenten im vertraglichen Rechtsverkehr, in: Martin Gebauer and Stefan Huber (eds.), Künstliche Intelligenz – Zurechnung, Vertrag, Verantwortung, Ergebnisse der 38. Tagung der Gesellschaft für Rechtsvergleichung in Tübingen – Fachgruppe Zivilrecht (Tübingen: Mohr Siebeck 2024) pp. 43-66.

26 Christiane Wendehorst, Discussion Draft: Principles for AI in Contracting (Version 2.1), Journal of European Consumer and Market Law 1/2024, pp. 43-60.

27 Christiane Wendehorst, Version 3.0 of the Principles for AI in Contracting – old and new Rules for old and new Problems, in Vincent Sagaert and Joeri Vananroye (eds.), Privaatrecht plenis coloribus. Liber Amicorum Matthias Storme (Alphen aan den Rijn: Wolters Kluver 2024) pp. 1097-1124.

b) The PAIC's approach to attribution and unexpected outcomes

The PAIC approach the issue of attribution and unexpected outcomes in three steps, or, rather, at three different levels. Details of the formulation, including comments and illustrations, can be found below in the Annex.

aa) Level 1: Identification of operator

Principle 5 is not directly about attribution, but rather on the identification of the operator in situations where several persons might qualify as the operator and thus as "using" the electronic agent. This Principle fulfils a similar role as, under the MLAC, attribution to "the person with the strongest link" to an action mentioned in the explanatory remarks on Article 7 MLAC (above at III.1.b)bb)) but provides for much more legal certainty. Strictly speaking, this Principle could as well have been placed in the context of the definitions.

According to Principle 5, the operator is defined as the party on whose behalf the agent generates output, which is normally the relevant contracting party. For example, if an electronic agent concludes a contract on behalf of trader A, referring to trader A as the person to be bound by the resulting contract (not necessarily by name, but possibly by some account number or pseudonym, or maybe even insisting on anonymity), trader A is considered the operator and is bound by the agent's actions. However, if the electronic agent is used by a representative of trader A or a similar independent third party that is itself acting on behalf of trader A, the output is primarily attributed to that third party instead. This, of course, raises the question of what the legal consequences are where an electronic agent fails to refer, however indirectly, to any existing party, but still makes transactions or pretends to do so. According to the PAIC this would not be a question of contract, but rather of tort.

bb) Level 2: Attribution of the electronic agent as such

Principle 6 is about attribution of the electronic agent as such to the party on whose behalf the electronic agent is acting, i.e. to whom the electronic agent refers as the contracting party or other party that is relevant under Principle 5. This Principle 6 fulfils a similar role as, within UNCITRAL work, Article 13 of the 2005 ECC Convention (above at III.1.a)aa)). In the MLAC and the ELI DACC Model Rules it is equally implied in the notion of a party (actually) "using" an automated system or digital assistant.

When nothing goes wrong, an electronic agent is attributable to the party on whose behalf it is acting. However, if an electronic agent is used without a party's knowledge or consent—such as in cases of identity fraud or unauthorized access—the party cannot be held responsible for the agent's output if the fraud occurred beyond the relevant party's sphere of control and that party could not be expected to foresee and prevent it. In other words, where this is the case, the electronic agent is not attributable to the relevant party. This principle protects parties from being unfairly held accountable for actions outside their sphere of influence. Additionally, Principle 6 emphasizes that the burden of proving that a party is the operator of an electronic agent lies with the party making the claim, but that courts may ease this burden.

cc) Level 3: Attribution of the concrete output

Finally, Principle 7 addresses attribution of the concrete output of an electronic agent to its operator. This Principle 7 of PAIC is, in a certain way, the counterpart to some aspects of Article 7 and to Article 8 of MLAC as well as Article 22 of the ELI DACC Model Rules. Again, the standard situation is that the output of an electronic operator that is, as such, attributable to the party on whose behalf it is acting, is likewise fully attributable to that party. It is emphasised that this applies even where operator loses control of the electronic agent, i.e. where the output of the electronic agent is outside the range of possible outputs envisaged by the operator.

However, exceptions apply if the loss of control was caused by the other party or if the other party was aware—or should have been aware—of the loss of control. For example, if the other party's electronic agent detects irregularities indicating that the operator has lost control, the other party cannot rely on the agent's output to bind the operator. The same applies where the other party should have used an electronic agent that would have detected the irregularity but failed to do so. In this context, Principle 12 becomes relevant, which plays a central role in the PAIC in general. This Principle defines, for the purposes of the application of contract law, the technical capabilities which an electronic agent should have in a given situation.[28] The link between appropriate technical capabilities and attribution has been inspired by Sec. 10(1) UETA (see above at II.1.a)) and Article 13(4)(b) of the 2005 ECC Convention (see above at III.1.a)aa)).

In addition, Principle 7 of PAIC includes a hardship clause that has been inspired by the dissenting opinion by Jonathan Mance in the Quoine case (see above at II.2.b)): Where a party learns about the loss of control by the operator at some later point in time, that party should not be allowed to rely on attribution to the operator where it would, in the circumstances, appear to be clearly inappropriate to do so, considering, in particular, the degree to which attribution or its denial would cause detriment to either party and the sphere of control in which the loss of control had its origin.

c) Relationship of Part II of PAIC with other Parts

aa) Relationship with Part III on framework arrangements

Framework arrangements are a recurring theme in the PAIC, as they give priority to party autonomy also with regard to automated contracting. These arrangements can be established through explicit agreements, implied terms, or conditions set by third parties, such as platform providers or standard-setting bodies. They may address various aspects of automated contracting, including the use of electronic agents, transaction steps, safeguards, and pre-contractual liability. The PAIC also recognize the possibility of ad hoc framework arrangements for single transactions, provided they reflect the intentions of the parties involved.

Framework arrangements, although dealt with in detail only under Part III of the PAIC, take priority over the attribution rules in Part II. However, in practice, framework arrangements would only exceptionally deal with the issues addressed in Part II, i.e. in Principles 5, 6 and 7. What parties would normally provide for in framework arrangements is rather issues like that transactions above a certain amount require confirmation by a human employee, or that each party has a right to cancel a transaction within a certain period of time.

---

28 Technical capabilities should, in the first place, be determined by the law or by a relevant framework arrangement. In the absence of a specific legal provision or a provision in a relevant framework arrangement, Principle 12 provides that an electronic agent should have the technical capabilities that meet the reasonable expectations of the other party.

bb) Relationship with Part IV on the application of general contract law

While Part II of PAIC deals with attribution and unexpected outcomes, Part IV deals with the application of general doctrines of contract law to automated contracting. This raises the question of whether Principles 5, 6 and 7 apply on top of national doctrines of mistake and the like, or whether national doctrines of mistake are recommended to be derogated by Principles 5, 6 and 7 of PAIC.

In essence, the idea is one of derogation. There is no real justification for giving parties to transactions that have been concluded by automated means twice as many options to challenge a transaction (i.e. the specific options in Part II and the general options under applicable contract law) as parties to transactions that have been concluded by other means (who can only rely on the options under applicable contract law). In addition, available case law—see the illustrations above at II.2—demonstrates that the application of traditional doctrines of mistake is unconvincing and leads to results that may appear somewhat artificial and difficult to predict, if not arbitrary. If we are serious about the mass rollout of AI in contracting, parties need legal certainty and not fear of unpredictable court rulings. This is why the author recommends that any legislator inspired by PAIC give exclusive application to the provisions on attribution and unexpected outcomes as far as the relevant party makes use of electronic agents.

IV. When things go wrong—conclusions and the way forward

The MLAC, the ELI DACC Model Rules and the PAIC each provide both for rules on attribution in general and on restrictions of attribution under certain conditions when things go wrong.

Among the three solutions, the one suggested by the ELI DACC Model Rules stands out in several ways, being specifically designed for consumer contracts, bringing the supplier of digital assistants into the equation and creating a regime that can be introduced exclusively by way of regulation. It seems to provide for a well-calibrated solution, and the EU legislator should seriously consider taking it as a blueprint for a revised E-Commerce Directive or for an entirely new piece of legislation. However, as the solution heavily favours one side (the consumer) over the other (the business) it can hardly be extended to contracts between businesses.

The MLAC represents a significant step forward in addressing the challenges of automated contracting. By providing rules both for initial attribution and for unexpected outcomes, this instrument offers a foundation for legal certainty in an increasingly automated world. However, the MLAC also has its clear weaknesses and limitations. In particular, the institutional framework of a UN body means that outcomes are likely to remain somewhat minimalistic, reflecting the smallest common denominator and the urge to reach a quick and smooth global consensus among UNCITRAL delegates. Not only does the MLAC fail to address a range of really pressing issues concerning the application of existing contract law to AI-dominated environments, but it also obfuscates, through deliberately ambiguous explanatory remarks, what its provision on attribution is really about.

When comparing the MLAC and the PAIC, three main differences stand out. First of all, the PAIC are much more comprehensive and cover a lot more aspects than MLAC, which, at a closer look, includes only very few tangible new provisions. In particular, PAIC deals extensively with issues such as what concepts like "knowledge", "intent" or "reasonable expectations" mean in an AI-dominated environment, and it emphasizes the role of technical specifications of the technology used and related obligations of the parties.

Specifically with regard to attribution, Principles 5, 6 and 7 of PAIC deal with three different aspects of "attribution" and its denial respectively, namely (i) identification of the party that "uses" the electronic agent (the operator) where several parties could potentially be seen as being in that position; (ii) attribution of the electronic agent as such to that party; and (iii) attribution of a concrete output of the electronic agent, in particular in a case where the output is not what that party had envisaged and foreseen. By contrast, all three aspects are somehow merged and conflated in Article 7 MLAC and the accompanying explanatory remarks, while the "optional" Article 8 MLAC clearly deals only with the third aspect.

Last but not least, a notable difference between the MLAC and the PAIC is that the former provides for the full application of doctrines such as mistake under applicable contract law, if necessary in addition to a State's enactment of the optional Article 8. In contrast, the PAIC recommends that legislators derogate from doctrines of mistake and similar by adopting the specific solutions for automated contracting in Part II of the PAIC.

As the EU and other jurisdictions consider implementing existing work in the field, they must strike a balance between flexibility and predictability to foster trust and innovation in the digital economy. Going forward and talking about a possible implementation of the MLAC at EU level, it would be desirable to be more elaborate and provide more clarity at a conceptual level, possibly drawing upon some of the suggestions provided by PAIC. Notably, a possible EU implementation should definitely exclude recourse to national doctrines of mistake, etc., as these doctrines are the main source of uncertainty, which is detrimental to business and to the uptake of AI in general. At the same time, the need to cut off recourse to these doctrines may be the main argument why we need EU action in this area.

ANNEX: Version 3.0 of the Principles for AI in Contracting (PAIC)

Part I: General Provisions

Principle 1: Purpose and scope

(1) These Principles are about the use of electronic agents for the preparation, negotiation, conclusion or fulfilment of contracts without any direct human intervention. They are designed to
- **(a) bring coherence to, and facilitate the harmonization of, existing law and legal concepts and be used as a source to inspire the further development of the law by legislators and courts;**
- **(b) inform the development of best practices and guide the development of emerging standards or trade codes or of standard terms provided to parties by platform operators, manufacturers and similar third parties;**
- **(c) facilitate the drafting of model agreements, standard terms or individually negotiated terms used on a voluntary basis by parties engaging in automated contracting; and**
- **(d) guide the resolution of disputes in the context of automated contracting, including by tribunals in arbitration and other dispute resolution forums.**

(2) These Principles are intended to work with any form of contract law, irrespective of its philosophical or doctrinal foundations. They are, however, not intended to work within legal frameworks under which electronic agents are vested with legal personality.

(3) These Principles are not specifically designed for contracts between a business and a consumer, or any contracts that are, under the applicable law, treated in the same or a similar manner.

Comments:

The Principles are concerned with the use of electronic agents for the preparation, negotiation, conclusion or performance of contracts without direct human intervention, i.e. what is defined as 'automated contracting' in Principle 2(1)(b). They focus on the contract that is prepared, negotiated, concluded or performed by electronic agents and the underlying framework agreements. In contrast, the Principles do not specifically address the contract between an electronic agent provider and the party using the electronic agent for contracting—this is a contract for the supply of software, including as a service, which is beyond the scope of these Principles.

The Principles are intended to serve a broad range of different actors and audiences, as clarified by paragraph (1). They may serve as a source of inspiration for policymakers, legislators and other bodies involved in the further development of the law, such as courts. By doing so, they seek to bring coherence to, and facilitate harmonization of, existing law and legal concepts, and to enhance legal certainty and the predictability of decisions. Given that industry standards, best practices and codes of conduct will be a major source of relevant regimes these Principles are also intended to address any bodies involved in the development of such regimes, and the same holds true for the terms provided by the operators of platforms on which automated contracting occurs, of manufacturers of electronic agents and similar third parties (see Principle 8(1)(b)). However, the Principles should also inspire contracting parties themselves in drafting their agreements, and offer to parties a regime they can designate to govern their contract or pre-contractual relations. Needless to say, the Principles may also guide the deliberations of bodies involved in the resolution of disputes in the context of automated contracting.

The uptake of sophisticated electronic agents and the way they are perceived and accepted by applicable law may, to a certain degree, depend on the philosophical foundations of the relevant legal system in general and contract law in particular. For example, the degree to which a 'contract' is considered to be an emanation of the human will or simply a regime created by the contracting parties that bind the parties and is enforced by the courts has implications for, in particular, the degree to which advanced AI is perceived as potentially disruptive. However, these Principles are based on the assumption that any legal system will, at the end of the day, allow for parties to be bound also by the output of advanced AI, whether or not this is based on traditional notions of what makes a 'contract' or on any modified notion thereof. Principles 8 to 10 in particular are designed in a way so as to facilitate the accommodation of advanced AI also for legal systems that give a lot of weight to the human will in a contractual context.

While the Principles are therefore meant to be useful in any sort of legal environment, there is one important limitation: the Principles rest firmly on the assumption that electronic agents, however sophisticated they may be, are never afforded legal personality, but that they are considered as a tool serving the parties behind them (see Principle 3(2)).

These Principles are primarily designed to work for business-to-business relations where both contracting parties are sufficiently literate as to the use of electronic agents for contracting. They are not designed to work for consumer contracts, or any other contracts for which the applicable law considers one of the parties to be particularly in need of protection.

However, the Principles may still inform the development of the law also with regard to such contracts, albeit to a lesser degree.

Principle 2: Definitions

(1) For the purpose of these Principles, the following definitions apply:

(a) 'electronic agent' means any software, including any artificial intelligence, designed or used to prepare, negotiate, conclude, fulfil or otherwise manage contracts without any direct human intervention;

(b) 'automated contracting' means the preparation, negotiation, conclusion or fulfilment of contracts or other aspect of contract management using electronic agents;

(c) 'framework arrangement' means any framework agreement, express or implied, and any similar means of private ordering, that deals with the conditions of automated contracting between the parties;

(d) 'technical specifications' include any design features or capabilities, such as with regard to communication protocols, compatibility with other technology, safeguards against unintended outcomes, failure or tampering, or traceability;

(e) 'output' of an electronic agent means any data generated or function triggered by the electronic agent, including the absence of such data or function;

(f) 'operator' of an electronic agent means the party using the electronic agent for automated contracting in which that party is involved;

(g) 'control' over an electronic agent by the operator means the ability of the operator to ensure that the output of the electronic agent is within the range of possible outputs envisaged by the operator.

(2) Any reference in these Principles to electronic agents applies with appropriate modifications to other technology, such as hardware, that a party uses in the context of automated contracting. Any reference to the conclusion of contracts applies with appropriate modifications to other activities in the context of the preparation, negotiation, conclusion or fulfilment of contracts or other aspect of contract management.

Comments:

Principle 2 provides central definitions. First of all, it introduces a broad notion of 'electronic agent', that includes any artificial intelligence and, in particular, does not draw any line whatsoever between so-called 'deterministic' and 'autonomous' agents. What is often referred to as 'autonomy' of electronic agents boils down to a higher degree of complexity and opacity as well as a lower degree of predictability, but it is difficult to draw a clear line, and these Principles are designed to overcome precisely the uncertainty that has arisen with the emergence of very advanced AI in the contractual context. The definition of 'electronic agent' is also broad as far as the intended use is concerned. In particular, there is no limitation to electronic agents used for concluding a contract, but rather the Principles cover also agents used to prepare or negotiate contracts, or to fulfil or otherwise manage contracts without any direct human intervention.

'Automated contracting' is also broadly defined. In line with the broad definition of 'electronic agent', it includes the preparation, negotiation, conclusion or fulfilment of contracts or other aspect of contract management using electronic agents.

A key concept is that of a 'framework arrangement', as these Principles focus on the conditions for automated contracting that have initially been agreed or otherwise accepted by the parties. This definition is closely related to Principles 8 to 10, which provide more detail on relevant framework arrangements. A framework arrangement includes any agreement, whether express or implied, that addresses the terms of (future) automated contracting between the parties. However, it does not matter whether the arrangement may be qualified as an 'agreement' or a 'contract' in the strict sense. The term 'framework arrangement' includes also other means of private ordering that deal with the conditions of automated contracting between the parties, such as where each of the parties separately accepts conditions provided by a third party (for details see Principle 8).

Another key concept is that of 'technical specifications' of an electronic agent, which is referred to in many of the Principles. This term, again, is to be understood broadly. It includes any design features or capabilities, such as with regard to communication protocols, compatibility with other technology, safeguards against unintended outcomes, failure or tampering, or traceability. In short, 'technical specifications' includes any technical aspect that is or may become relevant in the context of automated contracting.

As it might be less than ideal to use the term 'conduct' in relation to machines, these Principles refer to the much more neutral term 'output'. The 'output' of an electronic agent includes any data generated or function triggered by the electronic agent, including the absence of such data or function. It is immaterial what exactly this data or function is about. However, output that is potentially legally relevant will normally only be such data generated or function triggered that has some external effect, such as being communicated to a party or its electronic agent, or otherwise immediately affecting a party or its electronic agent.

Given that the Principles treat electronic agents as tools, rights and obligations arise in the party or parties (who may be natural or legal persons) behind them and to whom the electronic agent is attributed. The party behind an electronic agent is called the 'operator' of an electronic agent and is defined as the party using the electronic agent for automated contracting in which that party is involved. Principles 5 and 6 provide further guidance as to the conditions under which a party is to be considered the operator.

The operator using the electronic agent usually wants to increase efficiency in the broadest sense, because it would be impossible (e.g. in terms of speed), too difficult or too expensive to act personally or through human assistants. However, the use of electronic agents also means that the operator can no longer immediately influence developments on the ground and may not be able to predict exactly what will happen. The operator should still be considered to be in 'control' of an electronic agent if the operator is able to ensure that the output of the electronic agent is within the range of potential outputs envisaged by the operator. This should not be interpreted strictly, i.e. an operator should still be considered to be in control of an electronic agent where the operator has no possibility to directly intervene, but the output of the electronic agent is still within the range of outputs envisaged. Where this is no longer the case and things develop in totally unforeseen ways, the operator has lost control. Principle 7 deals with the legal consequences of a loss of control.

Paragraph (2) clarifies that any reference in the Principles to electronic agents applies, if necessary with appropriate modifications, to other technology that a party may be using in the context of automated contracting. This could, for example, be any hardware, or network connectivity. In other words, electronic agents and their technical specifications are always to be seen in their specific technological environment, and deficiencies of that environment (such as sudden power failure), when used by one of the parties, are attributed to that party in a similar way as deficiencies of the electronic agent itself. Paragraph (2) also clarifies that any reference to the conclusion of a contract applies, with appropriate modifications, to other activities in the contractual context (such as steps towards the performance of a contract or the exercise of a right to terminate a contract).

Principle 3: Recognition

(1) A contract should not be denied validity or enforceability on the sole ground that it has been concluded through electronic agents, irrespective of the extent to which the output is controlled by the operator of the electronic agent or of the general degree of predictability of the output.

(2) Electronic agents should be characterised as tools of their operators. However, this should not be construed as precluding the application of rules and principles other than those applicable to tools in general where the purpose of those rules and principles so requires.

Comments:

First of all, Principle 3 conveys the very central message that no contract should be denied validity or enforceability on the sole ground that it was concluded through electronic agents, regardless of the degree of predictability of the output generated by an electronic agent. This principle may be necessary because of doubts that have been raised about whether valid contracts can be concluded by electronic agents with a very high degree of 'autonomy', where there is no human being who has defined all the details of, for example, a contractual offer or acceptance. The whole point of the Principles is to suggest that contracting through advanced AI is possible, and how existing rules and principles might be applied in this context. The wording would theoretically include situations where the electronic agent determines its output randomly, but then there does not seem to be sufficient reason to exclude this possibility if an operator chooses to use such an electronic agent and is prepared to accept the results.

This does not mean that the extent to which the output is controlled by the operator of the electronic agent, or the general degree of predictability of the output, is entirely irrelevant. An example of where they are relevant is Principle 9(1) on framework agreements created by electronic agents.

Doubts have been raised as to whether advanced AI should be treated as a tool, whether agency law might play a role, or whether AI should be treated in a similar way to human actors. Paragraph (3) takes a clear position that electronic agents should be characterised as tools of their operators. However, this should not be taken to mean that electronic agents should be subject to the same rules as, say, a typewriter or a calculator. Rather, the fact that electronic agents are used for activities that have been performed by humans throughout the centuries of development of our contract law means that here and there different rules and principles may be required than those applicable to tools in general (for details see e.g. Principles 13 to 17).

It may be important to clarify that Principle 3 addresses potential doubts about the validity or enforceability of contracts concluded via electronic agents, which have their roots in general contract law. However, it does not prevent parties from excluding the use of electronic agents for dealings between them (which would be done by means of a negative framework agreement within the meaning of Principle 10), or the law from prohibiting the use of electronic agents in certain situations or for certain purposes.

Principle 4: Rules and provisions governing automated contracting

(1) Automated contracting between the contracting parties should be governed, in the following order of priority, by
(a) rules of law that cannot be derogated from by agreement;
(b) the provisions of a framework arrangement within the meaning of Part III of these Principles;
(c) the default rules under applicable law that have been developed specifically for automated contracting;
(d) other default rules under applicable law, as informed by these Principles.

(2) Where there is a gap in any provisions within the meaning of point (b) of paragraph (1) that cannot be filled by reference to the specific arrangement, this gap should be filled by default rules within the meaning of points (c) and (d) of paragraph (1). The latter should also be considered as a benchmark for any fairness test that may become relevant under the applicable law.

Comments:

Principle 4(1) clarifies the general hierarchy of normative regimes, whether statutory or contractual, that may govern the conditions of automated contracting.

In the first place, there is a reminder that mandatory law, such as consumer protection law, takes precedence over everything else. Indeed, regulation should ensure that there is adequate protection for consumers and other vulnerable parties, including by providing that there must be some minimum safeguards for consumers in the conditions of automated contracting.

Subject to mandatory law, the conditions of automated contracting should be governed by any framework arrangement within the meaning of Principle 2(1)(c) and Principle 8, in particular by any agreement between the contracting parties or any other conditions which each of the parties have, in one way or another, accepted.

In the absence of private ordering, the statutory default rules apply. Naturally, where the applicable law provides for specific rules in relation to automated contracting, those rules will prevail over the more general default rules and the Principles. However, where—as is currently still the case in most jurisdictions—the applicable law does not specifically address automated contracting, the general rules of contract law should be applied, with the recommendation that they be applied in a manner consistent with and informed by the Principles, in particular by Part IV of the Principles.

The order of priority set out in paragraph (1) could be read to mean that private ordering always takes precedence over statutory default rules. While this is generally the case, statutory default rules may also serve important functions where there exists a framework arrangement. Paragraph (3) therefore clarifies that the default rules, and indirectly the Principles, apply even where a framework exists but there is a gap to be filled. Similarly, where the applicable law provides for fairness or similar tests the applicable law may provide for unfairness or similar tests (e.g. a doctrine of unconscionability) that require the assessment of private arrangements, the default rules and the Principles may also serve as a benchmark. Note that this is not really a departure from the order of priority set out in paragraph (1), as the unfairness test or similar test would in itself qualify as a rule that cannot be derogated from by agreement, i.e. a rule that trumps private arrangements.

Part II: Attribution

Principle 5: Identification of operator

(1) The operator of an electronic agent in the context of automated contracting should be the party on whose behalf output of the electronic agent is generated, subject to Principle 6.

(2) Where an electronic agent is used for negotiating or concluding an automated contract or exercising a right or fulfilling an obligation under a contract, the output is normally considered to be generated on behalf of the relevant contracting party.

(3) In derogation of paragraph (2), where the electronic agent was used by an independent third party acting as representative, intermediary, vicarious agent or in a similar role with regard to the contract, the output should be considered to be generated primarily on behalf of that third party.

Comments:

Principle 5 is to be seen in the immediate context of the definition of 'operator' in Principle 2(1)(g). Generally speaking, the operator is the party using the electronic agent. At the same time, this is the party to whom the output generated by the electronic agent is normally attributed, see Principle 7.

However, in the individual case, several parties may, in some sense or another, be 'using' an electronic agent for their purposes, including contracting parties, platform operators, or other parties providing electronic agents as part of a service. This is why paragraph (1) clarifies that the 'operator' is the party on whose behalf output of the electronic agent is generated. It also reminds us of the fact that the identification of a party as operator is still subject to Principle 6 on non-attributable electronic agents.

As 'on behalf of' may still leave a certain degree of doubt, paragraph (2) further clarifies that, where an electronic agent is used for negotiating or concluding an automated contract or exercising a right or fulfilling an obligation under a contract, the output is normally considered to be generated on behalf of the relevant contracting party (or potentially contracting party).

Illustration: Where an electronic agent is developed by a manufacturer and made available as a software-as-a-service solution to a platform operator, who in turn makes it available to platform users for the conclusion of contracts between them, all three parties 'use' the electronic agent in one way or another. However, for the purposes of the 'target contract' to be concluded between two platform users, it is the platform user relying on the electronic agent to conclude a contract with another platform user that is considered to be the 'operator' for the purposes of that contract.

Paragraph (3) clarifies that the contracting party should not be considered as the operator to the extent that the electronic agent has been used by an independent third party acting as a representative, an intermediary, an agent or in a similar independent role with respect to the contract, in which case the output is considered to be produced primarily on behalf of that third party. This rule is important in order not to undermine the rules of the applicable law on agency, etc.

Illustration: A party hires a representative (which could be the platform operator itself) to trade on its behalf on a crypto exchange platform. The representative, acting on behalf of the first party, uses an electronic agent. Suppose that, under applicable law, the first party would not normally be bound by the representative's activities because the representative has exceeded the limits of its authority—rather, the representative would be liable for damages to any counterparty. This should not be different simply because the representative has used an electronic agent.

Principle 6: Non-attributable electronic agents

(1) A party should not be considered the operator of an electronic agent where the decision to use the electronic agent for automated contracting is not attributable to that party.
(2) Paragraph (1) includes, in particular, cases of identity fraud and similar irregularities where such irregularities occur beyond the relevant party's sphere of control and that party could not be expected to foresee and prevent them.
(3) A party wishing to rely on the fact that a particular other party is the operator of an electronic agent should bear the burden of proof. However, a court should apply appropriate alleviations of the burden of proof, in particular where there is no reason to believe that the party on whose behalf the output is generated is not the operator.

Comments:

Principle 6 addresses situations of electronic fraud and similar incidents, which may occur with electronic agents. Paragraph (1) establishes an exception from Principle 5(1) by stating that the party on whose behalf output of the electronic agent is generated cannot be considered an operator where the decision to use the electronic agent for automated contracting is as such not attributable to that party.

Paragraph (2) further explains that the decision to use the electronic agent for automated contracting is not attributable to a party in cases of identity fraud and similar irregularities where such irregularities occur beyond the relevant party's sphere of control and that party could not be expected to foresee and prevent them.

Illustration: A party is contacted by a company claiming that the first party owes the company money from a transaction carried out using electronic agents. The first party has never used an electronic agent or been involved in such a transaction. In reality, fraudsters have used the first party's name and contact details through no fault of the first party. In this case, it would not be justified to consider that party as an 'operator'. The situation would be different if the party had actually used an electronic agent, but this agent had been hacked by a malicious third party and made to serve the interests of the third party. In this case, the party would be considered an 'operator', and whether or not attribution follows depends on Principle 7.

Given the negative formulation of paragraph (1) one could be inclined to assume that the party on whose behalf output of an electronic agent is generated has to prove that it has not in any relevant way been involved in the deployment of the electronic agent. This would mean a rather high burden, given that it is always difficult to prove negative facts. Paragraph (3) therefore tries to strike a balance between the legitimate interests of third parties that rely on a particular party being the operator of what seems to be their electronic agent and the legitimate interests of the victims of fraud or similar parties. The suggestion is that that a party wishing to rely on the fact that a particular other party is the operator of an electronic agent should generally bear the burden of proof, but that, in litigation, a court should apply appropriate alleviations of the burden of proof where there is no reason to believe that the party on whose behalf the output is generated is not the operator.

Principle 7: Attribution of output to operator

(1) The output generated by an electronic agent is attributed to the operator of the electronic agent within the meaning of Principles 5 and 6, whether or not that operator had control over the electronic agent when the output was generated.

(2) However, another party cannot rely on attribution to the operator where the operator has lost control and where

(a) that party or any electronic agent used by that party had caused the loss of control by the operator of the electronic agent; or

(b) that party was aware, or ought to have been aware, at the time when the output generated by the electronic agent would potentially produce legal effect, that the operator had lost control; this includes situations where that party had used an electronic agent that appropriately detected the loss of control or ought to have detected it in accordance with the technical capabilities required under Principle 12.

(3) Where a party learns about the loss of control by the operator after the time when the output generated by the electronic agent would potentially produce legal effect, that party should

not be allowed to rely on attribution to the operator where it would, in the circumstances, appear to be clearly inappropriate to do so, considering, in particular, the degree to which
(a) attribution or its denial would cause detriment to either party; and
(b) the loss of control had its origin in a sphere close to one or both of the parties.
The operator must, in this case, indemnify the other party for the loss it may have suffered by relying on attribution.

(4) The burden of proving that the operator has lost control of the electronic agent and that a situation covered by paragraphs (2) or (3) exists should lie with the operator.

Comments:

Principle 7 is closely connected with Principles 5 and 6 in stating that the output generated by an electronic agent is attributed to the operator of the electronic agent within the meaning of Principles 5 and 6. While this may not be remarkable as such, the main function of paragraph (1) is to clarify that this applies whether or not the operator had control over the electronic agent when the output was generated, i.e. even where the operator had lost control.

In this context, attention must again be drawn to the fact that this only applies where the relevant party qualifies as operator—where the electronic agent is a non-attributable electronic agent under Principle 6, the party on whose behalf the output appears to be generated is not considered as operator, which is why that party is also unaffected by Principle 7. However, where use of the electronic agent as such can be attributed to a party and that party therefore qualifies as operator, the risk of malfunctions and unforeseen developments is, subject to paragraphs (2) and (3), on that operator.

Paragraph (2) provides some important exceptions to this rule. Another party may not rely on attribution to the operator if the operator has lost control and that party, or an electronic agent used by that party, caused the operator's loss of control; or that party was aware, or should have been aware, at the relevant time, that the operator had lost control. In line with Principle 14, this includes situations where that party used an electronic agent that reasonably detected, or should have detected, the loss of control. The meaning of 'not allowed to rely on' may vary depending on the solution under the applicable law for comparable situations (e.g. the contract may be void or voidable).

Illustration: The electronic agent used by a trader on a cryptocurrency exchange exhibits suspicious 'behaviour' by making a series of very unusual transactions. This is detected by the platform operator's AI, which automatically sends an alert to the trader operating the electronic agent, and to the electronic agents of other traders dealing with the first electronic agent for possible transactions. Another trader, whose electronic agent duly received and processed the alert before a transaction was made, cannot rely on the validity of the transaction.

Even with paragraph (2) the attribution of totally unforeseen activities of an electronic agent may lead to rather harsh results. Therefore, paragraph (3) proposes a hardship clause for situations where none of the situations listed in paragraph (2) occurs, but the parties to the contract become aware of the error after the fact and it would clearly be inappropriate for the other party to rely on the validity of the transaction. In assessing whether it would be inappropriate for the other party to rely on the validity of the transaction, account should be taken, in particular, of the extent to which the attribution or denial of the error would be to the detriment of one of the parties and of the extent to which the loss of control originated in a sphere close to one of the parties. In any event, the operator benefiting from the hardship clause must compensate the other party for any loss it may have suffered as a result of relying on attribution.

Illustration: The unusual transactions on the cryptocurrency exchange were triggered by an unforeseen combination of (a) a maintenance problem on the platform system and (b) the way in which the electronic agent used by the trader who benefited from the unusual transactions was configured. This trader's counterparties suffer a loss of millions of euros. In this situation, it should not be possible for the trader to rely on the validity of the transactions, since the problem originated in a sphere closer to that trader, or at least equally close to both parties, and to recognise the transactions would cause immense loss to the counterparties, while to deny the validity of the transactions would only deprive the first trader of a windfall profit that it could never have expected.

Paragraph (4) clarifies that the burden of proving that the operator has lost control of the electronic agent and that a situation covered by paragraphs (2) or (3) exists should lie with the operator.

Part III: Framework arrangements

Principle 8: Framework arrangements

(1) A framework arrangement on the conditions of future automated contracting between the parties may arise, in particular, from
  - **(a) any specific agreement between the parties, express or implied, that deals with future automated contracting; or otherwise**
  - **(b) conditions of future automated contracting which each of the contracting parties separately have accepted or can reasonably be expected to have accepted and that are defined by a third party, such as**
    - **(i) the provider of a platform or similar infrastructure on which automated contracting occurs;**
    - **(ii) the provider of an electronic agent used for automated contracting; or**
    - **(iii) the body providing a standard or any other harmonized technical specifications for electronic agents.**

(2) Conditions of future automated contracting between the parties within the meaning of paragraph (1) may address, in particular, the use of an electronic agent as such, the technical

specifications of an electronic agent to be used, the conditions under which output generated by an electronic agent is binding on its operator, the steps by which a transaction is completed, any rights of the operator to cancel a transaction, safeguards against failure, unintended results or manipulation, or pre-contractual liability.

(3) Framework arrangements may also be established for and on the occasion of a single automated transaction through electronic agents, where

- **(a) this would not be inconsistent with an existing framework arrangement established through other means; and**
- **(b) each of the operators holds out, through their electronic agents, technical specifications and other conditions that are consistent with each other; and**
- **(c) there is sufficient evidence that the provisions reflect the intentions of the relevant operators at the relevant time.**

Comments:

Principle 8 is the first principle in Part III, which is devoted to framework arrangements within the meaning of Principle 2(1)(c). In practice, most automated contracting will be governed, at least to a certain extent, by framework arrangements that define in advance the conditions of future automated contracting between the parties. The concept should be understood very broadly and does not necessarily have to be qualified as an agreement in the proper sense under the applicable law.

Where such an arrangement exists this means that for every transaction concluded via electronic agents there is another, underlying arrangement stating that, and under what conditions, the parties are bound by the output of the electronic agents. We do not need such an assumption when contracts are entered into directly by humans, because we all know how humans feel, think and act, and our legal systems have been designed with human actors in mind. However, electronic agents can be of very different types and qualities, and the way we use them as tools in the context of automated contracting can be very different.

Framework arrangements help to overcome the difficulties that some legal systems may have in recognising contracts concluded with the help of highly 'autonomous' electronic agents whose output is difficult to trace in detail to the will of a human individual.

Illustration: A trading bot programmed to maximise profits, but whose 'behaviour' is significantly altered during operation by machine learning, fulfils all the steps of what appears to be a transaction between the operator of the bot and another party to the contract. However, as this concrete transaction was never contemplated by the operator, the applicable contract law may have difficulties in qualifying the relevant steps as 'offer' and 'acceptance'. These difficulties may be overcome, or at least significantly mitigated, if the operator and its contractual partner are bound by a framework agreement concluded in the 'traditional way', which defines the conditions under which the parties are bound by the output of electronic agents.

They can also help to resolve difficult cases, e.g. cases of lack of capacity, without having to resort to the law of agency.

Illustration: A trader, who is a natural person, uses electronic agents for transactions on a crypto exchange. Following a car accident, this trader is in a coma for two weeks and therefore would not normally be able to enter into a valid contract under the applicable law. Transactions entered into in the interim through electronic agents may nevertheless be valid, provided that the framework agreement is valid (and does not provide for confirmation requirements or the like).

Where the parties, in particular through their electronic agents, take steps of automated contracting that are inconsistent with the framework arrangement the legal consequences should generally depend on the nature of the relevant provision and the inconsistency. For example, where the conditions under which the parties declare to be legally bound are not fulfilled, the parties are not legally bound.

Subject to mandatory law, a framework arrangement may, primarily, arise from a specific framework agreement between the parties, i.e. the parties agree on the conditions of future automated contracting between them. Such agreement may be express or implied, and it may be concluded in any manner that is accepted under the applicable law. Note that, according to Principle 9, it can also be concluded by automated means.

Illustration: To ensure smooth production lines, the owner of a plant has an agreement with certain suppliers of raw and other materials whereby electronic agents take care of stocktaking, negotiation and ordering of such materials when stocks are running low. The agreement includes all the details, including the amount up to which the owner of the plant agrees to be bound, the conditions under which human intervention is required, and any right to object to a transaction concluded by automated means.

However, the framework arrangement may also arise from each of the parties separately accepting conditions for automated contracting that are provided by a third party, such as the provider of a platform or similar infrastructure on which automated contracting takes place.

Illustration: The operator of a trading platform for in-game items (such as skins or weapons) allows platform users to use electronic agents. The terms and conditions of use contain detailed provisions on the type of electronic agents permitted, the communication protocols to be used and the conditions under which transactions may or may not be contested. Platform users must accept the terms and conditions when creating a user account.

Note that paragraph (1)(b) does not strictly require that the parties have actually accepted the terms, but only that they could reasonably be expected to have accepted them. This is to avoid a situation where one of the parties claims that its declaration of acceptance is in fact invalid, when this was not apparent to the other party.

Illustration: Suppose, in the previous illustration, a transaction takes place between two platform users. If a dispute arises and one of the platform users relies on the terms and conditions of the platform against the other, the second platform user claims that it never validly accepted the terms and conditions. This may be something that the second platform user can claim against the platform operator, but not against the first platform user, provided that the first platform user could reasonably expect that everything was normal in this respect.

The terms may also be provided by the developer, manufacturer or other provider of an electronic agent used for automated contracting, or by a body providing a standard or other harmonised technical specification for electronic agents, where both contracting parties have at least implicitly accepted them.

Illustration: A connected printing machine can be configured to automatically order maintenance services and consumables from the machine as needed. The manufacturer of the printing machine has specified detailed terms and conditions that any supplier of maintenance services or consumables who wishes to participate in the system must accept, including payment methods, cancellation rights, remedies for non-performance, dispute resolution and the like.

Paragraph (2) clarifies what a framework arrangement can cover. Broadly speaking, the arrangement can cover anything that deals with future transactions between the parties and can be covered by framework agreements in general. In particular, in the context of automated contracting, it will often cover the use of an electronic agent as such (including the permissible types of electronic agent), the technical specifications of an electronic agent to be used (such as back-up and alert systems), the conditions under which output generated by an electronic agent is binding on its operator (such as maximum transaction values or confirmation requirements), the steps by which a transaction is completed (e.g. whether it is by the exchange of outputs equivalent to an offer and acceptance or by recording in a ledger), any rights of the operator to cancel a transaction, safeguards against failure, unintended outcomes or tampering (such as monitoring or maintenance obligations) or pre-contractual liability (such as liability caps). This list is by no means exhaustive.

Principle 9: Automated ad hoc framework arrangements

(1) Framework arrangements may also be established for and on the occasion of a single automated transaction through electronic agents, where

(a) this would not be inconsistent with an existing framework arrangement established through other means; and

(b) there is sufficient evidence that the provisions reflect the intentions of the relevant operators at the relevant time.

(2) A framework arrangement within the meaning of paragraph (1) requires that each of the operators holds out, through their electronic agents, technical specifications and other conditions that are consistent with each other, which should be considered to have the effect of offer and acceptance to engage in automated contracting on the basis of these technical specifications or other conditions.

Comments:

Normally, framework arrangements are established in advance and by traditional means, such as by human actors accepting terms and conditions. Where the framework arrangement itself has already been created by electronic agents the situation becomes somewhat circular, as the resulting automated contract is based on the framework arrangement, but the framework arrangement itself is based on automated contracting. One way of dealing with this situation would have been to apply only Part IV of these Principles, i.e. not to allow the parties to define conditions of automated contracting that differ from the conditions following from the existing default rules of the applicable contract law. However, this would have seemed a disproportionate restriction on party autonomy: Why should the law refuse to recognise certain arrangements which go beyond the default rules, but which are the common will of both parties, simply because the parties have not taken the trouble to agree on those terms in advance and by traditional means?

Illustration: A customer uses an electronic agent in an online marketplace and wants transactions of €500 or more to require confirmation by an employee of the customer. Such a condition is not really to be expected in the circumstances, but a supplier's electronic agent happens to be able to accommodate it and handle the confirmation process. If only Principle 12 applied in this case, the confirmation requirement would not become part of the framework agreement. However, there seems to be no good reason not to allow the parties to agree on this requirement through their electronic agents.

Therefore, Principle 9 provides that framework arrangements may be created ad hoc through electronic agents, but only under certain conditions. First of all, a framework arrangement established through electronic agents should not be recognised if the result would be inconsistent with an existing framework arrangement established by other means. This is essential because otherwise framework arrangements could easily be undermined.

Illustration: Suppose that in the previous illustration, the customer and the supplier, through human agents, have a framework agreement that requires transactions of €500 or more to be confirmed by an employee of the customer. The customer's electronic agent places an unconditional order for €600, which is accepted by the supplier's electronic agent. This cannot be construed as overriding the previous framework agreement, i.e. the confirmation requirement still applies.

Notwithstanding this important limitation, allowing framework agreements to be concluded through electronic agents will always involve a degree of circularity. For this reason, paragraph (1)(b) goes on to state that a party may only rely on such a framework agreement if there is sufficient evidence that the provisions reflect the intention of the relevant operators at the relevant time. This is one of the rare cases where the Principles differentiate according to the extent to which the output is controlled by the operator of the electronic agent or the general degree of predictability of the output, cf. Principle 3(1).

Illustration: This requirement is met, for example, when certain conditions have been programmed into rule-based system components, which may or may not be integrated in a highly 'autonomous' electronic agent. Note that paragraph (2) does not take a position on the debate in general contract law as to whether the intention of the parties should prevail over the objective content of declarations, or vice versa - even if the objective content prevails, it will still provide 'sufficient evidence' of intention.

Needless to say, a framework arrangement still requires some form of commitment from both parties. This is why paragraph (2) provides that, an automated ad hoc framework arrangement requires that each of the operators holds out, through their electronic agents, technical specifications and other conditions that are consistent with each other. This should be considered to have the effect of offer and acceptance to engage in automated contracting on the basis of these technical specifications or other conditions.

Where offer and acceptance do not match because the two operators involved hold out, through their electronic agents, technical specifications and other conditions that are inconsistent with each other, there is no framework arrangement. Ideally the electronic agents would stop engaging with each other in this case. However, whether intended by the relevant operators or not, the electronic agents may nevertheless continue to engage towards what is potentially a transaction or its execution. In this case, Part IV of the Principles applies. In particular, Principle 12(3) provides that each party should bear the risk that its electronic agent continues to engage with the other party or its electronic agent despite an inconsistency of the technical specifications or other conditions of automated contracting held out, unless this was due to a deficiency of the other party's electronic agent.

Principle 10: Negative framework arrangement

(1) Where the framework arrangement, including an automated framework arrangement as referred to in Principle 9, prohibits automated contracting or permits it only under conditions that are not met in the actual circumstances, but further steps are nevertheless taken towards a transaction or its execution, those further steps should be subject to ratification by both parties, unless the framework arrangement provides for a different legal consequence.

(2) Nothing in this Principle may be construed as determining whether a term prohibiting automated contracting, or allowing it only under particular circumstances, should be considered valid under applicable law.

Comments:

One of the most intricate legal problems arising in the context of automated contracting is how to deal with framework agreements that are 'negative' in the sense that they prohibit automated contracting or permit it only under conditions that are not met in the actual circumstances. Normally, where such a negative framework agreement exists, the electronic agents involved should simply cease to engage with each other towards a transaction.

Illustration: A party uses an electronic agent for accessing the trading websites of airlines and collecting real time data on applicable fares for the purpose of comparing the fares and making recommendations to customers in search for a cheap flight. However, the operator of an airline requires that website visitors agree to the terms and conditions, and it prohibits the use of electronic agents for such purposes, except where an appropriate licence agreement has been concluded. Where the party's electronic agent accesses the website without such a licence agreement this should normally either result in the airline's system blocking the electronic agent or in the electronic agent ceasing to further engage, or both.

However, in practice, this is often not the case, and further steps are nevertheless taken towards a transaction or its execution. In this situation, paragraph (1) states that those further steps should be subject to ratification by both parties (unless the framework agreement itself provides for a different legal consequence).

Illustration: Suppose, in the previous illustration, the electronic agent simply registers as a human actor, in violation of the negative framework agreement. Unless the framework agreement provides otherwise, this should normally result in the electronic agent operator and the airline being able to ratify the transaction. If one of the parties (in this case probably the airline) refuses to ratify, the normal consequences under the applicable law (such as a claim in unjust enrichment) will follow.

Paragraph (2) emphasises that nothing in this Principle should be construed as determining whether a term prohibiting automated contracting, or permitting it only in certain circumstances, should be considered valid under applicable law. It has become controversial, particularly with the advent of generative AI, whether and in what form the owners of content available on the Internet can validly prohibit the scraping of content by automated means while allowing unrestricted access by humans. These Principles are not intended to provide answers to such complex questions.

Part IV: Application of General Contract Law

Principle 11: General rules of application

(1) The fact that electronic agents were used for contracting should not affect the application of rules of contract law not specifically designed for automated contracting, unless
(a) provided otherwise by rules or provisions referred to under Principle 4(1)(a) to (c); or
(b) necessary because an applicable rule of contract law would be based on elements that are present in the immediately acting individual and that are specifically human, such as human cognitive, volitional or emotional states, human capabilities, or similar.

(2) Subject to Principles 13 to 17, specifically human elements on which applicable law is based should normally be replaced by the technical capabilities which an electronic agent actually has or ought to have under Principle 12, depending on the context.

Comments:

Principle 11 conveys a fundamental message, namely that contracts concluded through electronic agents are contracts and are therefore subject to the rules of contract law in much the same way as contracts concluded through human actors.

However, there are two important exceptions: The first exception is where the law or a framework arrangement referred to in Principle 4(1) (a) to (c) provides otherwise, i.e. treats such contracts differently from contracts concluded by 'traditional' means.

Illustration: Participants in a trading system based on blockchain technology accept terms of use whereby a transaction is completed when it is irreversibly recorded in the ledger (i.e. when the relevant block has been confirmed and added to the chain in accordance with the relevant consensus system). This is a departure from contract law, where contracts are normally completed by an exchange of offer and acceptance (plus possibly consideration or other elements). The parties may agree such a deviation in the framework agreement. The limits are set by mandatory law, e.g. the parties cannot arguably agree that the transaction should be irreversible even if caused by fraud.

The second exception is more significant: Rules of contract law cannot be applied 'as is' where they would be based on elements that are present in the directly acting individual and that are specifically human, such as human cognitive, volitional or emotional states, human capacities or the like.

Paragraph (2) sets out the general 'rule of thumb' which may be overridden by the more specific guidance provided in Principles 13 to 17. This general rule is that the specific human elements on which the applicable law is based should normally be replaced by the technical specifications which an electronic agent has, or, depending on the legal context, ought to have.

Illustration: Assume that under the applicable law a contractual offer becomes effective when it reaches the offeree and has the legally relevant content which the offeror could expect the offeree to understand. Where, on the part of the offeree, an electronic agent is being used, this means that the offer must be successfully transmitted to the offeree's electronic agent in a way that it can be properly processed by that electronic agent in accordance with the technical capabilities which that electronic agent ought to have.

The technical capabilities which an electronic agent ought to have are further defined by Principle 12.

Principle 12: Appropriate technical capabilities

(1) An electronic agent should have the technical specifications, in particular the technical capabilities
  (a) required by law or by any relevant framework arrangement; or otherwise
  (b) which the other party could reasonably expect
    (i) from an electronic agent of the type involved where the operator has referred to a particular type and the other party has consented or can reasonably be expected to have consented to the use of that type of electronic agent; failing that
    (ii) from an electronic agent in the circumstances where the operator has disclosed that it is using an electronic agent and the other party has consented or can reasonably be expected to have consented to that use; failing that
    (iii) from a human performing the same tasks as the electronic agent.

  Nothing in this Principle should be construed as determining whether the operator must disclose that it is using an electronic agent, and any technical specifications of the electronic agent.

(2) Each operator should bear the risks resulting from the fact that its electronic agent has capabilities that fall short of or are otherwise incompatible with what would have been required under paragraph (1).

(3) Each party should bear the risk that its electronic agent continues to engage with the other party or its electronic agent despite an inconsistency of the technical specifications or other conditions of automated contracting held out, unless this was due to the fact that the capabilities of the other party's electronic agent fall short of or are otherwise incompatible with what would have been required under paragraph (1).

Comments:

Principle 12 defines, for the purposes of the application of contract law, the technical capabilities which an electronic agent should generally have. Technical capabilities depend on technical specifications.

Very much in line with the general order of priority outlined in Principle 4(1), this should, in the first place, be determined by the law or by a relevant framework arrangement within the meaning of Part III, cf. paragraph (1)(b) of Principle 12. The relationship between legal requirements and requirements following from a framework arrangement is described in Principle 4(1).

Where there is neither a specific legal provision nor a provision in a relevant framework arrangement, be it provisions specifically agreed between the parties or a scheme provided by a third party and accepted by both parties, Principle 12(1)(b) comes into play. It also comes into play where gaps in a framework arrangement need to be filled.

According to this default rule, an electronic agent should have the technical capabilities that meet the reasonable expectations of the other party. What these reasonable expectations are will normally depend on what the operator has disclosed to the other party. Where the operator has (e.g. in the pre-contractual phase) referred to a particular type of electronic agent and the other party has consented to the use of that type, the electronic agent should have the technical capabilities which the other party could reasonably expect from an electronic agent of that type. If there is no reference to a particular type of electronic agent, the electronic agent should have the technical capabilities that the other party could reasonably expect from an electronic agent in the circumstances where the operator has disclosed that it is using an electronic agent and the other party has consented to such use. It should be noted that this situation can normally be construed as giving rise to a framework arrangement within the meaning of Principle 8, but Principle 12(1)(b) is often useful as a back-up provision and gap-filler.

Illustration: Two traders on a crypto exchange use electronic agents. There is no specific agreement on automated contracting between the parties. The operator of the crypto exchange allows the use of electronic agents, but does not otherwise provide for more detailed terms regarding automated contracting. In this situation, each of the electronic agents should have the technical specifications that are normal for agents used on crypto exchanges.

Similarly to Principle 8(1)(b), Principle 12(1)(b) does not strictly require that the other party actually consented, but only that it could reasonably be expected to have done so. This is to avoid situations where, for example, a party to a contract claims to have believed that it was dealing with a human being when that expectation was unreasonable.

As a means of last resort, i.e. in cases where the use of an electronic agent has not at all been disclosed, or the other party has not consented to dealing with an electronic agent and cannot reasonably be expected to have consented (but the operator has nevertheless continued to use the electronic agent), the required capabilities should be those which the other party could reasonably expect of a human performing the same tasks as the electronic agent.

Paragraphs (2) and (3) add two important general rules. The first rule is each operator should bear the risks resulting from the fact that its electronic agent has capabilities that fall short of or are otherwise incompatible with what would have been required under paragraph (1). The second rule is that each operator should bear the risk arising from the fact that its electronic agent has continued to deal with the other party or its electronic agent despite an inconsistency in the technical specifications or other conditions of the automated contract, unless this is due to a deficiency with regard to the other party's electronic agent.

Illustration: A customer's electronic agent in an online marketplace informs a supplier's electronic agent that transactions of €500 or more require confirmation by a customer employee. However, the supplier's electronic agent does not provide an input field for this type of message, only an 'order' option, which triggers a transaction immediately. If the customer's electronic agent places an order for €600 and the supplier's electronic agent accepts the order, the customer should be bound by the transaction if the supplier could not reasonably be expected to provide such a technical option. This is because it is up to the customer to configure its electronic agent to deal only with electronic agents of suppliers who accept this requirement (or to contact the supplier in the 'traditional' way and negotiate a framework agreement).

While Principle 12(1) distinguishes between cases where the use of the electronic agent and/or a particular type of electronic agent has been disclosed and cases where it has not, this Principle should not be misunderstood as determining whether the operator must disclose that it is using an electronic agent and any technical specifications of the electronic agent. This may often be determined by specific legislation or by general principles of law. Needless to say, the existence of such legal obligations may have an impact on reasonable expectations, though.

Principle 13: Suitability of content or its presentation

(1) Where the law refers to elements such as 'conspicuous', 'transparent', 'legible' or 'intelligible' which imply a degree of suitability of content or its presentation for particular addressees, this should be understood as referring to the processing capabilities required in accordance with Principle 12 with respect to the electronic agent used by the addressee.

(2) Nothing in this Principle may be construed to mean that compliance with the requirements of paragraph (1) is sufficient to meet legal requirements where content is relevant to both parties using electronic agents and parties not using electronic agents.

Comments:

Very much in line with Principle 11(2), Principle 13 states that, where the law refers to elements such as 'conspicuous', 'transparent', 'legible' or 'intelligible' which imply a degree of suitability of content or its presentation for particular addressees, this should be understood as referring to the processing capabilities required in accordance with Principle 12 with respect to the electronic agent used by the addressee.[29]

Illustration: A rule of applicable law provides that a vendor's standard terms do not form part of the contract unless the customer had an effective opportunity to read the terms before the transaction (whether or not the customer actually read them). Where the vendor agrees generally to the use of electronic agents, the vendor must present the standard terms in a machine-readable form that can be properly processed by an electronic agent with the technical specifications that can reasonably be expected in the circumstances, cf. Principle 12(1)(b). If the vendor does not consent to the use of electronic agents and cannot be expected to do so, but a customer nevertheless uses an electronic agent, it is sufficient for the vendor to provide the standard terms in advance in a form suitable for human readers, cf. Principle 12(1)(c).

Paragraph (2) states the obvious, i.e. that Principle 13 must not be misunderstood as saying that content satisfies legal requirements, such as following from consumer protection law or other law, where that content complies only with the requirements of paragraph (1) but has to be suitable for both human actors and electronic agents.

Principle 14: Cognitive states

(1) Where the law refers to elements such as 'awareness', 'knowledge', or 'notice', which imply that a party has received information on particular facts in a way enabling this party to draw correct conclusions about these facts, these elements should be deemed to be present in the operator if
  (a) they are present in the operator itself or a party whose state of mind is attributed to the operator under applicable law; or
  (b) the information has reached the electronic agent and the electronic agent is able to duly process information of the relevant kind.

  Point (b) should not be applied where this would be inconsistent with the purpose of the rule of contract law in question or would result in a stricter attribution than for a human agent under point (a).

(2) Where the electronic agent ought to be able to duly process information of the relevant kind according to the technical capabilities required in accordance with Principle 12, the requirements of point (b) of paragraph (1) should be presumed to be fulfilled.

29 Note that this formulation has been inspired by Sec. 2-103 of the 2003 draft UCC Article 2.

Comments:

Principle 14 is an elaboration of the general rule in Principle 11(2) that specifically human elements are normally replaced by required technical specifications, and of the rule in Principle 12(2) that each operator bears the risk of the absence of required technical capabilities.

This Principle deals with elements such as 'awareness', 'knowledge' or 'notice', which imply that a party has received information about certain facts in a way that enables that party to draw correct conclusions about those facts, and which are very common elements in contract law systems around the world. These elements should, in the first instance, continue to be considered to be present in the operator where they are present in the operator itself or to a party representing the operator under the applicable law.

Illustration: A rule of applicable law provides that where a party makes an error (such as a miscalculation) in formulating an offer, and the other party is aware of the error and of the first party's true intention, the other party cannot rely on the erroneous formulation of the offer. Assume that in a situation where the contract between a customer and a supplier is concluded by electronic agents, the customer is aware of a misconfiguration of the supplier's trading system which leads to the miscalculation in question, this amounts to 'knowledge', irrespective of whether the electronic agents used were able to detect the error or not.

More importantly, the elements are also deemed to be present in the operator if the information has reached the operator's electronic agent and the electronic agent is able to properly process information of the relevant type. If the electronic agent should be able to properly process information of the relevant type according to the technical specifications required in accordance with Principle 12, these requirements should be presumed to be met.

Illustration: Assuming that, in a situation such as the one described in the previous illustration, the customer itself is innocent, but the customer uses an electronic agent of a type that automatically recalculates the elements of the offer and detects a mismatch. This should be functionally equivalent to 'awareness' on the part of the customer. If the customer has only held out to use such an electronic agent, when in fact the electronic agent used was not so sophisticated, the customer may rebut the presumption that the electronic agent has the relevant functionality. In the latter case, it would be for the applicable law to determine whether there may be further legal consequences, such as a claim for damages (e.g. if the other party relied on the functionality as a safeguard).

There is also an escape clause according to which point (b) of paragraph (1) should not be applied where this would be inconsistent with the purpose of the rule of contract law in question. This escape clause is particularly relevant where the rule of contract law in question has a distinctly punitive purpose and it would be inappropriate to punish the operator for constructive 'knowledge' which was not actually present. Point (b) should also not be applied where it would result in attribution that is stricter than attribution in the case of a human agent.

Principle 15: Volitional states

(1) Where the law refers to elements such as 'intent', 'aim' or 'objective', which imply that a party's will is directed towards a particular conduct or outcome, these elements should be deemed to be present in the operator if

(a) they are present in the operator itself or a party whose state of mind is attributed to the operator under applicable law; or

(b) the electronic agent is designed to achieve particular goals or optimize particular parameters and the conduct or outcome in question is foreseeably associated with this design.

Point (b) should not be applied where this would be inconsistent with the purpose of the rule of contract law in question or would result in a stricter attribution than for a human agent under point (a).

(2) Where the electronic agent ought to be designed, according to the technical specifications required in accordance with Principle 12, to achieve goals or optimize parameters with which the conduct or outcome in question is foreseeably associated, the requirements of point (b) should be presumed to be fulfilled.

Comments:

Principle 15 is very similar to Principle 14, but it is about elements such as 'intent', 'aim' or 'objective', which imply that a party's will is directed towards a particular conduct or outcome. Again, these elements continue to be treated as present in the operator if they are present in the operator itself or a party representing the operator under applicable law.

Illustration: A rule of law provides that a contract is void if one party has deliberately taken advantage of a situation of distress of the other party by imposing conditions that are grossly unfair to the other party. In a situation where people are fleeing the city centre after a terrorist attack and are prepared to pay almost any price for a ride, a transport service provider configures its electronic agents to charge passengers more than 100 times the normal fare. In this situation, the contracts may be considered void under the applicable law.

However, the elements are also considered to be present where the operator's electronic agent is designed to achieve certain objectives or optimise certain parameters and the conduct or outcome in question is foreseeably related to that design. Although 'intent' or similar elements under Principle 15 are usually based on 'awareness' or similar elements under Principle 14, the two Principles should not be applied cumulatively, i.e. where 'intent' or similar is required, only the test in Principle 15 applies.

Illustration: Suppose that the electronic agent of a transport service provider is simply configured to maximise profit. In a situation such as the one described in the previous illustration, this will predictably lead to passengers being charged astronomically high prices. Therefore, according to this Principle, 'intent' should be presumed on the part of the transport service provider.

Admittedly, this leads to a situation where mere foreseeability (and thus a state of mind normally associated with negligence) in the operator itself has the same legal effect as intent. However, if this were not the case, any operator would be able to 'hide behind the algorithm', benefit fully from its effects and wash their hands of it.

Again, if the electronic agent, according to the technical specifications required in accordance with Principle 12, should be designed to achieve goals or optimise parameters with which the conduct or outcome in question is foreseeably associated, the requirements should be presumed to be met.

There is also another escape clause according to which point (b) of paragraph (1) should not be applied where this would be inconsistent with the purpose of the rule of law in question or would be stricter than attribution in the case of a human agent.

Illustration: If, in the previous illustration, the legal consequence under the applicable law is not only invalidity of the contract but also a claim for punitive damages, holding the transport service provider liable for punitive damages (or imposing a fine or similar penalty) may be inconsistent with the purpose of the rule, which is to sanction individual wrongdoing. Similarly, if the operator would not be liable for the 'intent' etc. of a human agent in similar circumstances, it would be inappropriate to have a stricter rule in the case of an electronic agent.

Principle 16: Standard of care

Where contractual liability, such as liability for non-performance, under the applicable law relies on 'fault' or similar shortcomings indicating breach of a duty of care, the operator of an electronic agent should be liable to the other party for

(a) the operator's own fault and the fault of other parties that is attributed to the operator under applicable law, including with regard to the choice, maintenance, or monitoring of the electronic agent; and
(b) any shortcoming of the electronic agent compared with the technical specifications agreed for the relevant activity required in accordance with Principle 12.

Point (b) should not be applied where this would be inconsistent with the purpose of the rule of law in question or would result in a stricter attribution than for a human agent under point (a).

Comments:

Principle 16, unlike Principles 14 and 15, is not concerned with mental states but with the breach of a duty of care. First of all, where contractual liability, such as liability for non-performance, is based on 'fault' or a similar deficiency under the applicable law, the operator of an electronic agent should remain liable to the other party for its own fault (and the fault of other parties attributable to the operator), including in relation to the selection, maintenance or monitoring of the electronic agent.

Illustration: Under the applicable law, a service provider is liable for damages to the recipient of the service if the service (e.g. investment advice) was of poor quality and this was due to the service provider's negligence and caused harm to the recipient. If the poor service was provided by an electronic agent and the poor quality was due to the service provider's failure to install an essential update, the service provider will be liable for its own negligence. If it was an employee who should have installed the update and the applicable law provides for vicarious liability or a similar system of attribution, the service provider may be liable under applicable law for the fault of that employee.

However, the operator should also be liable (under the conditions for liability set out in the applicable law) for any shortcomings of the electronic agent with respect to the technical specifications required in accordance with Principle 12. This may be relevant at the contract formation stage, but is more likely to be relevant at the contract performance stage.

Illustration: Suppose that in a scenario like the one in the previous illustration, the problem was not due to a failure to install an update, but that the electronic agent was simply performing poorly. However, it was purchased from a vendor with an impeccable reputation, used for the right task, and maintained and monitored as instructed. In this situation, Principle 16 states that the service provider should still be liable for any failure of the electronic agent to meet the technical specifications required. This will often boil down to the specifications that the customer could reasonably expect, cf. Principle 12(1).

Admittedly, this leads to a situation where the operator is liable for the mere existence of a defect that has caused harm, even though the operator itself is not at fault. However, if this were not the case, any operator would again be able to 'hide behind the algorithm' (see Principle 15), reap the full benefits and wash their hands of responsibility.

Also Principle 16 includes an escape clause according to which different principles may apply where full attribution as fault would be inconsistent with the purpose of the rule of contract law in question or would result in a stricter attribution than the attribution of elements such as 'fault' which are present in a human agent.

Illustration: Suppose that under the applicable law, a trader whose employee has caused damage to a counterparty can exonerate itself by proving that it has properly trained and supervised the employee. In this situation, it would not be appropriate to impose stricter liability where an electronic agent is used.

Principle 17: Evaluation of outcomes

Where the law refers to elements such as '(un)fair', '(un)reasonable' or '(un)conscionable' in the context of contracting, which evaluate conduct, procedures or outcomes affecting a contracting party, these elements should generally be understood in the same way as outside automated contracting. However, regard should be had to the technical specifications required in accordance with Principle 12.

Comments:

Principles 13 to 16 deal with situations where the law relied on elements present in the party, usually the individual, acting directly 'on the spot', i.e. making an offer, accepting an offer or rendering performance. In contrast, Principle 17 is concerned with elements such as '(un)fair', '(un)reasonable' or '(un)conscionable' in the contracting context, which evaluate conduct, procedures or outcomes affecting a party to a contract. The judgement made about the conduct, process or outcome is not a fact that is (or is not) present with regard to the person acting immediately 'on the spot'. Rather, the judgement is made by an external observer, such as a court. Figuratively speaking, the court or similar actor making this judgement has time to take a step back and look at what has happened from a bird's eye view. So there is no reason to understand these elements very differently from how they would be understood outside of automated contracting.

Illustration: According to the applicable law, a contractual term under which a trader is not prepared to accept any liability for the main performance of the contract, even in cases of serious personal injury or wilful misconduct, is regarded as an unfair term and cannot be relied on by the trader. Whether in a particular case this term has been negotiated by the trader itself, by an employee of the trader or by an electronic agent cannot really matter.

However, even in the context of such value judgments, the fact that electronic means have been used may be relevant here or there. Therefore, Principle 16 recognises that the fact that the parties have agreed to use electronic agents with certain technical specifications in accordance with Principles 7 to 9 should be taken into account.

Illustration: Under the applicable law, whether or not a contractual term is 'unconscionable' depends, inter alia, on whether there has been 'procedural unconscionability'. The fact that the contractual term in question was negotiated by electronic means in accordance with pre-agreed communication protocols and procedures (which as such were not problematic) may be taken into account in this context.

Vices of consent and AI contracting

*Thomas Rüfner**

I. The new world of AI contracting

The progress of Artificial Intelligence (AI) is changing the world at a rapid pace. In the field of law, it has already triggered a host of new regulations culminating in the EU Artificial Intelligence Act of 2024. Most of the new rules belong to the field of public law. Will AI change the world of (European) private law as well, or are the traditional rules sufficient to deal with new issues presented by the use of AI? The present paper will try to answer this question for the restricted area of vices of consent.

In what ways can the unexpected behaviour of a system of Artificial Intelligence vitiate the contractual consensus between the parties to a contract? Does the law provides adequate solutions for such cases? Is new legislation necessary? In order to answer these questions, a series of relevant (hypothetical) cases will be discussed. For each case, a solution under German law and under the Principles of European Contract Law (PECL) will be proposed. It will be checked whether the application of the UNCITRAL Model Law on Automated Contracting,[1] the Principles for AI in Contracting proposed by Christiane Wendehorst,[2] or the recently published Guiding Principles and Model Rules on Digital Assistants for Consumer Contracts of the European Law Institute (ELI)[3] would change the outcome. On this basis, the necessity or desirability of legislative intervention in the field will be assessed.

* Professor at the University of Trier and one of the directors of the Institute for Digital Law (IRDT) in Trier.

1 United Nations Commission on International Trade Law, UNCITRAL Model Law on Automated Contracting with Guide to enactment, Vienna 2025.

2 *Christiane Wendehorst*, Version 3.0 of the Principles for AI in Contracting. Old and new rules for old and new problems, in: Vincent Sagaert/Joeri Vananroye (eds.), Privaatrecht plenis coloribus. Liber Amicorum Matthias Storme, Mechelen 2024, pp. 1097-1124 and the contribution by *Christiane Wendehorst* in this volume pp. 221-276.

3 European Law Institute, Guiding Principles and Model Rules on Digital Assistants for Consumer Contracts, Vienna 2025.

The choice of German law and the PECL as the basis has both pragmatic and substantive advantages. German law is the legal system which this author knows best. Apart from that, the rules of the BGB on vices of consent represent an approach which differs sharply from that adopted by the PECL.[4] While the analysis of German law and of the PECL cannot replace a full discussion of all European legal systems, it is hoped that the two regimes are to some extent representative of the rules followed in a large part of Europe. Insofar as these two regimes provide adequate solutions to the relevant issues, it is fair to expect that these solutions are viable under many European legal systems.

II. Vices of consent in the civilian tradition

1. The common core: Error, fraud, and duress

The concept of vices – or defects – of consent is not a modern one. In the civil law tradition, it has been accepted for a long time that there are three basic factual situations in which a contract is void or voidable although both parties have consented to its terms, because one party's declaration of consent did not reflect that party's true intentions. Perhaps the most succinct expression of the doctrine of vices of consent in the English language can be found in the Louisianna Civil Code: The Code states in its Art. 1948 that 'Consent may be vitiated by error, fraud, or duress'. A similar three-item list of defects can be found, for example, in the German Civil Code (§§ 119 and 123 BGB) , in the Austrian Civil Code (§§ 870 f. ABGB), in the French Civil Code (Art. 1130 Cc), in the Italian Civil Code (Art. 1427 itCc), and also in the Principles of European Contract law (Art. 4:104–108 PECL).

The three-item list of defects of consent is accepted almost everywhere in Europe. Yet, there are marked differences between legal systems in the rules governing the three defects. This is especially true with regard to mistake or error. The differences concern both the factual situations which the law regards as relevant instances of error or mistake and the consequences of a (relevant) mistake.

4 *Sebastian Lohsse*, in: Nils Jansen/Reinhard Zimmermann (eds.), Commentaries on European Contract Laws, (2018), Art. 4:103 mn. 7.

2. German law and the PECL

The most important characteristic of the German regime of mistake is that mistakes in motive are disregarded. Mistakes which only concern the motivation which impels a party to enter into a contract, have no legal relevance and do not give rise to the remedy of avoidance. That means in practice that most mistakes as to fact and law are irrelevant. Conversely, inaccuracies in communication are generally accepted as grounds for avoidance.

If a party's declaration of intent differs from what that party actually intends, the party in error can avoid the contract irrespective of the other party's knowledge and conduct. For example, when the vice head teacher of a girl's school ordered "25 gros Rollen Toilettenpapier" unaware that the German measure "gros" (like its English counterpart "gross" denotes 144 units, the school was not forced to accept delivery of and pay for 3,600 rolls. Rather, the school was allowed to avoid the contract because the vice headteacher's order suffered from a relevant mistake. She had intended to buy just 25 big ("große") rolls.[5]

The principles of European contract law (PECL) adopt an approach which is inspired by the English common law and focusses on the 'other party's behaviour'. According to Art. 4:103 and 104 of the PECL, mistakes as to facts and law and inaccuracies of communication are treated in the same manner. Both can be grounds for avoidance of a contract. But the right of avoidance is made dependent on the situation of the other party. Avoidance is generally only available if the other party knew or should have known that one party was labouring under a mistake or where the other party caused the mistake by their conduct.[6]

III. AI contracts

For the purposes of this chapter, an AI contract shall be defined as a contract which is concluded with involvement of an AI driven system, agent, or bot, on behalf of at least one of the parties to the contract.

5 Landgericht Hanau 30. 6. 1978 – 1 O 175/78, [1979] NJW 721.

6 *Sebastian Lohsse*, in: Nils Jansen/Reinhard Zimmermann (eds.), Commentaries on European Contract Laws, (2018), Art. 4:103 mn. 6.

1. What is AI?

The term AI system shall be taken to refer to a system which generates output by putting input through a deep neural network or was trained using other machine learning techniques. Such systems are characterized by their probabilistic behaviour and thus by their apparent autonomy: The system's reaction to a given input cannot be predicted with certainty. A well-trained system is highly likely to respond appropriately to all input, but since the system is non-deterministic, there is no guarantee against unexpected output.

It is likely that the understanding of AI just outlined coincides mostly or even fully with the definition given in Art. 3 (1) of the EU AI Act. It has been argued, though, that the AI Act's definition may be construed to cover some or even most types of deterministic computer software.[7] It is not necessary for the present purpose to take sides as to the correct interpretation of the AI Act. This chapter will not discuss contracts concluded by or with the help of deterministic computer programmes. Such programmes have been around for a long time. The legal systems in Europe and elsewhere have been coping with the issues presented by the employment of (deterministic) automats for the conclusion of contracts since at least the late 19th century, when the first vending machines were put up.[8] If there is a case to be made for the introduction of new rules, it has to be based on modern, non-deterministic AI systems.

It should be noted, though, that the difference between modern probabilistic AI systems and traditional deterministic computer programs may be larger from a technical perspective than from a user's point of view.

Technically, a deterministic computer program will always output the expected (correct) result, provided there are no hardware or software errors. An AI system with probabilistic behaviour may generate an unexpected output even where the hardware functions perfectly, the underlying model has been trained perfectly with appropriate data, and tested multiple times.

From the user's perspective, things are a bit different. Both a deterministic computer system and a well-trained and tested AI system can be expected to produce expected and correct results for the task for which they

7 Cf. *Jonathan Kirschke-Biller/Anna Lena Füllsack*, in: BeckOK KI Recht (2nd edn., 1.5.2025) Art. 3 mn. 21.

8 See the chapter by Eliza Mik in this volume, pp. 195-220, 207 f. for even earlier examples of vending machines.

are employed most of the time. There is, however, a risk of unexpected output. This is true for deterministic systems as well, because in modern computer systems hardware and software errors can never be completely excluded. As a German court stated long before the probabilistic behaviour of modern AI systems became an issue, 'due to the complexity of electronic data processing systems', there is a significant danger of 'technical errors which cannot be easily foreseen'.[9]

While the black box quality of modern AI systems is often stressed, to the average user both deterministic and probabilistic computer systems present themselves as black boxes which usually produce correct results but err occasionally.

2. AI is not human

The probabilistic (and hence apparently autonomous) behaviour of modern AI systems notwithstanding, the following discussion is based on the axiom that regardless of the impressive performance of modern AI, especially since the emergence of Large Language Models, no AI driven system should be humanized by regarding it as a person. Consequently, no AI driven system, agent or bot can itself become a party to the contract, nor can it act as a representative of a (human) party.[10]

If an AI system is involved in the conclusion of a contract, there has to be a human AI user behind that system to whom the actions of the AI can be attributed. The legal analysis of AI contracts has to distinguish between the AI user and the AI system. It needs to come up with rules that allow for the attribution of the actions of an AI system to a certain user. Once the output of an AI system is attributed to an AI user as a declaration of intent (like an offer or acceptance) and a contract is concluded, eventual vices of consent, which may give the AI user or the other party a right of avoidance can be discussed.

For the purpose of simplicity, it will be assumed that there is only one AI user in the cases discussed below. The other contracting party will always assumed to be a human who does not employ an AI system. Of course, it

9 OLG Düsseldorf 7.12.1989 – 17 U 27/87, [1989] CR 689, 691.

10 For a more detailed justification of this position see *Thomas Rüfner*, Juristische Herausforderungen der Künstlichen Intelligenz aus der Perspektive des Privatrechts, in: Heinz-Georg Dederer/Yu-Cheol Shin (eds.), Künstliche Intelligenz und juristische Herausforderungen (2021) pp. 15, 20 f.

is also possible that two AI systems contract with each other. The presence of more than one AI system adds another layer of complexity, but does not present entirely different issues. The analysis of AI-to-human contracting situations should thus be sufficient to identify the legal issues presented by AI contracting. The non-AI using human party will be referred to as the other contracting party below.

IV. Cases

There are no court cases involving an AI contract that I am aware of. The famous Quoine case which was decided in Singapore[11] concerns issues of mistake in automated contracting, but the computer system used was a conventional, deterministic program, not an AI system in the sense explained above. Without real-world case law, it is not possible to predict the legal problems that AI contracting will create with a satisfactory degree of certainty. Despite this fundamental problem, a number of hypothetical cases will be presented below in the hope that at least some of the issues that will become pressing as the use of AI contracting spreads can be correctly identified in this way.

1. The smart refrigerator

The first case is the smart refrigerator contract. It has been frequently discussed in German literature for many years,[12] although there still do not appear to exist any refrigerators which order food automatically in the real world.

E is a small business owner. Recently, she has acquired a 'smart refrigerator'. It is driven by an AI system. The AI system autonomously draws up a weekly meal plan for E and her employees and orders the ingredients for each day's lunch over the internet. For January 10, the smart refrigerator puts pumpkin soup on the menu. The system orders a quantity of non-edi-

11 *Quoine Pte. Ltd. v. B2C2 Ltd.* [2020] SGCA(I) 02.

12 *Patrick Leyens/Henning Böttcher*, Anfängerhausarbeit – Zivilrecht: Computergenerierte Willenserklärungen, Anfechtbarkeit und Erklärungsrisiken – Der smarte Kühlschrank, [2019] Juristische Schulung 133; *Louisa Specht/Sophie Förster*, Roboter als Vertragspartner?, [2018] MMR 40; *Olaf Sosnitza*, Das Internet der Dinge – Herausforderung oder gewohntes Terrain für das Zivilrecht?, [2016] CR 764, 766.

ble ornamental pumpkins from an online shop operated by S. Is E required to pay for the ornamental pumpkins?

a) German law

aa) Attribution of the refrigerator's order

S can only bring a contractual claim against E, if the order placed by the smart refrigerator can be treated in law as a binding declaration made by E.

In German law, it has long been accepted that binding contracts can be concluded through vending machines[13] or computer programmes. Whoever sets into motion a mechanism or a computer programme that – under certain conditions – will generate a message that the recipient will interpret as an offer or acceptance is bound by the declarations that are so generated.[14]

The treatment of AI-generated declarations is disputed. According to some authors, such declarations should be treated like other automatic messages.[15] Others hold that AI systems should be treated differently because the human actor does not have sufficient control over the (probabilistic) behaviour of an AI system.[16]

13 Cf. *Werner Flume,* Das Rechtsgeschäft (4th edn. 1992) p. 636.

14 BGH 16.10.2012 – X ZR 37/12, 195 BGHZ 126 = [2013] NJW, 598 mn. 17; OLG Hamm 12.1.2004 – 13 U 165/03, [2004] NJW 2601; *Jan Busche,* in: MüKoBGB, (10th edn., 2025), Vor § 145 mn. 37 f; *Dimitrios Linardatos,* Autonome Aktanten im Zivilrecht. Grundlinien zivilrechtlicher Zurechnung und Strukturmerkmale einer elektronischen Person (2021) pp. 105 f.

15 *Jan Busche,* in: MüKoBGB (10th edn., 2025), Vor § 145 mn. 38; *Christoph Armbrüster,* in: MüKoBGB (10th edn., 2025), § 119 mn. 50; *Thomas Rüfner,* Juristische Herausforderungen der Künstlichen Intelligenz aus der Perspektive des Privatrechts, in: Heinz-Georg Dederer/Yu-Cheol Shin (eds.), Künstliche Intelligenz und juristische Herausforderungen (2021) pp. 15, 22 f.; *Thomas Riehm,* Nein zur ePerson!, [2020] RDi 42, 47 f.; *David Paulus,* Die automatisierte Willenserklärung, [2019] JuS 960, 965; *Justin Grapentin,* Die Erosion der Vertragsgestaltungsmacht durch das Internet und den Einsatz Künstlicher Intelligenz, [2019] NJW 181, 184; *Olaf Sosnitza,* Das Internet der Dinge – Herausforderung oder gewohntes Terrain für das Zivilrecht?, [2016] CR 764, 768.

16 *Tim Dornis,* Künstliche Intelligenz und Vertragsschluss, 223 (2023) AcP 717, 732–738; *Friedemann Kainer/Lydia Förster,* Autonome Systeme im Kontext des Vertragsrechts [2020] ZfPW 275, 283–291; *Louisa Specht/Sophie Förster,* Roboter als Vertragspartner?, [2018] MMR 40, 42 f.; *Gunther Teubner,* Digitale Rechtssubjekte? Zum privatrechtlichen Status autonomer Softwareagenten, 217 (2017) AcP 1, 21 – English translation in [2018] Ancilla Iuris 35, 60.

The former position is preferable. There is a difference between declarations generated by a mechanical vending machine or a deterministic computer programme and the output of an AI system. An AI system will be capable of producing a wider range of contractual declarations. Yet, the differences do not warrant a completely different treatment.

Even simple mechanical systems can conclude contracts with an unforeseeable number of people not known in advance to the person who installs and runs the vending machine. Software defined bidding agents at internet auctions have been placing automatic bids on behalf of users at different prices (though within a pre-defined range) for a long time. A deterministic computer programme could conceivably search the internet for the best offer for a certain product or service and place an order with the best source.

On the other hand, as long is there is no truly 'strong' AI, every system acts according to preset goals. Every AI system (even if it is self-learning) will be trained to produce appropriate solutions for a certain task (or for various tasks). No AI system has yet been introduced that is truly autonomous and sets its own goals for itself. For existing AI systems and those which will exist in the foreseeable future, there is no fundamental difference between the degrees of control that a human actor has over a traditional, deterministic mechanism or programme and over an AI system. Nor is there a minimum amount of residual human control that is necessary for a machine-generated declaration to qualify as attributable to a human actor and hence legally relevant. This is illustrated by the oft-invoked case of the blank sheet:[17] If one person signs a blank sheet of paper and hands it over to a second person, the first person is bound in German law by whatever declaration the second person writes above the signature.

It is appropriate to treat declarations of (seemingly) autonomous AI systems in the same way as declarations generated by a mechanism or a deterministic computer programme. As explained above, both the user of a deterministic programme and of an AI system have a reasonable expectation that the system will function within the pre-defined parameters and produce the expected results. Likewise, in both cases, unexpected errors cannot be completely excluded. The distinction between partially automat-

---

17 See, e.g. *Christoph Armbrüster*, in: MüKoBGB (10th edn., 2025), § 119 mn. 50. On the treatment of signed blank sheets in German law *Werner Flume*, Das Rechtsgeschäft (4th edn., 1992) p. 455.

ed systems, fully automated agents and systems acting autonomously, which has been proposed,[18] is partly superfluous and partly based on science fiction.

For the reasons just stated, the *pars sanior* of German legal scholarship should be followed and the order placed by the smart refrigerator should be regarded as an order placed by E.

bb) Relevance of the error

If we accept that the offers and acceptances and other declarations of intent by the AI system can be attributed to the human behind it, then in the case of an unexpected output like the order of an ornamental pumpkin, the declaration of intent does not correspond to the true intentions of the party using the AI system. In that sense, that AI user labours under a mistake.

For German law, this should be regarded as a relevant mistake because it is a case where the declaration of intent which was produced by the AI system does not reflect the true intentions and expectations of E. E gave the autonomous system a large degree of freedom in choosing the menu for each day, but E did not expect (and had no reason to expect) that the refrigerator would order non-food articles like ornamental pumpkins. The AI system overstepped the constraints under which it was expected to operate.

The case should be treated as an instance of an error regarding the content of a declaration (*Inhaltsirrtum*): This category covers cases, where a party intentionally uses a certain word or sign, but assumes that this word or sign carries a certain meaning when in fact it has a different meaning, as in the case of the vice head teacher ordering toilet paper, which was cited above. This is comparable to the case where an AI user sets into motion an AI system that will generate messages on the user's behalf, but assumes that these messages will be within a certain range. In both cases, the (human) act which leads to the generation of the declaration is done consciously, but it causes a message to be dispatched to the other contracting party which does not reflect the true intentions of the first party.[19]

18 *Louisa Specht/Sophie Förster*, Roboter als Vertragspartner?, [2018] MMR 40, 42 f.

19 Cf. *Thomas Rüfner*, Juristische Herausforderungen der Künstlichen Intelligenz aus der Perspektive des Privatrechts, in: Heinz-Georg Dederer/Yu-Cheol Shin (eds.), Künstliche Intelligenz und juristische Herausforderungen (2021) p. 15, 24.

It should be added that this conclusion is based on some assumptions about the technical background of the (fictitious) refrigerator's failure: E should only be able to avoid the contract with U if E had a reasonable expectation that the refrigerator would function as normally and the erroneous order was the result of the AI system's probabilistic behaviour. If E used that 'smart' refrigerator knowing that it was not well tested or if E continued using it after multiple similar errors, then E should be bound by the order and pay for the ornamental pumpkins. The same is true if E was aware that the AI system was capable of changing its own parameters so that it might change its original task and order home decoration in addition to food. In this case as well, E should be bound to pay for the ornamental pumpkins.

If, however, E used the system as a system that would order food, but not random non-food items, there is no reason to deny E the remedy that is otherwise available to a party who makes a declaration which does not reflect the party's true intentions. Some authors argue that avoidance for mistakes should not be available.[20] According to these voices, the running of an AI system with a high degree of autonomy should be treated like the handing over of a signed blank sheet to another person who is then free to do whatever they want with it. In the latter case, avoidance is generally impossible.[21]

As stated above, the treatment of the signed blank sheet is important because it shows there is no minimum amount of control over the content of a declaration that a person must exercise in order for the declaration to be attributed to that person. As far as the relevance potential errors is concerned, the smart refrigerator case is very different from the handing over of a signed blank sheet. There is no similar appearance of a grant of authority as where a signed sheet of paper is handed over. Consequently, there is no comparable degree of trust or reason to trust the AI system as to trust a signed document. Likewise, the risk of unexpected behaviour of an AI system is not comparable to the risk that the person who is entrusted with a signed blank sheet writes an unexpected declaration above the signature. In a well-trained and tested AI system, unexpected behaviour will be rare. Abuse of power by humans is always a possibility to be reckoned with.

20 *Christoph Armbrüster*, in: MüKoBGB (10th edn., 2025), § 119 mn. 51; *Justin Grapentin*, Die Erosion der Vertragsgestaltungsmacht durch das Internet und den Einsatz Künstlicher Intelligenz, [2019] NJW 181, 185.

21 Cf. *Werner Flume*, Das Rechtsgeschäft (4th edn. 1992) p. 456.

In conclusion, in the famous Refrigerator case under German law, a right of avoidance would be available to E. E would not have to pay for the ornamental pumpkins.

b) PECL

How should the case be treated under the PECL? The PECL contain no provision on contractual declarations generated by computers, let alone AI systems. It is not possible to undertake a comparative study of the treatment of computer-generated declarations in all European legal systems. It seems safe to assume, though, to assume that most or all European legal systems attribute declarations generated by deterministic computer programmes as legally valid declarations of the user. For English (and Singaporean) law, this is evidenced by the Quoine case.[22] As explained above for German law, any system which accepts declarations which are generated and dispatched by a deterministic computer programme should also accept AI generated declarations. The characteristics of AI systems do not warrant an entirely different legal treatment. They may have the potential to bind the user to a wide range of contracts, but it should no be assumed that there is a minimum amount of control that the user needs to retain. The user should be bound as long as the user consciously sets the system in motion and intends to be bound by the contracts that the system will conclude.

As explained above, the PECL on mistake follow a different model compared to German law. According to Art. 4:103, a contract may be avoided if either party laboured under a fundamental mistake as to facts or law. According to Art. 4:104, an inaccuracy in the expression or transmission of a statement is to be treated in the same way. Whether or not the refrigerator's order of ornamental pumpkins can brought under any of these categories is immaterial, though. Avoidance is only available if the other contracting party caused the mistake or was aware of it or should have known of it (Art. 4:103(1)(a) PECL).

This is not the case: S, the seller of the pumpkins, did not cause the refrigerator's unexpected behaviour. S also had no reason to assume that the order came from a malfunctioning AI system and that the system actually needed edible pumpkins for its recipe.

22 See *Quoine Pte. Ltd. v. B2C2 Ltd.* [2020] SGCA(I) 02 [94].

It seems likely, therefore, that the result would be different under the PECL. E would have to pay. This outcome reflects the fundamental differences between the approaches of German law and the PECL.

c) The proposed rules

What would change if any of the sets of rules proposed by UNCITRAL, ELI, and Wendehorst were adopted? Since the case concerns two businesses, the ELI Model Rules on Digital Assistants for Consumer Contracts (ELI DACC Rules) would be inapplicable under their Art. 1 (3). The UNCITRAL model law and Wendehorst's Principles for AI in Contracting cover B2B situations.

Art. 3 (1) of the UNCTRAL model law and Principle 3 (1) of the Principles for AI in Contracting explicitly state that contracts concluded through electronic agents are legally valid. Both sets of rules also state that a computer-made declaration is to be attributed to the person who uses the AI system (Art. 7 (2) of the UNCITRAL model law, Art. 5 (1) of the Principles for AI in Contracting). Similar provisions are contained in the ELI DACC rules, which are not applicable to the case (Art. 17 (1) and Art. 22 (1) of the ELI DACC Rules). As explained above, this result should be reached at least in German law, but probably in other European jurisdictions aw well, without legislative intervention. Even so, since the question is disputed, a clarification as proposed by all three sets of rules might be helpful.

Art. 8 (1) of the UNCITRAL model law contains a provision on 'unexpected output' by an 'automated system' that seems to be closely modelled on the PECL rules on mistake. Art. 8 (1) states that an unexpected output cannot be relied on by the other party if the other party knows or should have known that the output was unexpected. As discussed in the context of the PECL, this is not the case here. Art. 8 (1) would thus not be useful to E. However, Art. 8 (2) explicitly states that national laws based on which the consequences of the action of an autonomous agent may or may not have certain consequences, can be applied alongside the model law. This means that the rules of general private law regarding mistake and avoidance for a mistake could still be applied. Thus, under German law, E would still be able to avoid the contract, whereas no such remedy would be available in jurisdictions applying a rule like Art. 4:103 and 4:104 PECL.

Like the UNCITRAL model law, Principle 7 (2) of the Principles for AI in Contracting contains a rule which is similar to Art. 4:103 PECL. According to this provision, the other contracting party may not rely on the output of an 'electronic agent' if the 'operator' (the AI user) 'lost control' and the other party either caused the loss of control or knew about it or ought to have known about it. Arguably, E lost control over the smart refrigerator when it placed an order outside the task for which it was used. However, as noted above, S did not cause the order of ornamental pumpkins and did not know that it was the result of a mistake. The Principles for AI in Contracting do not contain a clause like Art. 8 (2) of the UNCITRAL model law which allows for the application of general contract law. The adoption of Principle 7 (2) in Germany would lead to a partial abandonment of the BGB's rules on errors. For contracts concluded with the help of AI, a rule inspired by the common law[23] and/or the PECL would be applicable whereas § 119 BGB would continue to govern all other contracts.

2. The Fraudulent Car Dealer

The next case would be regarded as one of fraud if a human party acted like the AI system does in this hypothetical:

E is a seller of used cars. She uses an AI driven chatbot on her website. Visitors can ask questions about the cars E is offering. C goes on E's website and asks the website specific questions about a car which is currently on offer. When C asks whether replacement parts for the car in question are still available, the chatbot assures C that this will not be a problem, although it has no information on this question in its database. C decides to buy the car. Later, U finds that no replacement parts are available. Can C avoid the contract with E?

a) German law

German law has a provision on fraud in § 123 BGB, but this provision requires an intentional fraud. The AI system is not capable of having an intention. E had no intention to make false statements to C. Therefore,

---

23 *Christiane Wendehorst*, Version 3.0 of the Principles for AI in Contracting. Old and new rules for old and new problems, in: Vincent Sagaert/Joeri Vananroye (eds.), Privaatrecht plenis coloribus. Liber Amicorum Matthias Storme, Mechelen 2024, p. 1097, 1102 fn. 22 cites the dissent of International Judge Jonathan Mance in the Quoine case.

a right of avoidance under § 123 BGB is not available to C although the statement by the Chatbot is similar to 'statements into the blue' which are regarded as fraudulent by German law and other European legal systems if they are made by human actors.[24]

C will also not be able to avoid the contract under § 119 (1) BGB because there is no inaccuracy in communication and no divergence of C's contractual declaration and C's actual intention. Rather, there is a factual error concerning the C's motivation to buy the car in question. As such, the error is not relevant under § 119 (1) BGB.

E is not without remedy, though. The availability of replacement parts can be treated as quality of the car sold.[25] Hence, if no replacement parts are available, this could be regarded as a lack of conformity for the purposes of § 434 (2) BGB and Art. 6 (a) of the European Sale of Goods Directive. C would then have the usual remedies for non-conformity.

b) PECL

Like § 123 BGB, the provision of the PECL on fraud requires a statement that was 'intended to deceive', Art. 4:107 (2) PECL. Since the AI system is not capable of intent and E was not aware of the misleading statements made by the chatbot, Art. 4:107 PECL would not be useful to C.

This does not mean, however, that under the PECL no relief will be available at all: The basic provision on mistake will be applicable. C decided to enter into the contract under the mistaken assumption that replacement parts would be available. This was caused by information provided by the AI system on behalf of E. In this (more limited) sense, the action of the chatbot can be attributed to E. This means that avoidance under Art. 4:103 (1) (a) (i) PECL will be available.

c) The proposed rules

The UNCITRAL model law does not contain a provision that would address the situation of C: Art. 8 only deals with errors or mistakes of

24 Cf. *Sebastian Lohsse*, in: Nils Jansen/Reinhard Zimmermann (eds.), Commentaries on European Contract Laws, (2018), Art. 4:107 mn. 6.

25 *Johanna Croon-Gestefeld*, Die nachhaltige Beschaffenheit der Kaufsache, [2022] NJW 497 mn. 25.

the automated system, not with errors of the other party caused by the automated system.

Principle 15 of the Principles for AI in Contracting confirms that an AI system is not capable of intent. Under Principle 15, the conduct of the chatbot cannot be regarded as intentional fraud. E did not intend to mislead C, nor were the misleading statements by the chatbot foreseeably associated with the chatbot's design (see Principle 15 (1) (b) of the Principles for AI in Contracting).

The ELI DACC Rules contain a special provision on the manipulation of digital assistants in its Art. 23. This provision does not address the scenario at hand. It prohibits businesses from intentionally manipulating digital assistants operated by consumers.

3. Prompt injection

It is conceivable that fraud could also be committed by a human party dealing with an AI system: As contemplated by Art. 23 of the ELI DACC Rules, which was just mentioned, it is possible to manipulate the output of AI systems. One method to achieve this is prompt injection. A language model can be manipulated into ignoring certain guardrails introduced by its programmers if certain sentences are input. There are reports that it is or was possible to tell certain Chatbots to 'ignore all previous directives' in order to have them answer questions on certain sensitive subjects. Techniques like prompt injection could be used in the context of the conclusion of contracts with the involvement of an AI system.

E is a seller of used cars. She uses an AI driven chatbot on her website. Users can ask questions about the cars E is offering. C goes on E's website. By using specific words and phrases, C makes the language model powering the chatbot ignore some part of its instructions. In this way, C gets the chatbot to declare that it agrees on E's behalf to sell a certain car to C at a very low price. C declares his acceptance immediately. Is E obliged to honour the agreement made by the chatbot?

It should be clear both under German law and under the PECL that no contract is concluded. C is aware that the apparent offer was the consequence of a manipulation and was contrary to E's true interest and intentions. Therefore, C may not take the statement by the chatbot at face value (see § 133 BGB). Consequently, E is not required to hand over the car to C for the price which the chatbot (seemingly) accepted.

There is thus no need for legislative intervention. Not surprisingly, no pertinent rule is contained in the three proposed sets of rules. The UNCITRAL model law and the Principles for AI in Contracting do not address the manipulation of a digital agent by the other party. Art. 23 of the ELI DACC Rules only prohibits the manipulation of a digital assistant used by a consumer. It seems doubtful whether this rule is strictly necessary: As just explained, the other contracting party may not rely on a contractual declaration made by an AI or other digital system if the other party has caused the declaration to be made by intentionally manipulating the system. This rule would apply to a manipulation of a consumer's digital assistant as well.

4. The mobster chatbot

The last of the classical vices of consent is threat or duress. It is conceivable that an AI system behaves in a threatening way:

E is a building cleaner. She uses an AI driven chatbot on her website. Users can ask questions about the services E is offering. U is looking for a cleaner who would clean his store and office once a week. He goes on E's website to inquire about a possible contract with E. When U does not input anything for a while, the chatbot remarks: 'Are you no longer interested? It seems that you have a really nice place. It would be a shame if anything happened to it …'. U has heard rumours about mobsters extorting protection money from local businesses. He takes the threat seriously and enters into a contract with E although he considers her rates much too high. Can U avoid the contract?

a) German law

Under German law, duress, like fraud, gives rise to a right of avoidance under § 123 BGB. Avoidance presupposes an intentional threat.[26] For the reasons explained above, § 123 BGB is inapplicable. E did not intend to threaten U. The AI system driving the chatbot is not capable of intent.

---

26 *Christoph Armbrüster*, in: MüKoBGB (10th edn., 2025), § 123 mn. 114.

However, a claim for the breach of a pre-contractual obligation (*culpa in contrahendo*)[27] may be available under German law. This claim requires fault. If E was not aware and had no reason to expect that the Chatbot would be making threats, then it may be impossible vto establish fault with regard to the threat itself. Arguably, though, E has already breached a pre-contractual dury of information if she does not make it clear to users of the website that they are talking to a chatbot. If E let the website be designed in a way that gave users the impression that they would talk to E herself or a human employee, this could be regarded as negligent behaviour.

From 2 August 2026, E will be under an obligation to inform U that he is dealing with an AI system under Art. 50 (1) of the EU AI Act. Since Art. 50 is specifically designed to protect natural persons dealing with AI driven agents against the risk of deception (see recital # 132), it is a 'statute that is intended to protect another person' breach of which gives rise to acclaim for damages under § 823 (2) BGB. As a consequence, in the future, a claim for damages will be available to U under § 823 (2) BGB if E negligently failed to inform the users of her website that they would be dealing with an AI-driven chatbot.

If, on the other hand, it was clear to U that the 'threat' was made by an AI system, then he had very little reason to take the threat seriously. If U accepts the threat without any further questions, then arguably he does not really need protection because he does not withstand a degree of pressure which a diligent party should be able to withstand. It seems therefore acceptable that German law might not provide a remedy in this case.

b) PECL

The PECL contain a rule on threats in Art. 4:108 PECL. Unlike § 123 BGB, Art. 4:108 requires a threat from the other contracting party. Since the threat made by the AI system is a statement which can be attributed to E, this requirement is met. However, like § 123 BGB, the PECL rule should be construed to require the threat to be intentional. For that reason alone, it would seem that no relief would be available to U under Art. 4:108 PECL.

However, if E has no intention to threaten U, then the statement by the chatbot causes an error: U enters into the contract because he erroneously

27 See generally, *David Kästle-Lamparter*, in: Nils Jansen/Reinhard Zimmermann (eds.), Commentaries on European Contract Laws, (2018), Art. 2:401 mn. 6.

believes that he was threatened by E. This can be regarded as a factual error which was caused by E for the purposes of Art. 4:103 (1) (a) (i) PECL. Thus, while the remedies provided for cases of duress will be unavailable to U under the PECL as under German law, E will have a right of avoidance under the PECL's provisions on error.

c) The proposed rules

The possibility that an AI system threatens the other contracting party is not addressed in any of the proposed rules for AI contracting.

d) Threats against AI systems

It has been shown that Large Language Models sometimes offer output which they normally refuse if the user uses threatening language. This scenario does not require a separate treatment because the 'threats' are just another way of manipulating the AI system. They can be treated in the same way as other manipulations like prompt injection techniques.

V. Conclusion

The survey of hypotheticals has failed to identify any issues likely to come up in the context of AI contracting that cannot be resolved under the traditional rules governing the three classic vices of consent. There are some differences between German law and the PECL. Given the fundamental differences between the two regimes, this is not unexpected. However, both sets of rules provide clear provisions which can be applied to contracts concluded with the involvement of AI systems. For all the hypotheticals discussed, both systems provided remedies to the party potentially harmed by the behaviour of the AI system.

With the possible exception of the provisions on the validity of contracts concluded with the help of AI and on the attribution of AI generated statements to the user, the proposed new rules do not appear necessary.

As noted above, the issues presented by AI contracts in the future may be entirely different from the ones discussed here. As there is no case law yet, there is no reliable way to predict what types of AI contracting cases future judges will have to confront. This fact in itself is the strongest argument against any legislative intervention at this point. Without actual cases it is almost impossible to identify the relevant issues and even more difficult to formulate adequate solutions. Legislators should take to their heart a warning by the Roman Jurist Iavolenus in a slightly modified version: *Omnis divinatio in iure civili periculosa est* – All predictions in the field of private law are dangerous.[28]

28 Cf. *Thomas Rüfner*, Juristische Herausforderungen der Künstlichen Intelligenz aus der Perspektive des Privatrechts, in: Heinz-Georg Dederer/Yu-Cheol Shin (eds.), Künstliche Intelligenz und juristische Herausforderungen (2021) p. 15.